MEETINGS V
REMARKA
MAGICIA...

"A captivating exploration into the extraordinary life and magical practice of Carl Abrahamsson. Carl's passion for documenting and celebrating the often-overlooked aspects of the magical world is evident in every word. Through his vivid descriptions and intimate anecdotes, he brings to life a world where magic and mundane intertwine, leaving readers both enlightened and fascinated. *Meetings with Remarkable Magicians* is a testament to the art of storytelling. His willingness to share his experiences and insights is an invaluable gift, especially for those seeking a deeper understanding of the esoteric arts. This book is a must-read for anyone intrigued by the lives of those who embrace the hidden forces that shape our world and the extraordinary individuals who harness their power. I am grateful that Carl has chosen to share his incredible journey with the world. This book is destined to be celebrated and cherished for years to come.

BRI LUNA, FOUNDER OF THE HOODWITCH AND AUTHOR OF *BLOOD SEX MAGIC*

"Carl Abrahamsson's *Meetings with Remarkable Magicians* is an engrossing journey through the heyday of chaos magick and occulture. An essential read for young witches and occultists who want not only to do magick but live magick as well."

CHAWEON KOO, AUTHOR OF *SPELL BOUND*

"Carl Abrahamsson has done it again. In his new work, the master occultist once again displays his uncanny knack for being at the right place at the right time to ask the right people the right questions. And boy, does he get answers. From his formative years in the 1980s and '90s up to the present day, Abrahamsson has had his ever-sensitive finger on the always unpredictable pulse of postmodern occultism. In his new book, he shares the remarkable insights and adventures he has had along the way. A must-read for any student of the mystic arts."

GARY LACHMAN, AUTHOR OF
THE SECRET TEACHERS OF THE WESTERN WORLD

"On the surface, *Meetings with Remarkable Magicians* is an engaging and detailed record of a historic time when magick, art, and mainstream culture coincided. It's a tale populated by diverse and wonderful characters and places. But it's not just a description; this book is a work of magick itself, capturing a self-reflective arc of one man's journey to transcendence. This is your own opportunity to meet a remarkable magician: Carl Abrahamsson."

PHILIP H. FARBER, AUTHOR OF *BRAIN MAGICK*

"This book is no old-school hagiography, nor a simple recounting of ritual practices or name-checking remarkable and iconic figures in a magical and creative community. In fact, I would balk at describing it as a book and prefer to designate it as a high-order synaptic stimulant. *Meetings with Remarkable Magicians* is a fascinating, well-written piece of literature that buzzes with information, process, and art surrounding a group of people who chose to live their lives in a transformative, challenging, and often subversive but always creative manner. Simply enough, it's a great book that informs you, shakes you up, and takes you to places where there is no such thing as stasis—only endless creative, transformative movement."

CHARLOTTE RODGERS, AUTHOR OF *THE BLOODY SACRIFICE*

"Carl Abrahamsson is a gardener of outsider blooms, a curator of creators, and a maverick maestro of magick. He makes stuff happen. With his infinite enthusiasm for the weird and the interesting, he is a swirling galaxy of ideas. We need more of him in our world."

VAL DENHAM, VISUAL AND RECORDING ARTIST

MEETINGS WITH REMARKABLE MAGICIANS

Life in the Occult Underground

CARL ABRAHAMSSON

Inner Traditions
Rochester, Vermont

Inner Traditions
One Park Street
Rochester, Vermont 05767
www.InnerTraditions.com

SUSTAINABLE FORESTRY INITIATIVE   Certified Sourcing
www.forests.org
SFI-00854

Text stock is SFI certified

Cataloging-in-Publication Data for this title is available from the Library of Congress

ISBN 978-1-64411-848-1 (print)
ISBN 978-1-64411-849-8 (ebook)

Printed and bound in the United States by Lake Book Manufacturing, LLC
The text stock is SFI certified. The Sustainable Forestry Initiative® program
promotes sustainable forest management.

10 9 8 7 6 5 4 3 2 1

Text design by Virginia Scott Bowman and layout by Debbie Glogover
This book was typeset in Garamond Premier Pro with Editor, Gill Sans MT Pro,
Gin and Thrillers used as display typefaces

The Ordo Templi Orientis logo is a registered trademark of Ordo Templi Orientis
and used by permission. Poems by Genesis P-Orridge appear by kind permission of
the Estate of Genesis Breyer P-Orridge.

To send correspondence to the author of this book, mail a first-class letter to the
author c/o Inner Traditions • Bear & Company, One Park Street, Rochester, VT
05767, and we will forward the communication, or contact the author directly at
carlabrahamsson.com.

Contents

Foreword
Frater U∴D∴

It is generally held that magicians are of an egomaniacal disposition or, at the very least, an egotistical one. While Aleister Crowley's infamous *Confessions* may provide a case in point (depending on your personal view of the Master Therion), this mainstream assessment does not dovetail too neatly with the fact that actual autobiographies of practicing magicians, which we would accordingly expect to be inundated by, are relatively few and far between. Nor are they all necessarily as egocentric and narcissistic as one might assume: case in point being the present work by Carl Abrahamsson.

Primarily known to the general international occult public via the high-class magazine *The Fenris Wolf*, which he founded and continues to present us with on a more or less yearly basis, he has made his indelible mark as a top-level curator of Occulture and the various magical currents that are extant within this framework. His astute intelligence and brilliant networking skills, coupled with one-of-a-kind undogmatic open-minded pragmatism and an insatiable curiosity, have made him an ideal go-to point of documentation for just about anyone actively involved in present-day Dark Arts.

But there is a lot more than quantitative social connectedness to make his autobiography a most unusual—and equally most welcome—publication. As a participating observer, he manages to fuse the etic with the emic approach in an organic and enlightening way, which, even more importantly, remains constructive and does not play one point of view against the other. Here is someone speaking to us from hands-on experience: of ritual and of sigilizing, of sex-magic and results-magic, deeply rooted in his practical scrutiny and workings on the *inside* of occult orders such as TOPY and the Caliphate OTO, narrating his interactions over many years with influential figures of the occult current such as Genesis P-Orridge, Anton Szandor LaVey, and Kenneth Anger, to name but the most outstanding examples.

At the same time, Carl is a veritable master of contextualization, putting things very much into perspective along the trajectory of his multiple and vastly varied aesthetic interests. These range from his deeply informed, academically schooled expertise on cinema (both mainstream and underground), amplified by his own prolific filmmaking; to fringe and avant-garde music (again both theoretical and performative); and to experimental literature of all flavors, more than mildly spiced up with his voracious reading (and publishing) of occult authors in general, including Aleister Crowley and Austin Osman Spare in particular.

He also depicts in a perfectly nonjudgmental manner what LaVey termed (by Carl's quote) the—typically American if not Californian—"burlesquing" of the occult subculture from the 1960s to the present: ruthless Hollywood showbiz meets Disneyfied theme-park industry meets drug culture meets Eastward-looking spiritual neohippyism, and so on, and so forth.

Carl doesn't bother too much with abstract theory. Not that he is unaware of it. Someone as widely and thoroughly read as he is in the occult field is certainly able to engage in intellectual reflection and philosophical, existential musing. But his focus is different. As a self-confessed "occult lifer," he is far more interested in what the various disciplines, schools, sects, teachings, organizations, and collectives of Occulture actually have to offer in terms of *lived* and *living* application, of coloring and "magi-fying" the world both on the subjective and the transpersonal level—in short, as I would like to summarize it, his is the remit of *experiential gnosis*. This makes for quite a lot of delightful reading, taking us along on a ripping high-octane magical mystery tour of occult life with all its highs and lows, its shining peaks and gloomy abysses, its successes and failures, its geniuses and morons, its brilliance and its madness.

For all his easygoing eloquence, which more than once reminds us— in an entirely pleasant, relatable manner—of that other great Swedish raconteur, Lars Gustafsson, he never insults the reader's intelligence by spelling everything out too obviously. Hence, we are all well advised to read between the lines as well while we are at it. Not because there's any intentional obfuscation at work here—far from it—but because there's many a truth and insight, whether occult or not, that can only be intuited rather than made subject to facile ratiocination. After all, human language was never made for this: systemically veiling, not revealing, as any poet and bard worth their salt will mournfully tell you. And hasn't it been claimed since time immemorial that the mysteries, after all is said and done, will ultimately protect themselves?

There's a significant observation of Carl's that informs his entire narrative and serves exceedingly well as a key to understanding its motor:

> That is highly significant of real magicians: they weave webs in which others interact and sometimes start weaving their own webs. The intelligent magicians acknowledge the importance of the weaving masters as well as the past masters; the unintelligent are satisfied with claiming their own position while staring at their own reflective blinders.

It is his lifetime exploration of this particular aspect of Occulture that makes this autobiography so fascinating, enlightening, and entertaining. Moreover, it offers us a yarn very well spun, richly peppered with micro-biographies of the countless protagonists—heroes and rogues alike—who have molded, imprinted, impressed, and coined the entire occult ecosystem. To a considerable extent, they are still continuing to do so.

Whether it concerns the politics of a controversial poet like Ezra

Pound, or the antidemocratic elitism propagated in Crowley's *Book of the Law* or in the works of other authoritarian, anti-liberal figures, Carl can be relied on to take a strong, vociferous stand against what he terms the "invisible forces of fabricated moralities." It is quite obvious that today's ubiquitous monodimensional cancel culture and streamlined (screamlined?) commodification of artistic and metaphysical creativity are not for him. This lends an equally unfashionable and admirable quality to his approach that is very much in line with the common position of dedicated occultists as societal outsiders throughout history. Whether they are factually avant-garde and prescient, or reactionary and revisionist, it matters not in the slightest. Despite all the helpful services that spiritual technicians like shamans, witches, medicine men and women, cunning folk, houngans, mambos, sangumas, vitkis, sadhus, brujos, and curanderas might render to their communities, they have nevertheless always been seen as essentially *alien*. Such figures—who are perhaps best described from an optimist's point of view as the "spiritual-enlightenment-obsessed fringe"—seldomly become socially adapted beings subservient to their mainstream's currently projected braindead dogmas, creativity-busting regulations, and toxic prejudices. The same is true of artists. And, while I suspect he won't like this, for all his fulminant activities as a dyed-in-the-wool party animal and Occulture lounge lizard, Carl has retained that one critical quality that ranks him squarely and incontestably with his occultist forebears, his sorcerous contemporaries, and (it is to be hoped) his magical successors: the uncompromising, tireless exploration of what is behind the mirror of so-called reality—a looking glass that is often as shiny, blinking, and seductive as it is dull, blunt, and horrifying. What's more, for him it's not about the answers but rather the creative evolution and pursuit of open-ended (as opposed to closure-seeking) questions. (Perhaps Aleister Crowley's severely underrated little essay "The Soldier and the Hunchback" might contribute a thing or two to this discussion but that, as they say, is another ditty for another campfire . . .)

His observations on occult tropes such as the "Abyss," the

"Holy Guardian Angel," and that ever-looming elephant in the temple—the "Ego"—are revelatory and probably, to many, novel, since they are driven by hands-on, pragmatic experience. They may be subjective and individualistic, sure, but are nevertheless entirely appropriate and valid in just about every conceivable transpersonal sense. This is a rare mastery sadly lacking in most other magical autobiographies, whether they're of a self-avowedly overt hagiographic bent (such as Uncle Aleister's) or not.

Nothing presented here in loving detail comes over as monolithic or hewn into some stony stele in a silly conceit of captured, colonized eternity. Instead, things are and remain fluid and in flux, as they've always been from the get-go. Truth, lest we forget, is a cunning shape-shifter of dubious provenance, which is why it invariably requires the perennial trickster to make it stick. Ernst Jünger's figure of the Anarch offers us the indispensable archetype of the magician in a world so desperately set on shedding off its magic like a desiccated rustling snakeskin in favor of vainglorious discursive reasoning and its incumbent orgiastic cerebral contouring endeavors. "He that hath ears to hear, let him hear" (Matthew 11:15).

By the same token, it is acutely interesting to witness the evolution of Carl's assessment of both the OTO and Aleister Crowley, two prime sources of inspiration from which he quaffed for many decades. His involvement spanned the entire spectrum from original naive, romanticizing tyro enthusiasm to serious and engaged organizational activism, to distanced sobriety and sniper-precise, hard-nosed critique, albeit never disrespectful or malign. For many—though perhaps far too few—of today's more experienced magicians, this represents a paradigmatic and often inescapable omphalotomy: a failsafe indicator of genuinely accomplished personal maturation.

For anyone truly familiar with the process, it is anything but astounding to learn that it may require an entire lifetime of immersion to arrive at a conclusion such as this one:

One of the key concepts in magico-anthropology is *Sympathesis*, which means that we all (both as individuals and as collectives) construct the magical systems that we need in order to transcend (them). The more specialized, abstracted, and complicated our culture becomes, the more our magical systems will reflect these same tendencies. These systems become like a mirror of the soul, in which we can find temporary openings or cracks to peek through.

Please do read on then, esteemed reader, if you are seriously prepared—as if one ever could be!—to find out more, though possibly at the very real risk of having your mind blown in the sweetest of subversive old-school manners . . .

A cosmopolitan lover of nature; a seasoned explorer of the geographical world, scrutinizing it through the highly polished lens of its spiritual topography, on a never-ending pilgrimage through the multivalent manifestations of the inner and the outer realms and planes; an intellectually discerning, highly educated observer of the human mind and its frenzied carousel of individualistic and collective expression; a shrewd yet unwaveringly constructive critic of the politics, the histories, the economics, the sociologics, the sciences, the ecologics . . . in short: the *Culture*—yes, with a capital C!—of our times and beyond, Carl's is a voice of a kind we cannot hear enough of within the frequently all too parochial, smug, myopic, self-serving and self-exploitative global society of today in general and Occulture in particular.

So cordial thanks, Carl, for this veritable labor of Love under Will!

Frater U.·.D.·., founder of Pragmatic and Ice Magic, is Europe's best-known practical magician and contemporary occult author. He has written more than twenty-five books. His translations include works by Peter Carroll and Ramsey Dukes and Aleister Crowley's *Book of Lies*.

Introduction

What makes a Swedish kid from a cultured and secular upper-middle-class home devote his life to magic and occultism in all its forms, times, and spaces? I wish I had a simple answer to the question—because I am that kid. I would love to know, myself. All I can do is to try to look back, process the findings, and see what the future might bring. And I'm happy to share with you the journey thus far.

I am still amazed at the things I've experienced and all the magical people I've met. Some of these key players exist aboveground, while others remain underground. What unites them is the accumulated insight that there's always more to life than what we perceive with our senses. Not that there's anything wrong with our senses—on the contrary! But we do have inherent capacities to acquire and process knowledge and wisdom from hitherto unfairly unacknowledged quarters. I'm not only talking about dusty grimoires from ancient times, but rather what we can find within ourselves if we are courageous enough to look, and to take the process itself and the findings seriously.

This generalization has been called by many names and interpreted by many people and groups throughout the millennia. But it always boils down to the same essential things: *personal refinement, improvement, empowerment, and transformation through experimental means and methods.*

Some like to walk alone; they seek out isolation as something sacred—and invaluable. Others prefer to seduce the masses, to make the proverbial "big bucks" in public. What is or has been hidden is always fascinating and glamorous. There is power in secrets as well as in the ensuing promises of gradual revelation. If one moves occult teachings over to the visible sphere, they can be mass-marketed in ten easy steps of this and that. Or they can be fetishized and kept exclusive by bibliophile mentalities that often keep the buyers/readers locked in the symbolic realm—because the book's price tag apparently dictates its value, rather than its inherent potential for real change in life.

Magic exists within us all. It is in each of us, and within each collective and community—even those with which we might not "agree." Sometimes the expressed messages reveal unintentional draconian humor, as in mass political or religious movements in which the individual is emasculated while believing there is power in whatever fairy tale or dogmatic concoction is offered. Sometimes the teachings take on shocking and dramatic imagery in order to awaken the sleepers. And sometimes they speak clearly of what should be done, stripped to the core and devoid of allegiances or aesthetics.

Already as a teenager, I found all this fascinating. Why do some people invoke cosmic forces disguised as gods, angels, or demons? Why have systems been structured that promise that the seeker will find . . . something? And what is that something, really? A safe, comfortable, and invisible space among the like-minded? A pristine individuation based on a Nietzschean appreciation of Will? A cosmic escapism? A potential catharsis from early trauma? Et cetera (and I mean that—the list could go on for a long time).

As I set out on this journey in my teenage years, there was already a constructive foundation to build upon. As a newborn babe in Stockholm, Sweden, I wasn't only born into a solid situation of love and support. I also had a magical cradle. This might seem Harry Potter–like to some, but it's true. My father ran a famous jazz club in Stockholm called The Golden Circle. He loved jazz and had traveled to New York as a teenager in the late 1950s to immerse himself in the scene. He wanted to bring as much of it as possible to lovely but conservative old Stockholm. And he did, through The Golden Circle.

Around the time of my birth, January 1966, someone came by my parents' apartment, carrying a cradle for me. It was Ornette Coleman, experimental jazz guru extraordinaire, who was in town to play at the club. In that cradle I rocked and slept and dreamed and excreted both this and that, for months on end.

Although in my teenage years I hated jazz because it was my dad's interest, it didn't take me too long to realize how cool my initial rocking was: I had been graced by the hand of a genius artist right when I was born. *The hand that rocks the cradle . . .*

Growing up, I was immersed in my parents' interest in music, film, books, and art in general. At age two, I was at the opening of the legendary Andy Warhol exhibition at Moderna Muséet in Stockholm. Somewhere in my memory bank there should be visions of the pop artist from New York carefully walking around his show and saying, "Oh, that's great" to each and everyone.

As a child, I was a loner—or perhaps I should claim I was "picky" about whom I wanted to play with? This attitude has never really left me, and it has become the cornerstone of a healthy and contrarian worldview in which I make decisions and judgments based as fully as possible on my own impressions, assessments, and deductions. Sometimes you don't have to make "your own" mistakes in order to learn social skills; reading history and watching people around you will often suffice.

I did embrace the cultural input from my parents but of course wanted to seek out other sources for myself. Moving by attraction and intuition, I found my own fodder. In large part these came from a great bookstore called Hörnan ("the Corner"), which imported mainstream comics, underground comics, and science fiction from the US. My parents also had friends in the US who sent me comic books and American candy. Much appreciated!

Like many kids in the late 1970s, I was swept away by punk rock and its creative cousins post-punk and new wave. The music was great and the energy perfect for my contrarian mind-frame. Whatever these frustrated youngsters were actually singing about ("White Riot," "Protex Blue," "Tommy Gun," to cull a few exciting themes from the band The Clash), it was the energy itself that hit me first and foremost.

And more comics! More movies! More books! I was very hungry and curious, and loved to connect my own dots based on what I'd already found. I also knew early on that I loved to write, so a natural next step for me was to write about the things that thrilled me. This began in the world of comic books. Together with friends I started a fanzine called *Splasch* in 1982. It basically contained interviews with comic-book artists like Jean Giraud (aka "Moebius"), André Franquin, and Aldus Maurice de Bevère (aka "Morris"). It was exciting to talk to these artists and to process, write, and edit the material—and then cut and paste it all into pages that were printed and assembled. Absolutely magical!

In the mid-1980s I followed suit with the music and trash-culture fanzines *Lollipop* and *Acts of Interstellar Torture* (1985–1988). Learning how to write, edit, and take pictures as I went along, not to mention laying it all out on paper, while indulging in my own interests, was a fantastic education. I was also "empowered" by another fact: my experiences showed me that it was easier than I thought to connect with rock'n'roll people, regardless of whether they were real stars or struggling underground bands. All you had to do was be at the right place at the right time, and be persistent in the face of any initial hurdles. A great picture only takes 1/125th of a second to capture—you just have to pick the right micro-moment! The same goes for the interviews: if you want them to say something special, you need to ask a special question. I loved my time in the underground cultural trenches. In retrospect, it constituted the kindergarten years of my magical training.

As the 1970s turned into the 1980s, I grew more and more curious about what was called the nascent industrial music scene. The term came from a record label in London called Industrial Records. Their output was so influential that it created an entire "scene"—not just in the UK, but around the world.

The main band on the label, Throbbing Gristle ("TG"), was headed by a British artist called Genesis P-Orridge. In interviews, he talked about experimental art and music, surrealism, and occultism, and name-dropped several authors and artists that piqued my curiosity. As TG and Industrial Records folded in 1981, in favor of P-Orridge's new project, Psychic Television ("PTV"), the references just kept on coming. And there was the added allure of occultism proper, as the band had their own magical order called "Thee Temple Ov Psychick Youth" (TOPY).

Did I dive right in and get involved myself? Indeed I did, even to the point of starting a Scandinavian branch of the Temple called "TOPYSCAN." From then and on, everything snowballed in various directions. I was already reading Aleister Crowley and Anton LaVey, as well as some historical overviews about magic, so to suddenly be in the modern-day midst of something that was magical and experimental at the same time quite literally blew my young mind. I felt very strongly that I needed to connect with the current, so to speak, even if it would take me into unchartered territories. This is what I did—and it's the story that you're about to read.

As decades have passed and I'm now somewhat reluctantly approaching the (early) autumn season of my life, I feel compelled to share my experiences thus far. I have never been one for secrecy, but rather believe in blatantly inspiring others to set out on their own paths. If someone is too secretive or too beholden to a rigid system, it's probably best to keep your distance from them . . . inertia alert!

That said, I hope I haven't betrayed any oaths or confidences within these pages. If that should be the case, I claim immunity from the standpoint of necessity. If there is one thing I've learned over these decades, it's that magic as such is an integral, central part of our survival instinct. If there was ever a time to find new solutions to our overwhelming human problems, it is right now. The rapid occulturation* of hitherto

---

Occulturation is my term for when something moves from an occult(ed) sphere and into the mainstream of culture.

secret teachings into both the occulture and the mainstream are basically indications that our collective unconscious is telling us to wake up before it's too late. How hard can it be to understand? Acknowledging intuition, Indigenous wisdom, holistic approaches, and the psychological benefits of meditation and ritual will become increasingly crucial elements in avoiding human extinction, and/or possibly rebuilding a human culture after the seemingly inevitable deluge stemming from human hubris.

At this point in history, will we listen to the magicians? The ancient ones or the present ones—all claiming some little secret or wisdom that can "change your life"? We shall see! I don't claim to own any quick fixes, nor do I offer "ten easy steps." But I will assert that it's much easier to get to know yourself than you think. All you must do is listen—*to yourself.* If more people did that, we would have considerably less problems in the world.

In writing this book, I have listened to myself. I have enjoyed most of what I've said. It has made sense. If I had the chance to relive these experiences, I might go through some of them differently—but definitely *not* with a different attitude. To me, it's been simple enough: set out on the path, be honest, keep moving, swerve if you have to, document the work, cherish the mysteries, and just make sure to enjoy life—because for each of us it's *very* limited in time and space.

I once formulated magic as being "a neutral mind-frame that allows *all* the definitions of magic to pass through it." What that means in reality is that it could be a strictly causal, willed process; it could be an irrational orgy of overheated synapses; it could be cosmic stardust sprinkled on your perfectly still mind; it could be the gray area that filters a rainbow spectrum; it could be human fusion as genitals interlock, and the fission when the deed is done; or a gazillion other things and definitions, cosmic and mundane. You can define it any way you want—just don't shove your definition down someone else's throat (unless it's consensual).

Some of my friends from school have become millionaires, or more than that. I, on the other hand, have written much about "magic," based on my own firsthand experiences in a lifelong exploration of myself, the mysteries, and the potential merger of the two. Would I trade places? I think not. Money is great but it can only take you so far. Magic, however, is infinite, eternal, unbound, and, ultimately, proto-creative.

So, the first question before we set out would be: *Why settle for less when you can be immersed in a whole lot more?* And in this spirit, a little note on the structuring of this book: human perception isn't always perfectly chronological. I seem to think about the past mainly in palimpsestic impressions and through memories that poke each other in the fight for attention. In some instances, the chapters hold chronological sway, and in others I have preferred to intuitively arrange things by thematic or emotional kinship. I like to hold fast to the pleasant spirit of Quintilian: *Scribo ad narrandum, non ad probandum*—I write to tell, not to prove.

Vade Ultra!

PART I

1984–1989

 DO IT YOURSELF!

I graduated high school in Stockholm in 1984, at age eighteen. By this point in my life I was already very hungry for information of various kinds, including the occult and philosophy in general. Much of this was further fueled by my interest in experimental music. At around this time (the late 1970s, early 1980s) there was a vital and vibrant music scene in which people took concepts of musical normality and turned them on their heads, using new technology, a lo-fi attitude, and a "cottage-industry" sensibility that had been inherited from the punk movement and its "do-it-yourself" (DIY) ethos. Various bands, artists, and labels presented their work in a new way. Not only was it self-produced, controlled, and sometimes even self-distributed, it was also filled with references to their own sources of inspiration. In interviews, traditionally inclined artists might mention those who had influenced them—someone playing a similar kind of instrument, or another performer, writer, or poet. But this new scene, which was called "industrial" music, also contained many deliberate references, which might be overtly stated in informational pamphlets, record sleeves, and interviews, or covertly woven into lyrics. These allusions or associations were not meant to serve as demagogic propaganda, but as fodder for archeological forays in which one could uncover similar kinds of culture from previous eras.

One example would be the integration of the writings of William Burroughs and Brion Gysin, as well as many other beatnik writers, into the overall cauldron of bands like Throbbing Gristle and Psychic TV. Once I had awoken to all of the great music that was being made and put out in the late-1970s and early-1980s, I became like a sponge, eager to soak up information from all of the bands and artists that interested me through their fascinating music, and their inspiring ways of making records and creating a distinct culture. They left traces—intellectual, inspirational traces—in their trail. And I, like many others, followed up on the clues and it became a form of esoteric detective work to discover more of the same. So, this was not just a matter of consuming entertainment made by intelligent and intellectual people—it was also a networking search for information on different art and artists, and in this particular scene, it was also about magic and occultism.

One of the bands that I really enjoyed was the British group Psychic TV, or Psychic Television, or PTV for short. They were connected to their own magical order and information network called Thee Temple Ov Psychick Youth (TOPY). The key people in PTV, Genesis P-Orridge and Peter "Sleazy" Christopherson, had been involved previously with the band Throbbing Gristle, which I also liked a lot. This phenomenon of integrating esoteric material—whether literary, cultural, or magical—became a standard procedure for these people, a regular part of their output. The LP records contained musical structures, as well as textual explorations of a poetic nature. But there was also something intangible about their releases, which encouraged a way of thinking and acting that resonated with me greatly. Together with the records of Psychic TV, there was usually some kind of information attached, not seldom

Gothenburg, 1988
(Photo by Johan Kugelberg)

an encouragement to get in touch with this "mysterious" organization: Thee Temple Ov Psychick Youth. You could subscribe to their information for a very reasonable fee. I signed up and soon started to receive newsletters, mailings, and general information from their headquarters in London.

I was also collecting cassette tapes at the time through an international tape-trading network. This entailed exchanging or "swapping" cassettes, often live recordings of concerts, with others. Many of these recordings were of the band Psychic TV. And often one would find extra material that the people who spread them had added to the cassettes—usually interviews from the radio or interviews they had done themselves. This was the case with many of the Psychic TV tapes that I traded. There were interviews with Genesis P-Orridge in which he talked about the methods and aims of both Psychic TV and Thee Temple Ov Psychick Youth. This was very inspiring for me, and not only because I liked the music and poetry they created. Their work also represented a philosophy that favored individualism—pushing the individual to be strong and free and to have options in life, many of which TOPY claimed one could reach through unorthodox methods of magic and the study of certain esoteric or occult sources.

This open-mindedness was very appealing. As a teenager, I had already developed a passionate attraction to occultism. I had bought and read some books on the subject, such as Colin Wilson's classic study *The Occult*, Aleister Crowley's *The Book of the Law*, and Anton LaVey's *The Satanic Bible*—basically, (in)famous books that also happened to be somewhat readily available.

As I started getting into the philosophy of Thee Temple Ov Psychick Youth, it made me more curious about the references that they provided in their information, mainly having to do with two British magicians: Aleister Crowley (1875–1947) and the much less well-known Austin Osman Spare (1886–1956). These people were groundbreaking and radical in the sense that they had gone against the grain of "traditional occultism" (e.g., the sort presented via the Hermetic Order of the Golden

Dawn, which had been founded in the last decades of the nineteenth century). Crowley had studied and developed as a magician in the Golden Dawn. But he had also published their rituals without permission in his ambitious, almost encyclopedic work of ten books called *The Equinox*. This had led to controversy, in the wake of which he was kicked out of the Golden Dawn. Crowley then went on to create his own order, which he called the A∴A∴* In structure, the A∴A∴ resembled what Crowley found in the Golden Dawn, but it was informed by a much different philosophical perspective. This was based on an experience that he had in Cairo, Egypt, together with his wife Rose, in 1904, which had made him believe that he was the prophet of a "new age" he called the Aeon of Horus and of a philosophy he called Thelema (from one of the Greek words signifying "Will"). Around the new framework, he wove all his arcane magical knowledge that stemmed from the Western ceremonial magic tradition. Crowley was also a great synthesizer or syncretist, bringing in elements from Eastern traditions such as yoga and meditation, and from Jewish mysticism, including the Qabalah.

Austin Osman Spare was a much more freewheeling character who worked on his own, mainly as an artist. He had had connections with Crowley and other people in London at this time, but he was not an extroverted networker. He was more interested in his own work, and in how his art could be used for occult experiments and actual magical workings.

These two magicians were seminal in the philosophical corpus of Thee Temple Ov Psychick Youth, which also made references to surrealism, forgotten literary figures, and beatniks, and, to a certain extent, the hippies of the 1960s. These were all people and movements that went against the grain, having done so with the express purpose of securing individual liberty. The more these forgotten or ostracized people were brought to the light, the greater the chance that they would inspire

---

*Possibly short for Argenteum Astrum or Astron Argon (both meaning "Silver Star"), or Atlantean Adepts, or Arcanum Arcanorum ("Secret of Secrets").

young people specifically to evaluate themselves and the cards they had been dealt, so to speak.

TOPY's active integration of cultural expressions within a magical philosophy made it especially unique. It was something more than an initiatory magical curriculum through which the student or the seeker would be led gradually toward a greater realization of his or her true self. TOPY had dispensed with that classical, arcane mentality and its archaic way of organizing the work in a hierarchical structure based on degrees and initiations. However, there were different levels of commitment within TOPY. These mainly had to do with working within the local groups and taking care of various menial and sometimes boring administrative tasks, such as informational mailings and helping in the organization of events; in other words, real, practical work.

But there was also another level of commitment that existed within TOPY, and that had to do more concretely with magical work. The main form of this was called *sigilizing*. The concept came from Austin Osman Spare: he claimed that one can drop little symbols, signifying whatever one wants to achieve in the outer material world, into our subconscious mind by using ecstatic techniques and states of mind. These could include physical exhaustion, sexual exhaustion, or mental exhaustion—basically, frames of mind that are out of the ordinary and far removed from the rational. At the height of the ecstatic experience, one would then visualize, sensualize, and integrate a symbol that one has concocted oneself.

Within TOPY, this led to fervent experimentation and to an inclusion of the creative artistic process. This was never done in a dogmatically imposed manner; rather, it was an anarchic, self-imposed, experimental kind of work. No one really evaluated or judged the output of someone else. The main thing was to be true to the essence of the desire in question; how this was expressed creatively was an individual matter.

Regular engagement with the sigilization process and the kinds of artwork that it produced became an integrated phenomenon within the higher levels of TOPY commitment. By physically mailing these highly

personal artworks to the headquarters in London after each completion, you reached the level of becoming an initiate of sorts. This was not
something to be displayed as a status symbol. It was an individual process: something you did only with and for yourself. The fact that you
"released" your magical artwork and sent it away was in line with the philosophy of Austin Spare, and traditional occultism in general—meaning
that when you have worked with and experienced the ecstasy of "metaprogramming" (as I later came to call it), you have to completely disengage
yourself from the experience after it is over. You must divest yourself of
the irrational peak ecstasy, in order to prevent your rational mind from
trying to nitpick and analyze what has occurred. Because if that happens,
it will hamper and hinder the magical processes that allow for the goal
to unfold successfully. Although these artworks were collected and kept
safe at the three main TOPY "Stations" (administrative centers), they
were not meant to be displayed or used in any further way. Rather, it was
an archive of accumulated magical "trust"—trust in each other, but also
trust in yourself and your own magical, experimental process.

Another inspiring and important order was—and still is—the
Illuminates of Thanateros, also known as the IOT, or the "Pact." To
make a long story very short, they are an interesting mix of Austin Spare's
sigilizing theories and a loosely scientific approach that they called "Chaos
Magic." Central to the methods (and anti-methods) of the IOT are
ecstatic techniques wherein the practitioner exhausts the body and mind
to the point of "voidness" through exercise, sex, drugs, or other means. In
that moment, the practitioner declares the Will to themself, as well as to
the Universe. But this is just one among many techniques and approaches
developed by the IOT. They produced the great magazine *Chaos
International*, edited by Ian Read, which I lustfully devoured whenever
a new issue came out. Although the key players—which included Peter
J. Carroll, Frater U.'.D.'., Phil Hine, Ray Sherwin, and others—had also
written books of their own, I found the magazine to be wonderfully vital
and substantial to read. The Chaos crew had a genuinely open-minded
attitude, and they seemed happy to add to their repertoire *any* technique

that works. They took a pragmatic and experimental approach, avoiding the establishment of structures that were too rigid or too solid. Many of their writings still hold up very well, and when looking back at old issues of *Chaos International*, I can see how my own thinking was influenced by many of these people, such as Frater U∴D∴:

> In its pure form, the shaman or magician is not in need of spirits or other entities. The world is viewed as being "vitalized" by subtle forces or energies and his primary task consists in mastering the art of perceiving and manipulating them. As all phenomena are basically energetic in nature, the existence of an otherworld is strictly not required. Thus the magician is more of an "energy dancer" than a "fence rider" or go-between. But even here the key to the perception, charging and general utilization of these forces is again the magical trance or, as Chaos Magic terms it, gnosis.*

William Burroughs was allegedly a member of the IOT, and I'm sure many other notables were too. Much of the exciting occulture that grew out of the UK specifically during the 1990s seems to have been influenced in some way or another by the "Chaos current" and its sardonic open-mindedness—the output of the brilliant author Alan Moore is certainly one such example.

In late 1984, Psychic TV toured Scandinavia and passed through Stockholm. On the evening before the actual concert, there was a special video event at the one of the art colleges, presenting the work of "Psychic Television" (meaning the video-production side of the TOPY collective; this was a network of video-makers for which Psychic TV, the band, made music). I attended that screening in high spirits. TV monitors were stacked on the floor, and not that many people were in attendance; everything was quite informal. To me, it was very interesting because I had never seen any of the actual PTV films before; I had

---

*Frater U∴D∴, "Models of Magic," *Chaos International* 9 (1990), 3.

only read and heard about them. This was at a time when material like this was disseminated and distributed on VHS cassettes, and I had not yet gotten my hands on any of those experimental VHS anthologies in which these films were included. So, I was eager to watch them—all the more so since I was very fascinated by cinema in general at this time, and experimental film in particular.

I could also see how well the Psychic Television films fit into a tradition of surrealism. But it certainly wasn't surrealism of a happy or colorful kind, titillating the senses with puns and light intellectual word games. These PTV films were much more morose, gritty, and "hardcore" in the sense that wherever you looked, there was always a general reference to magic as a soul-searching and potentially transgressive way of changing yourself. The potential for change was inherent in the material, and many of the films included actual ritual footage. I found that clarity and signal very inspiring.

I had at this time already started to successfully experiment with the rituals TOPY recommended in their mailings and newsletters, but I had not yet become a sigilizing member. The video evening illuminated a link to something that was highly intimate and resonant for me in my private investigations: I realized that the personal process has, or can have, a tangible connection in the outer. And the filter or mediator in question is Art. This was at an *art* college, and they had made *art* films that also displayed and conveyed their philosophy in a similar way to their music.

On the following evening, there was a wonderful lineup at the club Kolingsborg, with Psychic TV headlining. They were supported by the Leather Nun, one of my favorite Swedish bands, and the American artist Monte Cazazza, who had been a friend and collaborator of P-Orridge's since the mid-1970s. Both the Leather Nun and Monte Cazazza had records released on Industrial Records (the label which had been established by Throbbing Gristle). This was therefore a very special evening—although it didn't quite turn out the way I had envisioned.

I had seen the Leather Nun live several times and really enjoyed their kind of heavy rock, which drew a lot of inspiration from Iggy and the Stooges. They were also part of this industrial music scene that was specific and very powerful, but quite violent in a certain way too. I think it mainly had to do with aesthetics. On this particular evening the club was packed with people waiting to see the new cult band from England, because Throbbing Gristle still had a huge following.

The atmosphere was very weird. There were two stacks of video monitors—probably the same ones they had used at the art school the evening before—and they were showing the same experimental art films, including elements that some people found very disturbing (footage of ritual cutting, for instance). There was a contingent of skinheads around and they were quite rowdy. Jonas Almquist, the singer of the Leather Nun, had been a skinhead at one point in the early 1980s. Now these guys were acting up and being aggressive and pushing people around. I was disturbed by this, as I wanted to enjoy the concert without idiots like that ruining it.

As I watched the Leather Nun play, they reached a crescendo with their song "FFA" ("Fist Fuckers Associated"), the lyrics of which came from a poem by Monte Cazazza. They performed it so beautifully; it really blew my mind. Cazazza joined in and sang, as did P-Orridge. To me it was like a meltdown-experience: something that was utterly cool and transgressive, but at the same time—via the philosophy of Psychic TV—entirely magical.

But the skinheads were continually aggressive and it freaked me out because I saw people being pushed to the ground and no one interfered; no one really stopped them. I realized that I couldn't enjoy the evening because of these cretins, which was deeply frustrating. I probably should just have found a more secluded spot and had a drink or something, but instead I decided to leave. Afterward I heard from people who were there that Psychic TV were, of course, amazing. I immediately acquired a pirated cassette recording of the concert. I had seen the video show, but I missed the concert. At least I got to experience Genesis P-Orridge and Monte Cazazza perform together with the Leather Nun, though, so there was some consolation in that.

HEADQUARTERS

By the mid-1980s I had already been to London several times. It was inexpensive to take a bus to Gothenburg from Stockholm, and then the horrible "booze boat" ferry to Harwich in the UK, and then a train to London. I usually ended up at some fleabag hotel in Bayswater.

I liked the grime and dirt of London. What today feels like urban heart-congestion was thrilling to me as a teenager. London's book and record stores were amazing—whether small, specialized shops or giant "megastores," they offered much more than I could ever take in. Not to forget the secondhand bookstores, filled to the brim with tomes I never even knew about (but certainly needed to). It was truly a paradise for a budding bibliomaniac and music lover like me.

In 1986 I went to meet Genesis P-Orridge for the first time. My fanzine *Lollipop* had been my main creative project for about a year, and I had been a TOPY "subscriber" for about two years. It made perfect sense to try to arrange an interview with Genesis. We set it up, and when I visited London in November of 1986, I took the "tube" to Bethnal Green and walked until I arrived at 50 Beck Road. I didn't pick up on it so much at the time, but this was a really grimy area with seemingly endless rows of small houses stuck together.

"Gen" opened the door and let me in. There was a small hallway and an office to the right. TOPY and the affiliated company "Temple Records" were expanding, and I immediately felt at home in this "cottage-industry" environment where the real hard currency was always postage stamps and "IRCs."*

I immediately took a liking to Gen. He was friendly and accommodating, eager to make me feel at home. Upstairs was the living room and kitchen. I met Gen's wife Paula and their young daughters Caresse

---

*International Reply Coupons were prepaid postal coupons that could be purchased from the post office and enclosed with international correspondence. The recipient would then redeem the IRC for return postage in their local currency.

and Genesse, and the German shepherd Tanith. There were also some other "Psychick Youth," or members of the Temple, around. I got a very typical "cuppa" tea, and we talked about this and that. Although I was there to interview him for my music fanzine, I realized I was even more fascinated with the whole TOPY angle than I was with Psychic TV. These people were living and breathing magic and art around the clock, and they were willing to share with others whatever they had found to be successful and inspiring in their magical work. It was an eye-opener and a mind-blower all at once.

I talked with Gen about musical things for *Lollipop*, and when the interview was over, we just kept on chatting—about Crowley, Spare, music, our mutual Swedish friends Freddie Wadling and Jonas Almquist, and what felt like a million other things.

Although energetic and enthusiastic in conversation, Gen also seemed tired, even exhausted. There was so much to do, and everything was invested with meaning. No time to waste. Already on that first visit, the attitude of a relentless work ethic made a deep impression on me. It was in some ways an initiation by osmosis onto a higher level of both awareness and efficiency.

As I departed Beck Road that evening, Gen made sure that the plastic bag I had arrived with (containing one Sony cassette recorder and one Pentax camera) was now filled with records, cassettes, badges, patches, and leaflets: a heap of fodder for the young Swedish sponge sorcerer!

I was leaving London that same evening. On the road, I remember listening to a cassette Gen had given me. It was the album *In Strict Tempo* by Dave Ball (the musical half of Soft Cell), which featured Gen on some of the tracks. It was such perfect autumn music for a bus ride through a dark and rainy London and its utterly ugly and depressing suburbs. It dawned on me that it's no wonder a place like London has produced so much talent and great art—and now also a magical guerrilla movement in TOPY. It was basically a matter of unveiling the survival instinct. Oppressive ugliness will distill great beauty. And now I had a whole plastic bagful of it!

PSYCHONAUTIC INDIVIDUATION

In 1987 I moved into my own space in Stockholm: a single room apartment with a kitchenette and bathroom. It was an unfathomable relief to leave my parents' home, and especially so because I wanted to experiment more with the magic I had already accepted as an integral part of my life. My parents were nice people who could cope with weird music, books, comics, videos, and my sometimes-erratic behavior, but the actual meditations and rituals felt far too private and intimate to share—even if I performed them in the privacy of my own room. Much better to create a spaceship of one's own.

The year of 1987 was mainly spent in the service of the Air Force, as all Swedish young men were required at that time to devote a year to the armed forces in some capacity. I cannot say I suffered. I was involved in "communications," which entailed working at night in a secret cave up north. Most of the time I was all alone. So, I spent my time during the nights there diligently putting together issues of *Lollipop* and reading Crowley's *Confessions*, while keeping a lazy eye on the secret military machines (which incidentally went out of date and service the following year) and a TV connected to a VCR with some horror movie or pornography to keep me awake and stimulated.

After my military service commitment was over, I felt like I was set free to return to my own space. This led to many great magical realizations, the most important perhaps being that one must use one's time well. As Sun Ra so eloquently put it, "space is the place," but time is undoubtedly the trickster. I realized that I had to be in charge of my time to the greatest extent possible. And even though I worked at a printshop to pay the bills, I could still motivate myself by having access to offset printing and great copying machines. I had definitely become an addict of printed matter. Whatever time was consumed on actual work for others, I could justify by having access to free printing. It was worth it.

My apartment became a "weekend spaceship" for a small circle of close friends, and it helped open my mind in many ways—not only through our various experimental experiences, but also as a result of my own role within these contexts. While I was comfortable being a lone "psychonaut," I was also just as happy to participate in a buzzing energy field made up of an assortment of turned-on goofies. We had a lot of fun, explored a lot of psychedelic culture, and in our own ways formulated our loose results under the banner of the "LIAC" (Lumber Island Acid Crew).* Many great things came out of this vortex, including the work of my friends Patrick Lundborg,† Stefan Kéry,‡ Max Fredrikson,§ and others.

My immersion in books about occult and spiritual topics filled me with great curiosity and inspiration. I thought that there must be some reason for this. After all, I wasn't disgruntled with life in any serious way. So, I don't think my budding interest was driven by a need for fairy-tale escapism, but rather a genuine curiosity based on initial resonance. What were all these magicians throughout time working with—and why? What was this strange sort of resonance I found in people that I had already met (like Gen), or would later meet (like Anton LaVey and filmmaker-magician Kenneth Anger), or even those I could never meet, since they were already gone (like Crowley and Spare)? They were all onto something; that much I could feel.

Experimenting with meditation—whether still, guided, or mantric—was important for me in this early phase. Not only because it was so simple to get started, but also because it provided a basis for all future work. When I first began meditating, it was a solitary pursuit for which I had little guidance outside of books. In retrospect, this was

---

*The name Stockholm loosely translates to "Lumber Islet."

†Patrick Lundborg (1967–2014), author of *Psychedelia—An Ancient Culture, A Modern Way of Life* (Stockholm: Lysergia, 2012).

‡Stefan Kéry (born 1963), musician and impresario behind the Subliminal Sounds record label.

§Max Fredrikson (born 1968), photographer and artist.

a positive thing as it forced me to be pragmatic. I also avoided any judgmental prejudice that I might have absorbed if I had been following the rules—the paradoxical dos and don'ts—of a particular magical order or school of yoga.

On the whole, that attitude has served me well. And it reflects a useful credo in the Satanic toolbox: *Don't take anything for granted.* "Cui Bono?" *Who gains?* At first, go against whatever it is in order to check the resistance. Provoke if need be, and always trust yourself more than others. For me it has been especially true in my magical explorations because so many of the avenues are lined with apparent exclusivity that always comes at a cost. It's not unfair to give something back to whomever is offering wisdom, but it is *always* unfair to yourself to accept and swallow readymade concepts without diligently chewing first. Stay true to your own intuitions!

This brings us to the wonderful idea of the "armchair magician"— something that I've seen myself as for my entire occult career! The phrase is often used dismissively about people who have supposedly not received the same quintessentially cosmic teaching from the very same master as whoever is saying it. It implies passivity, lack of action, and bookishness, whereas the "real deal" would be—what, exactly? I guess anything opposed to the sovereignty of the armchair in general, and, of course, anything that exclusively matches the critic's mind in particular.

In my own case, most everything begins in the armchair or in an "armchair state of mind." I get inspired by thinking by and to myself, and sometimes together with others. The first filtering that occurs is intellectual, usually poked at by something from the emotional sphere (which is an occulted quagmire).

For me, there's a good enough analogy in the relationship between rational empiricists and intuitive cosmic minds. Empiricism demands hard facts and trials to methodically get to "the truth," or at least to *a* truth. That's a beautiful attitude, but it often has a hard time acknowledging that the very fundament of empiricism is *speculation in irrational spheres*. Empiricism couldn't exist without speculation. If there were no crazy or wild ideas, notions, or speculations to kick-start and enthuse the scientific brain, then what would the empirical mind-frame occupy itself with?

Likewise, I believe that the intellectual formulation of a goal, desire, or quest is a prerequisite for it to become a substantial magical avenue on which we use a super- or supra-natural method and "Existech"* to achieve an ecstasy-driven, synchronicity-inducing life-enhancement in the pursuit of meaning and magical manifestation. If one throws oneself headfirst into the work of trying to control the symbolic without a solid foundation of identity and a conscious trajectory, it is very likely that things will become chaotic. It has been said, perhaps specifically in psychoanalytic discourse, that "thought is inhibited action." I would argue that the opposite is equally valid: "action is inhibited thought." In other words, "It's all good!" The proverbial armchair is the safe space from which you rise when you are ready to take the first steps. The armchair becomes the generous liminal space between evaluation and ecstasy, and back again.

In 1988 I started writing a diary. This development was not the result of some desire to document whatever I did, but because it was a practice that came highly recommended in the magical literature I was reading. Whatever was done ritually should be noted down and revisited later, in order to see patterns of behavior and results—negative as well as positive. This approach was a significant aspect of Crowley's concept of "Scientific Illuminism," expressed in the motto of his massive occult book series, *The Equinox*: "The Method of Science, the Aim of Religion." By meticulously chronicling whatever was going on, how you felt, who you met, and so forth, you at least have a knowledge base to look back at and "connect the dots."

I'm very happy that I adhered to this early advice. I've been keeping

---

Existech is short for Existential Technology, a term coined by the author when developing the Society of Sentience (SoS) in the 2010s. An Existech would be, for instance, an artwork of whatever nature (tangible, intangible, etc.) that contains a magical charge or symbolized desire.

a diary since then, early 1988, with very few interruptions. As I've been working on this book, I have found so many things, events, people, and twists and turns in my diaries that I had completely forgotten about. And I can now certainly see important changes in my behavior over time and how these changes can be connected to, or at least associated with, ritual experimentation and mind-frames. It's been a very rewarding interplay or cooperation between the symbolic and the real, between desire and manifestation.

DECORUM

A ritual behavior gradually emerged in my life, based as much on intuition as on intellectual study. TOPY ruled supreme in my initial approaches, with their hardcore attitude toward sigilizing. At the same time, sigilizers were encouraged to be very free in their aesthetic choices. How you build a dynamic ritual is essentially up to you alone, and sometimes that is not what young magicians are looking for. I threw myself headfirst into experimentation. I developed a method that involved obvious staples, such as candlelight and suitable music. In the early days it was often Carl Michael von Hausswolff's album *The Life and Death of PBOC* or Vagina Dentata Organ's *Music for the Hashishins*, or something similar. These were dramatic and evocative soundscapes without too much going on—on the surface. Experimental musical structures of this kind went beyond mere "ambient" music to become effective ritual mood-setters. Another favorite for more agitated rituals was the lovely *Brian Jones Presents the Pipes of Pan at Joujouka* LP, documenting the cosmic Moroccan sounds and rhythms of the Master Musicians of Joujouka.

Sometimes I created the sigil in question during the ritual, and sometimes it had been meticulously prepared beforehand. I often used my video monitor as an additional sensory ingredient, playing material that was symbolically relevant in some way. If there were other objects or symbols that I felt should be there, these were included on my altar table. The altar also housed a dagger, a cup, and eventually a disk and a wand.

Once everything was in place, I began by meditating on the subject proper and visualizing the symbol or "glyph" that was to be the literal key component of the working. Pornography was frequently integrated, either in the form of photos from hardcore magazines, or videos or Super-8 projections on the wall where the altar table was placed. Then I worked myself up to a sexual climax, taking my time, focused intensely on the graphic symbol, and blessed the artwork in question with the "libation of body and soul" or "OV," as TOPY called the sexual fluids (both male and female). Additionally, I used saliva and a little blood to truly personalize the artwork(ing), sometimes also including a few hairs from my body.

A certain amount of time went by before I actually started sending in sigils to TOPY (as recommended), but I was happy to experiment on my own—often several times a week. Some sigils, usually "mixed media" works on paper, I kept; others I burned or threw away.

The goals or objectives could be anything from financial needs, to greasing the machinery of work and projects. The more I worked with the process, the more I could see that it brought the results I was after. It certainly wasn't foolproof and instant. And in the cases where something really backfired or made it clear to me that this wasn't the right approach, then at least these all became pleasurable learning experiences. Working with different sigils, and continually, helped me to not think about what I had done or remember the symbols I had employed. It's important in this kind of work to let the glyph work its magic in the unconscious, and not be treated as a visual remnant of some rational, analytical process. The roots are in the soil, in the dark, and that is how it should be.

I would say this intense process of integrating ritual affected my dreams a great deal. It was like I had removed the petals to see the "jewel in the lotus" (to paraphrase the Buddhist image) or integrated a behavior that was new to me but, at the same time, timeless. Whatever it was, it affected me on deep levels. One diary entry from the autumn of 1988 reads:

> I visualized or rather sensualized how I found myself inside an archetypical vagina. The feeling was true to life, and it made me stimulated and excited, leading to a kind of obsession. Everything was very real. I imagined that I had an orgasm and then visualized the letters Z-O-S-K-I-A that drifted over each other and ended up as a sigil glyph. Pure art in sight. Right afterward I was taken by the "Devil" (more of a term or concept rather than something visual). I visualized a penis on my belly, very much like if the A in Aleister had been tattooed there, and I felt a great sexual strength. I fell back asleep, truly exhausted. I do not look upon this as a normal dream; especially not if I look back at the previous days. I have definitely entered a new level, and that requires more studies, more ritual practice, a greater awareness, etc. I have to prioritize what needs to be prioritized. My True Will consists of the studies as much as the artistic True Will. There is no separation, there are no boundaries or limits.*

In my frequent ritual frenzy, I also realized that magical capabilities have a lot to do with one's capacity for visualization or tapping the "I–I–I": the *Inherent Inner Images*, a flow of sensations and pictures on the inner, mental, or spiritual levels. We're still quite trapped in Freud's schematic overview of *das Es* (the "It," the unconscious instincts and drives), *das Ich* (the "I," our individual control center), and *das Über-Ich* (the "Over I," morals and more refined or advanced survival mechanisms), but of course the actual truth is much more complicated.

---

*Diary entry of 12 November 1988. *ZOS KIA* is a term from Austin Spare's work, referring (simplified) to pointed direction (ZOS) and infinite possibilities (KIA). The A in Aleister Crowley's signature often resembled a penis with testicles.

There are no distinct boundaries between these planes or levels. They are clever intellectual constructs. This actual malleability and flexibility that exists in-between psychic spheres can be used by the magician for bending both time and space, and thereby to affect change in the outer. It takes practice and determination, but once you have caught those first glimpses—meaning basically that you *allow yourself to trust what you experience* as valid and relevant "data"—the potential creativity is basically endless.

In my intellectual hunger, I bought as many books as I could afford. The occult bookstores of Stockholm were few but well stocked, and the people working in those shops actually knew what they were talking about. I existed on a spectrum where I bought everything from expensive Austin Spare facsimiles to cheap paperbacks from American publishers such as Avon. This was the company that had published the LaVey books as well as the "dreaded" *Necronomicon*, which opened up the gates not so much of Hell but rather a vivid imagination spawned by overdosing on the writings and mind-frame of H. P. Lovecraft.

Being ever attracted to the dark side, I found the *Necronomicon* fascinating enough but preferred to retreat into the writings of Lovecraft himself. To me, any trafficking with so-called demons belonged more to the world of role-playing games and the various facets of "metal" music, none of which appealed to me. Lovecraft, on the other hand, was a great author and magician who unconsciously brought forth change on many levels in Western culture—an obsessive ice-breaker on the vast and deep oceans of nineteenth-century fantastic fiction who not only paved the way for a renewal of this kind of literature but also for an adventurous approach to occultism, in which the human unconscious is directly and irrevocably linked to cosmic forces and processes (and vice versa).

In March of 1988, I wrote in my diary: "The question is *if* I want to evoke demons. What I'm already working with is interesting enough."*

---

*Diary entry of 19 March 1988 about the *Necronomicon*.

This was a reference to all of the projects I was then engaged with: making music and films, taking and making photos, writing, and so on. It is a question that has been with me actively for all my life. In Sweden, we a have a lovely saying: "It's like crossing the brook to go fetch water." To me, indulging too much in abstracted symbols instead of reaching for the real goals is essentially a waste of time and energy.

The entire "grimoire psychology"—that is, of resorting to the ancient and arcane out of personal laziness and romantic projections— has never been expressed in a more beautiful way than in the Disney magnum opus *Fantasia* (1940), directed by Ben Sharpsteen and others. The sequence in which lazy Mickey Mouse is the Sorcerer's Apprentice and conjures up too many brooms to help him clean the magician's quarters is not only funny and brilliant; it also leads to a stern warning from the magician to the acolyte about not using languages he doesn't understand. Apparently, any formula of gobbledygook can have an effect on the human psyche if the setting is seductive and conducive enough. Today, we need look no further than to social media and its simplistic memes to understand this!

CUTTING IT UP

A substantial element of my ambience and fodder in these early stages came from the creative minds of American author William S. Burroughs (1914–1997) and British-Canadian artist Brion Gysin (1916–1986). Their joint experimentations with the "cut-up method"* in various media and their general concept of the Third Mind†

---

*The cut-up method entails reassembling "cut-up" or separated fragments of original information in new and random ways. The element of chance decides where the fragments of the original information go in a new "structure," in order to create new narratives and possible interpretations of what was originally said in the original "transmissions" or expressions.

†When two (or more) minds meet and communicate, a third synthesis manifests.

had brought forth new approaches to magic, especially via TOPY. Whenever I was in London, I always rushed to the Compendium bookstore in Camden High Street, as they had all kinds of important cultural and countercultural nourishment, including material from the "Beat" scene. I got as much inspiration and fuel from tomes like Burroughs and Gysin's *The Third Mind* (1978) and Terry Wilson's conversations with Brion Gysin in *Here to Go: Planet R-101* (1982) as I ever did from Crowley's *Confessions* or *Magick in Theory and Practice.*

The reason was quite simple: they experimented with art and applied a magical mind-frame to both art's creation, and to its amorphous qualities, meaning: *It ain't over till it's over.* If you make a cut-up of some kind, or write or draw "automatically," or in any way welcome random developments in the creative process, this will feed back in very different ways than if every expression were "sanitized," as it were, by the rational mind. Although this was interesting in itself, it becomes even more so when actual magical aspects are brought in—that is, when Will enters the equation or big picture. Through the sigilizing, this creative magic was part and parcel of the TOPY bouquet, and it was a joy to try things out while inspired by the old boys (Burroughs and Gysin) to whom Genesis was also a living link.

A central item in this Burroughs-Gysin mythology is a device called the Dreamachine. This consists of a cylinder with symmetrical holes placed on a record player, with a lightbulb hanging down in the middle of the cylinder. When then cylinder spins, the light from the bulb is filtered through the perforations, which creates a psychedelic flicker-effect if you look at it with your eyes closed. TOPY provided a DIY template for cutting the properly spaced holes in the cylinder, and many people made their own Dreamachines out of cardboard and secondhand turntables for home use. I used mine for meditations, and also to create a "trippy" lighting effect when I was doing rituals in my spaceship-apartment, particularly with a red bulb instead of the commonplace white one.

HARMONY OF THE SPHERES

In the spring of 1988, my band the Altered States went into a studio and recorded two songs, "Sweet Jayne" and "Here to Do," which were slated to comprise our very first single. "Sweet Jayne" was a tribute song to the American actress Jayne Mansfield, and specifically to her involvement with Anton LaVey and the Church of Satan. Although suffering from youthful logorrhea and somewhat out-of-tune electric guitars, the songs made us very proud.

Unfortunately, just as we were about to proceed, we learned that there was a UK band with the same name. So, shortly before March 23rd, I came up with an alternative name: White Stains. This had many great associations for me—it was the title of Crowley's 1898 collection of erotic poetry (which includes my favorite poem of his, "At Stockholm"), but could also refer to the residue of semen, or unknown territories on maps, and other things. So, I focused on that name and on our success in my ritual of March 23rd, which was to result in my very first official TOPY sigil.

In great cut-up style, I also shot a Super 8 film for the "Sweet Jayne" track together with the other band members. When I got the raw film rolls back from the developer, I cut the sequences up and put them in a plastic bag, which I then swung in two directions over my head: twenty-three times widdershins and another twenty-three times deasil. Then I sat down by my editing "splicer" and took sequence after sequence from the bag without looking at them, and assembled it all together in random order. *Et voilà*: a bona fide magical "rock video" (which fit really well with the music when we eventually added that)!

In May of 1988 I started working with textual cut-ups along the lines recommended by Burroughs and Gysin. Instead of using other people's writings, I made sure to always include an expression of my own Will, in well-written form. This was then merged with another piece of writing that was of relevance to my goal. This synthesis and

Carl Abrahamsson and Thomas Tibert in an early White Stains
promotional shot (photo by Max Fredrikson)

disruption of the rational narrative is perfect for magical work, and it is something I have worked with ever since. The work can certainly just be "as is," meaning a textual collage of sorts. It can also be read aloud or recorded in various ways, and later it can be either destroyed or retained in whatever way one wants and feels is appropriate for the working.

This also led to applications within music—not only in the sense that some of my lyrics contained cut-ups, but mainly that they were (and still are) Will-driven. The integration of the statement of intent within forms that travel lightly out into the worlds is one of the best "systems" I've come across so far.

As we were about to record another song ("It's Yours If You Want It") for a compilation album, I wrote in my diary: "If you can succeed with cathartic objectives, a performance should also be able to bring pro-goals/results."* This song was very representative of most of the material I wrote. Being so infused and enthused with both high and low forms of magic, I turned every little lyric or poem into a demagogical call to arms in the service of the individual Will. Sometimes it worked, sometimes it didn't. But you can't blame a (psychick) youth for trying!

I wasn't fully individuated yet—far from it!—and hence couldn't know my "True Will." When it came to both reactivity and proactive goals, my focus was basically on current projects and material solutions to problems that may have been quintessentially immaterial. Why, for instance, have a band? To be able to make a record (which costs X amount of money to record—money that I might have to raise myself)? Well, it could also be for the pure love of music, or for whatever glamor there was just being in a cool band, or a mix of these, or a million other things . . .

I had such a strong will when it came to producing printed matter, music and records, and also films, that I just made a long list—what you might call a "supernatural to-do list"—of all the things I wanted to see manifested, and then worked both ritually and actually to make it all happen.

My appetites were "whetted" in all these fields: White Stains' first record made me push the band to achieve more, and myself specifically in the direction of writing more lyrics, and the one-off underground culture fanzine *Acts of Interstellar Torture* that I made together with a friend in Gothenburg, Johan Kugelberg, made me want to create a new fanzine filled with Occulture rather than rock'n'roll. Throughout the year 1988 I was also enrolled in film school in Stockholm, learning the tools of the trade and watching *a lot* of movies.

---

*Diary entry of 13 June 1988. A "pro-goal" is a term meaning something desired specifically as a positive goal—not as a cathartic movement or experience, but as a "programming" one.

PSYCHICK YOUTH

In the summer of 1988, I took two trips to the UK in order to hang out with the P-Orridges and make plans for a future that I felt very attracted to but didn't yet fully understand. First there was a concert with "Throbbing Gristle Ltd," a one-off project through which Gen wanted to emphasize how much the original "TG" had been the product of his vision. I was such a fan of TG that I simply had to go. Together with my friend Pontus Wedlund, who worked in the best record store in Stockholm, Pet Sounds, I took the boat from Gothenburg to Harwich. The concert was thrilling. Together with Paula, Richard Evans, Daniel Black, Scott Nobody, and Jordi Valls (whose project Vagina Dentata Organ I often used for ritual soundscapes), Gen showed that there is always magical malleability. What's in a name? A lot. And many of the ideas and angles from the original project that were distinctly Gen's were now again present, as this crew performed evergreen TG classics like "Discipline," "Persuasion," and "Hamburger Lady."

The main thing for me, however, was to reconnect with Gen and the Temple ov Psychic Youth. I had begun my monthly sigils and had been given my "Temple ID," which was "Eden 162."* I talked to Gen and the others backstage, and he told me that he had recently met Anton LaVey in San Francisco, and also showed me the Church of Satan membership card that LaVey always handed out to prominent people. Gen knew about my Satanic infatuation, and I had of course kept them in the loop regarding the "Sweet Jayne" record that had just been released. He suggested that I send a copy of the record to LaVey.

Before going back to Sweden, I also visited an exhibition of paintings by William Burroughs at the October Gallery in London, which included his first shotgun-art experiments (shooting at cans of spray

---

*Male sigilizers were given the generic Temple name "Eden," along with a specific number; female sigilizers were given the name "Kali" and a number.

paint in front of a board or canvas). Overall, the trip to England was a vitalizing "TOPY infusion," and Gen and Paula agreed that we should meet again as soon as possible.

About a month later I returned to London, and we traveled by car up to Cheltenham to look for the grave of Brian Jones, who had been one of the founding members of the Rolling Stones. It was July 3rd, and Jones had died on this very day in 1969, nineteen years earlier. After strolling around the cemetery, I found the tombstone. We laid down flowers and "Psychick Crosses"* (small ones made of steel, as pendants for necklaces) and were happy to see that a number of other visitors had also left fresh flowers there earlier in the day. I accidentally pricked a finger on a rose thorn in my bouquet, and I let a few drops of blood fall on the grave, right next to a paper with a poem I had written for him:

To go on . . .
Beautiful clothes, beautiful hair,
Fascinated fans, from here to there.
You played with great skill,
Everything that there was.
Still, still gives a thrill.
You're not here; it's a loss.

Yet we shouldn't look backward
And grieve and long.
We should always go forward
And remember the songs.
If your spirit could fill me
With colors and talent,
I would surely see
There's no need to lament.

---

*The Psychick Cross was the insignia or logo of TOPY: a vertical bar intersected by three horizontal bars, the middle one being shorter.

There are many who admire your genius much,

And a few who want to forget you as such.

We'll do our very best to keep you (on) high—

You deserve it, you see, we say with a sigh.

All we want is for you to be happy and bright;

Fill us with inspiration, energy, colors, delight.

Be here with us now in this small event,

And rise and rise from your long descent!

To go on at all times is a key to much.

For Gen, the Rolling Stones' founder had been an almost archetypal symbol of the genuinely experimental side of the "swinging sixties." This infatuation peaked with PTV's Brian Jones–adoring "Godstar" single in 1985, which saw them evolve from being experimental, occult weirdos to "hyperdelic" rock'n'rollers. And by the time of our field trip in 1988, PTV had already evolved into something else again—an

Genesis and me at the grave of Brian Jones, 1988
(photo by Paula P-Orridge)

"acid house" project. (The previous summer of 1987 had been called a new "summer of love" in the British music papers, and the mix of psychedelics and electronic dance music lingered on far into 1988, and beyond.)

Our excursion also took us to a pagan site, the Rollright Stones in Oxfordshire, where we (me, Gen, Paula, and a Psychick Youth named Chris) roamed around and tuned in to the powers of the site. It was then and there that we agreed I would start TOPY Scandinavia ("TOPYSCAN") as an official "access point" for the region, and I was overjoyed in every way.

Back in London, I celebrated by venerating Elizabethan Magus John Dee's magical objects at the British Museum and buying a far-too-expensive book at the Atlantis Bookshop: a facsimile edition of Osman Spare's *Book of Pleasure* put out by 93 Publishing in Canada. Spare was already an inspiration to me, and it felt great to solidify this book's importance rather than merely have a photocopied version of it.

Before leaving for Sweden, I spent time at Beck Road, interviewed Gen again, went through TOPY administrational things and stocked up on "propaganda" material such as informational flyers, stickers, badges, and the like. TOPYSCAN was now alive, and I had so many ideas brewing in my mind. It was a perfect leap from the trash culture of *Lollipop* and *Acts of Interstellar Torture* into the magical cauldron of Occulture!

One quote from the material I got that day resonated with me and provided inspiration on many levels: "Access Points should live Magick 24 hours a day, every DAY and night. We are never OFF duty. Thee entire Process is based on a cumulative effect, and thee perception ov ALL actions being INVOKATION."*

This of course resonated neatly with Crowley's concise and

---

*TOPY instruction, quoted in a diary entry of 1 August 1988. The odd spelling conventions were a trademark quirk of Gen's, an ongoing experiment aimed at laying bare the malleability of language and its meanings.

down-to-earth definition of magic(k): "Magick is the Science and Art of causing Change to occur in conformity with Will."* In other words, it's not just about the romanticized and exoticized hocus-pocus aspects, but rather a devotion to a process of *willed work*—whether rational/causal or intuitive/experimental. I had already met several occult "space-cases" whom I felt had become untethered in the spheres of the symbolic. It wasn't my place to be overly judgmental, but it was clear that most of them weren't able to see the lovely forest because they were so ardently burrowing into the root system of one specific tree.

In late August of 1988 I received a letter from Anton LaVey, and it was to become a life-changing experience for me. As mentioned, Gen loved the first White Stains record, and suggested I should send LaVey a copy. Since they had only recently met, Gen must have found the synchronicity poignant—as did I, and so I happily sent off a copy to the "Black Pope" in San Francisco. I didn't think much about it after that, until I received this most cordial response:†

Dear Carl,

I am honored that you have chosen me as a part of your inspiration, and Jayne would be more than pleased. It is through ongoing creations like yours, that she lives on.

Thanks to magical links like Genesis, more pioneers like yourself are coming forth to shake up the rest of the world. There's a new wave, a second emergence of that which began in 1966, and nothing will stop it now. Truly, their Apocalypse is right under their noses and they don't know it!

Please accept my appointment to membership in the Church of Satan and my best wishes for your future endeavors.

Rege Satanas!

Anton Szandor LaVey

---

*Crowley, *Magick: Book Four* (York Beach, ME: Weiser, 1997), 126.
†Letter from Anton LaVey to the author (18 August 1988, Year 23 "Anno Satanas").

Needless to say, I was catapulted into bliss. To be acknowledged by someone I respected so much was overwhelming. Although unique and spectacular, this wasn't a singular development as such; I increasingly felt more like I was surfing a wave of general magical progress—one that had constantly grown in magnitude since the *Lollipop* days. I was pushed onward by myself through very basic intuitions or insights: *One thing leads to another. Throw something out there and see what happens. When you're on the inside of something (or someone) be sure to make a good impression and an eloquent expression. You can be invited in thanks to someone else, but it's essentially up to you and you alone whether you get welcomed back or not.*

The feedback from the TOPY network was also great and inspiring. I sent out bulletins and other kinds of printed matter, and received similar things back, including responses with material I was looking for—at this time, mostly dealing with the work of the American filmmaker and Thelemite Kenneth Anger. Gen was showering me with praise too: "Everyone is truly impressed with your work and bulletins, you are thee perfect expression ov TOPY and Access Point meanings."*

My obsessions and interests were starting to create ripple effects in an occult community of sorts that I had previously envisioned as being untouchable, aloof, unattainable. But I did also bring my own experiences from my fanzine days in the mid-1980s to the table. Although at that time I was little more than a youthful fanzine writer/photographer, more often than not I was welcomed into all sorts of spaces—this held just as true for large press conferences with famous bands as it did when I knocked on the dressing-room door of some up-and-coming garage band playing in a basement club. These experiences instilled a sense of self-confidence when it came to "reaching out": I had absolutely nothing to lose when asking if I could come in and secure a chat and some photos. It was my will to do so, and that is exactly what happened most of the time.

---

*Genesis P-Orridge, letter to the author (15 November 1988).

The people I was now meeting in the occult network were a lot more interesting than egotistical and drug-addled rock'n'rollers, though, and by 1988 I had decided to create an entirely new fanzine, this time focused on occulture and magic: *The Fenris Wolf.* While working with TOPYSCAN, I let it be known that I was looking for material. LaVey was happy to contribute, as was Gen. I wrote to William Burroughs and got a nice handwritten letter back granting me permission to republish an essay from 1966:*

Dear Carl Abrahamsson,
Certainly you have my permission to reprint my article "Points of distinction between consciousness-expanding and sedative drugs."
All the best for TOPYSCAN.

Sincerely,
William S. Burroughs

Other interesting contributions rolled in too: one of my teachers at film school (where I spent most of 1988) wrote a piece about the nature of dreams, and introduced me to the work of Icelandic geologist and spiritualist Helgi Pjeturss; TOPYNA (North America) wrote on "Television Magick"; and I carried on in my infatuation with Jayne Mansfield by penning "Jayne Mansfield—Satanist," as well as a biographical article about Kenneth Anger. I was as excited as I had been during the first issues of *Lollipop* in 1985. I felt completely at home in the role as author, editor, and publisher, and the overall themes filled me with both knowledge and inspiration. When the first issue of *The Fenris Wolf* howled into the world in July 1989, I felt that I had found a perfect platform through which I could further expand my newly found occult network.

I picked the symbol of Fenris from the rich heritage of Scandinavian

---

*William Burroughs, letter to the author (23 November 1988).

mythology. Fenris is the wolf that devours the sun at *Ragnarök*—the end of the world as we know it. But this is a cyclical movement, and the apocalypse only happens so that the world can be reborn. Fenris is a necessary agent of change, facilitating the transformation from old to new. I found that symbol perfect for my new magazine; perhaps even more so than I consciously understood at the time.*

INITIAL PILGRIMAGE

Parallel to a desire to textually share my own enthusiasm through printed matter, there was the music. White Stains, the out-of-tune rock band, had dissolved after the "Sweet Jayne" adventure. Me and fellow founder Jan Ekman moved on to a new lineup, which included Peter Bergstrandh, a skilled bass player who had formerly been in a pop band I liked, Lustans Lakejer (the "Lackeys of Lust"), as well as his friend Thomas Tibert, who had a studio of his own at home. In the meantime, Jan and I had recorded and released a 7" single with a psychedelic monster called "The Energy" (and a flipside of cut-up chaos, "Phase of Madness," with lots of noise and voice collages). Being zestfully immersed in Crowley's Thelemic mythology, we pressed 100 copies of the single and then smashed seven of them so that the entire edition would be limited to 93 numbered copies.† To honor the 23-fetishism of

---

*For the tenth issue of *The Fenris Wolf* (2020), I wrote an essay about Fenris as a "libidinal liberator," elaborating on his/its force within a Scandinavian sex-magic context. The essay was also included in my book *Source Magic* (Rochester, VT: Park Street Press, 2023).

†93 is the most magical number for Crowleyites, as it pertains to his freestyle analyses of key Thelemic words/concepts filtered through the Qabalah. It is so ubiquitous that it is often used as a greeting phrase within the community. Instead of addressing a fellow Thelemite with the cumbersome Crowley exhortation "Do what thou wilt shall be the whole of the Law" (to which the respondent should reply, "Love is the law, love under will"—both being quotes from Crowley's *Book of the Law*), you can simply say "93!" to each other.

the TOPY mythos,* I had seen to it that 23 copies of the total 93 were pressed on red vinyl, thereby making the record a real talisman of my (literally) ejaculating creativity.

And so things continued. The new lineup kept recording at Tibert's studio, and there were two more singles that came out, "The Awareness" and "The Result," again in limited editions of 93 (with the 23 copies being pressed in blue and green vinyl, respectively). These were issued on the new TOPYSCAN label, which released a lot of records over the years that followed. The idea with these three "93-edition" records was to celebrate Crowley and his philosophy, and to poetically illustrate the student's path from Energy to Awareness and on to Result. On that willful note, a previous song that the old lineup contributed to a compilation album was titled "It's Yours If You Want It," while yet another single that came out in 1989 was called "Express Your Desire." And the flipside of "Sweet Jayne" was the song "Here to Do." Basically, this was more than just music with some random lyrics (or even cut-ups); it was *demagogic magic* from a young person obsessed with the occult. And this attitude remains unchanged for me even today: when I am inspired by something, I want to re-express it and inspire a similar interest in others. It's as simple—or complex—as that!

In December of 1988 I made a pilgrimage together with my friend Nicklas Kappelin.† We got Interrail passes and traveled through France

---

*23 was a most magical number for people in the TOPY community. The source for this was William Burroughs's fascination and frequent mention of the fact (?) that 23 seems to be a number that turns up more than others. In TOPY it was integrated in various ways, such as with the creation of the "23 sigilizing process": on the 23rd of each month, at 23:00 hours, TOPY initiates were to sigilize and then send in their talismanic artwork to a TOPY Station. Twenty-three completed sigils led to a new kind of status—one that wasn't necessarily visible to others, but it was something for the individual Psychick Youth to strive for. From a basic psychological perspective, you could argue that arbitrarily focusing on any particular word, number, or phenomenon will bring it more to the mind's attention when filtering outer stimuli. In my personal experience, "23" has been very, very present in my life, but I can acknowledge that this probably has to do more with my own early focus on the mythos itself rather than any objective phenomenon as such.

†Nicklas Kappelin (born 1964), a great friend, cofounder of *Lollipop*, and a seminal member of LIAC.

down to Spain. One of our goals was to visit Salvador Dalí's house in Cadaqués, outside of Barcelona. By this time in his life, he was infirm. We had no desire to disturb or even approach him, but just to pay our respects, regardless of whether we saw him or not.

Eventually, we found our way to the beach bungalow where we had been told he lived. When we were there on the beach, we could see people inside the house. As it turned out, Dalí himself was in the hospital (he would later die in January of 1989). But this was beside the point. What mattered was our effort in making the pilgrimage itself, our quest to validate our sources of inspiration.

And so it continued: we traveled down to the southern coast of Spain, where we took the boat over to Tangier. This turned out to be an overload of exotica, and not only due to the sensory impressions of a radically different culture. It too was a pilgrimage to a place that was "holy ground" for us young beatnik kids: this was the place where Burroughs and Gysin had been staying for a long time in the 1950s and intuitively constructed their Third Mind. Unbeknownst to me at this time, my father had also traveled to Morocco and Tangier in the late 1950s, and I'm pretty sure he ran into some of these old protagonists.

We soon discovered that Morocco can also be an overwhelming place if you're not used to people aggressively trying to sell you whatever they think you might need—drugs, alcohol, girls, boys . . . As young Swedes on the road, we must have radiated a glow of pure naiveté and gullibility, and we attracted local hustlers by the dozens. We both found this so irritating that we decided to cut our Moroccan trip short, and I remember thinking: *If it's this bad for the two of us, what would it be like for a young woman on the road in cultures like this?* As much as I love North Africa now (and I have returned multiple times) young Carl also realized that the best way to deal with the chaos of Tangier was probably to be constantly stoned. That was not on our agenda, however. We returned to the relative safety of southern Europe, making our way along the Mediterranean coast to Cannes.

Another pilgrimage site for us on the trip was Aleister Crowley's

Abbey of Thelema in the Sicilian coastal village of Cefalù. It was there, in a small villa, that the "Great Beast" had established a monastery of indulgence for a brief period in the early 1920s. Although he abandoned the place a few years later, it has taken on a mythic aura for Thelemites ever since. At this time I was obsessed with Kenneth Anger, the underground filmmaker and lifelong Thelemite. In 1955 Anger had traveled to Cefalù together with the American sex researcher Alfred Kinsey, where he worked diligently to remove layers of whitewash paint from the walls to reveal the amazing, sexual, magical and drug-fueled murals that Crowley had painted decades earlier. This I wanted to see!

But as we arrived in the village of Cefalù we were exhausted, and the local residents had little interest in helping us to find the ruined

Cefalù, 1988
(photo by
Nicklas Kappelin)

house. We tried asking about the "Abbazio di Thelema" and offering vague descriptions, namedropping "Aleister Crowley." This was the pre-internet era, with no "dark" or "weird" tourism websites to provide the exact location of a place like this, and I knew no one else personally who had been there before. We strolled around for a long time and ended up on top of the cliffs among some old abandoned and decrepit stone houses filled with Thelemic graffiti. *This must surely be it*, I thought. I performed Crowley's solar salutation, "Resh," at sundown, dressed in a white shirt that had Crowley's "Liber OZ" printed on the back.* We meditated, took photos, and wrote in our journals and notebooks by the houses. It was atmospheric, to say the least.

However, we found no mural paintings unfortunately, because . . . *they weren't there.* We were in the wrong place! The remnants of the Abbey of Thelema are down in the village proper, but we didn't find this out until we had returned home to Sweden. I then convinced myself that Crowley and his gang of occult experimentalists must surely have been up on those cliffs too, especially for the Resh salutations—and indeed it was insanely beautiful up there. Such are the compensatory justifications of a young pilgrim's mind!

We carried on to Rome to inspect the seat of Holy Corruption itself: the Vatican. It was interesting and depressing at the same time, but I didn't get a chance to philosophically speculate any further because some gypsy kids pickpocketed my passport, and I had to cut the trip short. A lot of naiveté on my part had certainly been shattered during our travels; it was an extended wake-up call that stretched over several exotic but exhausting weeks. In my anger and frustration, I performed a ritual to retrieve what had been lost. Although the ritual functioned mainly as form of catharsis, I did get a letter from the Swedish police a few weeks later, saying my passport had been found in Rome and that it could be picked up in Stockholm.

---

*"Liber OZ" is a condensed version of *The Book of the Law*, edited down to a handy propagandistic format of one page.

PANIC PROFITEERS

After the chaotic Interrail trip, I made another excursion to the UK. It was good to be back at Beck Road, talking to Gen, Paula, and Words and Jackie of the publishing imprint Temple Press, plus friends like Simon Norris, James Mannox, and others. The P-Orridges had moved to Brighton in 1988, but the house on Beck Road in London continued as a kind of TOPY space. On this trip I spent time alone there: sleeping, doing rituals, listening to music, and writing. These experiences gave me a big boost, and occurred right before an interesting event for us all: an international TOPY conference in Brighton called TOPYGLOBAL. People had come from the US (including the main organizer there, Tom Banger, who had supplied me with a wealth of archival bon-bons over the years and become a great friend), Germany, the Netherlands, and from all over the UK; I was the representative for dear old Scandinavia. We presented our local activities and experiences, and shared ideas freely. Being a kind of lone wolf since childhood, I'd never experienced anything communal before. I had a great time being a contributor to something greater than the sum of its parts. As I'm an early bird, I spent the mornings playing with Gen's daughters Caresse and Genesse, and looking at his library, while most others snoozed pleasantly. We held the conference meetings in an old church building, which felt very appropriate, and I got to know most of the people and their activities quite well. When it was all over and we shared our feelings and hopes for the future, Gen started to cry. He was overwhelmed by the realization that TOPY was apparently such a strong and vital network (or "nett work" as he liked to call it), with amazing potential to grow and succeed.

One of the things we discussed was security, in the most basic sense of the term. In England, as well as in the US at the time, there was something going on called the "Satan Scare" or the "Satanic Panic." Essentially, this was a moneymaking scheme that originated from evangelical Christian fringe groups, spewing their fire and brimstone against divergent and life-affirming individuals for profit. Television and radio talk shows, films, books, magazines, and other public events were used to spread preposterous and perverted fantasies—undoubtedly their own!—about a cult network that committed ritual human sacrifices and sexual abuse, all of which was allegedly going on in the name of "Satan." The authorities who investigated the claims—police, district attorneys, private investigators, and journalists—found no evidence whatsoever for the claims, which eventually were seen as the product of paranoid hysteria. But while the Satanic Panic wasted huge sums of the taxpayers' money in pointless investigations and court cases, it conversely served as a lucrative cash cow for those who perpetuated the tall tales in the first place. And these dark shenanigans had real and negative effects for many people. Idiots in San Francisco threw trash at Anton LaVey's beautiful Black House on California Street; on at least one occasion, shots were fired at the building. In Leeds, England, an occult shop called The Sorcerer's Apprentice had its windows smashed, and the store itself was firebombed. Individuals displaying "occult allegiance" were beaten up. Eventually, store owner Chris Bray and some of his associates established a "Sorcerer's Apprentice Fighting Fund" focused on legal aid. Parallels were drawn to the witch hunts of medieval times. The Sorcerer's Apprentice and the UK newsletter *Pagan News* regularly reported about vandalism and other attacks against various individuals and groups belonging to the "occult communities."

Whereas in the US the scare was obviously a vehicle for Christian moneymaking, in the UK it played out in a more chaotic—and therefore more dangerous—fashion. In both cases, it was essentially just a matter of exploiting an uneducated and disgruntled proletariat while scapegoating people who are different (in this case, those with interests in "the Occult"). Such dynamics never seem to go out of style!

At the TOPYGLOBAL meeting, we talked about what we could do in TOPY, and agreed that the best strategy was to be totally open about our activities. The general motto for the organization was always "Thee Frequency Ov Truth" (which was even printed on the TOPY UK stationery). It didn't take long for us to realize that this was a potential source of anger for others who were not so bright.

We could laugh among ourselves at these zealots' apparent stupidity when flipping through copies of, for example, the *Jesus Army Newspaper* from Northampton:

> But our greatest need is for God's army! An army of Christians! A "born again," holy army, motivated by love! A determined, win-at-any-cost army of converted people with the guts to blast the power of evil that stalks modern Britain, to challenge corruption, rescue multitudes trapped in degrading practices and prove the power of the Christian gospel.*

But since TOPY was involved in sexual experimentation in tandem with ritual magic, this naturally attracted a certain amount of attention—not all of which was positive. Gen was always willing to talk to the media about ideas, theories, and practices, and over the years he had received his share of negative exposure in the UK press. This had already occurred in the early 1970s with his art performance group COUM Transmissions, and it occasionally repeated with respect to Throbbing Gristle and now Psychic TV and TOPY.

In retrospect, our concerns over security were very well founded. Only a few years later, in early 1992, Scotland Yard raided the very house in which we had relaxed after the TOPYGLOBAL gathering: the P-Orridges' home. They were looking for video evidence of "Satanic" crimes (whatever that means) mainly based on spiraling hearsay having to do with the first PTV videos that were featured on a video compilation called *First Transmissions* (these were the same videos that I had seen in Stockholm at the art college Konstfack in 1984).†

Jesus Army Newspaper, issue 14 (1989), 1.
†COUM Transmissions (1969–1976) was a music and performance-art group founded by Genesis P-Orridge that would later morph into Throbbing Gristle (with former COUM members Cosey Fanni Tutti, Peter Christopherson, and Chris Carter).

Scotland Yard hauled away cartloads of material from Gen's archive for forensic scrutiny while Words and Jackie of Temple Press tried to make notes of everything that was removed. At the time all of this was happening, the P-Orridges were in Thailand, where they had stopped over on their return trip after an extended stay in Nepal. Their house had been essentially ransacked by the police and a vast amount of their archive and personal items were arbitrarily confiscated. Their attorney advised them not to return to the UK, as it was unclear what was going on. In many ways, it was like a raid of spiteful revenge after Gen's two decades of public provocations—with the added bonus of someone claiming it was all "Satanic."

The P-Orridge family never moved back. They emigrated to the US and rebooted their lives and careers there. Many years later, some—but not all—of the confiscated material was returned to Gen in the US. Ironically, it was eventually shipped *back* to the UK because the Tate had bought his archive, which had now become even more legendary and of greater value to art history!

Sometime around 2015, Gen sent me a list of what had been taken, along with some correspondence dealing with the case. Not only did Scotland Yard seize all of the video cassettes they could find—including such controversial material as *Madonna—The Immaculate Collection* and *Swiss Family Robinson*—but also such dangerous contraband as Caresse and Genesse's Pooh Bear sewing kit. And yes, a video anthology that I had compiled for my company Psychick Release in 1991 was in there too!

And why did the original raid take place? Because someone had deemed it fitting to denounce the P-Orridges—and, by extension, all of TOPY—because of their willingness to be experimental, and to be open and honest about it. Further exacerbating the situation was a media climate that relished in hammering down any alternative nails that might be protruding beyond the "stiff upper lip" of the British psyche.

Were we a bit naive? Probably. Gen and his attorneys had to spend many long hours and thousands of pounds and dollars to retrieve their possessions and make sense of the debacle, and to even get a complete list of what had been taken.

ACADEMAGIC

The occultism and ritual practice in my life developed quickly, something I ascribed to frequency, diligence, and creativity. It was no longer just a focused kind of masturbatory practice but rather a *Gesamtkreativität*, or "total creativity," that integrated new ingredients as I went along. One noteworthy ritual was performed in February of 1989. I had just re-enrolled at Stockholm University, in order to resume the film studies journey that I had begun in 1985. The focus of my research was the influence of Aleister Crowley on Kenneth Anger's films. Along with the library at the Swedish Film Institute, the TOPY network provided me with a lot of useful material relating to the topic.

I wanted to connect directly with Anger himself, however, so I sent out hopeful letters to a few contacts who might be able to help. I also created a ritual that contained an immersion in stimuli: Anger's magnum opus, *Lucifer Rising*, was playing on the VCR, and I had placed Rick Griffin's early poster for the film on my altar. There was a sigil prepared for the fulfillment of my goal and I had recorded myself greeting Anger—as if in conversation—which I had then treated and "looped" on a cassette so that it repeated over and over. In many ways my techniques here were a prelude to more "conscious" magical concepts that I would formulate decades later, such as "You have to learn to look at the future retrospectively"—in other words, you should treat an ideal, desired scenario *as if it has already happened*. My nascent application of psychodrama as a magical technique for acting out a desired scenario would later be deepened by my study of LaVey's Satanism.

It wasn't until my university thesis was ready and printed (and published by TOPYSCAN of course!), and the first issue of *The Fenris*

Wolf was out, that Anger started responding. I had proposed a biography project to him, to which he responded:*

> I will have to think about the biography idea. Unfortunately, I associate it with the idea of DEATH—as if my life is all over! I want to do *more*!

My return to the university had made me considerably less tolerant of just about *anything* that wasn't in line with my ideals and trajectory. One would assume that film studies on a university level would have to do with the study of film, and to a great degree this was thankfully true. But there were still some bitter remnants and ghosts of the 1970s around, lingering on in some kind of time warp and trying to force us students to hermeneutically appreciate positivism and Marxism—two approaches that were absolutely contrary to a magical worldview and appreciation of life. I could never figure out what any of this had to do with movies. I'd had similar run-ins with the very same teachers during my initial year of studies (in 1985), and it was just as incomprehensible now. The roots for much of this could be traced back to the disgruntled student uprising in Paris in May of 1968, which seduced a whole generation of comfortable communist crybabies and seeped into European universities. As for me, the trajectory was clear: I wanted to write—in this case, about my favorite filmmaker—and I didn't give a damn about French pseudo-philosophy. Later on in 1989, my academic "career" would end abruptly, something I'm still eternally grateful for.

SOURCE MAGIC

In late 1988 and early 1989 I also started integrating animal spirits in rituals, allowing for a temporary identification rather than

---

*Kenneth Anger, letter to the author (16 August 1989).

"possession." Through firsthand experience, it taught me how much the human mind or system can evoke and work within a conducive setting. In some ways it was my first real shamanic experience, integrating forces of nature in distinctly nonsymbolic forms for the purposes of deeper knowledge about a specific topic. Ritual as such was no longer just a causal "metaprogramming" of myself through the act of sigilization, but a more complex creation in time and space that allowed knowledge to flow back into the practitioner—an experimental epistemology, if you will.

This was so rewarding, useful, and inspiring that it also cemented my belief that everyone has shamanic or gnostic potential. (By extension, this also laid the foundation for my solid criticism of any kind of priesthood or structure that arbitrarily assumes the prerogative to disseminate its doctrines—but only to the obedient.) The "source"—or whatever we wish to call it—is always there and it can be approached by anyone, at any time. The creation of a dedicated—albeit temporal—ritual microenvironment for this purpose can be a great asset to the overall process. A piece of music, a small object, or an article of clothing can serve as a real gateway to deep-rooted knowledge within yourself, which can then be taken into "metaprogrammatic" spheres of desire.

In the late 1980s, the main protagonist of so-called neoshamanism was the American anthropologist Michael Harner. His book *The Way of the Shaman* (1980) became an instant classic and fueled a new interest for people to seek answers within themselves via an openness to nature as such and to the natural forces we cannot *intellectually* perceive. Harner's studies and practices had already begun in the early 1960s, and thus ran parallel with the work of fellow anthropologist Carlos Castaneda and his chronicles of the Yaqui sorcerer don Juan. But it was only when Castaneda's star was beginning to fall—partly as the result of considerable academic criticism (or was it envy?) and an increasing sobriety among the reading public—that Harner's book was published and became a great success. That there was a baton-passing of sorts was inherent in Castaneda's blessing of *The Way of the*

Relaxing on a
runestone at the
shamanic workshop
in Vallentuna
(photo by
Boris Hiesserer)

Shaman: "Harner really knows what he's talking about."* Incidentally,
Harner was also an acquaintance of Anton LaVey and visited his Black
House in San Francisco many times.

The Norwegian shaman Arthur Sørenssen had been a participant in Harner's workshops and classes in Stockholm as well as at the
famous Esalen Institute in the US. He had written a book of his own
called *Den Stora Drömmen* (The Big Dream), and we got in touch
thanks to a mutual friend, Arild Strømsvåg from Bergen, Norway. As
"Frater Evmaios," Strømsvåg was responsible for the establishment of
the OTO in Norway, having been initiated by Crowley's disciple Grady
McMurtry during one of his European "initiation tours" in the early
1980s. We corresponded and quickly became friends. Strømsvåg's
interest in music with occult associations, not to mention new forms
of occultism like TOPY, made me feel comfortable about eventually
entering the fraternal structure of the OTO. But before this would

---

*Back-cover endorsement of Michael Harner, *The Way of the Shaman* (New York:
HarperOne, 1990).

happen I wanted to organize shamanic initiations or workshops in Stockholm for the TOPYSCAN crew, and so Sørenssen needed to come visit. This took place in May of 1989, and we brought those interested out to Vallentuna, a rural area outside of Stockholm where my aunt and her family lived in an beautiful seventeenth-century homestead, surrounded by nature.

The workshop was a great success. We were instructed by Sørenssen in the fundamental basics of "underworld" journeying to the rhythm of a drum, and "overworld" journeying states of mind induced with wooden "click-sticks." We were encouraged to find our totem animals in the underworld, and supporting and benevolent spirits in the overworld. Among other things, we experimented with automatic writing and drawing while in the overworld, the prophetic qualities of sticks and stones, methods for visualizing the body's energy fields, and techniques for finding and singing your own power songs alone or together with others.

It was a mind-blowing experience for me, as I hope it was for the others. In many ways, it served as a justification for much of my own initial work on the inner planes. Western minds are essentially authoritarian and need someone to tell them what is real, good, useful, valuable, and so on. I'm probably no exception—or at least I wasn't back in the late 1980s. So, it was a great revelation to have a shaman instruct me in his particular method or tradition, without critically commenting on whatever else I had been up to myself before this. It also became clear to me that my earlier intuitive explorations had essentially been shamanic.

The bottom line: *Whatever we find is ultimately as real as it is an illusion.* If you experience something with your inner eye (or the *Hug Auga*, as I had begun to call it: the "mind's eye" in archaic Swedish), it is absolutely real to you—and thus useful for further examination. In another context, it is also technically an "illusion" as it will probably never be able to be validated by established science, so-called, nor by *anyone* else.

I had read Harner's book before the workshop and returned to it afterward. I pencil-marked one section, specifically, as perfectly expressing my own perspective:

In the SSC [Shamanic State of Consciousness], the shaman typically experiences an ineffable joy in what he sees, an awe of the beautiful and mysterious worlds that open before him. His experiences are like dreams, but waking ones that feel real and in which he can control his actions and direct his adventures. While in the SSC, he is often amazed by the reality of that which is presented. He gains access to a whole new, and yet familiarly ancient universe that provides him with profound information about the meaning of his own life and death and his place within the totality of all existence. During his great adventures in the SSC, he maintains conscious control over the directions of his travels, but does not know what he will discover. He is a self-reliant explorer of the endless mansions of a magnificent hidden universe. Finally, he brings back his discoveries to build his knowledge and to help others.*

Through Arthur Sørenssen I also got to know the people at the bookstore Vattumannen (Aquarius) better. This was strange in the sense that they were in Stockholm, as was I. Until that point, Vattumannen had been a store that occasionally had interesting books, but I hadn't really connected with anyone working there. As it turned out, some of my new friends at the store had a group called Yggdrasil, and they worked with the Nordic mystery school (rune magic, *seid* and *galder* work,† etc.), something I found increasingly interesting.

On a personal level, I strongly identified with the god Bragi (modern Swedish: Brage) in the Nordic pantheon. He is the god of poetry and

---

*Harner, *The Way of the Shaman*, 27.
†Rune magic is any form of magic that actively utilizes the runes. *Seid* is a ritualized system of oracular magic in which (most commonly) a priestess/female magician goes in a trance to retrieve information or otherwise "metaprogram" external events. *Galder* is a kind of singing or chanting that can be used in different contexts (including seid-rituals). On a basic level the word could be translated as a "vocal spell." That there was a great respect for this kind of magic can still be sensed in present-day Swedish: the verb *att gala* refers to the cock crowing in the morning, heralding the sun; the adjective *galen* means to be insane, as if someone had cursed you via a galder spell.

storytelling, a son of Odin and the husband of Idun, who with her apples keeps the gods young and healthy. Already in 1988, I started ingesting "eucharistic" apples daily in honor of Bragi. Basically, I carved the runes of his name in the apple and then reverentially ate it, and this went on for years. It was part of a budding and practical interest in a pantheon and mystery school that is incredibly rich in symbolism and psychic strength. I was also regularly using runes in my sigils, as their angular form lends itself so well to assembling them into what are usually called "bind runes." To connect with other groups like Yggdrasil and Telge Fylking was valuable to me.* This was especially the case since by then the "market" had already been flooded with mainly American interpreters of ancient Nordic magic, and they always made me cringe. To meet with fellow Scandinavians who were carrying on with these kinds of traditions, rituals, and ceremonies was inspiring and a great learning experience.

A VORTEX OF INSPIRATION

It was exciting to exist in a kind of vortex of energized enthusiasms and discoveries. Not that I had anything else to compare it with, really—for several years I had been eking out a living by working in a printshop, but I had plunged fully into magic and was now immersed in it on multiple levels. I even wrote in my diary: "I have become addicted to magic. Great! When I can't channel all my energy on my true will I just get nervous and restless."† And that really summarized a lot. I had a kind of stereoscopic view of everything that happened: on one hand, there was Crowley's concise definition of magic as the "Science and Art to cause Change in conformity with Will," and LaVey's category of "lesser" or manipulative magic. And on the other hand, there were the amazing

---

*Yggdrasil is the name of the World Tree in Nordic mythology. Telge Fylking means a formation of flying birds (*fylking*) coming from the area of Södertälje (outside of Stockholm).
†Diary entry (20 February 1989).

benefits and lessons of inner journeys and mind-expansions, and, in extension of this, psychodramatic explorations of the concept of "ritual" in itself. I was not "religious." I did not adhere to one system. I did not stay away from supposedly dark and dangerous stuff. On the contrary, the more "warning signs" I came across, the more I explored exactly those avenues: not as an end in itself, nor as some kind of contrarian obsession, but rather because my own experience tells me that people who actively promote or "dis-promote" something usually want to promote themselves in the bargain. I believe there are useful and inspiring gems in every school, tradition, philosophy, and religion, and I believe it was my early openness and enthusiasm that lay the foundation of that approach. It just made a whole lot of sense.

I increasingly saw my developing persona through the feedback of others—not just in distinctly magical contexts like TOPYSCAN meetings and workshops, but also in everyday settings. Friends I worked with creatively told me how much I inspired them, and of course that was delightful to hear. But I was never looking for acknowledgment per se as much as I was for new experiences on both the outer and inner planes. Even my mother, who was uncomfortable with me being on Swedish TV and radio talking about Satanism and magic, hypocritically asked me to curse people a few times! Now, why would you do that if you didn't believe in the process as such, and in me as a magician? From an early point my persona became associated with the "Devil"—a phenomenon I described as a nonpersonal core of energy whose only function is to encourage people to be themselves. The Devil is an agent of culture and cultivation in so many ways, and a force that goes against all of the petty hypocrisies, neuroses, prejudices, and projections of those who—for many reasons—lack the courage to look themselves in the mirror.

The symbol of the Devil always felt close to me. This was a resonance and conversation with a principle that was *within myself*—it never had anything to do with external forces dreamed up by perverted and psychotic monotheists. I did, however, bear a grudge against Christianity as I found them guilty of most everything that had gone wrong in human culture. I was never a Christian, but I certainly have never had a problem being an anti-Christian. This was evident from an early point in my life, and I have often wondered what brought it on so strongly. As mentioned, I do believe there's something useful in every cluster of teachings, but Christianity as such will always be "guilty" due to its association with rigid structures and paradoxical powers and all their detrimental effects on the human psyche and planetary health.

As TOPYSCAN was preparing for the release of the Psychic TV album *A Real Swedish Liveshow*,* Genesis asked me to write the liner notes. I composed a freestyle rant, partly inspired by a recent visit of the Pope to Sweden:

An open letter to that ignorant and confused part of humanity, not yet aware of Magick and Nature, nor of the importance of them becoming integrated as soon as possible for the survival of the Human race!

Do what thou wilt shall be the whole of the Law.

"Nature slowly decays" is something you hear quite often. Well, it isn't really so . . . Nature always evolves, always develops in directions given by the components and forces within it. Nature and the Earth will always exist, be it even in forms of burnt-out lands and hordes of cockroaches. The statement "Man's nature slowly decays" is closer to the truth!

Our environment that we need to live and regenerate in IS decaying . . .

There isn't one single person who can deny this today. It's a sad fact, but even sadder still is the fact there are people actually opposing human development. There are people violently struggling for their own security and wealth, believing that this will save them and that's the only one thing that matters . . .

---

*This was a recording of Psychic TV's 1984 Stockholm concert and became the sixteenth LP in PTV's monthly issuing of 23 live LPs in total.

Well, pardon me if I laugh at you dying of cancer and spit merrily on your graves!

You are despicable and such cowards that you won't even share your dead bodies with the Earth, but put them inside wooden and metal coffins to "protect" them. From what?

What are children taught in school? How to act and behave in a clockwork structure, working in a destructive downward-spiral . . . "Be good and you're welcome to heaven . . . Sacrifice yourself for the greater good . . . God knows best . . . He is omnipotent . . . You are small and worthless . . . Just be good and everything will be alright . . ."

This is a feeble, sick and, most importantly, unnatural morality that we should all help to eradicate. It has no value or justification today, when we should all work together for the restoration of our essential Mother Earth.

There is no god but man. Omnipotency comes from actions that alter the surroundings, mental and physical. If those actions are destructive (for instance, dumping toxic waste into the sea), you'll be sure to get what's coming to you (cancer as a result of toxic ground-water). If those actions are good (for instance, planting trees and flowers), you'll get immediate results (there will be more oxygen in air). You are the judge, as you are God.

Christianity and its fellow criminal religions Islam and Judaism exist today merely as vehicles of Control, merely as modes of thought to keep people from acting and thinking for themselves. Judaism = Christianity = Islam = Communism = Capitalism, etc., etc., and so on, ad infinitum, ad nauseam. Just different words denoting the very same unnatural perversion and illness. Which is the fact that YOU ARE NOT FREE!

When they realize that times and morality have changed, and this time NOT in their favor, they become afraid, like small children who start to scream because their mother says "No," although they are very well able to express themselves. They become ultra-paranoid, in need of extreme polarities, a black-and-white way of regarding the world. And there is violence and death, as always in times of change. 2,000 years ago there was the Roman Empire succumbing to Christianity, in times of wars and civil wars.

And today? The 23rd pope arrives at Stockholm in the 23rd week of 1989, saluting the Swedish catholics (mere thousands—a piss in the ocean . . .) and praying for peace in the world. At the very same time there is a potential civil war in China, where communist soldiers kill students who think freedom lies in a red-and-white soft-drink can. There are train-crashes and pipelines exploding in Russia, corruption having a higher priority than public safety. Ayatollah Khomeini dies and falls out of his coffin into the hands of millions of insecure, and thereby fanatical, Muslims. The world trembles . . .

Yes, pray on, old fool, because you may very well need it. There is no Christianity anymore (Praise the Lord!). Sweden has never been a Christian country. You've failed, you are all failures, and you are so aggressively neurotic because you know it's true.

Scandinavian mythology has always lived on, through the times of your oppression and contemptuous misunderstandings of Nature and its fantastic forces. The Runes are part of the Scandinavian DNA-structure. Pagan activities have never died, not anywhere, and today it's all coming back to you. A Magickal appreciation of history and Life in the work for all peoples' common future.

There is a good definition of a free person, and that's one who is completely honest with her/himself in every situation, and who's thereby working for the procreation of WoMankind. The honesty becomes the medium. The work is the goal in itself.

Love is the law, love under will.

In this kind of frantic Fantazius Mallare mind-frame,* it's easy (and fun) to rant about others. But I was never prone to sit tight and mope; I'd much rather create positive change.

---

*Fantazius Mallare is the violently bitter protagonist in Ben Hecht's novel of the same name, originally published in 1922.

THE MELTING POT

During that summer of 1989, the constructive experimentation was focused on TOPYSCAN's first "Rotorite"—a time of hosting rituals for visitors from other places. We returned to Vallentuna to perform a Scandinavian Midsummer *blot* (ritual offering) together with members from Sweden, the US, and Germany. I had composed the ceremony based on historical sources and incorporated elements of sacred drama.

On our way out to the place in the woods we noticed that there was a rainbow in the sky. Nothing could have been more auspicious, as the rainbow is traditionally a bridge between Midgard and Asgard, between the sphere of the humans and that of the Gods. I acted as "Gode" (priest), and after Thomas Tibert had given us nine beats on his mighty drum, I welcomed all friendly forces and cursed all the foes, blessed the site and the participants, and read from the *Poetic Edda*. We all greeted the Gods and Nature as such. Then we positioned ourselves in runic postures (physically emulating the specific runic forms) while intoning or singing the same runes. It was quite a powerful opening of the ritual and we felt safe and enclosed in our space—a little clearing within the forest that contained some big stones. It was also the summer solstice, so despite the late hour, the sun was still shining brightly, blessing us with its rays of energy and warmth.

Each participant then made a personal offering (*blot*) in a slow and atmospheric pace. I had brought a sigil that I burnt in the open fire. I opened a bottle of red wine, had a few sips, and then poured the rest out as a libation for Odin. Then I did the same thing with three apples I had brought: had a bite of each and then placed them down on the ground as a gift for Odin. All those present had different styles and personal touches, basically acknowledging the unique moment and power of the solstice as well as its beneficial energy within one's own strict focusing of desire for the coming period. As a final stage, we all sang runic intonations together, finding each other's frequencies and eventually coalescing in a perfect harmony and resonance.

Our guests stayed on for a few days, and we agreed to make a video sigil on June 23rd for a TOPY compilation project in Brighton. Two Edens and two Kalis participated in the work, which included making video edits of already existing material, filming an intimate ritual, and eventually making a piece of soundtrack music that included cut-ups as well as runic singing. The final film, *Psycollection 23*, was included in screenings and on a VHS compilation at the time, and much later ended up on a DVD that accompanied the first edition of the revised edition of *Thee Psychick Bible* in 2009.*

Left to my own devices after this amazing Rotorite, I wrapped up the first issue of *The Fenris Wolf* and started sending it out. The journal had been a great labor of love and was printed by myself and my friends at work, Peter Bergstrandh and Michael Matton, with considerable production help from others too. It was a symbolic as well as tangibly real beginning of a new phase in my life: Occulture and Magico-anthropology in full Flow Motion!

I celebrated a few days later by getting my first tattoo at the legendary Doc Forest studio in Stockholm: a bind rune placed over my heart. It's been protecting me ever since.

In these days there was a lot to keep up, in terms of correspondence. There was a constant stream of inter-TOPY communication going on, plus inquiries from the public that arrived at TOPYSCAN, and fan mail to White Stains. But it was always the letters and talks with Gen that really inspired me. I loved all the things I was doing under this occultural umbrella, but sometimes the to-do lists were daunting and stressful. Gen definitely felt the same way and we sometimes would call each other and just let off steam. In mid-July of 1989 he telephoned me,

---

*Genesis Breyer P-Orridge, et al., *Thee Psychick Bible* (Port Townsend, WA: Feral House, 2009).

asking if I was happy. It was obvious that he was not, so I tossed the question right back at him.

"I'm depressed," he confessed. "I can never really catch up, and it feels I'm always doing things for other people." Although in many ways we were different, there was one thing that united us. It wasn't the magic per se or the acknowledgment of the importance of past masters whose work we were carrying on in very distinct traditions. It was that we both wanted to *write more than our circumstances allowed.* I often felt stressed by all the fun and creative things that went on around me, because they also served as distractions. The good things that were happening became almost paradoxical reminders that there was an even more important matter to which I should attend—namely, creative writing. I could only imagine how Gen felt, considering the much heavier projects and responsibilities he was carrying on his shoulders. "When I need to, I just sleep for a day or two," he confided. "You should do that too sometimes. It's important magic." Whenever I could, I reminded him to do more writing, and it was reciprocal. "Your work is thee most perfect and consistent in TOPY and TOPI,"* he told me, also in July 1989, and of course a pep talk like that hit home, as it should. I tried to do the same for him whenever I could, provided we didn't have more urgent matters to discuss.

It was in equal part Gen's words and his voice that had originally inspired me to get more involved (plus the magic, of course). At about this time, I started planning for a project together that would include his words and voice combined with White Stains' music. I knew this would inspire Gen to write more and to have the real poetic essence of his mind documented through his own recorded voice.

Inside my own mind swam the poet-magician Genesis P-Orridge and the ever-inspiring vision-maker Kenneth Anger. And there were always the mischievous shenanigans of "The Great Beast 666,"

---

*Toward the end of "Phase One" TOPY (1981–1991), we also started integrating "TOPI" as an acronym for "Thee Temple Ov Psychick Individuals."

aka Aleister Crowley. My thesis documenting Crowley's influence on Anger was well received at the university, and I left in the spring of 1989 making sure the wonderful Cinematheque in Stockholm was booked on "Crowleymas"—Crowley's birthday, October 12—for a screening of Anger's films. To me, it was a huge triumph (and an early piece of relevant occulturation), especially as White Stains' third and final "93-edition" single was released on the same day. Hence, we had journeyed from the *Energy* to the *Awareness*, and on to the *Result*.

Crowley was my staple daily reading and this never really ended, considering that he was such a prolific writer. I particularly appreciated his massive *Confessions* tome, because what I liked most about him—and still do—was his way of life. This included his philosophy of Thelema, of course, but it was his provocative audacity that had stirred my initial interest in him. My favorite text was his collection of peculiar aphorisms and riddles, *The Book of Lies*. I noted in my diary that I especially liked chapter 64 ("Constancy"):

Constancy

I was discussing oysters with a crony:
GOD sent to me the angels DIN and DONI.
"A man of spunk," they urged, "would hardly choose
To breakfast every day chez Lapérouse."
"No!" I replied, "he would not do so, BUT
Think of his woe if Lapérouse were shut!
"I eat these oysters and I drink this wine
Solely to drown this misery of mine.
"Yet the last height of consolation's cold:
Its pinnacle is—not to be consoled!
"And though I sleep with Jane and Eleanor
I feel no better than I did before,
"And Julian only fixes in my mind
Even before feels better than behind.
"You are Mercurial spirits—be so kind

As to enable me to raise the wind.
"Put me in LAYLAH'S arms again: the Accurst,
Leaving me that, elsehow may do his worst."
DONI and DIN, perceiving me inspired.
Conceived their task was finished: they retired.
I turned upon my friend, and, breaking bounds,
Borrowed a trifle of two hundred pounds.*

Although cryptic and mysteriously funny, there's a lot in there (as is always the case with Crowley). I can't remember what attracted me to it in 1989, but I suspect the lines "Yet the last height of consolation's cold: / Its pinnacle is—not to be consoled!" rang an existential or perhaps even psychosexual bell. After a few years of intense productivity, I had noticed that I cared less and less about indulging in the finished product itself. I usually felt happy and even proud about the end result, but the point was never about proving to myself or anyone else that I could do it—*I already knew I could.* So, the process itself took over, and it fit well with my essentially Lutheran work ethic of fulfilling a duty to my True Will. The work needs to be done, and that is the most important thing. I still feel that way.

Perhaps that is also why I had an almost epiphanic resonance when I watched one of Werner Herzog's documentaries on TV in early 1989: *Gasherbrum—Der Leuchtende Berg* (1985).† The film consists of an interview with Austrian mountaineer Reinhold Messner as he and his climbing partner Hans Kammerlander are about to ascend Gasherbrum in the Karakoram region in Northern Pakistan. Essentially, it's a conversation in the romantic scenery of mountain ranges to be "conquered" without oxygen but by pure will power. What the climbers set out to do, they succeed with. But the underlying narrative is more interesting, as Herzog tries to get Messner to talk about *why* he is trying so

---

*Crowley, *The Book of Lies* (York Beach, ME: Weiser, 1980), 138.
†The English title is *The Dark Glow of the Mountains.*

hard to master peak after peak after peak. Messner breaks down in tears when he tells the story of meeting his mother right after his brother had fallen down a crevasse during another expedition, but still . . . It's a pathology, an obsession, and a more or less (un)conscious integration of Nietzsche's psychodynamic *Übermensch* or Overman. One must press on relentlessly to the next thing on the agenda, at whatever cost, appearing if not dissatisfied with, then at least detached from whatever goals have just been accomplished. And although Herzog has later critically suggested that this approach of "mastering" peaks and goals through elaborate expeditions (i.e., going beyond the personal, psychic spheres) is a symptom of our civilization's disease, it applies just as well to his own attitudes about work in general and filmmaking in particular. The relentless pursuit of ecstatic truth is not a "way of life"—*it is life itself.*

And there they were in my own life: Crowley, Spare, P-Orridge, LaVey, Anger, and a whole army of poetically minded truth-sayers, artists, and magicians, pushing on because they had to, without necessarily needing to understand why. That was exactly what I was striving for. And that's why a contemporary platitude like "Work smarter, not harder" has no meaning for me: it sounds like a euphemism for cutting corners. In my mind it's always much better and more rewarding to work harder.

SELF-INITIATION

The summer of 1989 was eventful, and Crowley was definitely part of it. I had applied to join the Ordo Templi Orientis, the German fraternal order that Crowley had developed during the 1920s, and I wanted to express and externalize the process creatively too. Crowley had written a ritual of self-initiation called "Pyramidos"—as was typical of him, he clothed it in Egyptian terminology and "occult" symbolism that obfuscated what was going on. I wanted to perform it but not by the book, so to speak, not to the letter. Instead, I talked to Thomas Tibert and Jan Ekman, my White Stains partners, about making a live performance called "Pyramidos" that would absolutely not be rock'n'roll but rather an introspective expansion and a mind-bending expression of sound and vision. I ritualized my desire, and it was very much in sync with the upcoming "Hultsfred" festival, which was the biggest music festival in Sweden at the time. Our "concept" proposal was accepted for the festival's experimental stage, and we worked hard to make it special.

I shot material on Super 8, mostly archival stuff off my video screen, and spliced together a 23-minute journey of bizarre sequences and macabre montages. In Thomas's studio, we prepared a backing track that also included sampled voices. When the time came, the film was projected on stage while I played an old synthesizer with effects, Jan played a very loud guitar (as usual), and Thomas mixed it all together with a synapse-challenging backing track. We had called this adventure "The Purple Glow Mind-Blow Show" and the effect was, as desired, powerful. We liked it because it was a new experience to us—in fact, it was White Stains' very first live concert. People in the audience who didn't appreciate the cacophony screamed at us to stop, some skinheads yelled with delight (and thanked us afterward, asking for autographs), and at least three young women fainted (one of whom later became my girlfriend!). It was not necessarily a strict Crowleyan "Pyramidos" performance, but it was definitely a self-initiation into something new: the power of amplified sounds, words, and moving images together opened my mind to many magical possibilities—quite a few of which I've continued using to the present day.

In September of 1989, TOPYSCAN organized another workshop with Arthur Sørenssen. I had been greatly inspired by my first initiation, and worked on my own with a steady drumbeat I had on cassette. I mainly focused on communications with my totem animal, and it was incredibly rewarding. The new workshop focused more on overworld work, and how interconnected or interchangeable it was with the occult terms and concepts in the "Western Ceremonial" tradition. This did not come as a great surprise, since shamanic journeys and experiences constitute the very source of all religions and occultisms that people have dreamed up and constructed throughout time. The real breakthrough was that I allowed myself to become fully interactive and engaged, rather than merely an amazed voyeur.

While in the overworld, I asked to meet Austin Spare. I explained that I was genuinely interested in automatic writing, and received some symbols visually that were explained to me. One of them looked like an arch or the top of a circle. A voice that I understood to be Spare's told me: "Know the Earth!" I asked what death was. "A trick of life . . ." I asked if he was happy where he was. "As happy as I was down there." Amazed at this conversation of sorts, I asked if I could see him. "What for?" was the curt reply. I then petitioned Odin to assist, but the attitude remained the same: "What for?" Spare did, however, promise to help out with my explorations of automatic writing, as agreed, and he seemed to me warm, sympathetic, slightly bitter or cynical, as well as intelligently and sardonically humorous.

Sørenssen was a wonderful shaman and magician, and that same weekend he took me to see Arild Strømsvåg for the first time, as Strømsvåg had a layover at the Stockholm airport. We went out there to have a few beers and talk about what was coming up—namely, my own trip to Bergen, Norway, to join the Ordo Templi Orientis, the storied German occult fraternity that Crowley had invested with his philosophy of Thelema.

My initiation into the Minerval (guest) degree of OTO took place on the autumnal equinox of 1989, and it was pleasant and inspiring—nice people, wonderful ritual, and overall a great reception of myself into their midst. It wasn't a big group, but enough people to initiate new members and also to perform Crowley's Gnostic Mass. Before my arrival, there had been a few other Swedish members in this revived/revitalized OTO,* but they seemed to have disappeared from active duty. So, I was the "new kid on the block" and people were interested in me. Strømsvåg of course knew about everything I'd been up to, so I

---

*After the death of OTO leader Karl "Frater Saturnus" Germer in 1962, there was some confusion as to who was allowed to take over and carry on leading the OTO. This matter was settled in the 1970s when the American Grady McMurtry ("Hymenaeus Alpha") gradually assumed leadership of what came to be called the "Caliphate" OTO.

had a good guide in him. To strengthen my bonds with Odin's son, the storyteller, I took the magical order name of Frater Brage.

As an unexpected and welcome surprise/synchronicity, I received a letter from Kenneth Anger two weeks later, along with a gift: Thea von Harbou's magnificent novel *Metropolis*. As an unexpected and unwelcome surprise, I also had my first asthma attack. In my magical interpretation, I was welcomed into the grand cabal of asthmatic magicians, but in actual fact it was just my bad idea to start smoking a pipe at age twenty-three that caused this unpleasantness! Bizarrely enough, the lovely old American paperback of *Metropolis* contained a cigarette ad as an insert: "I'd heard enough to make me decide one of two things: quit or smoke True. I smoke True. Think about it." How fitting to find this in such a beautifully dystopian science-fiction classic!

The film version of *Metropolis* (directed by Fritz Lang in 1927) was a favorite of mine at this time, so Anger's gift was perfect. Reading it also made me appreciate the prescience—let's rephrase that literally as "pre-science"—of good science fiction, and how intertwined fiction is with the magical perspective of the "Is-To-Be":*

And the machine, having neither head nor brain, with the tension of its watchfulness, sucks and sucks out the brain from the paralyzed skull of its watchman, and does not stay, and sucks, and does not stay until a being is hanging to the sucked-out skull, no longer a man and not yet a machine, pumped dry, hollowed out, used up. And the machine which has sucked out and gulped down the spinal marrow and brain of the man and has wiped out the hollows in his skull with the soft, long tongue of its soft, long hissing, the machine gleams in its silver-velvet radiance, anointed with oil, beautiful, infallible—Baal and Moloch, Huitzilopochtli and

---

*Whatever is presented as fiction that people will consume will have an effect on the outcome of the future. This tends to be a hard-learned lesson. It's worth remembering that the generations of boys and girls who devoured sci-fi in the 1930s and 1940s went on to develop and launch real space rockets only a few decades later.

Durgha. And you, father, you press your finger upon the little blue
metal plate near your right hand, and your great glorious, dreadful
city of Metropolis roars out, proclaiming that she is hungry for fresh
human marrow and human brain and then the living food rolls on,
like a stream, into the machine-rooms, which are like temples, and
that, just used, is thrown up . . .*

Whether this prophetic image is interpreted literally as a giant city—and
today "Monstropolis" would probably be a more fitting term—or perhaps
as the internet or "social media," von Harbou's dark and poetic depic-
tion of the gluttonous void enters the gray area between fiction and magic
that two of my sources of inspiration, Anger and LaVey, had already made
their own. Sometimes the artistic evocation of *emotional* images and
sounds becomes more real than what we as humans can see and hear.

DROPPING OUT, DROPPING IN

The autumn of 1989 was tumultuous on a personal level. I had begun
my first semester of journalism school, and my parents were overjoyed
that I was finally headed in some kind of (accepted) direction. But what
I found there was so horrendous and soul-killing, I had to drop out
when the semester was over. I could never become a journalist like that,
I decided—someone who worked in an editorial office, churning out
clichéd and formulaic pieces about things and people that were of no
interest to me. I wanted to write and be a journalist of my own design.
For me, the key to a good life was—and is—to control your own time,
and never lose track of the insight that Time is a currency strongly
linked to our perception of freedom. True Will needs to be merged
with Time: that's a solid formula for successful magic.

I remember having great conversations with Gen about this, and it

---

*Thea von Harbou, *Metropolis* (New York: Ace, 1963), 29.

seeped into our respective writing too, with statements like "Time is that which ends" (CA), or "Life begins when time stands still" (CA), or "Time is that which Emits" (GPO), or:

> It seems to me Magick is about movement and change, about Time passing. Thee medium ov Magic is Time itself, and thee Belief ov Magic is Action.*

After having "traveled through" the seventeenth tarot trump (the Star)—that is, after having used that tarot card as a gateway into a lucid inner trip—Gen once told me that Time could perhaps even be a person or being and not a linear apprehension or interpretation of change. That would imply possible manipulation or communication if we could find the correct frequency of that being.

I had often used Crowley's *Thoth* Tarot deck for oracular advice and intuitive pointers myself, and I did so specifically toward the end of the semester, as part of my process of deciding whether I should stay or leave college altogether. I had something big up ahead—my first-ever trip to the US, which would be full of life-changing encounters—and school really seemed pointless. Even before I went, I knew the trip would become one great initiation for me. When I drew the fourteenth trump, "Art," that was it—my mind was made up. I needed to dive headfirst into the great adventure of art, creativity, and magic, and see where it would take me.

In one conversation Gen confessed that he felt lazy when he thought of all the things I was doing. The remark caused an amazing twist in my mind, as it was *his* zestful multi-creativity and supreme work ethic that had been one of my own attractions to TOPY in the first place. How nice to hear from your main inspiration that you in turn inspire them! "I'm very happy to have gotten you started," Gen said. So was I.

The main thing that was going on at this time, November 1989,

---

*Genesis P-Orridge, "Notes from a Magical Diary 1967–87," in *Esoterrorist—Selected Essays 1980–1988* (San Francisco: MediaKaos/Alecto, 1994), 26.

was preparing for a P-Orridge visit to Scandinavia, and the recording of an album that Tibert and I had already begun making the music for, in collaboration with another great friend and musician, Pär Aronsson. Toward the end of November, Paula and Gen came over to Stockholm. We had dinner at my parents' place, as they wanted to meet these weird artists that I had talked so much about. They all got along nicely, and my mother even gave Paula some jewelry. On the following day, Eden 140 (aka the video artist Fetish 23), my dearest and most active TOPY ally in Stockholm, drove us all down to a poetry festival in Gothenburg. Paula had a flight case with six cassette decks and mixed various samples while Gen read from new and old texts, including "His Name Was Master" (about his mentor and magical teacher Brion Gysin). And underneath it all was the music that White Stains had made especially for these performances. It was a great success in every way. We had dinner together with my friends from the amazing cutting-edge record label Radium, some gentleman heavily into body piercing, and the photographer Lars Sundestrand, who had known Gen since the TG days and whose fanzine *Funtime* had inspired my own endeavor *Lollipop*. It was a great time, and I stayed up late with Radium's Carl Michael von Hausswolff, knocking ourselves out with champagne. In my pocket I had a gift that Gen had given me on the way down: a necklace with a blue and quite natural-looking glass eye that I still have and occasionally wear to this day. To me, it very much signifies the eye of Odin—he had sacrificed one eye to the Well of Mimir in order to see clearly on the inner planes. Whether the eye on the necklace represented the one sacrificed or the one remaining, I still haven't figured out, but it turned out to be an important symbol for me over the coming years.

In true rock'n'roll fashion, we returned to Stockholm early and prepared for a performance at the club Lido. It certainly wasn't like its grand Paris mother with perpetually smiling and scantily clad dancers, but instead was a rather small club for anxious intellectuals dressed in black. Whatever the case, it was another great success. I had provided Gen with the poem "At Stockholm" from Crowley's youthful 1898 collection of erotica, *White Stains*, and he wove it into a miasmic flow of his own words as Paula created an enticing collage over the trippy White Stains backing track.

At Stockholm

We could not speak, although the sudden glow
Of passion mantling to the crimson cheek
Of either, told our tale of love, although
We could not speak.

What need of language, barren and false and bleak,
While our white arms could link each other so,
And fond red lips their partners mutely seek?

What time for language, when our kisses flow
Eloquent, warm, as words are cold and weak?—
Or now—Ah! sweetheart, even were it so
We could not speak!*

---

*Aleister Crowley, "At Stockholm," in *White Stains* (Stockholm: Edda, 2011), 38. The poem celebrates Crowley's initiation into homosexuality. In his *Confessions*, Crowley writes: "Two main events were destined to put me on the road toward myself. The first took place in Stockholm about midnight of December 31st, 1896. I was awakened to the knowledge that I possessed a magical means of becoming conscious of and satisfying a part of my nature which had up to that moment concealed itself from me. It was an experience of horror and pain, combined with a certain ghostly terror, yet at the same time it was the key to the purest and holiest spiritual ecstasy that exists. At the time, I was not aware of the supreme importance of the matter. It seemed to me little more than a development of certain magical processes with which I was already familiar" (London: Routledge and Kegan Paul, 1986, 123–24). The man in question was later referred to as James L. Dickson in Crowley's *Not the Life and Adventures of Sir Roger Bloxam* (1917). In his introduction to Edda's edition of *White Stains*, William Breeze suggests that the man was James Lachlan Dickson (1855–1927), a married Scottish machinery manufacturer's agent from London. I believe it was rather James Fredrik Dickson (1844–1898), a Scottish-Swedish nobleman and businessman who was the stable master for Swedish King Oscar II, and a supremely decadent and extravagant bon vivant in every way. In honor of her overspending husband, his widow Blanche built the lavish Tudor style castle Tjolöholm outside of Gothenburg, which was used as the set/backdrop for Lars von Trier's magnificent film *Melancholia* (2011).

As that was a late concert, we had time in the evening to do TOPY work, constantly strategizing and making plans. Both Gen and Paula expressed that they wanted to make more art, like what we were doing on this mini-tour, and less of draining administration, and I could only second that emotion. But, I reasoned, we were also doing exactly that as we were talking about it, so I guess we just felt there needed to be a healthier balance.

The following day we flew to Copenhagen for a performance at the lovely Saga theater. The performance was well received and afterward we all went out to dinner with Nick Cave, who was also headlining the festival. Our shaman friend Arthur Sørenssen was also present, as was my girlfriend, Beatrice Eggers. We could see how engaged the local Copenhagen Psychick Youth were, helping out whenever they could. It was a pleasant time in so many ways.

When we finally arrived back in Stockholm, it was time for some serious studio work. Thomas and I had completed all the music, but now we needed to record Gen and Paula properly. The three live performances had very much been like rehearsals for the recording of the album that had the working title "Thee Tarot Ov Abomination" (the name of the tour).

We recorded the pieces one night each, and it was a seamless process. Paula was skilled in weaving tapestries of human voices and other samples—a way of making music in itself. And Gen's recordings were basically all first takes, read to a single flickering candle in an otherwise dark studio. We were all enchanted and mesmerized not only by the brilliance of the material, but also by Gen's seductive voice. Hearing that voice enmeshed in our music still gives me the shivers to this day.

We decided to magically use the opportunity to spread some inspiring propaganda too, with Gen recording "Message from Thee Temple" in English and I doing so in Swedish.* Ultimately, these

---

*"Message from Thee Temple" was an introductory text included in the basic information packets from TOPY. It had also been recorded by tattoo artist and body piercer "Mr. Sebastian" for Psychic TV's first album, *Force the Hand of Chance* (1982).

tracks ended up on one of the album's compositions, one voice in each stereo channel.

After the P-Orridges had gone back to the UK, I made my mind up and resigned from journalism school. I already had a taste of an ideal life, and I wasn't going to give that up. The money would come from somewhere, I was sure. As long as I could use any technology or printing facilities or whatever, I was totally fine with having a regular job "on the side." But I was already in a state of magical frenzy and hardly had any time to think about these things.

In mid-December of 1989, I put on the "Visions of Occulture"* show at a venue in Uppsala. I was amused when fundamentalist Christian protesters decided to show up, but disgusted by the fact that they tried to prevent people from going inside. On the one hand, I felt like compassionately offering them a cup of coffee (it was cold outside); on the other, I wanted to tell them to fuck off and stop interfering with my show. These zealots were charming in a naive kind of way, subjugated and defenseless—as they secretly yearn to be—and the evening was a great success in spite of them.

IF YOU'RE GOING TO SAN FRANCISCO . . .

The winter solstice of 1989 brought me to America for the very first time. Touching down for a brief stop in LA, I met up for a tour of Hollywood with Sissi Bauman, a friend from Gothenburg who was there working as an au pair. It was bizarre to see the discrepancy between the fabricated image of Tinseltown and the real grit of Hollywood Boulevard (which was a lot rougher back then—perhaps not quite on par with New York's

---

*"Visions of Occulture" was a TOPY traveling film show that included films by Alejandro Jodorowsky; the film *Mondo Magic* (1975); the Church of Satan documentary *Satanis: The Devil's Mass* (1970); and the 1968 Antony Balch version of Benjamin Christensen's *Witchcraft through the Ages* (1922; original title: *Häxan*), narrated by William Burroughs over a jazz soundtrack.

42nd Street, but definitely not a safe area). I immediately loved it. Perhaps this was inevitable, since I had already immersed myself for years in what I would later term "Highbrow Lowlife," a kind of transcendental approach to the delightful clashes between the Imaginary and the Real—and especially the American varieties. It felt like I was peeking into a dream of sorts, driving down the streets and boulevards, and seeing so much beautiful neon, the streetwalkers, the panhandlers, the limousines, the plastic façades of the Scientology edifices, and of course the hordes of tourists worshiping the fabricated demigods of a magical moving-image industry that was still going strong, and in many ways more so than ever.

The first real stop was San Francisco, and my guide and host was Tim O'Neill. Tim was at this time part of the esoteric underground scene in this lovely city, and basically knew everyone involved in interesting things. He took me to see many of his friends, like the great musician Kris Force who would later develop the project Amber Asylum. I could also browse amid Tim's amazing library of magical books. He was gracious enough to have set me up with a space of my own, thanks to a friend who was away over the holidays. I was thrown into a vortex of inspiring minds, just like I had hoped for.

At this time, San Francisco had a number of world-class bookstores like Fields, City Lights, and Green Apple, and it turned out to be a dangerous visit—to my already ailing wallet, that is. But I knew that everything would work out somehow, and couldn't resist the talismanic osmosis that I would receive from fine editions of Kenneth Grant and LaVey books.

I also met up with Boyd Rice, the infamous prankster, performance artist, and noise musician. We had been in touch for a couple of years, and he had written me just before the trip to say that LaVey had showed him the copy of "Sweet Jayne," and they all looked forward to meeting me in person, adding that "Anton speaks highly of your work."

Boyd was kind enough to lend me a copy of a book that was really hard to get at the time: Burton Wolfe's *The Devil's Avenger* (1974), the first real biography of Anton LaVey. I was overjoyed, and Tim immediately took me to the nearest copy shop so that I could get it xeroxed. In many ways, and in my TOPY-network mind-frame, certain photocopies were worth more to me than overpriced first editions.

I also met local TOPY members, as well as some OTO members. Quite often there was a crossover, as there was within myself. These people were so devoted and friendly that if I had ever harbored any doubts about whether the fraternity/sorority was "real," I now realized it was very much so. There was lots of curiosity about TOPY specifically, and we talked and made excursions to Golden Gate Park and the museums of Berkeley, all the while incessantly talking about magic and culture. I made friends especially with a magician who now goes by the name Aidan Wachter and his girlfriend Laura, who were involved in both groups and with whom I felt a great resonance. They were kind enough to give me a copy of the oversized "doorstop" edition of Israel Regardie's *The Golden Dawn* book, something that made my luggage even more (pleasantly) overweight.

Aidan is another great magician who would bloom out of this very free era of experimentation, writing inspiring books and also creating some stunning magical jewelry (up until 2019). At the time we kept in touch via letters and I could see he shared my attitudes vis-à-vis the crazy Christians—a hardline approach is better than seeing them as the meek and mellow people they actually aren't:

> We are apparently meant to up the signal to noise ratio and make this world worth living in . . . And I believe that you are right . . . The Aeon is in full effect . . . The predominantly Xtian self- and world-tyrannical feeding frenzy is just about over . . . The "Satan Scare" is mainly the shark eating itself, and the wolves watch laughing and egging them on . . . The world is our oyster and we know how to get into the goodies.*

---

*Aidan Wachter, letter to the author (31 May 1990).

At this time there was a considerable overlap between the magical/ pagan communities and the tattoo-and-piercing scene. The San Francisco–based imprint *RE/Search* (whose owners I also met and became friends with on this trip) had just published an anthology called *Modern Primitives*, to a great extent influenced by Genesis—ever the cultural engineer.* These two scenes were similarly intertwined in London and other places in Europe, and of course have been part of Indigenous ritual practices since time immemorial. Affecting change on or in the physical body, in the sense of extreme and signifying adornment and modifications, appealed to young magicians who were desperate to leave the rigidity of the then almost paradoxically collectivistic "individualists" who inhabited the older occult order structures. And I'm sure people in the body-modification scenes, with their inherent shamanic leanings, felt the same way: it was time for a new kind of cultural visibility.

Today, as we know, tattooing and piercing are mainstream and almost de rigueur practices. It's been an interesting journey to follow from esoteric symbol and signal, through occulturation, and into the mainstream of culture. As he often did, LaVey hit the nail on the head when he was interviewed in *Modern Primitives*:

> You can put the various forms of bodily adornment in classifications. Fakir Musafar has been at his activities for so many, many years: infibulation, nipple piercing, constriction, etc. I saw a lot of *that* sort of thing when I was in carnival work (late forties). At that time tattooed people had to live in almost a twilight world: a society set apart from ordinary society. They were really aliens. Now many supposedly "respectable" people are able to celebrate a secret or

---

*Some years earlier *RE/Search* had published a book that had almost become like a bible for me and my friends in Stockholm: *Incredibly Strange Films* (1986), edited by Boyd Rice and another friend of Anton LaVey's, Jim Morton.

fetishistic life. That's a motivating factor that didn't exist so much in the past: the satisfaction of knowing that one is different underneath one's business suit.*

Fakir Musafar, aka Roland Loomis (1930–2018), the world-famous advertising executive who really pushed the boundaries of body modification and the use of such practices for inducing altered states of consciousness, was a true gentleman. Tim brought me to the Channel 25 TV studio on Folsom Street, where an episode of *Madeleine's Variety Television* was about to be recorded. The guests were Fakir Musafar and Jim Ward, the founder and owner of the Gauntlet body-piercing empire. It was great to hear them talk about their work and fetishes. A highlight was when the ever so correct Loomis stripped and became Fakir Musafar, attaching a TV camera on heavy hooks through his chest and then filming parts of the show. To me, it wasn't only fun and bizarre (although it was that too!); it was a show of force from people who made no compromises whatsoever in their choice of lifestyle. Some days later, I visited Jim Ward at the Gauntlet store and he was equally friendly and cultivated. He provided me with issues of the magazine *PFIQ (Piercing Fans International Quarterly)*. It was a center for this kind of modification culture that Gen and Paula P-Orridge had been featured in at some point, as had Mr. Sebastian (aka Alan Oversby), the famous London body-piercer who narrated TOPY's original "Message from Thee Temple" on the first Psychic TV album, *Force the Hand of Chance* (1982).

Although I have never felt sexually attracted to the hardcore leather scene of San Francisco nor been attracted to extreme shamanic body modifications à la Fakir Musafar, meeting these two gentlemen made a strongly positive impression and reinforced my view that *life is essentially what we make of it*—in action as well as in attitude!

---

*Anton LaVey interviewed in V. Vale and Andrea Juno, eds., *Modern Primitives* (San Francisco: RE/Search, 1989), 92.

THE BLACK HOUSE

After some telephoning back and forth, I made arrangements to visit 6114 California Street: Anton LaVey's infamous Black House where the Church of Satan was founded in 1966. I was nervous, to say the least. What had begun as teenage fantasies about Jayne Mansfield, seeped into the rock'n'roll projections of White Stains' "Sweet Jayne" record, had then been spurred on by Genesis's advice straight into the Devil's Den. Getting to meet this iconic magician wasn't easy either—LaVey was, by this stage of his life, very reclusive and exclusive. At the agreed time, I knocked on the door. The rest, as has often been said, is history.

Having viewed Ray Laurent's Church of Satan documentary *Satanis* (1969) so many times over the preceding years, I had created an elaborate and vivid image in my mind of what the Black House would be like. To step onto this "sacred ground" was exciting, needless to say, and it turned out to be grander than any preconceived vision. The first thing that struck me was that the light in the corridor you came into was subdued. I almost tripped over a box by the front door that LaVey later explained had belonged to "Skippy," the dog who played the chipper Asta in the successful *Thin Man* series of films between 1934 and 1947. A great entrance!

The main living room, the "purple parlor," was quite small but it still had the items I had seen in photos and film clips: bookshelves, a nice couch, two easy chairs, a coffee table made from a tombstone, some decorative peacock feathers, and a TV set.

Blanche Barton served me a drink and asked me to have a seat. The "Doktor" would soon be with us, she explained. And suddenly there he was, coming out of the kitchen with an outstretched hand and a big smile: elegant, powerful, and indeed very Satanic-looking, dressed entirely in black. Any nervousness I had felt quickly dissipated amid this genuinely friendly and curious reception and the conversations that followed.

Both LaVey and Blanche heaped praise on the first issue of *The Fenris Wolf*, and this of course made me very proud. What in my mind was merely a brave attempt to make a fanzine about something other than rock'n'roll bands and trashy pop culture had suddenly established itself in ways I could have never foreseen. But there it was: the wolf was out and a-howling, and now I found myself in the purple parlor talking to Anton LaVey about it!

LaVey had allowed me to reprint an old essay of his from the Church of Satan's newsletter, *The Cloven Hoof*, and he was pleased with how it had turned out in print. But his enthusiasm was even more apparent when it came to the article I had written specifically for the first issue of *Fenris*, which was "Jayne Mansfield—Satanist." LaVey apparently appreciated any and all attempts to keep Mansfield's memory and legacy alive. I was more than happy about this: Jayne Mansfield had definitely been my late teenage crush, and her life story was fascinating in a number of respects, not least of all her connection to LaVey.

After dinner at MacArthur Park, we returned to the Black House in LaVey's elegant black Jaguar. LaVey suggested we move to the kitchen, and I knew what this meant: a musical extravaganza performed on his many synthesizers (organized on racks so that he could play several at the same time). He looked at me and Blanche and then just hammered away. Being a supremely skilled musician, LaVey seemed to enjoy performing in a humorous way, and often in weird and contrapuntal medleys that really took you on rollercoaster rides. He knew some pretty rare pieces of music, and I just tried to memorize as much as I could. Wagner's "Ride of the Valkyries" merged with the "Horst Wessel Lied" and then into something I recognized as a theme song from a Hollywood comedy. And there were many others too. He made them merge seamlessly, and always appreciated our smiles and spontaneous applause. He was a natural-born entertainer.

As White Stains were recording a new album in Stockholm

at around this time, I asked LaVey if he knew anything decidedly Scandinavian. After a short pause, he played a lovely and upbeat folk tune that I recorded on my SONY cassette recorder and included on our album as "The Satanic Hambo." Later on, I figured out that the tune was an old Danish Christmas melody, and I could only wonder how he had come to absorb it into his vast musical memory bank!

After this inspired musical interlude, there was more conversation in the purple parlor. I told them about my new publishing venture, Psychick Release, and that I wanted to publish *The Satanic Bible* in Swedish, and possibly anthologize LaVey's brilliant essays from *The Cloven Hoof.* All of this sounded great to LaVey and Blanche, and I was overjoyed. But that was not all. As the hour was approaching dawn, they suggested I come back the following evening to talk more.

LaVey in his front parlor and library room, 1989
(photo by Carl Abrahamsson)

I had made it. I had passed the test and gained top Satanic Security Clearance, and I couldn't wait until it was nighttime again.

On the next evening, we watched *The Falcon's Alibi* (1946), with LaVey emphasizing that I should always be on the lookout for movies featuring Elisha Cook, Jr. A good piece of advice! We kept on talking, mainly about movies. At some point very late in the evening, LaVey took out a copy of Ben Hecht's dark and perverted 1922 fantasy *Fantazius Mallare—A Mysterious Oath* and started reading from it. At times, he cast a glance my way to see if I was paying attention. And indeed I was: to hear Hecht's words in LaVey's distinctly American voice was a knockout. Following on this trail, he pulled down Hecht's *A Guide for the Bedeviled* (1944) and read sections from that book to me. This, by contrast, was no dark fiction, but rather Hecht's attempt to make Americans—perhaps specifically American Jews, and even more specifically American Jews in Hollywood—wake up to what was going on in Germany at the time. Hecht had often been a rabble-rouser and through his massive success as a scriptwriter in Hollywood he could indeed wield a bright torch. At the time, I got the impression that LaVey wanted to emphatically show me Hecht's supreme versatility, and how he put it to use in various ways. It was a special moment that made an impression on me—an impression that led to not only a documentary film thirty years later but also a book about LaVey and his magical ways of sowing seeds inside the minds of those he found Satanically fertile.* The magic worked in mysterious ways, inside and across time.

One of those fertile minds at the time was definitely Boyd Rice. He dropped by after midnight and we celebrated our Hechtian focus by watching the Marx Brothers in *At the Circus* (1939), a film that was written by Hecht and Buster Keaton. We then watched clips from the macabre mondo film *Death Scenes* (1989), which LaVey had narrated in

---

*This is my *Anton LaVey and the Church of Satan: Infernal Wisdom from the Devil's Den* (Rochester, VT: Inner Traditions, 2022).

his exquisite and dramatic voice. LaVey also told us that he had been instrumental in promoting Herschell Gordon Lewis's classics *Blood Feast* (1963), *Two Thousand Maniacs!* (1964), and *Color Me Blood Red* (1965), as well as Tobe Hooper's *The Texas Chain Saw Massacre* (1974).

LaVey's love of movies was present in almost every conversation, and perhaps only overshadowed by his love of music. I think it was a significant part of the reason why I was welcomed back after this first San Francisco visit. I had spent the greater part of my teenage years curating my own cocktail of weird movies, contrarian occultism, and highly evocative, cutting-edge music. Thanks to satellite TV, VHS cassettes, and the wonderful Cinematheque in Stockholm, I could indulge a lot in all the "highbrow-lowlife" culture I immediately felt belonged to me. I connected the dots early on—there *is* magic in movies!—and I think LaVey could see right away that I "got it." Due to its immersive quality, a medium like cinema is a perfect one in which to cast spells and leave clues—for use in the moment or much, much later.

To key me into the Satano-Gnostic, cine-magical vibrations, LaVey name-dropped a lot of titles that I tried to remember and then fervently write down after I had returned to Tim's friend's apartment. Mostly these were films with which LaVey had some degree of involvement. In *The Devil's Rain* (1975, directed by Robert Fuest) he played the part of Devilish High Priest, but there were other less visible connections too.

In *The Omen* (1976) the two cars—a Buick Electra and a Jaguar—were directly "inspired" by LaVey's well-known ownership of the same. In the second *Omen* film (1978), the team wanted to actually film at 6114 California Street—according to LaVey, it was to have been a kind of "Satanic bar mitzvah" scene.

Influences were present in Bernard McEveety's *The Brotherhood of Satan* (1971), in which LaVey had also had a hand; he called it an "incredibly magical film." And there was Bruce Kessler's *Simon, King of the Witches* (1971), which LaVey claimed to have partly inspired. Nor could we forget Ted V. Mikels's surreal and Satanic masterpiece *Blood Orgy of the She-Devils* (1973)!

As I discuss in detail in my book *Anton LaVey and the Church of Satan*, the film that LaVey found most magically powerful, and also the one that he felt most pride in having been involved with (ex post facto) was Tod Browning's outsider odyssey *Freaks* (1932). This classic sideshow drama, including many real circus freaks of the day, had a short and controversial life in the 1930s, after which MGM tried to terminate it through neglect. It wasn't until much later that a somewhat decent print was found in the same theater where LaVey had played the organ for burlesque dancers in the late 1940s (and where Russ Meyer used to be a projectionist!), which could be used for striking new prints—at LaVey's recommendation and insistence in 1956 to the Camera Obscura Film Society of San Francisco. Thus began the film's long journey back to well-deserved accolades and appreciation. "It's something I'm very, very proud of," LaVey told me.

The theme of this film, and the people involved in it, were integrated in LaVey's magical corpus and teachings—and not only passively, as a "cool" reference within occulted cinema history. Nor was this just a nod to director Tod Browning's genius, or because of the fact that LaVey knew a lot of the freaks personally from his days working at sideshows (Johnny Eck, Koo-Koo the Birdgirl, Josephine Joseph, to name but a few). It was also based on the realization that power exists in being feared and different. The Satanic angle is one of *natural outsidership*, and these special people were all real stars enjoying a high status in the sideshow "circuit." Outside of the confines of their own habitat, they were feared as abominations, and made the "normies" show their most intolerant and cynical sides in uncontrollable ways—which paradoxically revealed them to be ethical freaks themselves (as they were mostly Christians). It was one of LaVey's favorite mockeries: the people with a "good-guy badge" who try to impose a general morality (or moralism), usually to hide their own shenanigans (LaVey loved to call these people "candy-ass do-gooders," "stupid baboons," and other lovely Americanisms). This is basically the theme of the film too. If you're genuinely welcomed within the cabal of these powerful, misshapen, and rare birds, you know you're genuinely special. If you break that trust, however, there's basically only one way out.

This a powerful nugget of Satano-Gnostic wisdom: *Being on the outside looking in is usually more revealing than being on the inside looking out.* If you feel you don't "belong" to a given environment, don't be sorry. Find or create your own environment instead—it will definitely be filled with more interesting people!

During our conversations, it also surfaced that LaVey appreciated Werner Herzog's films because of their "weird narratives about supermen." I couldn't have agreed more! According to LaVey, they had discussed different scripts and ideas, specifically for what was to become Herzog's classic remake of *Nosferatu* (1979). LaVey claimed to be the stylistic inspiration for Klaus Kinski's appearance in the film, and that his daughter Karla (whom I also met during the course of this darkly enchanted night) had been the inspiration for casting the slender brunette Isabelle Adjani rather than some voluptuous blonde vampire-magnet.

A gem of a statement surfaced in our movie talks during the night. LaVey said, speaking of Hollywood in the Golden Era, that "in those days, art followed life, and not vice versa." I had forgotten about this remark until I came across it written down on a page in my (early morning) notebook as I was working on my aforementioned LaVey book in 2021. I must have integrated it in my mind somehow because it became the main magical mantra in one of my "Cotton Ferox" texts (more on this later): "Life Mimics Art Mimics Life . . ."

What I think LaVey meant was that the fabric of life (with its concomitant stories) was richer and in many ways more colorful back then; there was simply a lot to make great books or movies *about*. I don't believe this holds as true today, when we live in an aesthetically egalitarian and pruriently paranoid postmodern monoculture and would rather be inspired in life by the art we claim to prefer—or simply the one we find shoved down our throats.

The dissolving fluidity that surrounds us now is great for conscious magicians aware of its potential, but rather unhealthy for passive "consumeroids" who, for instance, believe that all of cinema history can be found via the online streaming services and who gladly fashion themselves after the most bland and unthreatening of commercial models. To go outside of these limits is inherently heretical and thus blatantly powerful. In the context of our LaVeyan wisdom it could mean cherishing and watching a rare DVD (or even VHS cassette!) of some forgotten film you love because something else equally mind-blowing led you to the effort of seeking and acquiring it—rather than just plugging into one of the streaming platforms and passively watching whatever by talentless gutter regurgitators like Ryan Murphy. There's a very Satanic/contrarian logic in any culture's relationship with time: whatever is highly successful today will not be so tomorrow; whatever desperately clings to the moment will be forever associated with it.

PART II
1990–1994

HAPPINESS & ANGER

On New Year's Eve, I went with Aidan and Laura to the OTO Thelema Lodge in Berkeley. They served as officers in the Gnostic Mass, and it was very different to the one I had experienced in Norway a few months earlier. It was performed in a designated temple space and was beautifully executed. The lodge in question was then the oldest one still running in the world, having been chartered by Crowley's disciple Grady McMurtry ("Hymenaeus Alpha") in 1977. For better or worse, the rebooting or restructuring of the OTO in the mid-1970s was definitely colored by the Californian environment, and was even boosted by a newspaper like the *Berkeley Barb*:

> Since nobody else in the late Sixties seemed to be doing anything, McMurtry decided to declare himself OHO ["Outer Head of the Order," meaning de facto leader], and to take over what was left of the OTO until such a time as the Order again had sufficient lodges and members to hold a proper international election for an OHO. After knocking around the Bay Area for a few years, he finally decided to try some "fairly heavy magick" last spring, opening up the Order to an influx of psychic energy from the ancient Egyptian Gods worshipped by the Order. KAPLOOIE!! The hippie-commie-pervert-weirdo-heathen occultists of Beserkely descended upon him en masse, to check him out. They found a hard drinking, hard thinking crusty old man, with one of the world's greatest collections of humorous Al Crowley stories.*

As soon as Mass was over, there was a party. Although the members were nice and curious about me as a Minerval from exotic Sweden, most of

---

*Philip Jameson, "How Aleister Crowley Came to Berkeley," *Berkeley Barb*, issue of December 9–15, 1977, 7.

them were high, stoned, and/or drunk, and proudly flaunting it. I am certainly no moralist, but there was definitely something loosely ominous in the air, signaling a potential Satanic Panic–type disaster. What I didn't know at the time was that there *had* recently been a police raid at the lodge, sparked by rumors of drug use, drug dealing, and other conflicts. It just didn't feel like a cool or wise move to use the temple space for indulging in illicit substances. I specifically blamed this on a lax California attitude, as I had been part of the Norwegian experience, and the naughtiest thing the Norwegians had done was probably laughing too loud.

Instead of hanging around, I headed back to San Francisco with Aidan and Laura and toasted the new decade on the stroke of midnight, filled with many impressions of and connections to magics both past and future, and amazed at just what an incredible year it had been for me.

The beginning of the new year certainly didn't disappoint, either. I left San Francisco and traveled back to Los Angeles. I had already made arrangements to meet Kenneth Anger, and Anton LaVey had surprised me by letting me know that he had also been on the phone with Anger, singing my praises. Anger had then told LaVey to instruct me to come straight over to his house from the airport. Which was exactly what happened.

As the airport shuttle arrived at the address on Barton Avenue, close to the Hollywood Forever Cemetery, Anger came out from the house to help me. He said we should hurry, and as soon as we were inside, he bolted the front door securely. I soon realized why. Just about a minute later there was a helicopter hovering over the street and police cars drove up with sirens and lights. There was a raid taking place on a house directly across the street. "There's a gang there," Anger explained. "A neighbor was shot recently, and also a dog." It was a surreal combination: hearing the violent chaos outside while being safe inside in what I can only describe as a sanctuary. Anger smiled as I looked around. I knew he had great collections of Hollywood memorabilia—after all, he was the author of the scandalously entertaining *Hollywood Babylon* books—but to be immersed in it was a real bliss. It also re-evoked

LaVey's house in that it was obviously designed and decorated to create a magical effect: the "total environment." Anger's part of the house was an art-deco dream filled with exquisite vintage furniture and posters and lobby cards from movies such as *Goin' to Town* (1935; directed by Alexander Hall and written by Mae West), the Clara Bow classics *The Keeper of the Bees* (1925; directed by James Leo Meehan) and *Red Hair* (1928; directed by Clarence G. Badger), and life-size promotional cutout figures of Boris Karloff and Elsa Lanchester as Frankenstein's monster (and his love interest). It was like time-traveling to Hollywood in the 1930s.

We talked about current projects, my thesis, and seeing LaVey in San Francisco. Anger told me he was working on a film of Crowley's Gnostic Mass, and I told him I had been at Thelema Lodge only a few days earlier. He did not seem impressed by what they were getting up to in Berkeley.

We walked to a nearby motel where I would stay. We then went out to dinner at a Mexican restaurant and kept talking about Crowley.

Kenneth Anger at his home in Los Angeles, 1990
(photo by Carl Abrahamsson)

Anger emphasized that he was not a member of the OTO, and I gathered that he was probably a member of the A∴A∴, Crowley's magical order that was based on the structure of the Hermetic Order of the Golden Dawn. He mentioned being a friend of Cameron,* the widow of Crowley's California disciple Jack Parsons, and that she had been an important catalyst for his early interest in Crowley and the Thelemic teachings. The house where Anger now lived was the one where he had shot his classic occult art film *Inauguration of the Pleasure Dome* in 1954. It was owned by Samson de Brier, who also stars in the film as Osiris (and other characters). De Brier was still living in another part of the property. My mind was blown: this wasn't just the house where Anger had shot his legendary film; it had also been the location for de Brier's salons that attracted Los Angeles cool folks like Dennis Hopper, Sal Mineo, Curtis Harrington, Marjorie Cameron, Michael Bowen, and Wally Berman of the influential Ferus Gallery.

After a nice Mexican feast, Anger suggested we should go to the movies. I could hardly believe my ears! Going to the movies with Kenneth Anger! So, after I had treated him to dinner, he treated me to Oliver Stone's *Born on the Fourth of July*, starring Tom Cruise, in 70 mm. It was a great experience, and certainly greater than the film itself. Afterward we concluded that Tom Cruise is a very talented actor and that he basically carried the film on his shoulders. The evening ended outside my motel with Anger telling me I have very attractive eyes. Why, thank you, Mr. Anger! That was one of the times I genuinely wished I had been born gay or been more sexually adventurous. Instead, we retired—each to his own abode—after having made plans for the following day.

The next morning, following breakfast together at a diner, we sat down properly in Anger's living room. I interviewed him for the second issue of *The Fenris Wolf*, and he was very accommodating. I felt like

---

*The mononym used by Marjorie Cameron Parsons Kimmel (1922–1995). More on her in due course!

I wasn't only experiencing a dream—I was now an active part of it. I knew well from my vast archive of Anger interviews that he could be tricky and snippy, but this certainly was not the case here. When the interview was over, he enthusiastically showed me his library of occult books in general and Crowley books in particular. As with the movie memorabilia, most of his books were first editions and in great condition. He also pulled out Ben Hecht's *Fantazius Mallare* as well as the second volume, *The Kingdom of Evil*, and recommended I get them. I mentioned LaVey had talked a lot about Hecht too. "He was one of a kind," Anger said. "He made a lot of money writing screwball and comedy movies but there was a darker side to him too. Anton loves that combination. I do too. Hecht was definitely touched by genius."

Anger insisted I borrow two books from him, even though I was living so far away: the fairly recently published volume of *The Equinox*,* signed by its editor, Hymenaeus Beta; and Crowley's wonderful book of erotica, *Snowdrops from a Curate's Garden* (which had recently been republished by Chicago-based publisher Teitan Press). He also mentioned that both books were important for me, as I was on my way into the OTO. And if this weren't enough, he said he wanted to give me something. I remained standing there by his bookshelf, flipping through *Snowdrops*, when he returned with a rolled-up sheet of paper. He unrolled it. Inside was a large photograph of Aleister Crowley. "It's from the Yorke collection in London. It's Crowley dressed as a lesbian dandy,"† Anger said and smiled. I thanked him and shook his hand. I was flabbergasted by his generosity. When it was time to return to the motel and then leave Los Angeles for Palm Springs, I refused to pack

---

The Equinox was published by Crowley between 1909 and 1913 in ten issues plus a supplement (usually called "Volume One"). The book Anger lent me was volume 3, no. 10, a special issue about the OTO and its history.

†Later on I found out that Crowley was dressed as "Saladin" in this image, the Muslim leader who fought the medieval Christian crusaders, and who plays an important symbolic part in the first OTO initiations. That only added to the drama of Anger providing me with a foretaste of what was to come (rather than what I had already been through, via the introductory Minerval degree).

the roll in my suitcase. I carried it in my hand as if it were a sacred magic wand. And in many ways, it was.

Before I returned home after this eventful first American trip, I spent a few days with friends in Palm Springs. They were active in arranging film screenings and festivals, mainly of old Hollywood classics and silent films, and they had been instrumental in helping me to arrange the meeting with Anger—although I do believe the parallel occult connection via LaVey had helped considerably more. Through them I met Eric Burdon from the band the Animals, who lived close by, but the most interesting thing that happened was that we had lunch with the artist Sésame Thanz-Buckner and her husband (also friends of Samson de Brier). I knew she sold collectible books, and I asked if she had anything by Ben Hecht. She said no, but then called to check with a friend and fellow bookseller: later that afternoon, I could pick up early editions of *A Guide for the Bedeviled* and a few other Hecht titles from her friend. My journey was complete! The icing on the cake came with the return flight back to Sweden. The man in the next seat turned out to be Sven Nykvist, Ingmar Bergman's main cinematographer, and like me a Leica camera aficionado. We spent the whole flight engaged in conversation. He had just been working in Hollywood and, as we talked, it dawned on me: *so had I.*

PSYCHICK RELEASE

When I returned home to Sweden, I was filled with ideas. I was also in love. In September I had met a delightful woman, Beatrice Eggers, at one of the TOPYSCAN "Visions of Occulture" film screenings, and we had fallen for one another. She couldn't join me on the US trip, but I went to her town in the south of Sweden as often as I could afford, and she visited me in Stockholm too. The previous short relationships I had had so far had been disappointments. This was partly a result of my inexperience, but also because those girls had been completely "unmagical," meaning that they were locked in a causal, rationalistic groove, and with no willingness to peek and pop out of the proverbial box. But this new love object was different, and eager and curious to learn new things. It didn't take long before we started to experiment with ritual magic together, and it was literally phenomenal. She started sigilizing and became a TOPY Kali, and this led to much ritual work for us together too.

There was a book waiting for me when I got home from the US. Gen had sent me a copy of Crowley's *Little Essays Toward Truth*, and I found that relevant and meaningful as I was feeling the pull of the more structured work of the OTO and Crowley's Thelema. I felt that with TOPY I had jumped into a pool of delightful and life-changing wonders, but I was becoming more and more drawn to the various streams that fed into the pool. Thelema was one of these streams, and Gen shared my interest in many aspects of Crowley for the very same reasons. We could all learn a lot from his mistakes—as a person, as a magician, and as the leader of a magical order. *Little Essays* was an important book as I embarked on the next stage of my journey.

> There is in fact only one Magical Operation of whose propriety we may always be sure; and that is the increase of our sum of Energy. It is even indiscreet to try to specify the kind of Energy required, and worse to consider any particular purpose.
>
> Energy being increased, Nature will herself supply clarity: our Vision is obscure only because our Energy is deficient. For Energy is the Substance of the Universe. When it is adequate, we are in no doubt as to how to employ it; witness the evident case of the will of the Adolescent. It is also to be well noted that moral obstruction to the right use of this Energy cause at once the most hideous deformations of character, and determine the gravest lesions of the nervous system.
>
> Let therefore the Magician divest himself of all preconceptions as to the nature of his True Will, but apply himself eagerly to increas-

ing his Potential. In this discipline (moreover) he is beginning to fit himself for that very abdication of *all that he has and all that he is* which is the essence of the Oath of the Abyss!

Thus then do we find one more of those paradoxes which are the images of the Truth of the Supernals: by destroying our own highest morality, and relying upon our natural instinct as the sole guide, we come unaware upon the most simple, and the most sublime, of all ethical and spiritual conceptions.*

One of the first things on my agenda for the new decade was to set up a proper company: Psychick Release. It was to be all the things that TOPYSCAN had sketched out in terms of releasing both books and records, and arranging events and film screenings. I wanted everything to be more organized and legitimate, as Crowley had written in *The Book of the Law* (III:41): "All must be done well and with business way."† To pay the immediate bills, I got a job at a comic-book publishing company so that I could access their computers, laser printers, reprographic camera, and so on. I could not consider working anywhere where I couldn't allow at least half of my brain—probably the right side—to work on my own projects. I specifically wanted to publish *The Book of the Law* in Norwegian and Swedish, and I had also started translating LaVey's *Satanic Bible* into Swedish.

In February of 1990, I returned to the UK, this time with my girlfriend. We spent time in London at the Groucho Club with Gen and Paula, and appeared on the *Buzz* TV show talking about magic and TOPY. There was also some substantial TOPY business to go through, and we went down to Brighton to have a strategy meeting. Together we decided that I should create TOPY EUROPE as a "Station" and start administrating sigils and general correspondence (this had previously been handled by members in the Netherlands,

---

*Crowley, "Energy," in *Little Essays Toward Truth* (Scottsdale, AZ: New Falcon, 1991), 58–59.
†Crowley, *The Book of the Law* (York Beach, ME: Red Wheel/Weiser, 2004), 60.

but they had run out of energy). I was more than happy to do it: I loved being part of improving and restructuring organizations, and I was also very good at it. Furthermore, I was happy to feel the confidence from an organization that really inspired me, and which was inevitably growing and in need of smooth administration. Gen and I celebrated by going out and buying me a gray clergy shirt and collar in a Christian store. Gen already had some and was wearing his garb when we went inside. It was utterly hilarious to hear him talk and be talked to as if he were a parish priest and not an underground rebel artist with occult leanings.

I brought home a 16 mm print of Benjamin Christensen's classic film *Häxan*, in the Antony Balch edit called *Witchcraft through the Ages*, which was narrated by William Burroughs (the same film that we had screened as part of the "Visions of Occulture" show). After Balch died in 1980, Gen had rescued a great deal of Balch's films with Burroughs from being lost, and was preparing a sale of them all.* In the meantime I was allowed to take the film back with me to Sweden and screen it wherever I could, which felt like a great step forward as I had already been showing it occasionally on video. (I loved traveling around with films, and the earlier "Visions of Occulture" program had served as my basic training in this regard.)

In Stockholm, Thomas Tibert and I worked on mixing the album that would soon be released on my new label, Psychick Release, and which was now simply titled *At Stockholm*. We were so proud of the entire process and Gen and Paula were overjoyed with the result too. Looking back on it today, the album still packs a real magical punch, and to me it still feels completely timeless. One of the greatest acknowledgments I received was hearing Coil talking warmly about the music we had made; we exchanged records at around this time in the early 1990s. Our song "The Result" had been an obvious inspiration for a

---

*For more on this fascinating story, see Breyer P-Orridge et al., *Brion Gysin: His Name Was Master*, 50–60.

Coil track called "Amethyst Deceivers," and Sleazy told me in London in 1997 how much he liked *At Stockholm*.*

CINEMAGICIANS

The spring of 1990 was as intense as the previous years had been, if not more so. Psychick Release was happening, and me and Thomas were already recording new material. As I was now back at the printshop, I made several new books, including facsimiles of the great runologist Sigurd Agrell's books on rune magic. I loved showing films, so I conceptualized a film club or society in Stockholm that would show underground classics. It was all part of my psychological structure: wanting to share whatever it was that had inspired or entertained me, whether it was contemporary occultism and occulture, or cool cult films that no one in Stockholm had ever heard about—preferably combined with great parties afterward.

I traveled with the print of *Witchcraft through the Ages* to Copenhagen and Berlin before I had to send it back. In Berlin I had a meeting with "Ritus," who ran TOPY Germany, and it was great to catch up on what had happened since we had met in Sweden for the Rotorite. I could sense a fatigue that was similar to what had occurred with the members in the Netherlands. People were *busy*, expending energy in other areas such as relationships, jobs, studies, and all the normal things one goes through in life. TOPY was always genuinely Thelemic in the sense that we encouraged people to go exactly where they wanted to go. It was never a cult, never a doctrine that put the collective first. There was no expectation or demand that individuals adapt to it and set their own goals aside. I was happy about this and certainly did my share to uphold the spirit of tolerance and respect. It was an essential sentiment that most of us shared.

---

*Coil was the musical project created by ex-PTV members Peter "Sleazy" Christopherson (1955–2010) and Geoff Rushton (aka John Balance, 1962–2004).

Wherever I went, I brought either a Super 8 or 16 mm camera and shot as much film as I could afford. In Berlin for instance, we were lucky that my friends in the band Union Carbide were playing. I filmed some snippets from that show and was basically using the camera as an extra diary of sorts, like two of my cinematic heroes, Andy Warhol and Jonas Mekas. The same was true of the still camera I always had on me (a Minox, which was very lightweight and good). It was almost as if I wanted to document my great life because it felt kind of unreal, or dreamlike. This "documentarian" approach had been with me since my fanzine days, when I often appreciated taking some rock musician's picture more than I did actually talking to him or her. In what better way could I "convey" to others all the interesting people I had met?

That spring I edited a Super 8 film called *Thee Tarot Ov Abomination*. It was material I had shot during the P-Orridge spoken-word tour, and again I used a more or less random cut-up process for sequencing the images. The result was a magical little cine-poem that far exceeded its merely documentarian aspects, especially when I added the musical soundtrack to it from our album. The film became a gateway not only to my memories but also to an entire philosophy or system of magic.

The master for me in this regard was still Kenneth Anger. I called him in April to see how he was doing. He was a bit depressed at the time as he needed to move out of Samson de Brier's house. I didn't press him about what was going on, but told him that I had framed the photo of Crowley and that it was hanging prominently in my apartment. That made him happy. He asked about the books he had lent me, and I said I was enjoying them greatly and that I would return them promptly. He said that there was no rush, and that I should read *Snowdrops* with special attention. I was very happy Anger had directed me to it, or rather it to me, as it was indeed a wonderful book, filled with transgressions against that typically British (Victorian) mind-frame of hypocritical attitudes toward anything sexual:

She entered into his desires and abandoned herself to the new vice with rapture. Again and again she deluged him with love-drops, and the warm odour of their bodies went up, a delicious steam, till his head withdrew, foaming, and fell upon her reeking lips again to lick salacious kisses and gently chew her gentle eyelids when she turned her mouth again to an even dearer object.*

> There was a young man of Cape Town,
> Who acquired European renown
> By sucking his come
> From his bugger-boy's bumb
> Swallowing it, and keeping it down.†

Young Crowley at his best! (And as these citations show, the book would resurface again in my life some twenty-five years later when I issued a new edition, illustrated by Fredrik Söderberg, via my company Edda Publishing in 2013.)

In terms of ritual, I was keeping up a daily schedule of meditation and sigilizing in the evenings. Whenever I was together with my girl-friend, we drifted into heavy sex-magic experimentation and learned a lot by just *doing*. There is only so much you can do in theory on your own when it comes to this kind of magic. For obvious reasons, I was usually exhausted at work during the daytime, but still managed to copy books, print books, and have fun with my friends Peter Bergstrandh and Michael Matton.

I was in the habit of strumming some things on a guitar at home, recording it, and then giving the cassette to Peter. His skill as a musician was phenomenal and he structured bass lines and arrangements for most of the conventional tracks White Stains recorded. Throughout

---

*Crowley, "After the Fall: A Page from the Book of the Recording Angel," in *Snowdrops from a Curate's Garden* (Stockholm: Edda, 2013), 117.
†Crowley, "Limericks III," in *Snowdrops*, 151–52.

1990 we were delving full force into the second album, which I wanted to call *Dreams Shall Flesh*—a deliberate nod toward Austin Spare's influence on my creativity.

FRATERNAL OCCULTURE

In May I went together with some friends (incidentally, all TOPY people) from Gothenburg to Bergen, Norway. They took their Minerval degree and I was initiated into the first degree of the OTO. I felt ready for it, and it was a very pleasant experience. The group in Bergen was as friendly and curious as during my last visit, and I had great discussions with many people that weekend. Everything felt just right, as my

In Norway, 1990
(photo by Björn Sanden)

interest in Thelema and Crowley seemed to be constantly developing. It didn't take long before I started making plans for establishing a more formal OTO presence in Sweden too. It was in my nature to get involved beyond the level of mere membership.

An increasing crossover environment developed in which my doings in Stockholm left traces in many minds and environments. TOPY would hold more workshops with Arthur the shaman, during which we would also talk about the OTO. Film screenings were arranged by our newly formed "Cinematick" society (for instance with American underground filmmaker Richard Kern and the German director Jörg Buttgereit), and there would always be TOPYSCAN information around at the parties that followed. White Stains would make new music to accompany, for instance, a screening of F. W. Murnau's *Nosferatu* in Gothenburg, and at the same event I showed the film of the "Pyramidos" performance before it was time for me and Arthur to give lectures about magic and shamanism. There were *Asatro* blot rituals open to anyone interested.* Psychick Release arranged performances by The Hafler Trio in Stockholm and Gothenburg, but since the main protagonist of that project, Andrew McKenzie, was also a friend of both Gen and TOPY in general, it was to an equal degree a ritual containing intellectual and emotional fodder on many levels.

It was like being in a melting pot with strong alchemical implications and applications, and I had become the energetically crawling spider in a very productive and satisfying web. I had truly created an environment and a lifestyle that provided optimal catalysts for me to develop. This was true of the things I created alone or together with other people. In particular, our album *At Stockholm* often served as a soundtrack for my meditations and led to many epiphanies as I listened to it in different states of mind. It was like an extremely positive magical feedback loop: I created a work of art or event filled with desire, which then affected the

---

*The Swedish word *Asatro* corresponds to the Icelandic term *Ásatrú*, meaning "belief in the Æsir," in other words, the old Nordic pagan pantheon. The anglicized version of the word is Asatru.

surroundings and other people, which in turn brought about the desired change or experience. This inspired me to do more, and while this process rolled onward I also learned more about my own tastes, likes, and dislikes. A creative kind of individuation process had now begun to move of its own accord after a few years of being frantically pushed by my (at the time) still too causally oriented brain. The boundaries were gradually worn down and allowed for me to fully bloom in new and interactive ways. For a long time I had grasped only intellectually what I was now *living*, full time: whereas much in life is a total illusion based on convenience and agreement, magic is the ultimate reality in which the human being can flourish and move both biology and psychology forward. I had now become part of it, because *I had created it.*

The same was true for the second issue of *The Fenris Wolf*: I received more material than expected and turned it into a book instead of a "fanzine," which in turn attracted even more material. It had suddenly become renowned in the occult underground, and people wanted to be in it. Jake Stratton-Kent, an early colleague who published the Thelemic magazine *The Equinox* (not the same as the official OTO publication) at the time, reviewed the second issue:

The subject matter is interesting, and it is well dealt with. Carl, we deduce, obviously has some contacts . . . The magazine has shifted to paperback format as he has found this is the format given most respect—astute guy. Not only does he have contacts, he has brains and resources (important thing that, I've learnt the same lessons but don't have some of the resources . . . I think I'll be a Swede in my next life . . .) Some of it is obviously more Gothic than I usually like, but it is more interesting than I usually find such material. All in all this is good material, well handled and of sufficient interest to occultdom at large to do well. Presuming some of us can forgo the odd gallon of lager that is!*

---

*Stratton-Kent, in *The Equinox*, vol. VII, no. 7 (1993), 360.

I also worked with my OTO inspiration more and more: I corresponded, produced the Scandinavian newsletter *Ratatosk*, and studied Crowley more diligently through his books and OTO-degree compendiums. In the autumn of 1990, I took my II° in Denmark, and its symbolic title was "Magician." It was relevant and suitable as I basically looked at everything in my life through the Magician's eyes.

BACK INTO THE DEVIL'S DEN

In late 1990 it was time to return to the US, this time together with my girlfriend Beatrice. We were very much in love, and I wanted to share all the things that I had experienced the year before (when we had only just met, and she couldn't go). Again, the host was Tim O'Neill, and he did his best to make sure we had an interesting time. He took us to meet Jay Kinney, the editor of *Gnosis* magazine; artist Kristine Ambrosia; and the occultists Kyle and Luna Griffiths.

Tim also made sure we visited the delightful Rosicrucian Park in San Jose (created by the order of AMORC). I found it beautiful and ultra-American in the best possible way: taking a signal, jazzing it up, and then building a theme park to prove its worth! That fine line between real magic and—as LaVey would put it—"burlesquing" it was one that I still greatly enjoyed stepping over. Whether you come across it in India, Africa, or the US, it shines a precious light on the essential fact that all gods and religions are human creations, and how they remain in the narrative basically has to do with the quality of the artists chiseling it all into *eternitas in potentia*. The Rosicrucian Park is also one of the places where legend has it that the ashes of Aleister Crowley were spread, the other spot being under a pine tree in New Jersey. It inspired me to write the following poem (as "Christian Rosencreuz, Jr."), which was included in the TOPY EUROPE bulletin of January 1991:

To run AMORC in the park

Amidst Egyptian buildings tall,
A taller pine tree makes a hall
Under which, rumor has it,
Lies the aeon's greatest asset
A poet-warrior, knight and knave
("Bury me in a nameless grave!")
Of an overwhelming kind
By far the century's greatest mind!

Some ashes here, some ashes there
In fact, it could be anywhere—
Mediterranean mounts or Scottish lakes
Or is Binah the sea just what it takes?
Did disciples mix it with cocaine,
Or is it just my fevered brain
Bewitched, bothered, and bewildered
By those tiny three roses oh so red?

As my girlfriend and I were both active in TOPY and OTO, we revisited most of the friends I had met only a year ago; most of them were similarly active in both environments. We visited Thelema Lodge again, to attend a performance of Crowley's Rites of Eleusis. Unfortunately, I was left with the same impression as the last time: the atmosphere at the lodge was much too relaxed and liberal for its own good, but it was still interesting to have been there. I donated a copy of the second issue of *The Fenris Wolf* and the *At Stockholm* CD to their lodge library.

This visit, as well as the overall Thelemic OTO infusion in my system, definitely affected my dreams. One dream was particularly interesting:

I was alone in a desert, at night, and the stars were out and crystal clear against the pitch-black night sky. I was welcomed into a tent by an oasis, where an exotic, dark-haired woman seduced me. When I climaxed inside her, my mind literally exploded and the infinite number of mind particles joined the stars in the sky.

It was highly relevant not only to the initiatory symbolism I had experienced thus far within the order (moving from the status of "guest," to that of Man, and on to that of Magician), but also on a higher, cosmic level in which the Egyptian goddess Nuit arches her body over the night sky, waiting for potential to be fulfilled.

A few nights before this dream occurred, I had one in which the setting was the "Abyss." It may sound dramatic and negative, but in the tradition of Western ceremonial magic it's just something you will encounter sooner or later if you're diligent: you come to a point of no return, basically, and you must decide whether you "trust the river" (i.e., yourself) or not. In other traditions, there's the forking path, the crossroads, the great sea, and many other culturally significant images or symbols. Are you real or not real? Honest or not honest? I was not yet facing the Abyss—that would come much later!—but the inherent message was interesting. I was being told: *It's all an illusion.* "It" being—at least in my mind, at this time—even the different esoteric frameworks that I was now working so diligently within. There is no solid ground, nor any ultimate truths. Concepts like "degrees," "abysses," and "initiations" were about as unreal (or real) as the ice cream I was enjoying, the conversation I was having, the book I had just bought, or the sex I had just engaged in.

I wasn't specifically looking for these kinds of magical pointers, but they came anyway—and often in dreams or meditations. I felt very comfortable with integrating this concept of Illusion. My attitude was already one of absurdist amazement that frequently bordered on misanthropy, but even this detached and often critical stance was malleable, flexible, and reframable because of this insight that *nothing is essentially what it seems to be.* It was to become a cornerstone of my own magical thinking and structure, and one that still largely permeates it.

Andrew McKenzie of The Hafler Trio and my friends from

Radium in Gothenburg happened to be in San Francisco at this time, and we visited a McKenzie-curated exhibition of Dreamachines that was really interesting. Beatrice and I also got tattooed by the artist Deborah Valentine, and had lunch with Vale from *RE/Search*. As Vale knew that I was now friendly with Dr. LaVey and Blanche, he confided to me that he had approximately one hundred hours of interviews with LaVey stashed away in a secret safe, which were originally meant to be the fundament of a special *RE/Search* issue on the Church of Satan. Unfortunately for the world, they had had a falling out at some point and the project never happened. Later on, I heard that Vale had destroyed the cassettes, but I am not sure I believe he could ever do that.

As for me, I had remained on good terms with LaVey since our first meetings, and received much praise from him for all my projects over the past year. And now I was so happy to be able to bring Beatrice into the mix. During our first evening together on that trip, after a dinner at Joe's in Daly City, we asked LaVey if he would consider marrying us while we were in San Francisco. I knew that he wasn't active in that "old school" sense anymore, but it certainly couldn't hurt to ask. After thinking about it for a while, he smiled and said yes. He suggested New Year's Day as a symbolically suitable date, and we were all overjoyed.

It would turn out even better as New Year's Day arrived. I can't recall exactly what I had expected, but it was probably something along the lines of a laid-back wedding ceremony with some talking and blessings. But no. We were ushered into the Black Chamber, the very holy of holies for Church of Satan romantics like me. This was the room where all the meetings and rituals had taken place in the Church's heyday in the 1960s and 1970s, and the energy could be felt viscerally as you entered the room: it was a timeless space of accumulated power that now bid us to enter and partake of its generous offerings.

LaVey showed us all the priceless items that were such an integral part of his own magical development: Rasputin's rocking chair; Francis Dashwood's chair from the Hellfire Club; a Knights Templar sword; the skull of a pope; Bram Stoker's ashes inside an Egyptian statue; a

Conn organ; the house's previous owner, "Madame" Mammy Pleasant's photo of her son built into the fireplace with cobblestones and debris from the 1906 San Francisco earthquake; several statues and paintings made for LaVey; and of course the majestic altar "Baphomet" pentagram, the main symbol of the Church of Satan.

LaVey told us to face the Baphomet, which hung right over the fireplace, where so many naked ladies had been "living altars" during the Church's nighttime rituals. By now I felt almost dislocated in time and space, as the entire experience was more like a dream than a rational and chronologically sequential event. I could tell that Beatrice was feeling something similar. We looked at each other in excitement and anticipation.

While Blanche was standing behind us, LaVey pulled up Francis Dashwood's chair and sat down right behind us. He started telling us about our new union being a cell that has tremendous power because our commitment to each other and even mutual dependency creates freedom in a way that you can't develop alone. It leads to a unified force field that can be used for magic and creativity. It was a fairly short speech, probably about ten minutes, after which he declared us man and wife, "In Nomine Satanas!" A most infernal group hug followed!

Afterward we hung around in the Black Room drinking champagne, and LaVey proudly showed us many of the objects in detail. My sense of happiness was overwhelming, and it just kept on flowing: a celebratory dinner at MacArthur Park, and then back to watch movies. We visited them again on the next evening, which also included more extravagant musical medleys from the Luciferian repository of LaVey's mind: "Get Thee Behind Me, Satan," "Old Devil Moon," "Somewhere over the Rainbow," as well as the Russian national anthem, and many more, in a hysterically funny and simultaneously powerful mélange.

I don't know if it was the ritual itself or the happiness of being newlyweds, but we both felt an excitement and general "sensualization" that we hadn't really encountered before. It was like a mix of orgone and ozone: a vitalizing, life-enhancing energy on a deep level. I knew that LaVey had preferred to keep the Black Room hermetic or almost sealed because it was such an invaluable storehouse of memories as well as energies. Apparently, these could be tapped into—and that is undoubtedly what had happened. The magic moment for me and Beatrice was of course the wedding itself, but to be embraced by LaVey and Blanche inside this dark, cosmic space was definitely an initiation of sorts.

Writing much later about these visits in my book *Anton LaVey and the Church of Satan*, I concluded that one was afterward "always infused with a solid mix of intelligence, humor, orgone, and *joie de vivre*. When you eventually woke up in the afternoon, the borders between dream and waking states were always pleasantly blurred."[*]

The entire ritual of marriage was as overwhelming as everything else in the presence of Dr. LaVey and Blanche. It was like being in a dark fantasy world of pure and creative magic. In hindsight—when the relationship with Beatrice was eventually over and we were divorced, and I had read LaVey's essay "Satanic Weddings: Why I Don't Perform Them" in 1998—I felt even more honored that he had said yes to our request. Perhaps he had made an exception because he really liked us? Or perhaps he missed the feeling and function of being inside the Black Room once in a while? Maybe both were true. Years later, when our relationship was falling apart, Beatrice said angrily that I had wanted to marry LaVey, and not her. Perhaps there was something to that, after all? As with many things, LaVey was far ahead of the matrimonial curve too:

> Marriage imposes rules where none are wanted. An "ideal" marriage is a non-marriage where no rules apply and both parties are "free" to go their own ways. There is nothing wrong with that. But why call it marriage? Why formalize what is intended as informal? Does not the stigma assumed by formalization place greater stress upon an already tenuous responsibility?[†]

---

[*]Abrahamsson, *Anton LaVey and the Church of Satan*, 19.
[†]LaVey, "Satanic Weddings: Why I Don't Perform Them," in *Satan Speaks!* (Venice, CA: Feral House, 1998), 119–20.

As for the city of San Francisco itself, on this trip I was also deeply impressed by the de Young Museum and the Japanese Tea Garden in Golden Gate Park. In my mind, there was something so inherently healthy in Asian cultures that was lacking in the monotheist ones, and of course it mainly had to with art and iconography being fully integrated on all levels: a refined sense of aesthetics that was completely integrated into the general culture.

Back in Stockholm, there was a performance by the Tibetan Institute for the Performing Arts (TIPA) in the summer of 1990. It was phenomenal. The music and dance, and the overall impact of something so refined, really blew my mind. At that point in my life, I had some basic knowledge about Buddhism and found it as interesting as most other things. But this was different. The Tibetan performances were filled with an understanding of ritual and magic, and of rhythm and frequency, that I hadn't come across before on these general levels. At home, I had a few books by Swedish explorer Sven Hedin, who had mapped out large parts of Tibet at the turn of the twentieth century. I quickly jumped back into these books to read more. The Ethnographic Museum of Stockholm housed Hedin's vast collections of Tibetan artifacts and I started going there regularly to try to understand what this newfound resonance in me was all about. Visiting the de Young Museum in San Francisco had boosted that inspiration too.

PSYCHICK FATIGUE

Soon after we returned from the US, we organized a workshop and performance with American percussionist-magician Z'EV in Stockholm. He was within the TOPY circuit, and it was a delight to invite him. He performed at the experimental venue Fylkingen, and I used the overwhelming sonic experience to travel on the inner planes and declare various intentions. I also made sure Thomas Tibert would have some time with Z'EV in a studio to record his brilliance in drumming and creating sounds for Thomas's newly initiated sampling CD project.

For the TOPY locals, Z'EV held a workshop on the Qabalah, and it was of course fascinating. We decided then to make a book together based on his insights, and he was very happy to be "contextualized." I often felt that despite his serene manner, Z'EV was always about to burst with wisdom and knowledge of many kinds. I remember we had some very inspiring conversations about how different brands of occultism related to the Earth proper, and how important it was to create a new kind of terminology that transcended specific allegiances: a nontechnical and nondenominational occult language. Z'EV was a unique magician. The book in question, *Rhythmajik*, would explain that to the world:

> It is a grammar, as it were, of beat patterns. In the same way I worked at the workshop, this book explains the form and function of the use of rhythm, with something like 600 beat patterns. It will be of use to the total spectrum of the occult—from Shaman to Anglo-Egyptian to Satanist to Wiccan . . . Anyone who wants to beef up their ritual with the appropriate rhythm.*

With respect to TOPY, however, rhythm and energy were dwindling. In the summer of 1990, there was much back and forth with Gen, with both of us venting about chores and the quantity—rather than quality—of work involved. Tom Banger of TOPYUS also seemed tired of it all. For my part, I felt sort of in between and undecided. I had become accustomed to keeping up a high tempo, and all the more so now that I had a company to run after my day job and was in a new relationship. But I was wearing myself down and thin.

While Gen and Paula had been away in the summer of 1990, money and objects had disappeared from their home. Accusations flew back and forth, and some key TOPY members left the scene for good. I was glad I wasn't there. Gen nurtured an almost hippie-like faith in

---

*Z'EV, undated letter to the author (received 4 March 1991).

people, and there they were living a quasi-communal lifestyle. This was something I knew I could never handle. The idea of multiple people intimately sharing time and space, as well as a core belief system, never really resonated with me. Moreover, it never seemed to work out in the long run, and these situations could easily be viewed in a negative light, as cultlike, by others outside the group. Such developments were always counterproductive. Anyway, Gen was devastated now that the Brighton core had become unraveled, and this was on top of all the other things they were trying to do. I tried to be supportive from my end. Toward the end of the year it reached the point that Gen asked me to take over the administration of *everything* from Stockholm: in other words, we would now fold TOPY UK into the structure of TOPY EUROPE.

The arrival of *At Stockholm* in November provide a much-welcome boost of faith. The album was well received by everyone who heard it, and in many respects it was an ultra-TOPY document/testament, especially with us including "Message from Thee Temple" both in English and Swedish. We focused on the album and tried to license it to several US labels, such as Wax Trax and Important. Wax Trax loved it but were afraid that it would confuse the American market, which now (apparently) viewed Psychic TV strictly as an "acid house" project. This made me realize that there's more to music than expressing an emotion in frequency and rhythm. I had made enough records by then to realize how hard it was to actually get them out there into the world, and I could only imagine the trials and tribulations of bigger yet fiercely independent projects like all those that Gen had been involved in. The business side of things can quickly become tiresome when all you *really* want to do is create something significant, magnificent, and intelligent, and get people to indulge in it.

In March of 1991, "Words"* from Temple Press called and told me that Tom Banger had left for South America and didn't want to be part of TOPY anymore. I knew that Tom had been experiencing an

---

*Nickname for Paul Cecil.

increasing sense of burnout for some time, so the news didn't come as a shock. I then followed suit in the summer, writing a letter to all the key people and letting them know that I just couldn't do it anymore. It's always a relief to make decisions and let them be known, but it was bittersweet in this case. I had felt so involved and creative, and together with very magical people in a network that had provided me with so much material, inspiration, and support. I felt somewhat superstitious, thinking I would lose a lot of myself in the process of "dropping out."

But I didn't. We had all run this back and forth so many times, not blaming ourselves for any inadequacies or shortcomings, but gradually coming to the realization that perhaps the "time is up." Gen had already tried, consciously or not, to effect some change of focus by integrating an I instead of the Y (or, as he put it, "the Eye instead of the Why") in the name and acronym. During the last years of this "Phase One," there were frequent mentions of TOPI (Thee Temple Ov Psychick Individuals) rather than TOPY (i.e., Psychick Youth), and it was a natural progression.

The way I see it now, TOPY Phase One (1981–1991) is all about Youth and the preparation for real Individuation. Hopefully, those who remained with the idea and concepts in (youthful) defiance of the inevitable found their own way eventually. Most of the old-timers seemed to have had no problem easing their way into new adventures. Sometimes they disengaged completely, but more often they drifted in and out of contact during the decades that followed.

It only took about a month before I received a package from Gen with a nice letter and a lovely goat's head ("Baphomet") necklace he had had made in three copies: one for himself, one for me, and one for Dr. LaVey. We were free to roam as we pleased, because we were individuated and as nonreactive as we could possibly be. Sometimes it just takes a bit of soul-searching and turmoil to fully realize it.

Some exterior projects fell by the wayside because of my decision. Z'EV pulled his book *Rhythmajik* from Psychick Release as it was no longer a TOPY-affiliated endeavor. It soon ended up with Temple Press instead, and the result was a magnificent book—much better than I could ever have made it during those chaotic circumstances.

 "THE GREAT BEAST"

My ritualistic experimentation evolved from being primarily sigilizations (works on paper including resounding residue of the ecstatic moments) to blooming into psychodramatic manifestations that involved sound (suitable music and often recordings of myself either rolling with a mantra or talking as if the goal had already been achieved), vision (video, photography, and Super 8 projections), and behavior that was symbolically or concretely relevant to the desired outcome. The behavior could include dressing up (or down) to accentuate gender traits, as well as purely personal ones—basically, amplifying whatever was relevant in such a way as to leave the "norm-core" rational mind behind, merely "thinking" about what I wanted to achieve.

In many ways, the more elaborate and extensive these rituals became, the more efficient I found them to be. Instead of just blurting out "I want this or that" to some temporarily receptive sphere of my psyche, it became an elaborate seduction in which everything was pleasantly malleable and possible. While never losing track of the peak moment and the desire itself, I was willing to go on tangents and detours in the moment to enhance a certain quality or emotion. I realized that the magic happens as the focused inner intent is right on its way out through the physical. This fragment or slice of "in-between time" is what I later (in the "Society of Sentience" project) termed "prejack" and "projack."*

When reading through my diaries from this particular era, the early

---

*"Prejack" = Prejaculation, "Projack" = Projaculation. The first term signifies the first physical sensations of orgasm, when the ejaculation becomes inevitable. This is the focus time. A projaculation is a fully charged or sentient orgasm including ejaculation. For females, this corresponds to the time between "Encliteration" (inevitability) and "ProPax" (the positive paroxysms of pleasure in orgasm).

1990s, I find that I sometimes used the term "pandrogen" to indicate that I had assumed a role that was more or less feminine within the ritual—usually in a theatrical/dramatic context where I took on the role of a force or actual person relevant to the ritual symbolism (more concretely, this could also take the form of mimicking a "real" person who was an object in some way within the ritual narrative).

Gen came up with the term "pandrogeny" early on and gradually developed it into an entire lifestyle project that bordered on performance art. The terminology was meant to distance it from mere "androgyny" and to include not only the concept of "pan-" as signifying an inclusive transcendental movement, but also that of "Pan"—the pagan mythic figure of ecstasy of the Mediterranean cults and cultures. Naturally, it also contained a Gen-based in-joke of the sort that academics have such a hard time understanding: it's called "pandro*geny*," *not* "pandro*gyny*." However, in the noun form it can certainly be a "pandrogyne."

For me, at this time, "pandrogeny" more had to do with the realization that small symbolic changes within the space and time of my own temple could have massive psychological effects on me, which would then continue projecting into and onto the outer world even after the ritual. This kind of "fluidity" has also been very interesting to explore with a partner when we are able to act out different roles starting only from very basic agreed-upon or preconstructed narratives. We know where it should all end up from the perspective of ritual psychology, but the road there can be startling, innovative, funny, arousing, and deep—sometimes even terrifying. Basically, this is a matter of acting out scenarios that have been only very loosely scripted (or not at all).

Since joining the OTO, I had become increasingly interested in Crowley's massive corpus. He had written so much and to me it was obvious that his head was screwed on right. I could feel the intelligence and dynamic sensitivity in his rituals and ceremonies. Some of the elements had been appropriated from earlier sources, of course, but I had no problem with this. On the contrary, it was pure TOPY and pure Chaos Magic in many respects, and not entirely different from the cut-ups of Burroughs and Gysin in spirit: take something and improve it in experimental ways, and see what actually works. It is also in keeping with the nature of human thought and intellectual history in general. Culture is very much a stream of consciousness, and as such has a life of its own. Humans—whether magicians, artists, scientists, or whatever sort—may add to the equation, but they can never really claim to "solve" it on their own, once and for all. Those who do make such claims are usually religious (I use the term here as a euphemism for borderline psychosis) and should be avoided at any cost.

Crowley took the cosmic structuring of the Golden Dawn's ceremonial magic and infused it with his own Thelemic flavors and fireworks. Besides the actual initiation rituals of the OTO, which were already in place when Crowley joined the gang in 1910, he created a vast number of poetic texts and instructions. Typically, these were garbed in Egyptian symbolism—an inheritance from the Golden Dawn along with his own epiphanic experiences in Egypt in 1904.* Although he claimed to be the prophet of a "new aeon," the magic as such was all pretty old school. Here in the Western sphere, the remnants of the Greek Magical Papyri, the Neoplatonists, and Renaissance flirtations with magic have all left a legacy that has permeated much of what's been going on. So, in actual fact, Crowley's claims of ushering in a "new aeon" must be taken with a pinch of salt. To build a new foundation upon whatever you supposedly rejected because you were disgruntled is as normal in the magic business as it is in any cultic environment (such as religion, business, music, psychoanalysis, etc.). That being said, no one can really deny Crowley's mastery as a syncretist and synthesizer. His integration of yoga, meditation, and other Eastern techniques on a path of personal empowerment was groundbreaking, in part because of his own zest in selling it to the curious "inepts" who were hoping to one day become adepts.

---

*During a visit to Egypt in 1904, Crowley "received" a channeled text called *The Book of the Law* from a "discarnate intelligence" called Aiwass. This manuscript became the fundament of his teachings from then on.

The daily integration of the "lesser banishing ritual of the pentagram" (elemental) and that of the hexagram (planetary) led to a focus within me: bringing me back to what's important even in the most banal daily chores—namely, to remain aware that I am on the path and need to interpret things as to whether they have any relevance to whatever it is I want to magically achieve. The same was true for his "Liber Resh" which is a four-times-per-day celebration of the sun. It works like a celebration, but the main advantage is to regularly remind yourself that you should be focused on your Will—that's really what matters, be it sunrise, noon, sunset, or midnight . . . Focusing your mind and body in connection with the solar energy provides the same dual advantage: that of the energy in itself, plus the mental activation of focus.

During 1990 I had set up the Auga Odins ("Eye of Odin") Camp of the OTO in Stockholm, allowing for a networking presence and a chance to host meetings, events, and eventually initiations. I felt compelled to ensure that philosophies of a magical nature be present in the social surroundings of Sweden. And it worked. My circle of friends, who had always been interested in mind-expansion and fringe philosophies, became the first to hover around, and as I translated *The Book of the Law* into Swedish there seemed to be an uncorking of energies. Back then, Crowley was not as big of a "brand" as he is today, but he was certainly more well known than Genesis P-Orridge and Anton LaVey.

By late 1991 I had received my third degree and soon afterward I was entitled to start initiating others. Over the decades that followed I performed hundreds of initiations in various countries. The cultural kinship within Scandinavia led to a lot of traveling: facilitating initiations, the Gnostic Mass, and an increasing number of gatherings and parties. As this environment attracted more people, it was possible to rely on more individuals with both specialized and general skills. Members were eager to help out, and even though circumstances were quite primitive (key terms at the time were "battlefield conditions" and "temporary temples") there was great and inspiring joy to be found in the mutual construction of magic.

This was especially true for the performance of the Gnostic Mass. It is such a beautiful ceremony when performed correctly, and it was a great and arduous learning experience to get everything right. But that was exactly what made it so magical. The OTO at this time was still "rippling" from the European visits by Grady McMurtry in the late 1970s and early 1980s, meaning that an attitude and sensibility of overcoming primitive difficulties was still very much alive in the general OTO body. This was good in the sense that it led to real work, real initiations, and real Gnostic Masses despite whatever shortcomings might exist in terms of experience or resources. But it also had some drawbacks and negative aspects as we were still developing even in the 1990s, as there was a "habit" of accepting things that were not perfect in every sense, simply because they had become the "tradition." I could see the situation was improving over time, however, and I'm sure it's much better now than it was when I was active and initiating.*

"MR. SATAN"

I have always been vocal about my interests and activities, but some topics are certainly more attractive than others. Anton LaVey had already figured this out in the 1960s. If I talk about "occultural networking" or "ceremonial magic," it isn't half as interesting as when there's talk of "Satan" or "Sex Magic," or why not "Satanic Sex Magic"? Then the curious will flock. They will be outwardly critical and dismissive, of course, but inside their heads, they're salivating in hot fantasies.

I lectured publicly about Satanism from time to time, and it usually drew big crowds. On one occasion in 1991 I talked about Satanism at the University of Uppsala, and the usual bunch of Christians were praying for me (I guess) outside, while the rest of us in the lecture hall

---

*I was a member of the OTO from 1989 to 2019 and took part in initiations and similar activities internationally up until 2007.

were having fun. There were also articles being published about me and it all seemed to confuse people. Here was a guy who actively and officially disliked *any* form of metal music, dressed impeccably, and could speak more eloquently than the academics about subjects he had *actually experienced*. This was really a brand-new concept in those days, and probably still is.

There were usually a couple of lost kooks who contacted me after events like that, or some girls looking for a "bad boy" (which I'm definitely not). But overall, the genuine interest was intelligent and quite substantial. A young author, Alexander Ahndoril, who was a friend of one of my neighbors, tagged along to a few events and eventually interviewed me for a thesis at Stockholm University that was titled "En människa som kallar sig satanist" (A Man Who Calls Himself a Satanist).*

I had some pleasant times with a few intelligent journalists too. I could read people quite easily and see whether their intentions were fair (most weren't). David Lagercrantz was one of the fair ones. He interviewed me for *Expressen* (The Express, one of Sweden's biggest tabloids) and wrote a piece called "Satans Sändebud på Östermalm" (Satan's Messenger in Östermalm).† It was amazing to see how easy it was to get attention as long as you had some kind of hot keyword as a gateway. In the interview, I talked about Nietzsche and very sensible ideas, but these ideas would never have gotten any attention if it hadn't been for dear old Satan freaking people out.‡

Although I laughed heartily at the headline and enjoyed it, my parents certainly did not. Nor did people at the printshop where I was still working. There was also a death threat left on my answering machine (probably by a Christian). I was not unaffected by these negative

---

*Ahndoril later took on the pseudonym "Lars Kepler" (together with his wife Alexandra Coelho) and has been writing a bestselling series of "Nordic Noir" crime novels.
†Östermalm is the part of Stockholm where I grew up and still lived at the time. The equivalent would be the Upper East Side of New York, or Mayfair in London.
‡David Lagercrantz later became the bestselling author of "Nordic Noir" crime novels in the "Millennium" series after its original author, Stieg Larsson, died in 2004.

punches, but on the whole it made me feel even stronger in my conviction that it was right to use powerful symbols in the dissemination of healthy ideas. Not that I was feeling like Don Quixote in any way, but I just didn't believe in backing down because some morons were too afraid to look *themselves* in the mirror. And, as you might have guessed, I wasn't killed. Instead, the experience became just another great booster in my youthful quest for Occulturation.

In the spring of 1992, I traveled with my dear old TOPY friend Fetish 23 to Kraków in Poland. I had been invited to screen some of the "Visions of Occulture" films (including Antony Balch's films with Burroughs and Gysin) and to deliver a lecture at a student club at the university. It was an important and crystallizing trip. To travel, to be invited, to share of myself and my interests, and to document the experience as well as I could: all these things have been fundamental parts of my life and essence. This particular trip also opened my eyes in two distinct ways, both having to do with collective systems of control.

Outside a cathedral there was a market, and we immediately found some insanely beautiful devil figures carved out of solid pieces of wood (but with detachable tails and penises!), which we immediately bought. (More than thirty years later, mine still resides as the main piece on my personal altar dedicated to my own creativity.) The interesting thing was of course that this was a *Catholic* market, not a devil-worshipping one. As much as I have always loved the camp and kitschy Christian iconography of devils and demons, mainly because of what they symbolize (integrity, intelligence, ingenuity, defiance, etc.), they are, after all, a fabrication by a control system—cleverly designed by manipulators who are drunk with the power they wield over other human minds. And such symbols eventually come back to bite the powerful in the butt in ways they could probably have never imagined. This always happens: over time, paradigm-shifts occur and the symbols take on new meaning(s) within cultures.

While we were in the vicinity of Kraków, some friends took us on a visit to the remains of the nearby concentration camp, Auschwitz. As

I entered the grounds, I had my still camera and Super 8 movie camera, and I took pictures of things that appealed to me aesthetically—as I usually always do, wherever I am. But when we were back at our hotel and I had put my tools away for the day, the accumulated impressions of history hit me over the head. The shock and disgust of controlled mass murder was overwhelming—in part, disgust of what had been going on there in its systematized, clinical precision, but also shock at my own behavior. It's not disrespectful to document things, but the way I had done it disturbed me: my tools had made me a detached voyeur; they had allowed me to not react emotionally in the moment; they had protected me in a way I did not appreciate.

As in the case with the devil figures mentioned above, the massive demonization of one element will have averse or even reverse effects in another time and context. An overdose of antithetical energies will create its own reaction—this is just pure physics, filtered through human psychology and emotional reactivity. When that happens, what should be a humane monument of compassion, information, and warning will become a source of psychosexual pornography. That is what George Santayana meant by his maxim: *Those who cannot remember the past are condemned to repeat it* (which we had integrated into TOPY as well). That memory needs to be reformulated at regular intervals; otherwise, the iconography itself will take on new meaning(s) for those who are not in sync with the control system as such—whichever this may be.

Cultures that promote individualism are safeguarded from the sort of collective hysteria that eventually leads to systematized mass murder. This is a dynamic that transcends strictly political environments: we have seen time and time again, specifically within monotheist environments, how a religiously based demonization of other kinds of believers easily leads to persecutions, pogroms, and mass murder. Whether political or religious, it's always a matter of abuse of power.

My lecture at the student club in Kraków was titled "The Demonic Glamor of Cinema" and it reflected what my mind was focused on at the time: inspiration from Kenneth Anger was still flying high, and my love of movies was stronger than ever. To reconnect all of this with my ideas about magic seemed suitable, and the lecture was well received:

> Experimental cinema has always led the way to new developments in the medium, technically as well as generally on all levels. The experimental filmmaker is most often someone who loves the medium so much that he or she isn't content with just telling a story or conveying a feeling, but rather wants to explore for the sake of exploring, to find new worlds and new ways of showing these discoveries. Like all true magicians, in other words.
>
> Non-, or rather, anti-narrative film tends to provoke the viewer to a point where he/she either opens or closes the mind to the confusing impressions. If one chooses to open the mind, there is suddenly an extremely clear picture, an exposé, revealing what techniques are used in, for instance, commercial cinema to seduce the viewer. Why is this part cut to that one? Why is there such strange music here, but not there? Why was this scene shot from this angle, and not that one?
>
> And, as I've mentioned before . . . It's the same thing in magic: if one chooses to let go of rational ways of thinking and analyzing the processes and goings-on around oneself, and opens up the mind to see with a subconscious or inner vision, everything appears in more or less perfect clarity. If one chooses to accept one's dark nature with all its aspects and qualities, then one can go on in the work of improving oneself.*

I remember watching Balch's films with Burroughs and Gysin in a slightly new light on this trip. I had always associated them with TOPY proper, and with my own readings of Burroughs, specifically. But after having been shaken by the visit to Auschwitz, everything made even more sense: the mechanisms of blind control always have extremely detrimental effects. This was something that Burroughs had pointed out

---

*Abrahamsson, "The Demonic Glamour of Cinema," in *The Fenris Wolf* 1–3 (Stockholm: Edda, 2011), 192.

over and over. However, to be specifically critical toward one side or phenomenon means running the risk of becoming engaged and thereby attached. It is much better to actually be detached from the specifics, and cock a critical eye at the very mechanics themselves. Burroughs's, Gysin's, and Balch's experiments with cutting up and randomly reassembling words, sounds, and images laid bare the dynamics in a healthily critical perspective that was entirely devoid of allegiances—especially if the fodder used in the experiment *comes from* the discourse of deception. It is not far-fetched to call the cut-up process "oracular," or at least "magical," as it displays facts or information that were previously known in an entirely new way, and it almost always brings a sense of fresh meaning to the table of interpretation.

Many of my friends found these old beatnik icons too cynical and paranoid to be "magical," but I certainly didn't see it that way. On the contrary, it was extra-important to acknowledge those who had dared to point their fingers and flashlights at decay and hypocrisy—in whatever way. That was one of my main attractions to the symbol of Satan in the first place: the truth hurts, and that's why most people tell lies (to themselves, most of all).

I never felt any attraction to what emerged as "New Age" philosophy at the time. It was too washed-out, diluted, and faint to stir me in any way. I lived a life of my own making in which I allowed myself to be intuitively guided by my own attractions and harmonies. Texts like Hakim Bey's short "Instructions for the Kali Yuga" would shake me to the core, in that it is a lovely *personal* recollection of experiencing magic, while also contextualizing the experience as such. The thrust of Bey's essay resonated with the twenty-something, budding magician Carl:

> Her Age [the Kali Yuga] must contain horrors, for most of us cannot understand her or reach beyond the necklace of skulls to the garland of jasmine, knowing in what sense they are *the same*. To go thru CHAOS, to ride it like a tiger, to embrace it (even sexually) & absorb some of its shakti, its love juice—this is the faith of the

Kali Yuga. Creative nihilism. For those who follow it she promises enlightenment & even wealth, a share of her temporal *power*.*

My days were continually full of magic. While walking or traveling, I would focus on a mantra of relevance and relegate it so that it was on "automatic" in the back of my mind. At home in the evenings, I would work causally with correspondence, production of new books, or recording new music. And then the ritualizing would take over, with experimentation and intuitive "gelling" of my three main sources of inspiration: TOPY, Crowley/Thelema, and LaVey's brilliant syncretism. As an example, I could prepare the temple space with the basics (candles, suitable audio and/or video, incense), open with a Lesser Banishing Ritual of the Pentagram (LBRP), invoke suitable forces, and then have the rite follow the structure of a compassion ritual from *The Satanic Bible*. But instead of burning a note with an expressed wish, as suggested in LaVey's book, I would delve into an "Ov Power"† session with a sigil, before drifting back, and then out again, via another LBRP.

I often traveled on the inner planes to commune with levels of myself in specific god-forms or forces, asking specific questions that "they" would know about. Later on, I would come to call this particular kind of work an "infocation" rather than the classic "invocation" (a "calling in" of a force). As I was—and still am—very much a "metamagician," many of these communications were with Odin—the master magician and the ultimate shaman. The inquiry usually concerned the principle of magic itself, or specific questions about the meaning of certain runes. And the runes were swirling all around me at this time: the local OTO body I founded was called Auga Odins (the "Eye of Odin"), my order name was Brage, and I republished the four main books by Sigurd Agrell

---

*Bey, "Instructions for the Kali Yuga," in Adam Parfrey, ed., *Apocalypse Culture* (New York: Amok, 1987), 66.
†*Ov* is the TOPY term for "charged" sexual fluids, both male and female. "Ov Power" is a reference to the Psychic TV musical composition of the same name from the album *Force the Hand of Chance* (1982).

that dealt with aspects of rune magic (and worked with them); I was also keeping track of all the goings-on in the rune-magic book market (mainly American authors interpreting European material).

Jonas Almquist, the singer of the Leather Nun, was already an Asatro "believer" when I got to know him in the mid-1980s, and he instructed me in basic bind-rune magic. Another important person on the Scandinavian "scene" who was merging Scandinavian magic with Crowleyan teachings was the Icelandic musician Hilmar Örn Hilmarsson (aka HÖH, who was a member of Psychic TV for a while during the early to mid-1980s). We were in touch briefly in 1992 to discuss a possible film project about the Ásatrú "Allsherjargoði" (High Priest) Sveinbjörn Beinteinsson, who was still active at that time but elderly (he died the following year).* I felt very much at home in my own native magical culture.

As generally recommended by all the people who instructed me (including Genesis, Anger, and LaVey), I made detailed notes or records about my magical work in diaries. Later I would return to them to evaluate what worked and what didn't. The diary was—and remains—an invaluable asset if one wants to maintain at least a modicum of "quasi-scientism." To show others that "magic works" in some kind of empirical way has never been my motivation; I'm much more eager to simply let people know that *magic exists* and *magic is.* This attitude seems to inspire others much more than trying to convince them exactly how or why it *possibly* functions. However, for the private use of the individual magician/psychonaut/artist (et cetera), the personal records are invaluable.

STOCKHOLM OCCULTURE AND A GOLDEN DAWN

Stockholm in the early 1990s had a very vibrant occult scene. And thanks to the efforts of myself and my closest companions, the OTO

---

*Today, Hilmarsson successfully serves as the religious leader of the Icelandic Ásatrú community.

now had an active presence here: not only as a private esoteric order, but as a known entity that was a part of the larger scene. As I've mentioned earlier, the Vattumannen ("Aquarius") bookstore was run by several people who were interested in real magical work. They had a Rosicrucian group called the Merlin Order, which took a freestyle approach, incorporating various Freemasonic rites and whatever other things they were interested in. They were also active in exploring the Nordic mysteries through the group Yggdrasil, focusing on the runes and other magical aspects of Northern lore. And they were very sympathetic toward whatever I was up to (that said, I was also a very good customer in their store!). So, for instance, the OTO occasionally conducted open (semi-public) Gnostic Masses that some of them attended, and the Merlin Order also performed Crowley's Gnostic Mass within the confines of *their* order. We would show up at each other's events and social gatherings, and it was a very encouraging and open-minded environment.

Stockholm, early 1990s
(photo by Max Fredrikson)

Another group in this scene was an order called Dragon Rouge, which still exists and has grown considerably in the meantime, thanks to the relentless efforts of founder Thomas Karlsson. I attended some of their meetings and rituals early on. They had a "darker" approach than other esoteric groups, yet their "vibe" was something distinct from what I had experienced in the Church of Satan or in my own researches. They were much more focused on Western ceremonial magic, but specifically the shadow side—in Qabalistic terms, the "Qliphotic" side of the Tree of Life—as suggested and exemplified by British author and Crowley-disciple Kenneth Grant.

Dragon Rouge was definitely doing some interesting work, but it didn't appeal to me on an immediate level. The atmosphere with them was much more "metal" and aesthetically dramatic (in fact, the group's membership included a number of musicians from famous metal bands). Whatever dark energy I needed, both personally and magically, instead came from the Church of Satan and LaVey's blend of contrarian highs and lows. Nevertheless, I have always felt a great respect for Thomas Karlsson, because I know what a tough job it is to "run a show"—not just in the sense of attracting members by glamour (and substance) but also in terms of successfully leading and administering the group.

In late 1992 at one of the open evenings arranged by the Merlin Order, a colorful American man showed up who was approximately ten years older than me. His name was David Griffin. He was a very "solar" character—beaming and extroverted. The lavish, magical gold jewelry he wore was clearly custom-made. All of this made a noticeable impression on the witchy ladies of the scene. He also displayed knowledge of Western ceremonial magic in a very solid way. This, however, was not the thing that appealed to me about David. It was his sense of humor, his intelligence, and the fact that we could communicate more or less immediately. In other words, we hit it off and in no time were yapping about all things occult.

David was definitely a presence in the Stockholm occult scene, because for six months of the year he lived in Sweden together with a

Swedish wife and their young son, and he was able to use his time as he wished. The other six months he worked as a tour guide, mainly in California and the southwestern American states. We had a good rapport and decided that we should get together and talk about all the hocus-pocus stuff that fascinated us. To me, it was very interesting because here was someone who was a strange bird in this environment that I already knew so much about. In a real sense, I was a key player in the occult circles of Stockholm. David Griffin's entrance into the scene was perhaps not vitalizing specifically to me, but I did suddenly feel that here I had a peer, someone I could talk to about *magic*—the rather abstract, philosophical concepts of magic that I felt that I couldn't really share with anyone else. There were some people with whom I could discuss such concepts in America perhaps, but certainly not in Sweden.

So, we started meeting and talking. It dawned on me through various details in our conversations that David was active in a group or order. I had suspected as much because of his behavior and knowledge; it was clearly more than mere intellectual posing. Eventually, we got around to working together in a practical sense. He was living in an area of Stockholm that I knew quite well, only a couple of blocks away from where my grandmother had her apartment (and to which I would soon move). So, we were basically living in the same part of town. David's wife, a Swedish woman working in graphic design, was very nice. She had no interest whatsoever in the esoteric, but they had a wonderful little family going and seemed happy together.

One evening when the wife and kid were gone, David showed me what he had been working on in the basement of their apartment building. He had ambitiously turned his family's little storage compartment into a full-fledged temple, complete with painted walls decorated with angelic and planetary sigils. It was like stepping into a secret bubble of Western ceremonial magic. I recognized many of these symbols from my studies, specifically of the Golden Dawn. As mentioned, when I had been in San Francisco in 1989 my friend Aidan Wachter had given me a copy of the "doorstop edition" (so-called on account of its size) of

Israel Regardie's book *The Golden Dawn*, which contained their rituals and much more. Just like Crowley before him, Regardie republished the rituals of the Golden Dawn, and he was at this time, in a way, a kind of semi-official caretaker as he had been initiated into the "Stella Matutina" branch of the order.

So, I was familiar with the designs and the structure of the Golden Dawn, and I recognized these symbols that were painted in visually striking hues in this tiny storage space. We then ingested what David called the "sacrament"—something that I was also familiar with from previous and, I would say, non-occult-related experiences: lysergic acid, or LSD. Being "turned on" in that confined space, lit solely by candlelight, amid the splendid ocular bouncing of beautiful complementary colors, really made me understand the aesthetic implications of how the symbols and symbologies of arcane systems are ingeniously designed specifically for their capacity to open up the mind in ritual situations. Whether the situation is psychedelic, or meditational, or ecstatic is beside the point. The symbols are there to act as mediators, as door-openers into a specific mind-frame. Within the ceremonial-magic tradition, for example, if your magical aim relates to success, it could be relevant to work in a Jupiterian context, invoking the divine force through the planetary sigils of Jupiter, and so forth. If, on the other hand, your aim relates to love or sexuality, it would be pertinent and relevant to work with the powers and sigils of Venus.

We worked diligently all through that first night, stating various personal intentions and getting to know each other. LSD induces a state of heightened consciousness in which you are both powerful and vulnerable, and I was happy that I was already "experienced" (as Jimi Hendrix would put it). David was obviously experienced too. So, for us, this first session was more of an establishment of a deeper or perhaps higher level of friendship than anything else. The magical aspect of it was wonderful too, and I got a little insight into something that I immediately realized had to do with the Hermetic Order of the Golden Dawn. Initially, Dave didn't reveal what his own affinities were, but he did tell me he was interested in taking the Minerval degree of the OTO* and asked if I could facilitate. I think that David at this time was a networker, securing his own position within a larger stratum of occultism in particular locations around the world. He was already familiar with California and with some other places in Germany, and now he lived casually for half of every year in Sweden. I got the impression that he was very concerned about having a "presence" in these specific places. Part of the way he did so was by seducing certain people into eventually joining his group, which turned out—as I had suspected—to be the Hermetic Order of the Golden Dawn in the Regardie tradition. For my birthday in January of 1993, he gave me a copy of Regardie's book, inscribed: "I think you will find this a most valuable reference . . . back to the roots."

Our collaborative explorations of ritual magic continued for many years, sometimes with the added infusion and inspiration from LSD, but most often not. It was always interesting work. And almost immediately in the wake of our first ritual collaboration, we had become fast friends. We had regular sessions in which we "third-minded" a lot of topics and mysteries, always coming up with revelatory explanations and fanciful twists and turns.

This could range from solving the "cipher" of Crowley's *Book of the Law* ("the cipher is a trick/trap—only Thelema in itself is valuable") to trying to blend and merge Germanic magic with Jewish magic in order to make "peace" between the two. In hindsight—usually on the next day!—we would question what we had "solved" or "received" or "constructed," but quite often there were some substantial and useful "takeaways" that one could add to the philosophical cauldron. The moment itself was the real mystery, message, and blessing: when we worked together, things emerged that couldn't have done so otherwise. This *in itself* is a fundamental part of magic—and human existence! We can do a lot on our own, but for real transcendence there needs to

---

*This is an introductory or "guest" degree designed to allow candidates to get to know the environment before they become properly initiated into the I° degree.

be a challenge of energies, be they sexual, intellectual, philosophical, or emotional. It is in these moments that we really learn new things—especially about ourselves.

Sometimes we took on magical personae in psychodramatic contexts. Dave was enamored with Samuel Liddell MacGregor Mathers, one of the founders and certainly the "poster boy" of the Hermetic Order of the Golden Dawn. And I was the perfect Aleister Crowley in these ritual games: knowledgeable and literally representing the OTO, not yet ready to rebel but definitely happy to provoke the conversations sufficiently to bring new revelations to the table. This led to insights about the nature of "Aiwaz," for instance: the "discarnate intelligence" Crowley claimed was his Holy Guardian Angel and the facilitator of the "reception" of *The Book of the Law*. Our main symbol or apparition in this regard was a (temporarily) humanlike figure with a beard, stepping out of cosmic fire, and wearing a "pentadent" (like a trident but with five fork-points). His message was very similar to others present in this particular age or planetary phase: all beings have to seek out Aiwaz *on their own*, in the sense of *gnostically* communicating with the direct source. Since the pendulum has swung away from the malaise and corruption of the old structures, an era of magic and inner journeying will play out over a long period. Any proxies or structures are absolutely anathema at this time. To simplify things further, the real magic becomes manifest in moving from "I was" (misunderstood by Crowley and others as Aiwaz, Aiwass, etc.) to "I am." In other words, a constant process of individuation in the present is what it's all about.

Being a Thelemite, this was hardly news to me, but it was certainly interesting embarking upon these "pathworkings" together with someone on the same level. They brought not only insights and knowledge, but also a respect for the kind of inner work that has been very rewarding for me over the decades. There is an overarching wisdom in this as well: *You have to value the experiences you have for what they are, and trust your own intuition when it comes to guidance and trajectories.* To be overly compartmental and dismissively discard something that makes no "sense" in the moment or immediate aftermath of an epiphanic moment, for instance, is to deny yourself the possibility that there's more to life than what meets the senses and mental cogitations.

Experiencing inner visions that contain symbolic representations of an assortment of things and beings—many of which might be unknown or even threatening to you in the moment—is the beginning of the interpretation process that will lead you to a deeper insight about the issue at hand (and about yourself). The obvious analogy is that of dream experiences—an equally irrational sphere that we have integrated culturally as "existing" and filled with useable fodder for deep interpretation.

To balance out the quite conservative Golden Dawn energy and structure, I was working every day with developing the OTO in Sweden together with a small team of great brothers and sisters. We conducted initiations, translated Crowley texts into Swedish, arranged parties—usually under the banner of the "Babalon Bar," with many of our talented musician friends performing—and also arranged a gathering for Scandinavian members at Midsummer of 1993. It was the first time that the Gnostic Mass was performed by the OTO on Swedish soil. I served as deacon as I wasn't yet ordained as a Gnostic priest, and it was a great moment for everyone involved.

We also cultivated a very joyful fraternal spirit at these get-togethers, which always included members from the Scandinavian countries as well as from further abroad. There was surely work to be done, but for me the real magic lay in the "glue" that made the fraternity real in so many ways: conversations, arguments, cooking, eating, drinking, listening to musical performances, and so on. "Hanging out" in itself was important alongside the institutional customs. The order's structure and its rules may have had individual, beneficial meanings, but the real fuel for me was the shared experience of initiation and how that made a lot of the normal prerequisites and demands of social behavior quite redundant. If you had passed through the same degree rituals—whether in Sweden, Israel, the US, Germany, or wherever—you were already mutually trusting friends, in a way.

Parallel to all of these communal OTO activities, I focused a lot on my own inner work. I was aware that the overarching force or spirit that was so dear to me, and with which I interacted symbolically in ritual contexts, was not the "proverbial" Holy Guardian Angel that one reads so much about in the dusty tracts of historical magic. How did I know this? *Because It told me so*—or because I told myself so (after all, it might all be the same . . .). But it was still a very helpful guide in my orientation: a tangibly real, personal supra-layer of guidance and decision-making.

I did feel I was on the right track, with my guiding spirit poking and pushing me ever onward. Early on in the TOPY days, I had taken a magical motto, and it was one I often used as a final sign-off in written correspondence: "Vade Ultra!" It's Latin for "Go Beyond!" in reference to medieval Catholics using "Vade Retro!" ("Step Back!") as a magical spell whenever they felt threatened by temptations, usually of a sexual kind (placed on their path by the so-called Devil, of course). At this point in time, I felt completely immersed in "Vade Ultra-ism" and worked very hard and visibly to inspire others to do the same.

In my mind, my overarching work or project was called "Operation Weltanschauung" (German for "Operation Worldview"), meaning examining and laying out the options for an optimal individuation process. I also changed my magical name in the OTO from "Brage" to "N.A.L.R." The acronym stood for "Nirameg AL Lupon Rex," which was an anagram for "Germania AL Lux Per Nox": my cultural sphere + (Liber) AL (the original name of Crowley's *Book of the Law*) + "Light Through Darkness" in Latin).

BEATIFIC FLICKER IN THE USA

David invited me to go with him on a trip to the US during the summer of 1993. In the summertime, as mentioned, he worked as a tour guide, taking tourists from all over the world on weeklong scenic bus rides through beautiful parts of California and the Southwest. I thought that this sounded excellent—mainly to go with him, but it was also an opportunity to visit America again and reconnect with people whom I had gotten to know, like the brothers and sisters of the OTO. I could visit LaVey too, of course, and Genesis, who was now living in California after having moved there from the UK via Nepal in 1992. So, David's suggestion that I go with him on this trip was like the proverbial icing on the cake, or the cherry on top.

All through that spring of 1993, David and I continued working our ritual magic in his little basement temple. After those experiences we would relax up in his apartment, listen to nice "world" or psychedelic music, and talk about magical things. I found him to be very intelligent and knowledgeable, particularly with respect to his tradition. And, at least initially, I felt that he was curious about what I had to bring to the table.

The more I got to know him, however, it became clear that David was not really curious about any perspective besides his own. And his interest in other people was basically of a narcissistic nature: he wanted to see where he could fit in, and how other people could help him maneuver onto center stage in these new environments and places.

Eventually, much later, I would realize that our communication had been a kind of one-sided exchange. The things I felt he could benefit from, he actually couldn't, because he didn't have the capacity to integrate information from other people. But while it lasted, it was a deep and very magical friendship. This was amplified even more during that summer, as we traveled together in the American Southwest.

The summer of 1993 would bring a major shift for me, and I sensed it beforehand. I anticipated that things would change for the better. But I could not foresee the extent to which this trip specifically helped me attain a new level of magical realization. One key element in this was what Crowley had called a "beatific" experience. And shortly after arriving in the US, I had such an experience in Central Park in New York. I had decided to spend some time in New York before I left for

California, mainly because I hadn't been there yet, although I knew even beforehand how much I loved the place.

A number of people I knew from Stockholm were also in New York at this time. My friends from high school, Gustaf Broms and Max Fredrikson, were apprenticing as photographers, with Richard Avedon and Bruce Weber, respectively. And my first real girlfriend, Lotta Hannerz, was taking herself to new artistic heights while spending a long time in this creative Monstropolis-vortex. I could easily see myself doing something similar, focusing on my writing as well as walking onward on the "path."

I was basically exploring the place on my own, staying with Peter Gilmore and Peggy Nadramia of the Church of Satan in the Hell's Kitchen area of Manhattan. I would just roam around and enjoy the hustle and bustle of this great city, which revealed itself in the best possible ways: bookstores, buildings, and an endless supply of weird people. There were still even a few remnants of sleaze in the 42nd Street area that was now quickly becoming "Disneyfied" for the sake of tourism.

While strolling in Central Park one day, I decided to sit down on a bench in the sunshine to relax for a bit. The sun was filtered through the crowns of the overarching trees, and the fluttering interplay of the leaves created a kind of "flicker experience" that was extremely pleasurable. I don't know how long I sat there, for time felt suddenly suspended. It may only have been a few minutes. But for some inexplicable reason, this moment affected me in a way that I can only describe as "spiritual" and blissful. It was warm, bright, and relaxing to all my senses, providing peace. It touched me on deep levels. I was cast into a state of *not thinking*, only feeling. I remember that the essence of the realization I experienced while in this reverie had to do with the path that I was on: a magical path, an occult path. But it was completely "nondenominational": it didn't refer to anything specific or to any of the groups or orders or even people I'd been involved with thus far. It only had to do with me being in the right place at the right time, resulting in a wondrous feeling of complete presence in Central Park.

The experience became a part of the way I saw the world at this time: as a big, enchanted playground, in which magicians interacted with me, and taught me things just as I could teach them. This kind of communication was—and still is—very important to me: the sharing of information, results and findings, and expecting something in return. This is not a barter system, but rather a free-flowing exchange of ideas and information.

Later it dawned on me that Brion Gysin had had similar experiences while traveling on a bus to Marseilles in 1958. He was passing by trees that filtered the flickering sunlight and made him "trip out" temporarily in his seat. This experience led to his developing, together with mathematician Ian Sommerville, the Dreamachine, the device that had become revered—and much used—in the TOPY mythos. Gysin immediately wrote about it in his journal, and in a letter to fellow psychonaut and creative partner William Burroughs:

An overwhelming flood of intensely bright patterns in supernatural colors exploded behind my eyelids: a multidimensional kaleidoscope whirling out through space. The visions stopped abruptly when we left the trees. Was that a vision? What had happened to me?*

Flickering light triggers things inside us, just as darkness, twilight, or bright sunshine does. And apparently it can trigger a sense of deep existential belonging and bliss in tandem with magical movements in life.

In New York, I got to know Peter and Peggy quite well. I really enjoyed staying with them. Their tiny apartment in Hell's Kitchen on 10th Avenue was absolutely jam-packed with books and videotapes from floor to ceiling, as well as interesting art. I could relate to the environment. There were so many things that spoke to me in terms of resonance, like the sublime and Satanic mix of classic horror fiction

*Brion Gysin, quoted in John Geiger, *Nothing Is True—Everything Is Permitted: The Life of Brion Gysin* (New York: Disinformation, 2005), 160.

Peter Gilmore and Peggy Nadramia with Countess Karloff in their Hell's Kitchen apartment, New York City, early 1990s (photo by Carl Abrahamsson)

and movies as an aestheticized backdrop for real and highly personal magic. It felt like being at home. In the daytime Peter and Peggy were working, and in the evenings we had dinner, took strolls around the neighborhood with their dog Countess Karloff, and also went to the movies.

Of course, the great affinity I felt for Peter and Peggy, and their apartment (and, later on, their house in upstate New York), extended further to the Church of Satan, because that was essentially the organization they were representing. I am sure we would have had a great time talking about different things in "neutral gear," so to speak, but it was the references and the framework of the Church of Satan that was the social or perhaps even magical glue that held us together.

One of the experiences I had in New York was meeting Bill Breeze, also known as Hymenaeus Beta, the head of the OTO. Because of the fact that I had by 1993 taken the OTO in Sweden to a substantial level, and was also working on *The Fenris Wolf* and some OTO publications, I'm sure he was curious to meet me to see how I could potentially be of use. We had been corresponding by mail for some time, and he had contributed to the just-published third issue of *The Fenris Wolf*, providing me with a memorial text about his mentor of sorts, the recently deceased artist and experimental filmmaker Harry Smith.

We had a wonderful time in Williamsburg, Brooklyn. Before we went out, Bill showed me the real *sanctum sanctorum*: his office. It was incredibly inspiring for me at the time, because the environment was not one of "hocus pocus" of any traditional kind. It was more of an intellectual workspace—a powerhouse office in which Bill produced his magnificent Crowley editions, basically devoting his life to becoming a master bookmaker. And he has, ever since that moment, certainly inspired me a great deal in my own publishing endeavors, and particularly with respect to occult publishing.

For dinner, we were also joined by Bill's wife, Dustin, and we spoke about various things: my upcoming trip to California; the earlier experiences I had had in Berkeley; and also what was going on with the OTO, both in general and in Sweden, Denmark, and Norway. During the dinner, Dustin complained a little bit about feeling a pain in her stomach. She was at the time, I think, eight months pregnant, and I had touched her big belly, fascinated that there was a new life in there waiting to get out. Her pains were not something that made us immediately worried; perhaps she had eaten something that didn't agree with her. But the discomfort didn't subside. After a while, it was decided that they would take me a bit on my way and drop me off, and then go straight to the hospital to check on her status. We got into Bill's little orange BMW and drove through the hectic streets of Brooklyn and Manhattan. Later on, I learned that Dustin had given birth that night to a perfectly healthy son. That was to be the first of two similar experiences I had on this particular magical journey.

LEGACIES & POLICIES

When I traveled onward to California, David was already on the road with a group of tourists. I therefore stayed with his Golden Dawn mentor, who would also become mine. Patricia Behman, aka Cris Monnastre, was Israel Regardie's only acknowledged student of magic, so it was a great honor to meet her. For me as a Crowley-romantic, the meeting wove myself into the web of occult lineages. Whereas I had been initiated into the OTO by Frater Evmaios and (later on) by Hymenaeus Beta, who had both been initiated by Grady McMurtry (Hymenaeus Alpha), who in turn was initiated by Crowley, now it was time for another lineage. The Golden Dawn work and initiations together with Cris connected me to the Regardie-Crowley lineage and at the time it felt like a "big deal."*

I stayed with Cris in her apartment in Burbank while David was away. I helped her organize her vast Golden Dawn archive, which included many personal and magical items that had belonged to Regardie. It allowed me to study a lot of the material and prepare for my initiations into the order. I felt honored to be not only invited in but also given a kind of VIP treatment in this tradition. And indeed, I could count myself lucky, as by this point in life I had already experienced a similar sensation in a number of other environments.

The archives were fascinating, containing essays by members, old and new, miscellanea, ritual notes, nice editions of old books, and items and magical weapons crafted by Regardie himself. I helped out by making a filing system and an index so it would be easier for Cris and other temple administrators to find whatever they were looking for.

I got along well with Cris and we had a constructive time together in Los Angeles. When she was not working (as a clinical psychologist),

---

*In the late 1920s, Israel Regardie served as Aleister Crowley's secretary and attempted to be his student.

Cris Monnastre in
Los Angeles, 1993
(photo by
Carl Abrahamsson)

we drove around Los Angeles, and I got to visit Manly P. Hall's beautiful Philosophical Research Society Library (a mind-blower, and an inspiration for me to this day); the Theosophist Besant Lodge; two great bookstores, Bodhi Tree and the Psychic Eye; the Tesla Coil at the Griffith Observatory; and Israel Regardie's grave. In the evenings Cris instructed me in basic but powerful traditional rituals like the "Opening by Watchtower" and the "Middle Pillar" meditation, and she helped me study for my initiation exams. Cris and Dave were intent on me cramming as much as possible so that I could fly through the initiations while I was there in Los Angeles. It was intense work, and I did feel a need to change gear at times.

I called Marjorie Cameron on the phone, as Bill had provided me with her number.* We talked about possibly making an edition of Jack Parsons's *Songs for the Witch Woman*, which would have her illustrations, and just chit-chatted away. She sounded fairly tired, which was not surprising as she was suffering from a brain tumor. I didn't want to push for a meeting if I didn't have anything more substantial to bring to the table.

I also studied the Tarot with Crowley's magnificent *Thoth* deck instead of Cris's recommendation of the classic Rider-Waite deck. And I delved into the "Satanic" one day by visiting LaVey's dear friend Nick Bougas, who provided me with much wonderful material, including a VHS copy of the brand-new LaVey documentary that he had made: *Speak of the Devil*. It was a much needed break from the quasi-Christian Golden Dawn mind-frame that I otherwise found myself immersed in "24/7."

Cris wanted very much to write a biography of Regardie but was frustrated that she could never find the time. I was familiar with that feeling but felt that I was doing great in my overall focus and trajectory. As a thank-you gift I bought her a nice notebook and a fountain pen at one of her favorite spots in LA: Alexander Stationers in Hollywood. She later reported that she was indeed writing material for her book in the notebook I gave her.

Cris also set up a meeting with Donald Michael Kraig, author of the bestselling Golden Dawn–inspired tome *Modern Magick*. Donald was a very nice guy and we had a great rapport. He was unusually savvy about what was going on internationally, and was aware of the work of both TOPY and the IOT. He also liked music a lot, as I recall. Ever on the lookout for great material, I asked if he wanted to write something for *The Fenris Wolf*, and he said yes.

Cris had suggested earlier that she could talk to Carl Weschke

*Cameron (1922–1995) was an American artist and the widow of Crowley acolyte John Whiteside "Jack" Parsons (1914–1952). Both Cameron and Parsons were key figures in the American Thelemic environment, specifically after Crowley's death in 1947.

at the publishing company Llewellyn about giving me a job if I ever wanted to move to the US, and Donald agreed that would be a good idea—he also worked for Llewellyn at this time.

During our conversation, it surfaced that Donald had worked in the "adult entertainment" industry and this topic brought out some inklings about intolerance in the overall Golden Dawn environment. Cris was cool about most things but asked me not to mention my "allegiances" to any other temple members (I met a few of them); she had also made extra-sure that they wouldn't know that I was an OTO member and a de facto Satanist who knew Anton LaVey. To me, the very notion of trying to hide such things was absurd. Why should anyone bother or care about what someone else believed or worked with? I played it down, but amusedly so. Donald didn't seem to care at all, so who were these other people with such strong views?

There were some other American Golden Dawn players at the time, making money off of people's interest, and milking their friendships with Regardie specifically. For some uninteresting reason they bore a grudge against the OTO. In terms of their belief system, they were essentially Christians. Be that as it may, Cris gleefully showed me some wonderful photocopies in the Golden Dawn archive (that I duly helped to file properly) of ads from a gentlemen's club, starring a stripper who was then also a high-ranking member of another Golden Dawn group. It amused me greatly. Was it because of these hypocrites that Cris had to make sure that it wasn't known that I had other allegiances? David had also earlier hinted that I should "be careful," but I assumed he was joking. It was my first real insight into occult politics and how banal most of the people involved actually are.

Several years later it became clear to me that the negative emotions came as much from Cris as from anyone else. We met again in Las Vegas in January of 1995 (at the pyramidal Luxor Hotel, fittingly enough) and I could sense she wanted me to get more involved in the order, perhaps to balance out David. The strategy was to make me a "Chief." Throughout the years I let her know that I was increasingly busy, and that I certainly favored the OTO, as I felt that meant constructive and stimulating work locally in Stockholm, and that there was at least a meaningful philosophy that underpinned the order. Cris grew more and more frustrated and wrote me in an email:

> Regardie had nothing but contempt for thelemites . . . he called them "termites" . . . (although he respected Crowley) which is why Grady got all of Regardie's referrals re thelema/OTO, because Regardie had no use for any of it.*

She also emphatically stated that I was *not* ready for my upcoming degree of "5 = 6"—as if I would care.

David got his fair share of Cris's vitriol too. In the autumn of 1994, he wrote me saying he wished Cris would accept that he was only in the US for six months per year. She apparently regularly felt abandoned, and at times said she would "divorce him on all levels" (whatever that meant). It sounded like a weird love affair to me, in which they both did care about each other, but under a cloak of paranoia. David dramatically told me that we needed to be prepared for the worst and be ready to go on in the Great Work without her, in the event that she eventually abandoned us due to her personal "stresses."

Despite the petty personal drama involved, the Golden Dawn system was of great interest to me at the time. I viewed it as being at school, with a very particular curriculum. Cris, David, and I worked almost every evening and night in Los Angeles, specifically with the "Watchtower" ritual, and with my initiations. I also had to pass the tests of the Golden Dawn "knowledge lectures," which I did. David would take on many different roles in the rituals and sometimes other temple members helped out too. I got the feeling that somehow Cris wanted to rush me through the degrees. I didn't mind this at the time, but I also started to sense that the situation was more "political"

---

*E-mail from Cris Monnastre to the author (31 August 1995).

By Regardie's grave in the Hollywood Hills, 1993
(Photo by Cris Monnastre)

than altruistic. At times David was with us, and on other occasions Cris and I worked alone. The real magic happened when we were all together. One evening Cris brought out the Enochian chessboard and pieces that Regardie had crafted himself, and we all played the game that had originally been conceived of by Golden Dawn founders William Wynn Westcott and MacGregor Mathers. I can't remember anyone "winning" the game (or if that's even possible) but it was a very beautiful and in many ways timeless experience to play this four-dimensional, multicolored mind-opener by candlelight in the surroundings of a full temple.

ELECTRIC SKIES

Eventually, it was time to go on the road with David. He was entertaining and highly competent as a tour guide. I could not see myself doing something similar, as had been suggested by David and some of his colleagues with whom I had become friendly. You got to see a lot of beautiful things and make a lot of money, but to be constantly hounded by tourists asking questions about this or that didn't appeal to me.

We traveled on the tour bus south to San Diego, and then moved on to Arizona. I found the landscapes extremely beautiful—about as beautiful as the American architecture we passed was bizarre and ugly. A very strange mix! At a gas station in Yuma, Arizona, I found some cassette tapes of albums with Yma Sumac and Les Baxter (both of whom I loved), and they provided perfect, contrapuntal soundtracks to the dry and scorching-hot landscapes we traveled through.

At night in Phoenix, David and I lay on our backs floating around in the hotel swimming pool, staring up at the most violent and impressive show of thunder and lightning I have ever seen. This was a bit reckless on our part, of course, but we had just come out of a ritual and found it highly fitting that our "extended temple" in outer reality was supercharged with electricity.

I used all these wonderful places for my own magic as well. I had developed a three-part series of meditations and rituals to jumpstart my new "Operation Weltanschauung" life in Stockholm: Nox Per Nox, Lux Per Nox, and Lux Per Lux. The first one, *Darkness* (or "Night") *through Darkness*, included burning a photograph of myself on which I had written my major weaknesses. It was time to let these go, and preferably as soon as possible. That thunder-and-lightning show was pure "Hammer of Thor" and to burn an image of myself to ashes in *Phoenix*—well, nothing could be more appropriate!

In Sedona we paid homage to the spirit of Regardie, who had lived there for several years; it was also where Cris had studied with him between 1981 and 1983. After this, we stayed by the impressive Grand Canyon, and as soon as the stars were out, so were we in our magical pursuits. I performed the *Light through Night* (Lux Per Nox) ritual and went through its meditation, dealing with a sense of allegiance and magnetism toward specific groups and individuals I was attracted to at the time. At sunrise we flew in a small Cessna plane over the Grand Canyon, which was a magical experience in itself, only to land in the city of artificial light par excellence: Las Vegas! Here, amid the bright and buzzing neon and decadent hyper-bling, I wrapped up my cycle with *Light through Light* (Lux Per Lux), which was also the first time I performed Regardie's "Opening by Watchtower" ritual by myself. Time to shine!

After this I just sat back and enjoyed the ride: Nevada, Yosemite, Mammoth Lakes, the Grand Sequoias, Mariposa Grove, and magnificent redwoods like the "Grizzly Giant" and the "Faithful Couple." I loved the experience of getting closer to American nature. There is immense power in this immense land (as of course there is everywhere), and to work ritually on sacred grounds that have been kept "active" and revered by brave and resilient Indigenous nations, despite enormous hardships, was an honor.

To roll back to San Francisco after these majestic natural experiences was weird, but what could I do? I was very happy to be back in the city that had meant so much to me on various magical levels. I made arrangements to see LaVey and Gen, who was now living north of San Francisco. The morning after my arrival, Gen and his daughter Genesse picked me up at my hotel. We drove up to Cazadero, where they lived in a nice house surrounded by nature and very open-minded old hippies. I was delighted to meet their German shepherd Tanith again, who had been around at Beck Road in 1986.

Gen and I enthusiastically talked and talked, catching up with one another about what had been going on in our lives. A sad affair at the time was Gen's divorce from Paula, and I arrived into the midst of a lot of bickering and bitterness. But that didn't stop us from making new plans for new records (specifically a new spoken-word album called *Original Vision Control*) and other projects, and just generally having a good time. Gen suggested I move to the US too, so we could work together more closely, and it was certainly an appealing possibility at the time.

One evening we watched *Home Alone 2* on video, and after Genesse had fallen asleep, we retreated into Gen's office. In candlelight I performed the banishing rituals of the pentagram and hexagram* to protect Gen's space and time and being, moving around him slowly with a Japanese samurai sword that David had given me in Los Angeles. When that was done, Gen blessed me with ashes from the fire outside the Pashupatinath Temple in Nepal, which they claim has been burning for over a thousand years. He had brought the ashes from Nepal the previous year. He said that the ashes were special to the Aghori Baba tradition, living life on "the path of no distinction." He also gave me an Aghori necklace, allegedly made of human bone.

Through Gen, I also got to know a fellow Thelemite, Adam Rostoker (aka Adam Walks-Between-Worlds). This big, bearded, witchy guy was simpatico and easy to get along with. He was also an exceptionally talented writer whose Thelemic analysis of Robert Heinlein's classic novel *Stranger in a Strange Land* ended up in an issue of *The Fenris Wolf* many years later.

While Gen was working in a studio in San Anselmo with fellow musician Larry Thrasher, Adam took me to meet Bill Heidrick, the OTO's treasurer at the time. Heidrick was basically the administrative brains of the international OTO, handling membership files and a million other things in a computer system it seemed he had built himself. Very much in the Thelemic style of Grady McMurtry and Harry Smith, Heidrick appeared as an old, bearded hippie who had somehow gotten stuck in the mental labyrinths of the Qabalah. His house was dark

---

*These elemental and planetary banishings are done to "clear" a space before and/or after a ritual.

and filled with books, papers, and old pizza boxes, and I wondered if he was someone who could make it in the real world. Of course he could! Heidrick was a genius in many ways, balancing not only the financial books, but also the sometimes-conflicting wills of Lodge masters of the OTO, and the lax and too liberal attitudes of the Californian OTO that I had experienced some years earlier. As the order developed in Sweden, the responsibility fell to me of sending in regular reports about membership dues, initiation fees, and so on. Unfortunately, I was never very good at handling these administrative duties. As time passed, I came to admire Bill Heidrick more and more for his seemingly endless patience.

My last stop on this California trip was San Francisco again. Adam had already given me a ride into town for a meeting with the label Silent Records, and then it was finally time to head over to 6114 California Street. The latest wonderful news was that Blanche was pregnant. LaVey was tired yet beamed with pride. "See, Carl, I can still cut the mustard!" he said and smiled his most devilish smile. With permission, I put my hand on Blanche's belly and realized this was the second time for me this American trip.

We had dinner at Le Trou, a nice bistro, but unfortunately there were some coked-up cretins at the next table who wanted to push the boundaries of social courtesy, making remarks about LaVey's flamboyant looks (they probably had no idea who he was). I remember Blanche secretly showing me a beautiful gun with a mother-of-pearl grip in her purse, and mentioning jokingly (?) that she was ready to deal with the situation. It worked as a magical ritual, and I could also see LaVey's intense hatred toward these yuppie jocks gleaming in his eyes. All of a sudden, they got up, threw some money on the table, and left—meals still unfinished.

Back at the Black House we kept on talking until 4:00 a.m. Both LaVey and Blanche praised what I had been up to recently, and there was a lot: the third issue of *The Fenris Wolf*, several new records, and also re-securing the publishing rights for a Swedish edition of LaVey's *Satanic Bible*. As usual, they provided a sense of support, belonging, and respect that I greatly appreciated.

I think at this point I had already formulated a strategy: *The only way you can substantially change things is through culture.* It's by way of ideas embedded in literature, movies, music, and art that inspiration and thoughts are transmitted to a wider sphere than the immediate one, from which point they can then "snowball" onward. Gen helped me see this through his devoted work with "cultural engineering" over the decades, but LaVey was definitely another pioneer in this sense. You have to leave the obfuscated arena of the symbolic and change things in the sphere of the real through willed aesthetic expressions that touch other people more deeply than just on a surface level.

Another important key to LaVey's brand of Satano-Gnosis was the encouragement of personal fetishisms, the ultimate empowerment. In the dark of our last night together we discussed my interest in beautiful pens (a passion he shared), and he also showed me some of his guns and "Al Mar" knives. These were tangible objects of art and great mechanical beauty that are radiantly peaceful when still, touched, and admired—but can be ferocious and even deadly if their owners are provoked.

Although one can certainly write on a computer, or with a cheap BIC ballpoint pen, or fight someone with a baseball bat or one's bare hands, there is undeniably something so utterly civilized—bordering on decadent—with tools of *any* trade that transcend their mere functionality and efficiency and take on a deeper mythic gestalt through refined aesthetics. LaVey's thoughts on this affected me greatly:

> Every magician should have at least one strong fetish. Though the word *fetish* is usually linked with sex, it is actually the same meaning as "amulet," "talisman," or "charm," in the strictest magical sense. A fetish, if properly employed, can be used to generate the highest degree of controllable magical energy and useable power.*

---

*LaVey, editorial in *The Cloven Hoof*, vol. XIII, no. 3 (1981), 1.

I would say that we're unconsciously attracted to the right fetishes for us. Whether or not we understand this initially, our psychic constitutions will demand the right tools, filtered through aesthetics as much as utilitarianism. If we can "get on board" with this and set sail, we will have a strange and satisfying journey ahead of us. As a self-defined journalist (and long before I dropped out of journalism school), physical pens and cameras have been immediate "objects of desire" for me rather than just useful "tools." Many of my cameras, for example, have been much more than mere workhorses—they have been door-openers to psychosexual vistas I couldn't have reached otherwise.

The same goes for the pens, both on a philosophical level and in the writing itself. What do I write and with what? A whole psychological interpretation model could be developed based on the history of fountain pens, for instance. Are you a crescent- or a button-filler? A piston- or twist-filler? Or perhaps you're a Scheaffer vacuum-filler? Which is your immediate choice: An Aurora Edacoto hatchet-filler or a LeBoeuf celluloid, or perhaps a dare-devilish Chilton Wing-Flow?

The encouragement of fetishes—sexual, psychosexual, objectified, or what have you—is important. It is literally the cataclysmic union of "nature" and "nurture"—two words we have usually been taught need an "or" or "versus" between them.

I often dreamt about LaVey on this particular trip. Perhaps it was an unconscious effort on my part to maximize his presence, as this would turn out to be our last meeting *in vivo*. Some of the dreams had an initiatory or magical quality. A few weeks before the meeting in San Francisco, I dreamt that LaVey was upset about something. I told him that it didn't really matter if we were together in the same space because we had an energy link between our heads (which became visible in the dream). "That's right," he said, "and we have *this*." He shook my hand and made a twisted half of the face, which I replicated. To me, it was a secret sign with a great sense of humor—something much more at home in our beloved magical movie *Freaks* than in any somber lodge hall with "occultnik" brethren. The background set of the dream, the Purple Parlor, then morphed into a pet store, signifying (for me) the importance of loving and appreciating animals in general, but also how civilization basically consists of consensual cages of varying kinds, restraining our animal natures. In the dream, LaVey held back the animals that were his in this space, in order to not upset a lady with a family of ferrets.

I returned to New York and the tender, loving care of Peter, Peggy, and Countess Karloff. I was exhausted from all my impressions and felt knocked out. But after a good night's sleep I was ready again for the "Big Apple." One of the absolute peak moments of the entire American odyssey was visiting the Coney Island amusement park together with Peter and Peggy.

On our last evening together in Manhattan, Peter played me some of his favorite pieces of music: Gustaf Allan Pettersson's seventh symphony, and Gustav Mahler's tenth. It was a perfect way to wind down, and I could feel the Swedish composer Pettersson specifically beckoning me to come home.

ON THE ROAD

Needless to say, this American trip inspired and fortified my position a great deal. Over the course of autumn, I soul-searched and tried to formulate a perfect solution to move me forward. My own experience tells me that the best way to do this is with the method of "Dolores"—namely, doing what hurts the most first. I certainly was not going to keep my job at the print/copyshop, as it was too draining. Nor did I want to be slaving away alone with Psychick Release. I did not wish to get stuck in a relationship (my by now ex-wife had moved to Copenhagen, and I liked being alone on a personal level) or any kind of "groove." So, I decided to upend everything and see what would happen.

I sublet my apartment and moved in with my grandmother. I quit my job and made plans for a new company that would be "the same but different"; I would also run it jointly with another person. Creatively, there were also exciting things going on: White Stains (which now consisted mainly of myself and Peter Bergstrandh) had been offered a tour together with the Hamburg-based band Cassandra Complex. I had met the singer, Rodney Orpheus, in OTO contexts on several occasions in Hamburg and Stockholm, and I appreciated his "devil-may-care" attitude. So, we made plans for a European tour, in which White Stains would be the support act. I would also film Cassandra Complex performing each night, and the signal would be mixed into a live video feed projected on stage. It all sounded great to me.

Peter and I had made the album *Misantropotantra* in 1992, and had just wrapped up a new one, *Why Not Forever?*, in the summer of 1993. It was perfect timing to take our form of non-vocal experimental music on the road.

We prepared some basic samples from movies and my collection of audio cassettes with weird vocal sources (Crowley, Marinetti, and Willy Wonka, to mention but a few), and Fetish 23 made a darkly trippy background video for us, integrating scenes from one of my all-time-favorite movies, the Japanese *A Page of Madness* (1926), which poetically depicts the inside of a lunatic asylum. We were all very happy to jettison the traditional rock'n'roll approach and mind-frame behind, and delve into an entire world of electronics and samples.

We left for Hamburg, got to know all the people involved, and were excited to head out on a new occultural adventure. Almost every evening I wore a Horus T-shirt on top of a turtleneck, as well as the bone necklace Gen had given me in California. I integrated a new wand that I had found in the US into the performance, holding on to it and occasionally directing energy through it. It was still only bare wood but was being put to work anyway. In most of the gigs, intentions were woven poetically into our music, which we described tongue-in-cheek as "tech-yes" (as opposed to "tech-no").

It was interesting to see the difference between eastern and western Germany. It had only been a few years since the unification in 1990, and it felt like a privilege to get a glimpse of how bleak and dreary the eastern part of Germany actually was. Unemployment was high and it reflected in the mind-frames of the audiences too. They were hungry for input and stimulation, depressively licking the deep wounds from an enforced socialism that had depleted the people and the culture for more than forty years.

I had no intention of merely "playing a concert" on this tour. We had tried that when we were a rock band and it quickly felt like I was going through the motions, singing and posing. I was never comfortable in that role. But as soon as there was real, evocative music and I had something to send out, I got excited. It was true on this European White Stains tour, and even more so later with the project that followed, Cotton Ferox. Whenever we played live, there was *intention*, and whatever structures we had in terms of music and poetry were there to facilitate the ritual work.

There was only one moment in the rock'n'roll days that I can recall had an instant magical effect or charge. In 1992, White Stains played at the alternative venue Månefisken in Oslo on the vernal equinox. Our set was made up of songs from the *Dreams Shall Flesh* album plus a few new ones, including "Citizen of the Infernal Empire" (honoring LaVey), "I Love the Wolf Man" (honoring Gen), and "I Cannot Die" (honoring magic as an eternal flow through life and nature). These new songs were considerably less Thelemically demagogic and contained more of a personal signal. As we performed "I Cannot Die," I got real shivers and somehow sang in a much more powerful way. I was free of any intellectual shackles and just let go. Something was unleashed at that moment in Norway: a pure, dark, and feral energy expressed via my youthful poetry and our amplified new wave music. Whether it was only relevant for me or also for others, I don't know. In part I think it had a lot to do with the band. Not only was Peter as excellent as ever on his bass, but we also had Christer Hellman on drums that tour. Peter and Christer had been the rhythmic backbone of one of my all-time-favorite Swedish bands, Lustans Lakejer (the

"Lackeys of Lust") and it was a thrill to have them whip up the frenzy I needed on stage.

The performances of our 1993 European tour were short, bright moments in the otherwise dreary life on the road. After the concerts, it was just getting into the bus, most often drunk, and moving on . . . Hamburg, Bremen, Dortmund, Nortrup, Frankfurt, Siedlingshausen, Hannover, Magdeburg, Berlin (where I reconnected with my friend from Gothenburg, the Polish Nietzschean noise-musician Zbigniew Karkowski), Cottbus, Chemnitz (until recently known as "Karl-Marx-Stadt"!), and on and on. One charmed moment was getting out of the tour bus at an Autobahn roadside grill in Bayreuth in the middle of the night, with everyone singing or humming Wagner's "Ride of the Valkyries."

After the concert in Nuremberg, we arrived in Prague a day early and decided to go to the club that evening. Death in June was playing on a bill with Boyd Rice there, so I thought it could be fun to reconnect after so many years. The overall attitude in our entourage toward Death in June, as well as toward Boyd, was chilly to say the least. Personally, I just wanted to say hi and talk about LaVeyan good times. Which we did. I had some moments with Boyd backstage before the concert, chatting mainly about the recent birth of LaVey's and Blanche's son, Xerxes. We wrote a postcard together to the new parents, featuring a really big nude model, with heartfelt congratulations:

Hello all! I'm here in Prague with Carl A. Will call as soon as I'm back. Best regards, Boyd.—Prague is a magical city and look who popped up! Congratulations on the baby! Well done! I'll get back to you more in detail—lots of stories from the road. A tough life indeed! Vade Ultra! Carl*

Then I noticed some other familiar faces backstage: James Mannox and Simon Norris, both of whom had been involved in TOPY UK. It was

*Postcard, undated (1993), Church of Satan archives.

lovely to see them again but to me they seemed almost embarrassed to be caught in the act of playing together with this overtly "martial" carnival sideshow. That said, I have to admit that Boyd was quite powerful on stage in his exclamations of Social Darwinism, whereas battlefield romantic Douglas Pearce just strummed his guitar ever so delicately, flanked by James and Simon playing marching drums and whatnot. It was a bizarre evening indeed, and I'm happy that Simon (as "Ossian Brown") landed on his feet in the project Cyclobe some years later.

We traveled on to Munich and Vienna and played great concerts. At the impressive Hofburg museum I consecrated my wand-to-be by the mythical "spear of destiny" that allegedly had pierced the side of the crucified Christ. This myth of immense power invested in the spear had been gradually amplified by famous people who had owned the object over the millennia, including my ancestor and grail-romantic Charlemagne (more on this later in our story), as I had recently and enthusiastically read in Trevor Ravenscroft's bestselling 1973 book *The Spear of Destiny*. So, to secretly bring out my stick of wood, as yet unadorned, in that amazing museum and let it touch the glass protecting the powerful talisman was quite overwhelming. There's something to be said for human projections into and onto seemingly inanimate objects. And sometimes, if you accept the dynamics of the relationship, the objects can project right back at you!

Invigorated by this experience, I traveled onward to Linz and Salzburg with the entourage. In Salzburg, I met with Saulus and Tim, two fellow magicians and old friends of David Griffin. They too worked as tour guides in the US and enjoyed half of the year in Europe. We had met in Stockholm in the spring and had gotten on well together. They were representing a different tradition, one which was essentially more mystical, and invited me to be part of their "cabal." They were very interested in time travel and history, and how one can go exploring and sometimes even correcting historical events. I found this very intriguing, and a great balance to all the systematized mental occultism I was getting fed through the Golden Dawn and the OTO. For many years

I had a great correspondence with Saulus, and he helped me untangle quite a few psychological dilemmas relating to my "quest" or individuation process. It was also quite remarkable to meet magicians who were not after any kind of limelight or attention. In this sense, they were/are genuine *occultists*, and quite content with being involved with the mysteries in themselves. No flaunting or stress needed!

That said, my own more visible occult traveling continued at an ever-faster pace. Right after I returned home from the European tour, I left for Bergen in Norway again to be initiated into the fourth degree and some extra degrees that connect the first two degree triads ("The Man of Earth" and "The Lovers"). It was exciting and energizing, to say the least. We were all amused by the fact that the Olympic flame passed through Bergen on the very same day as the initiations. The flame was being ceremonially brought up further north, to Lillehammer, where the winter Olympics of 1994 were about to begin. I didn't miss the opportunity to use the occasion for further magic. I rode up on a funicular to the mountain range surrounding this lovely coastal town and made the final consecration of my wand, immersing it in the freezing snow and ice while the divine fire of Mount Olympus was passing through the town below me.

Back home again, exhausted and penniless, I was happy to stay with my beloved grandmother. She was probably the only relative who supported what I was doing without necessarily really needing to understand it, and compassionately so. My parents knew what I was up to, for sure. My father was an intellectual beatnik kind of guy, immersed in his jazz nostalgia, and certainly more of an outsider (in the Colin Wilson sense) than a bourgeois insider. My mother was a highly cultivated and refined woman who was well aware of Crowley and other similar minds in culture. When cleaning out the papers after her demise in 2018, I found a 1962 clipping from *The Village Voice* in which she was quoted as saying, "The object of all knowledge is action."* I have no idea how that

---

*Margareta Lindman, quoted in John Wilcock, "The Scattershot Technique," in *The Village Voice*, issue of 27 December 1962.

came about. Whatever it was that they had possessed in their youth, I had apparently carried on in mysterious ways. But the difference now was that I wasn't a teenager anymore: I was approaching my thirties, and they were annoyed at having to explain about my irregularities and occult antics to their friends—some of whom kept feeding them with American press clippings and notices about LaVey's ongoing alimony case with his former common-law wife Diane Hegarty, as if in glee.

As New Year's Eve approached, I was elated and mystified at the same time. Whatever would come, would come.

PART III
1995–1999

A TWO-WAY LOOKING GLASS

It was impossible for me *not* to run a publishing company, but I was definitely done with Psychick Release. As I returned from the White Stains tour of Europe in late 1993 with a net profit of two German Marks (about $1), I probably should have licked my wounds and gone back to work. Instead, I started a new company together with Michael Matton: Looking Glass Communications. We teamed up with a bookseller friend, Jens Näsström, and moved into a little basement in the same part of town where I was living. It felt like a fresh start in many ways.

As Looking Glass expanded and I worked hard to make money to finance it all (ad work, graphic design), we were also looking to the future. Whereas the efforts with Psychick Release had been ambitious, I felt hindered by being alone in these efforts. I preferred to exist in a greater context, and the new collaborative venture with Matton and Jens provided that. Although I was in charge of the day-to-day operations, which usually amounted to twelve-hour shifts, their input was valuable. Not only did we publish Rodney Orpheus's *Abrahadabra: A Beginner's Guide to Thelemic Magick*, but also the Swedish translation of LaVey's *Satanic Bible* that I had failed to publish on Psychick Release, and a new and nicer looking edition of my Swedish translation of Crowley's *Book of the Law*.

Whereas I had talked to Marjorie Cameron on the phone in 1993, discussing an edition of Jack Parsons's *Songs for the Witch Woman* with her illustrations, Bill Breeze suggested we could take it one step further and buy the rights for *all* of Parsons's work from her. She was aging, ill, and in need of money, and we needed new material to publish. I thought that was a great idea and we steamed ahead, finalizing this deal in early 1995 before Cameron eventually succumbed to her cancer that summer. Thanks to the fine brokering by Bill, this little Swedish publishing company would now become a real player on the international market. Not only that: we also bought a share of Bill's company, Spirit Vision, which in turn owned the classic imprint for supreme editions of Crowley, 93 Publishing.

Visiting Bill Breeze in North Carolina in early 1995 solidified all these business aspects. We talked about various projects inside and outside of the OTO, and I was especially interested in seeing the progress he was making with revising the definitive and massive edition of Crowley's *Book Four—Liber ABA* (a project I had seen the beginnings of already in 1993 in New York). I brought him a gift of a notebook and a nice pen, just as I had for Cris Monnastre in LA. My intention was to inspire him to write more himself, as he is a very talented writer.

Bill let me roam freely through the OTO archive, which was incredibly interesting and inspiring. And of course I was always on the lookout for fascinating material for *The Fenris Wolf*! A great and surprising climax was him taking me to a bank vault, in which I could try on Crowley's original gold ring (a copy of which Bill most often wears) and flip through Crowley's original manuscript of *Liber AL— The Book of the Law*, dictated to him by his wife Rose Kelly in Cairo in 1904. Naturally these were ecstatically talismanic moments for Carl the Thelemite, as well as for Carl the Magico-anthropologist!

I was dizzy after that experience, and later in the day my shamanic totem animal came to the rescue, suggesting that I divest myself not only of occult paraphernalia but also of allegiances—that I become "clean" in the sense of "independent." I was told quite fiercely that I wasn't a "stamp collector," and that my own "Institute of Comparative Magico-anthropology"* was "more than enough and much better" for me. The real message was: *You have enough power in yourself.* This vision or experience happened as Bill was on the phone with Martin

---

*This was a development of the "Institute of Comparative Misanthropology," which had been an umbrella of sorts for some of my early activities like the fanzine *Goggle-Eyed*. In early 1994 it was transformed into the Institute of Comparative Magico-anthropology, which has remained active to the present time, mainly as the overseeing entity for *The Fenris Wolf* journal.

Starr of Teitan Press, another long-time Thelemite. I had at some point expressed interest in Crowley's other group, the A∴A∴, and Starr as well as Bill were both involved. Perhaps my totem animal had had enough of my seemingly endless branching out? That evening, I did ritually and temporarily divest myself of objects carrying "weight" of attachment: a golden ring I had received from David Griffin, an Omega watch that had belonged to Saulus, and the Baphomet necklace that Gen had given to me (and LaVey). That small ritual or experience provided much food for thought, and for quite some time.

Another equally inspiring "initiation" came about when Bill showed me an episode of the amazing 1960s TV series *The Outer Limits*. After this I was hooked on this perfect television expression of EC Comics, pulp horror, science fiction, mind-bending twists, and superb storytelling. It became a perfect complement to my admiration for straightforward sci-fi and horror writers like Ray Bradbury, who can evoke entire universes through quite modest literary means.

Another lovely meeting on this trip was with Jack Hogg, Bill's mentor and the bishop in the Ecclesia Gnostica Catholica (EGC)* from whom "my" particular Gnostic lineage within the OTO stemmed. Hogg was also the man who once upon a time had put Kenneth Grant in touch with the gnostic magician Michael Bertiaux.

NECROMANTIC NAMEDROPPING

Working with the Gnostic Mass and the EGC under the aegis of the OTO in Stockholm was exciting, perhaps even more so than initiating a steady flow of curious Thelemites (by the mid-1990s there were already OTO groups in Stockholm, Gothenburg, Malmö, Lund, and Uppsala). The ceremonial structure is more or less perfect, and when it

---

*EGC: Ecclesia Gnostica Catholica, a loose association of Thelemic neo-Gnostics "housed" within the OTO.

flows it creates a very special form of beauty that definitely transcends mere ritual theater. In my mind, the Gnostic Mass is Crowley's best piece of writing when it comes to actual ritual.

One interesting aspect is the segment that deals with the "Gnostic saints." When the priest has been purified and consecrated by the priestess, and he, in turn, has blessed and consecrated her on the altar, the deacon goes through a long list of names in the middle of the temple, blessing them all within a strictly Gnostic context. It's a bit of cooling down before the magic of the communion happens for all participants up by the altar, hammering the "good folks" into the psyche of all those present, invoking them as tangible spirits and forces. This is a brilliant inclusion by Crowley as Thelemic-Gnostic schoolmaster and it is what people take away from the Mass in the long-term perspective.

Esoteric namedropping has been a vital part of my own schooling, and working with the Gnostic Mass made me realize it's an important part of keeping a magical tradition alive—and one that goes all the way back to the earliest names included. Where I could read about weird surrealists and magicians in obscure Coil fanzines, for instance, or track down books by certain authors that were included in actual lists in publications like *RE/Search*, *Vague*, and *Rapid Eye* in the late 1980s, the Gnostic saints (as given by the "Great Beast" Crowley) have become a more specialized infusion while at the same time representing a wider spectrum of minds.

I will give the list of them all here, just for the benevolent hell of it:

Laotze and Siddartha and Krishna and Tahuti, Mosheh, Dionysus, Mohammed and To Mega Therion, with these also Hermes, Pan, Priapus, Osiris and Melchizedek, Khem and Amoun Mentu and Heracles, Orpheus and Odysseus; with Vergilius, Catullus, Martialis, Rabelais, Swinburne, and many an holy bard; Apollonius Tyanæus, Simon Magus, Manes, Pythagoras, Basilides, Valentinus, Bardesanes and Hippolytus, that transmitted the Light of the Gnosis to us their successors and their heirs; with Merlin, Arthur, Kamuret, Parzival, and many another, prophet, priest and king, that bore the Lance and Cup, the Sword and Disk, against the Heathen; and these also, Carolus Magnus and his paladins, with William of Schyren, Frederick of Hohenstaufen, Roger Bacon, Jacobus Burgundus Molensis the Martyr, Christian Rosencreutz, Ulrich von Hutten, Paracelsus, Michael Maier, Roderic Borgia Pope Alexander the Sixth, Jacob Boehme, Francis Bacon Lord Verulam, Andrea, Robertus de Fluctibus, Giordano Bruno, Johannes Dee, Sir Edward Kelly, Thomas Vaughan, Elias Ashmole, Molinos, Adam Weishaupt, Wolfgang von Goethe, William Blake, Ludovicus Rex Bavariæ, Richard Wagner, Alphonse Louis Constant, Friedrich Nietzsche, Sir Richard Payne Knight, Hargrave Jennings, Carl Kellner, Forlong dux, Sir Richard Francis Burton, Paul Gaugin, Doctor Gérard Encausse, Doctor Theodor Reuss, Sir Aleister Crowley, Karl Johannes Germer, and Major Grady Louis McMurtry—Oh Sons of the Lion and the Snake! with all Thy saints we worthily commemorate them worthy that were and are and are to come. May their Essence be here present, potent, puissant and paternal to perfect this feast!*

It's a meaty list, and not one containing only traditional Gnostics but rather minds that have *acted* gnostic in the service of humanity; to facilitate direct initiation and individuation through art and magic, basically. Thus, we have Mosheh side by side with Catullus, Laotze with Manes, and so on. The wonderful and often paradoxical eclecticism makes sense, seen from Crowley's attitude of cultural and thereby actual alchemy. In the original list from 1913 he attached himself at the end as a pinnacle of sorts, but there's no denying that these mythical and/ or actual people changed things in themselves that in turn allowed for

---

*This is the current and slightly expanded list used in the Gnostic Mass today, as reproduced in James and Nancy Wasserman, *To Perfect this Feast: A Performance Commentary on the Gnostic Mass*, rev. 3rd ed. (N.p.: Sekhmet, 2013), 38–39; for the original version, see Crowley, "Liber XV: The Gnostic Mass," in *The Equinox*, vol. III, no. 10 (New York: 93 Publishing, 1990), 131.

change in other people—and that is certainly valid for Crowley too. In a dire and *"realpolitik"* hindsight, we might today have problems with a few of these names and forces, but can they really be blamed for how other and contemporary people have interpreted and acted upon their teachings? I think not.

Already during my career as performing priest and bishop of the EGC, critical voices were raised about the fact that no women were mentioned in the list, and that women should also be included. This was perhaps a gentle "pre-quake" of the massive representational avalanche that followed suit in the 2010s, disrespectfully even insisting on changing things that had been written in another time, by another human being with the full right to express himself or herself in any possible way (please see Crowley's excellent call to arms in *Liber OZ* for more on that crystallization of liberty*). If you're not happy with what you read, then go read something else. Or even better, write something different yourself!

That being said, I have never much appreciated sacrosanct dogma. For one of the first masses I helped set up (Denmark, 1991), I included Anton LaVey and Austin Osman Spare in the list of Gnostic saints. This actually caused a minor upset/roar/hiccup and some ensuing kindergarten snitching among the devoted Danish Crowley kids, and I decided to stay away from similar antics after that—although I do believe those two should be in there, along with many others (Jack Parsons and Marjorie Cameron, Albert Hofmann, Hermann Hesse, Ludwig Klages, Rudolf Steiner, Rémy de Gourmont, Genesis P-Orridge, Timothy Leary, Ram Dass, Ralph Metzner, Olga Fröbe-Kapteyn, Carl Jung, Maria de Naglowska, Paschal Beverly Randolph, Hilma af Klint, and Nicholas Roerich, to mention but a few).

As for women and the Gnostic sainthood, I today believe they *should* be included, as should any other gender identity. After all, the only time is now, and the times they are a-changin'. But . . . *only based on their own merit as Gnostic individuals* (like all those on the existing

---

*Crowley, "Liber 77: OZ—The Rights of Mankind," in *The Equinox*, vol. III, no. 10, 144.

lists) and certainly not for reasons of socio-mathematical representation.

But let's also not forget the main ex post facto argument *against* this: "May their Essence be here present, potent, puissant and paternal to perfect this feast!" The saints mentioned are male, and seemingly deliberately so to invoke the "potent and paternal." The woman-priestess is enthroned on her altar and worshiped by the priest as well as the congregants. Although perhaps nameless, she is definitely the eternal and ultimately real source of power here, whereas the males named on the list are all pretty imperfect humans (and some nonhumans) with karmic and other problematic issues of personality.

This kind of necromantic namedropping is not only fun—it can also be a conscious strategy of revitalizing certain "spirits" or currents. Anton LaVey understood this well and included lists of de facto historical Satanists and sources of inspiration in many of his books. Thus, in the first paperback editions of *The Satanic Bible*, we come across Satano-Gnostic saints like Friedrich Nietzsche (crossover!), Ragnar Redbeard, Wilhelm Reich, Fritz Lang, P. T. Barnum, Jayne Mansfield, Marilyn Monroe, Reginald Marsh, Mark Twain, and William Mortensen, to mention but a few.

BABALONIC MIND-FRAMES

One peak of the mid-1990s OTO work was an international gathering that we arranged and hosted in Sweden in 1995. It was a great success and a lot of fun, with people coming from all over the world to attend, including Bill Breeze. And we used the fraternal aspect in more ways than merely symbolical, which pleased me. We organized an auction and asked individuals and OTO "bodies" to donate things for it. The proceeds went to brothers and sisters in the Balkans, who were then suffering from the war that eventually NATO had to put an end to. For me, it was magic and fraternity in action in the best possible way. I acted as auctioneer and greatly enjoyed making a clown of myself (at least it was for a good cause!).

At the gathering I met a sister who called herself Lilith von Sirius.

She was quite beautiful and artistically inclined. The interesting thing about her was that she was a genuine devotee of Babalon, one of the Crowleyan concoctions or reinterpretations that have since almost generated a cult of sorts.* Many sisters of the OTO acknowledged and were inspired by Babalon but (at least in my experience) no more so than by any other force or god/dess within the Thelemic pantheon. Lilith not only acknowledged the inspiration—she lived in a transgressive state and used it for magical purposes.

She wanted to talk to me about the possible publication of her writings and promised to send me a disk with her poetry, which she later did. She also brought out a bunch of papers for me to look at. We sat down on her bed and I flipped through them. It was a slave contract, which would give me license to do anything to her or treat her in any possible way. She said it would be part of the book too, as a poem of sorts, but that it was also meant for me.

I replied that I was honored by her offer, which was true. But sexually I'm much more of a voyeur than a full-time sadist; I think and feel in images rather than feeling any need to impose my whatever-will on the partner—and this in addition to the physical hoopla of attraction-friction. I have often been criticized by women for being either too self-ish *or* too kind or considerate "in the sack" (as well as in general), but usually this only tells me more about them and *their* needs. I am quite happy to just be me. If I can have a camera or two along for the ride, then all kinds of play are possible: the projection of the ideal image outward is reflected in the scene and "frozen," which generates new angles, temperatures, and literal and libidinal exposures. The "Kundalini of the Camera" rises in real time so that the situation and eventual congress essentially becomes a sexual feedback loop that generates new images all

---

*For more information about Babalon, see my articles "Babalon: The Psychology of Supra-Sexual Transformation" in *Reasonances* (Scarlet Imprint, 2014), 59–68, and "Sexual-Dynamic Polarity as a Magical Formula: Aleister Crowley's Views on Gender and Transcendence," in *Occulture: The Unseen Forces that Drive Culture Forward* (Rochester, VT: Park Street Press, 2018), 156–67.

along the way to the climax. And let's not forget that after the fact you hopefully have some wonderful images to look at . . .

My mind was very stressed at that time as I was the main organizer/ spider at the gathering, as well as the priest for one of the Gnostic Masses, and I was acting as the initiator. I told Lilith I would consider her offer, but that we would have to resume talks later. It intrigued me a great deal though, and I asked her who or what Babalon had been in her inspiration and work, as her collection of poetry even bore that name in the title. I expected to hear of meditations with and on the Lust trump card of Crowley's beautiful *Thoth* Tarot deck (which has become so emblematically iconic in the latter-day Babalonic approaches and devotions), but Soror L told me something in passing that stuck with me:

> Babalon is in the crossing over; that's where things happen. It goes both ways. Nice to naughty, naughty to nice, male to female, straight to gay, back and forth, whatever . . . You have to embrace the opposite and that's where you can tap in.

I then asked her if her "normal" self was the opposite of the sexually advanced being that Lilith was. She nodded:

> That's exactly it. I'm a nice girl, a poet, dancer, dreamer. But when I'm in sexual ritual and am dominated in any way they want, there is a boost I can't describe. It lifts me; it's beyond the mere pleasure we feel. But it would work equally well the other way around: the slut or whore suddenly dressed in pretty white lace and romantically meditating on her own peace and love would be equally lifted.

Lilith von Sirius unfortunately died in 1997 at age twenty-five, and we never got around to publishing her poetry via Looking Glass Press. But our brief conversation opened my mind in the sense that it pushed the traditionalist-fundamentalist interpretation aside for one of deeper psychological implications that touches even on physics "proper" (opposites attract, magnetism, fusion and fission theory, supernovas and black holes, etc.). Crowley was brought up in a fundamentalist Christian home (and those were certainly more moralistically rigid days in general), so of course he would have fantasies about a super harlot straddling the Lion/Beast (the Great Beast, of course, being his own "nom de plume") and tying it in to the psychotic ramblings of the Biblical "Revelations," as well as the transgressive wife-swapping adventures of John Dee and Edward Kelly, who, while in inebriated states, were "channeling" Angelic sermons that included the Babalon gestalt in their overheated male Christian psyches!*

But when viewed as an imperative to go exploring, transcending, and, importantly, transgressing your own psychosexual rigidity, Babalon is indeed a tangible force that can take on *any* shape your psyche so desires. This force can help you with things in ritual situations and contexts. And the fuel it requires is nothing other than your own honesty and courage to catapult yourself out of inert comfort zones occasionally, to facilitate new perspectives on how to make your life experience even greater.

> now the next big mission
> and the next step in life
> is to grant a freedom of movement
> to that wild Babalon beast in that kinky heart of mine
> welcome, white nights
> black days are over forever if I ever play the game
> there's a fantastic voice
> there's that fantastic choice
> strive ever to more, to more
> more fun, more joy
> more pleasures, more search and destroy
>
> LILITH VON SIRIUS, "BABALON"†

---

*See the previous note regarding my texts on Babalon and the related history.
†Lilith von Sirius, excerpt from "Babalon" in her collection of poetry, *Liber 156* (unpublished manuscript in the archive of the author).

But then we have the challenge of "Hegelian dialectics": If Babalon is an antithesis rebelling against the original "thesis" or imprint, where is the actual synthesis? The answer, I would argue, is: a more aware and extra-sentient "heightened" being; someone who is conscious of the dynamics involved and who chooses to work with them to evolve. As it would turn out, Gen was on a parallel path, although much more expressly and publicly so. After all, one of Gen's central mottos and attitudes was: "When in doubt, be extreme."

PANDROGENY

After our meeting in California in 1993, I kept in fairly regular contact with Gen, who was now much more settled after the divorce from Paula. He was in a new relationship with Jackie "Lady Jaye" Breyer from New York, a nurse and also a sex worker/dominatrix working for our mutual friend Terence Sellers at her dungeon in New York (both of these women were definitely Babalon devotees!). Except for artistic work and music via the "Transmedia Foundation," Gen's focus now lay on reviving or remodifying "The Process" (Church of the Final Judgment), the old Scientology spin-off group that had made a splash mainly in the UK in the late 1960s and early 1970s. We had already been interested in them back in the peak TOPY era, and I remember getting photocopies of their magazines and early articles about them, as well as a copy of William Sims Bainbridge's classic study of The Process, *Satan's Power*, via the TOPY network. Friendships with original Process members like Timothy Wyllie in New Mexico encouraged Gen in this overall inspiration. These social-emotional boosts could be clearly perceived in our general communications, which pleased me:

My mind is so full ov ideas agen. E think Miss Jackie is inspiring me. E am also becouming much less gender specific in my clothes and thoughts. E think there is a hint ov this need in HORUS, and to leave thee old Aeon, we must become AS GODS/ESSES. Which E all ways felt was P-ANDROGENOUS. Positive, or charged androgeny, power through transcendance ov imprinted gender programming. As ever, your own experiences synchronize with my own. Which really pleases me, Calle.* We seem to have a deep connection. E still believe we can gradually initiate a truly modern perception ov how magick and shamanism, gender, and technology, are mere manifestations ov thee FIRST true change in our paltry species!!!†

This pandrogyne image was a classic model or archetype in our worlds, perhaps defined best in the ultra-iconic image of "Baphomet" by Éliphas Lévi, first published in the second volume of his book *Dogme et Rituel de la Haute Magie* (1856). It shows a goatlike being with one hand point upward to the skies and one downward to Earth, with angelic wings, displaying a great set of breasts and an erect "caduceus" flanked by two snakes, a pentagram on its forehead and the words "Solve" and "Coagula" emblazoned on each arm. Embracing human, animal, male and female aspects, and a whole lot of magic, Baphomet's mythic origins have been studied and alleged to derive from Knights Templar sources (i.e., being a symbol of their dealings and exchanges of information with esoteric Islam as well as teachings from further East). No matter what the exact origins, it is undoubtedly a symbol that has permeated the Western ceremonial-magic psyche. And it is perfectly encompassing as a magically potent synthesis of transcended or transgressed opposites: the quintessential upheaval of dualism, as favored and preached by Gnostics, Daoists, and many others.

Incidentally, the symbol of the Church of Satan, which is also called "Baphomet" and features a goat's head within a pentagram, was first

---

*Calle is a Swedish nickname for Carl.
†Genesis P-Orridge, fax to the author (3 March 1995).

developed by French author-occultist Stanislas de Guaita in his 1897 book *La clef de la magie noire* (The Key to Black Magic). Fin-de-siècle France was undoubtedly a hotspot of romantic diabolism—in both fiction and fact!

In 2022, I commissioned the ultimate Baphomet image from my favorite artist, Val Denham, for the cover of *The Fenris Wolf* 12. In a pulp-paperback style, Baphomet is seated on planet Earth, flanked in the sky by two skulls and on the grassy earth by two voluptuous women. The phallus (no euphemistic "caduceus" objects here!) is erect and penetrates the Fenris Wolf "FW" logo that is resting on its lap. The central "spine" of the logo shoots up toward the left breast of Baphomet, connecting to its very heart. On its lower arms the old alchemical "Solve" and "Coagula" have been replaced with the words "Fenris" and "Wolf." For me, it's the ultimate development of a traditional symbol that has lost much of its value and power over time into a more vibrant one with a distinct place in the active end times of the Kali Yuga: by uniting with the mythic Fenris, Baphomet has become a force to be reckoned with in our present-day Ragnarök!

The overcoming of duality has been a staple ingredient in esoteric history and philosophy, constantly challenging and provoking the status quo. One of the wisest things Crowley ever said was that "The true Magick of Horus requires the passionate union of opposites."* The Judeo-Christian relationship between "God" and "Satan" is perhaps the most emblematic and problematic one, as it seems culturally resistant to any mediation, let alone a transcendence in union. The old Gnostics were wiser and allowed this union free reign in, for example, the figure of Abraxas. The Process Church of the Final Judgment developed this necessary union in (somewhat) contemporary times. There are many similar examples in religious and mythological history: Odin's integration of Loki (and their occasional transgender manipulations), as well as the interplay between Set and Horus, and

---

*Crowley, *Little Essays Toward Truth*, 89.

in the merging of Exú Duas Cabeças within Quimbanda, and in all twin-based mysteries and myths. "Pan" is a key to these mysteries, because it connotes not only a distinct force of violent ecstasy (in the Mediterranean mythologies, and in the origin of the word "Panic") but also one of union/wholeness: pan-sexuality (positive indiscrimination), Pan-American (an airline for all of the Americas), pan-theism (striving for Oneness), pan-creas ("wholly of flesh"), pan-drogeny (a transcendence of the binary), and so on.

The problems that arose from too much rigidity leading to actual global inertia were addressed in my novel *The Devil's Footprint* (2020), in which the God-Satan conspiracy (as well as their teamwork) begets not only a new aeon but also a whole new heiress to the queendom of Earth. In part (without spoiling any details of the novel), I was directly inspired by Gen's and Jaye's conceptualizations of pandrogeny when I worked on the book. What's been divided needs to be united in the search for an overarching sense of Wholeness or Oneness, as Gen described it:

> We could argue that actually it's probably better to be pandrogyne as these are magically aware of the alchemical implication. A trans-gendered person isn't necessarily interested in that iconography at all; that's one of the differences. But there's definitely something bubbling beneath the surface in the culture. One of the symptoms of whatever it is that's bubbling under the surface is the acceleration of interest in she-male transsexuals and body modification to neutralize the archetypes. I don't think it's anywhere near as clear cut as people used to assume. I know it's not. It wasn't that classic thing where I'm a man trapped in a woman's body, or I'm a woman trapped in a man's body. We should know that a pandrogyne is simply just trapped in a body. And the body has to become a part of the dialogue in terms of control over the narrative of your life.*

---

*P-Orridge, *Sacred Intent—Expanded Edition* (Vimmerby: Trapart, 2021), 159.

A PARA-ACADEMIC ANTIDOTE
TO INTELLECTUAL INERTIA

In the mid-1990s I considered going back to university. My parents were academics and my father had a Ph.D. in history, a subject that interests me as well. Perhaps I could combine my interest in esotericism with an academic career? Henrik Bogdan, my good friend from Gothenburg, had already started paving the way by writing about the Golden Dawn, Freemasonic rituals, and other similar subjects at the University of Gothenburg. I knew there were some related activities at Uppsala University too, but as it turned out, these would make me lose all interest and faith in academia. In retrospect, I can only say I'm very grateful!

Enrolled in a licentiate degree program (a Swedish postgraduate degree between the M.A. and Ph.D. levels) at Uppsala for a long time, a guy called Erik Rodenborg was working away on a thesis about Aleister Crowley. I found this exciting, but the more I researched the researcher (a journalistic duty!) I found troubling information. Rodenborg was some kind of fringe communist and wrote for an anachronistic old-school magazine, *Internationalen* (The International). Rodenborg was literally biting the beast that fed his own academic career, and—lo and behold!—soon crossed paths with me, the OTO, and Looking Glass Press. He wrote about Crowley's *Book of the Law* and LaVey's *Satanic Bible* in *Internationalen*, and included all of the lowest clichés about violence, eating babies, and so on—just like idiotic British and American extremists had done during the "Satanic Panic," and in a similar way to what QAnon is doing today.

We sat on a few open academic panels together, discussing his blatant errors (which I told him about to his face, because he was so ridiculously predictable in his argumentations). He painfully tried to wiggle out of it like a worm one lifts from the ground and exposes to scrutiny, and he always failed miserably. He also mentioned Looking Glass Press in these hack pieces, thereby painting himself into a corner. I consulted one of the best attorneys in Stockholm, who said that I could win a libel case but that it would mean running up a large legal bill, which the guy would eventually be ordered to pay (but probably couldn't), and that there wouldn't be any extra compensation (like in the US), probably only a mandatory yet minimal note in their magazine admitting they had made a mistake. So, I withdrew my aggression and potential lawsuit, and was sure that he would at least not get his dissertation approved, given that it was filled with actual factual mistakes and subjective, slanted points of view.

I followed the process and attended his public "defense," for which Professor Mattias Gardell was the external reviewer or opponent. Several students, as well as myself, had pointed out the errors in Rodenborg's dissertation but nevertheless—it was approved by the examining committee!

This blew my mind and rubbed me in all the wrong ways. It made me furious. I had always regarded Gardell as one of the "good guys" in Swedish academia (and in general) and hoped that he would put an end to this farce. To make the process smooth and easy, Gardell had even borrowed several books from me and others,* with added information about Rodenborg's deliberate errors. But to no avail . . . I just couldn't figure out why they would let this ferocious *faux pas* of a thesis be accepted as a work of scholarship.

Later I found out why (and no shadow should fall on Gardell here, as he was merely the reviewer, not the actual examiner): the faculty in the department wanted to get rid of Rodenborg at any cost, as he had been a meandering shit-disturber in Uppsala for years. By granting him his degree, they could finally show him the door, and that was the end of it. This was also when and why I decided *not* to go into academia myself, and to instead pursue similar kinds of subjects as a private scholar.

---

*These included Crowley's *The Law is for All* and *Magic Without Tears*, Regardie's Crowley biography *The Eye in the Triangle*, and Francis King's *Sexuality, Magic, and Perversion*.

In the early 1990s I jokingly defined myself as a "misanthropologist," enjoying the bizarre and absurd daily shenanigans of humans all over the world. When working at the printshop, we used whatever spare time there was to cut out weird news from various newspapers and assemble it in a fanzine that we called *Goggle-Eyed*. And we found a lot! It was highly symptomatic of young misanthropes who didn't want to adapt to any norms but would rather have a loud laugh at *la comedie humaine*.

As my interest in the occult and magic grew, instead of dissolving into enforced normality, I changed the concept into "magico-anthropology" instead. Being a magico-anthropologist was a wonderful and all-encompassing identity that could include traits and research attitudes from many journeying heroes: Aleister Crowley, William Seabrook, Sven Hedin, Alexandra David-Neel, Heinrich Harrer, Thor Heyerdahl, Nicholas Roerich, and Ernst Lothar Hoffmann (aka Lama Anagarika Govinda), for example. They had all written amazing books that touched people precisely because they were *not* hamstrung by academic bondage. They could look at the world as human beings and write as real writers. Naturally, that's a much better way to communicate what's "out there" to us readers still "in here" rather than having to churn out dry prose while endlessly regurgitating footnotes from other compulsive footnoters.

So, *Wham Bam Shazam! Abrahadabra! Hocus Pocus Focus Locus!* Suddenly, I had created my own Institute of Comparative Magico-anthropology (on January 1st, 1994), with myself as resident Professor Emeritus! It was one of the best things I've ever done, and to this day "ICM" work fills me with joy and happiness—especially the editing and publishing of *The Fenris Wolf*. Slightly later in the story, around 2010, I formulated a tighter yet very accurate description of its essence: "The Institute of Comparative Magico-anthropology is a four-dimensional artwork that preserves, filters, and sends out its own signals—specifically dealing with the Magic of the World and its revelation through Academagical Ethno-pluralistic Epiphanaticism." Now, if that's not a clear definition, then I don't know what is!

HIMALAYAN HIGHS

It didn't take long before I planned an expedition together with three other ICM alumni and dear friends: Henrik Bogdan, who was at this time working on his Ph.D. at Gothenburg University, the Danish traveler Peder Byberg, and an old friend from high school and LIAC, the photographer Max Fredrikson. We all shared an interest in Vajrayana Buddhism and specifically its ritual aspects. We decided that perhaps it would be best to gain pace in the safer environment of Northern India, where the Tibetan government-in-exile resides and could help us with our research. After about a year of preparations and communications, we set off to India in October of 1996.

After flying to Delhi, resting a bit, and getting sick (as one does), we traveled onward, arriving late at night in the town of Dharamshala, and then continued up by taxi to the village of McLeod Ganj. We were utterly exhausted but couldn't wait to leave our luggage at the hotel and take a walk in the warm night. The smells and twilight sights were enticing to me in every possible way. Tibetan monks passed by, smiling and greeting us with *"Tashi delek"* ("Hello!").

Something inside me told me I had to be up for sunrise and film it (I had brought a clunky but good video camera for documentation). I managed to stick to my hunch and got up on the hotel roof with my camera very early in the morning. The sky was already glowing and I stood in awe of the light that was taking over the sky and, by extension, our lives. As the sun rose over the majestic mountains, I burst into tears. This does not happen often to me, but the sheer beauty of the moment was overwhelming. I managed to film a little, but soon set the camera aside. It was ridiculous and utterly vain to try to capture or preserve this kind of magnificence, anyway—better to just experience it. If one wanted more, it was just a matter of getting up there again the next morning, which I did.

I had fallen immediately in love with the Himalayas, and it's a love supreme that has never dwindled, although I've been there far too seldom. I can get excited by the European alps and other mountainous regions too, but the Himalayas are literally the "top of the world," and when in their vicinity, so are you.

The goal of the expedition was to discover what the general relationship is between magic and ritual in the (exile) Tibetan Buddhist community. Vajrayana Buddhism is very ritually inclined, and much of their insanely complex iconography is essentially a cluster of maps for inner traveling/meditations. Whereas the southern forms of Buddhism, like the Theravada, are more focused on meditation and general compassion, the Mahayana (northern) and specifically the Vajrayana ("Tibeto-Buddhism") forms are much more active, ritualistic, and engaged with artistic expressions for achieving the desired change in the mind. In that sense there is a lot of kinship in both form and content with other schools and traditions of magic proper.

The more I read about Tibetan Buddhism, the more fascinated I became. There was an intersection here of a very interesting kind. There was surely a reason why Tantric "thangkas" (intricate paintings on fabric) appealed more to me than merely another "great golden Buddha" statue.

Upon our arrival, we were immediately helped at the Department for Tibetan Culture and Religion, the Library of Tibetan Works and Archives ("LTWA"), the Norbulingka Institute, the Gyoto Tantric University, and many other places and monasteries. Everyone was so concerned that we should be well treated and that we should be able to access whatever we needed for our research. In so many ways, it felt like a magico-anthropological wet dream! At times it was difficult to reconcile a sense of Scandinavian time and order with how things proceed in India, but for the most part our planning went smoothly enough.

All four of us were sick at various points, mostly due to the different kinds of bacterial cultures in the food. At one point I had to consult a Tibetan doctor, and it was interesting to say the least. She diagnosed a lot just by taking my pulse at the wrist, and then gave me little round pills that were very bitter and looked like fecal matter from a small animal. I forced myself to swallow them although they tasted horrible (perhaps it's true that ill-tasting medicine makes you get well faster?). She also gave me some advice that made me realize we were on the right track: she looked me in the eyes and told me that I shouldn't look up so much but stick to my own level. It wasn't long before I felt healthy and strong again.

When we weren't working in the library, studying, and preparing questions, we trekked in the nearby mountains. Pretty much wherever you go there are Buddhist prayer flags and small *stupas* (monuments) commemorating some teacher or legendary figure in Tibetan history. Initially, it feels exotic and like eye candy for tourists, but at the same time everything is consciously infused with magic. The prayer flags that have become so iconic of the Tibetan "brand" are a wonderfully intelligent and efficient example of the "butterfly effect": with every flutter of these small swatches of cloth, the prayers and Buddhas that are printed on them fly out to every corner of the multiverse. How many *"Om Mani Padme Hums"* have rippled out there thus far, one might ponder?

We had a general letter of introduction from the Department for Tibetan Culture and Religion, so we could essentially contact whomever we wished in the community, with the exception of the Dalai Lama. However, we did get to meet him on a public blessing day, when he received Tibetans and tourists alike. People who have recently crossed over from Tibet always have first priority at these meetings, and it was very moving to see the mix of sadness and joy in everyone's faces. Only the Dalai Lama seemed to remain forever smiling and calm, as he greeted hundreds of people, one by one, with a handshake, after which you get a white *"khata"* scarf that retains the blessing.

For me, shaking his hand was so magical, because as with phenomena like projections and pilgrimage, everything is a mix of your own anticipations and the reflective surface offered. That said, many reflective surfaces accumulate real power by these projections so that the dynamic becomes a being or a force field in itself—almost a cosmic *perpetuuum mobile*, one might say. Is the Dalai Lama holy because he inherently is so, or because people have projected the holiness on him since 1937, when it was "discovered" (by magical means) that he was the reincarnation of the previous Dalai Lama? That's a tough nut to crack, even for experienced magico-anthropologists, but I would say—diplomatically!—that the answer lies in a mixture of both interpretations.

In a culture so heavily steeped in magic and philosophy that it might actually be the most advanced and civilized one on this planet, there are no set boundaries between rational and irrational, or between "this" and "that." Historically, this process of reincarnation is completely natural and integrated for the Tibetans. Do the transgenerational projections, acknowledgments, and acceptance give psychic life to esoteric concepts that for other cultures can seem totally arbitrary and weird? Absolutely.

The closest we got to the higher echelons of Tibetan leadership was the medium for the State Oracle of Tibet. The nation has its own Oracle who is consulted about important matters, and mediumship is highly regarded and respected. When we met the then-current one, Thupten Ngodub, he was as friendly and "normal" as any of the other monks, politely answering our questions and perhaps being a bit surprised that we understood and respected his perspective right from the start, whereas other Westerners would raise an eyebrow when it comes to forms of magic like this.

One speculative perspective is that this phenomenon is a remnant of more distinctly shamanic times, when the shaman of the village or nomadic community would go into trances on behalf of his people. It is still more present in the older religion in Tibet, Bon, but it is actively worked with in Tibet proper and in the exile communities. From Bon the techniques and reverence spilled over into the first specifically Buddhist sect, the Nyingma (founded by the Indian Tantric saint Padmasambava in the eighth century CE), and from there it seeped into Tibeto-Buddhist culture in general.

EXCELLENCIES IN EXILE

For me as a book-maker and publisher, it was very inspiring to meet Gyatso Tschering, who was then the leader of the Library of Tibetan Works and Archives and almost solely responsible for having published more than four hundred books about Tibetan culture and religion. What an incredible feat! Many of the books issued by the LTWA are distinct pieces of the important puzzle of preservation of Tibetan culture. Where normal monks work diligently for their own release from samsara—and, by extension, that of all other sentient beings—devoted intellectuals like Mr. Tschering worked around the clock to write, edit, translate, design, publish, and distribute books like *Overview of Buddhist Tantra: General Presentation of the Classes of Tantra*, *Captivating the Minds of the Fortunate Ones*, *Lectures on Tibetan Medicine*, and *The Dzogchen Innermost Essence Preliminary Practice*—just to mention a very, very few. I could entirely relate to that focus of manic devotion, and to this day I feel like I can still tap into the inspiration from Mr. Tschering.

One of the most fascinating experiences for me was the interview we did with a monk, approximately seventy years old, by the name of Tenzin Choesang. He was incredibly frail, tiny, polite, and serene, and thanks to an interpreter we learned of his horrendous experiences of imprisonment and torture in Tibet after the Chinese communist invasion. Yet despite all this, he felt no remorse or anger toward the Chinese.

Most of his comments about Tibetan Buddhism in the interview were fairly "run of the mill," but he also spoke quite freely in response to our questions about magic.

However, I could feel there was something going on between us. I got caught in his gaze and stayed there. Suddenly, one part of my mind was listening to what he was saying and what I was then saying; another part of me realized that he was communicating with me *telepathically* at the very same time. He said I was welcome in that space, and I of

Me and the telepathic monk, Dharamshala, 1996
(photo by Max Fredrikson)

course thanked him. *"These things are as natural as anything else,"* he conveyed. I wondered, *"What things?"* and he replied that he was referring to the matters we were asking about in our magico-anthropological quest. I spaced out, perhaps in disbelief that it was happening, and he smiled (also in the other, non-telepathic conversation)—*"But we have to make priorities, even in our acceptance. I am a mere old monk. It's been a hard life, but for me it makes perfect sense. It's transitory; everything vanishes. I accept what you are talking about, but I seek emptiness."* This was not expressed in a (telepathically) accusatory tone at all; it was just a statement of his focus. I thanked him for being so wonderful and honest. *"The Jewel is really there . . ."* he conveyed before he returned to our strictly rational conversation. I assumed he was referring to the *Om Mani Padme Hum* mantra, "The Jewel in the Lotus," and that I should just carry on looking for this jewel within my own Lotus flower of life. That is my own Thelemic interpretation, of course, but I didn't really feel any kind of Buddhist "proselytizing" from him or from anyone within the Tibetan communities we visited.

We spent weeks traveling to different monasteries (for both monks and nuns) that represented the four different sects of Tibetan Buddhism. The Norbulingka Institute was particularly beautiful, with its grand temple, a Japanese garden, and small pools with fish; a true sanctuary amid the lush, junglelike scenery. In the Kalachakra room of the main temple, we could witness monks being trained in logic and Buddhist dialectics in their particular and animated fashion, with lots of laughs, heated energy, and handclapping or slapping.

We also visited the Gyoto Tantric University, which had been established with the support of Japanese donations and was to be officially opened by the Dalai Lama only a few weeks later. These centers for advanced Buddhist studies and practice have become crucial for the survival of Tibetan culture. It was emotionally moving to realize how many people around the world *do* care about the Tibetan diaspora, and how successful the work of the Dalai Lama and his administration has been. The question of whether the Chinese communist aggression and obvious malice have unintentionally *helped* to spread Tibetan culture is a justified one that borders on magical thinking or speculation. We can certainly see within the African diaspora religions how faiths, philosophies, and practices have been spread in a conserved form, but also as new mutations in new territories.

BACK TO ROOTS

Before we returned to Scandinavia, we also traveled to the Menri Monastery in Dolanje (about eighty miles south of Dharamshala), where the Tibetan Bon religion has its main seat. We were warmly welcomed by the abbot (and equivalent of the Dalai Lama within Bon), Sangye Tenzin (aka Menri Trizin aka Lungtok Tenpai Nyima). He had lived and taught in Oslo, Norway, before he was elected Head of the Order in 1969, and he humorously told us about some of his memories and difficulties he had with Norwegian language.

The Menri Monastery was quite different from what we had experienced so far. Although everything basically looks the same at first sight—the Bon monks have a bit of blue in their maroon robes, they chant and drum and play similar instruments, they are Tibetan to the core, they love intricate iconographies, and there is a great degree of philosophical-religious overlap—the Bon are coming from a more visibly preserved line of animism and shamanism.

Their main protector, Thonpa Shenrab, is said to have existed already some 18,000 years ago (while the good old Gautama Buddha lived a mere 2,500 years ago) and settled in the Zhang Zhung region near Mount Kailash, where he began teaching compassion. It's obvious that there has been a certain degree of cross-fertilization here between the two main religions over the millennia. Whereas much of Tibetan Buddhist teaching has been written down (for instance, the founder of the Gelug sect, Tsongkapa, was a prolific author who helped define Vajrayana Buddhism during the fourteenth to fifteenth centuries), the Bon transmissions were for a long time strictly oral and thereby prone to influence and outer development.

We were also invited to stroll around as we pleased. I sat down in what was called the "Protector's Room" together with monks who performed a ritual, drumming and chanting intensely. For me it was like being in any genuine magical temple—an exquisite feeling of refined and pure human culture. I was holding on to my video camera but couldn't keep my "real" eyes from watching the focused monks creating a sorcerous symphony of and for the senses. The dark walls were ornamented with golden and silver details and images, and adorned with thangkas. From the ceiling hung a ritual dagger (*phurpa*), and on the altar there were not only wicks burning in butter-oil lamps, but also strange painted sculptures made of butter as well. My immediate association was to the writings of H. P. Lovecraft and his psychic images of cosmic monsters "best left dormant." There was something very darkly cosmic about the room itself. No wonder: every day monks work here with opening up their minds, alone and together.

We got to watch and listen to a ceremonial chanting session, and it was amazing in its use of frequency. There was also a recurring steady rhythm evoking a shamanic incentive to journey inward, plus the crashing cymbals within this vast ocean of sound. I remember thinking how most of the weird, experimental music I had enjoyed throughout the years was essentially nothing but an intellectual pursuit, like being in a hot tub of frequencies that you could easily get out of, whereas devoted and focused sonorous sensibilities like the Bon and Buddhist ones could drop you into an existential ocean deep and wide, in which you have to learn to swim—inward!—in order to not drown in confusion and fear of your own superficial mirror image.

Some of these ritual Bon parameters are certainly present in regular Buddhist monastic practice, but usually in large congregations and spaces—it feels freer and lighter in many ways. Inside a dark, confined space, it's a different story. You are literally immersed in frequencies you've never heard before and it becomes like an assault on the senses. I let this moment and the space itself be an inspiration for the design of my own temple room in Stockholm: walls painted black, and with golden, silver, red, and blue decorations within a pretty strict Thelemic aesthetic, but with many objects from the big world of magic that added to the genuinely pragmatic "cauldron" I love so much. When everything is said and done, we are all essentially working the same magic. The faster we shed the trappings of dogma, the faster we can understand and focus on our similarities rather than our differences. In these my first romantic roamings of Asia, I was inspired by the Russian mystic, magician, and artist Nicholas Roerich (1874–1947), and specifically by his book *Shambhala* (1930):

> Remembering the conjurations and evocations of the sorcerers of the Malabar coast one could not overlook the very same rites of the Siberian Shamans, the Finnish witches, the clairvoyants of Scotland and the red-skinned sorcerers. Neither the separation of oceans nor continents had affected the essence of the folk conception of the

forces of nature. One recalled the necromancy of Tibet and compared it with the black mass of France and the Satanists of Crete . . .
By counter-opposing the facts, exponents of East and West found
themselves speaking about identical things: The seeming diversities
became only various degrees of human consciousness! These two
conversationalists looked at each other with astonishment—where
was the East and where the West which one was so accustomed
to contrast?*

The abbot suggested we should all come back at some later point and
study. For me, in many ways it was a fantasy of sorts—to potentially
stay at a magical compound like this and study the fascinating original
Tibetan religion and its magic. Who knows, perhaps someday it will
happen? Unfortunately, the amazing Sangye Tenzin died in 2017, but I
am happy and honored to have spent at least some time with him.

Before it was time for us to leave, I was offered to buy a Bon drum
of my own. I hardly had any money left as this was toward the end of
our trip, but I couldn't say no. A monk painted the skins on both sides
of the drum in their traditional green color and left it to dry in the hot
Indian sun. I still have that deeply resounding Bon drum and use it
occasionally in my own rituals.

As we left, Sangye Tenzin blessed us all with holy water and gave
us a little red yarn-cord for our wrists, along with a traditional khata
scarf, just like the one we had been given at the Dalai Lama ceremony
in McLeod Ganj, plus a color image of Thonpa Sherab. Feeling totally
blessed in every possible way, we then made our way home.

In Dharamshala I had a big metal box made and painted by Tibetan
artisans to contain all the books and objects I bought during this mind-
bending trip. Consensus reality then hit me in the head when we arrived
at the New Delhi airport and went to the Aeroflot (cheapest airline)

---

*Roerich, *Shambhala* (Kathmandu: Pilgrims Book House, 1997), 283. As this quote
illustrates, Roehrich was a pioneering magico-anthropologist.

With Abbot Sangye Tenzi at the Bon monastery in Dolanje, 1996
(photo by Max Fredrikson)

counter: my luggage was heavily overweight and the additional fees they wanted far exceeded the amount of money I had left in my wallet. I was in a state of panic. There was no way in hell I was leaving behind all those LTWA and Indian University Press books! I am usually serene and nonconfrontational in my disposition, but facing these Russians, I blew my lid. Although they were totally in the right, I managed to loudly haggle the price down to exactly what I had, plus my Sheaffer fountain pen that was part of my magical pen kit. I'm sure these Aeroflotskis were pleased as they pocketed every Rupee as well as the pen, but so was I. All the books came home with me, safe and sound. Close call!

ANCESTRAL MEDITATIONS

Although this had been a truly fantastic trip in a number of ways, it was great to be back home and at the office. While Max got to work on developing his many rolls of film and printing exquisite images in his darkroom, the rest of us pondered on how to best proceed. One thing was clear: despite the fact that we had just collected such great material, we would need to go to Tibet and also Nepal to talk to more people and document more things and environments.

At the same time I was catapulted into the vortex of Looking Glass Press, doing soul-crushing, grinding advertising work to pay for it all, and keeping the OTO expanding and active. There were now OTO "bodies" of varying sizes all over Sweden; initiations were held regularly, and Gnostic Masses performed. Everyone was riding high after the international gathering in Sweden in the summer of '95, and it was great fun to work with it all. My girlfriend at this time, Soror H, who was also the priestess in our local Mass, was a great help for me, as were the Looking Glass guys, and many other brothers and sisters. The communal aspects really worked for a time and proved to me that things have to move forward at their own pace—as much as I might want to, I can't push everything (or everyone) according to my own ambitious whims. Everything needs to grow organically, preferably slowly, and based on local, individual needs. Although I greatly enjoyed my own career and work as initiator and Priest of the Mass, the things I liked doing the most were always and ever the same: making *Ratatosk* and *Nornia* (the Scandinavian and Swedish OTO newsletters), ensuring that the level of local inspiration was always high, and corresponding with Bill and other order bigwigs. Once a printed-matter-producing networker, always a printed-matter-producing networker!

The occulture of the time was also very inspiring, and I perceived that the overall atmosphere was friendly and supportive. Andrew Chumbley, an innovative magician, author, and publisher (of the Xoanon imprint) involved in exciting developments of the Austin Spare school of magic expressed interest in writing for the fourth issue of *The Fenris Wolf.**

---

*This issue didn't see the light of day until much, much later—and only after I had completely "rebooted" the journal in 2011. Unfortunately, in the meantime Andrew had died in 2004.

He produced some excellent books of fine quality, paving the way for many of the contemporary occult publishers. Before Looking Glass Press, I had only printed books and booklets at the very basic print-shop where I was working, and sometimes the quality wasn't the best. Andrew commented on this from time to time, but things got better as Looking Glass Press used normal, commercial printshops: "Material of such quality must be presented in such a way as to last, thus it may be read and re-read. There are only a few such publications—it is a shame in some ways—but true inspiration can never become a commonplace."*

Kenneth Grant was also on my list for *Fenris* 4, as I had enjoyed his writings and speculations so much over the years. But it didn't work out at the time. Grant wrote me: "Sorry—too busy at present, but wish you every success with your project."† It was symptomatic of the times somehow, for reasons I couldn't figure out. Luckily, I have been blessed with a vast sense of patience!

While visiting the Frankfurt book fair in 1995 and attending to some OTO business as well, I came across the town's prominent statue of Charlemagne, the Germanic Roman Emperor who had died in Aachen in 814. His claim to fame/infamy was his frenzied and not so meek Christianity, which led to a failed conversion event in 782 in Verden at which 4,500 pagans were beheaded. On the whole, however, he was very successful in his pursuits and is generally regarded as a kind of early unifier of Europe. That aspect of his legacy might even be seen as foreshadowing the development of the European Union more than a millennium later.

The reason I mention Charlemagne at this point is that my historian father had recently put together a family tree or pedigree list for me. This had been fairly easy for him to do, as my mother stemmed from a mix of the Swedish noble families Ridderstad and Stackelberg, who both had correct genealogical records that extended far back in

*Andrew D. Chumbley, letter to the author (20 September 1995).
†Kenneth Grant, postcard to the author (10 August 1994).

time—indeed, all the way to Charlemagne. In the mid-1990s, I was too busy to understand all of it, or care, but more recently I have found this very intriguing. And I must have sensed it already in Frankfurt, as I insisted on having my picture taken by the Charlemagne statue. At some point, the concept struck me that perhaps everything I was up to in life was unconsciously making cosmic amends for the horrendous atrocities that this Emperor inflicted on many pagan regions of Europe?

Sometime in 2020 I wrote a text about this "concept" for the Patreon webpage that my wife and I had just set up, and it's relevant here in that it beams us right back to my mind when I was standing there by that statue in 1995:

Transtemporal Recognition

We are all composed of different kinds of memories. We are familiar with the memories we call "our own"—those we accumulate during our temporary lifetime. But let's not forget about DNA, which to an equal degree constitutes an amorphous and malleable part of consciousness that integrates experiences, and then passes these on at the moment of new conception. And then there is the tricky concept of the "soul" or "consciousness" itself, which—if we accept its transcendental and migratory capacities—must surely contain a veritable storehouse of impressions and interpretations from many, many incarnations and their related journeys.

Our own memories are tied in to our life. Either they fizzle out in dementia; foreboding an imminent demise. Or they become compensatory, comforting fodder in extra vivid form; perhaps also foreboding an imminent demise. The fear of dying—and of becoming forgotten—has undoubtedly been history-writing's best friend.

The soul is a mysterious force/sphere, and only very elevated states of mind will allow us to truly connect with it. Transitory states of birth, death, and other major shocks to the system that allow a proximity to these strong experiences can make us see—if but for a brief moment—our holistic connection to all pasts and futures. The relevant question then pops up, specifically in regard to (re)incarnation: "If I have already been someone else, then who am I?" (times X amounts of possible incarnations!)

DNA is slightly more concrete than the soul—yet equally mysterious. It contains two very basic levels of tangibility: one of actual passed-on biological programming, and one of the actual historical pedigree. Both these aspects are embedded in our "heritage"— a memory which is not our own, yet becomes our own with time, whether we want it or not.

This is the sphere of the ancestors, and, as such, it is a vast sphere of potency and potential. In many cultures, the ancestors are venerated and integrated in daily life as well as in specific magical workings. If you are there for them, they will be there for you. It's not some corny concept stemming from an increased contemporary interest in "diasporic," indigenous, or "folk" customs—it is a practice integrated in every culture on the planet—if even on the most minute level of remembering some relative who died during our own lifetime. Actively respecting those who have walked before us helps our own gait become much steadier.

Most people only know their own genetic backstory spanning a couple of generations, but that can be a great start. As can genealogical explorations of historical sources. As can DNA "testing," which is commercially available in many forms today.

A more intriguing form of psychological-magical genealogy is, of course, if you actually have an elaborate family tree. And even more particularly so if this family tree consists of noteworthy, "historical" people.

In the photograph accompanying this text (taken in Frankfurt, Germany, in 1995), I stand before a statue of Karl the Great, or Charlemagne (approx. 742–814). The reason for this is simple: he is an ancestor of mine. A mere forty-one generations ago, he added to the pool of experience that has helped me become who I am today.

If you know a bit of history, you realize that this can be a problematic (yet irrevocable) genetic identification for me. He was a fierce Christian proselytizer/missionary, who helped eradicate European paganism by force and systematic murder. His diligent violence was generously rewarded by Rome. In addition to being king of large parts of Europe via his own ambition and ability, he was also made "Holy Roman Emperor" by the papacy.

The price for his worldly power was incredibly high—for others. At the bloodbath in Verden, Saxony, in 782, Charlemagne allegedly had 4,500 pagans beheaded. The main pagan sacred site in the region, and its "Irminsul" tree/monument, was destroyed. That the people eventually gave in and "converted" to Christianity is not really that surprising.

Thinking about this is sometimes painful and can very well have led me to the paths of magic and paganism, as well as potentially being the very source of my fierce disdain for monotheism in general, and for Christianity in particular (although there are of course other and more "rational" arguments against Christianity too). I wouldn't be surprised.

Am I proud of this kinship? Looking at Charlemagne's track record of an almost incomprehensible brutality, I would say no. Looking at his stature, power, and determination in (re-)shaping Europe and culture, I would say yes. But this ambivalence is, of course, true of all our bloodlines and relatives. We might not love our parents, and yet the river runs deep. They have given you life and form: in part by their own individual design, but in part also with what their ancestors brought to the genetic table.

Having a tangible heritage can undoubtedly be a two-edged sword. I can invoke and commune with Karl the Great when it comes to certain things, but I wouldn't bring up specifically magical requests or ruminations. He is a great energy for big projects and constructions, for massive ambitions and an overall sense of cultivation—sort of "history in the actual making." In that sense of kinship evaluation, I know that I can also effect change on major levels (nonviolently, of course!).

Charlemagne basically gave all his riches away to charity, which is a truly Christian thing to do. But whether that was strategic (in order to avoid inheritance issues, for instance) or perhaps a way to alleviate a genuinely bad conscience for having been such a brutal instigator of wars and superviolence, we will never know (and if I find out, I'll probably keep it to myself). I'm positive he had "issues" as a result of his behavior, and these may still linger on.

History, like magic, is not a compartmentalized "thing" we should deal with only at certain times, when we feel so inclined. We are it, and it is us. History is not necessarily the past. It is to an equal degree the very present, as it's this present that will become fodder for future analyses, deductions, and conclusions. History-writing is only an encapsulation of history proper. History is what's being created in each moment. It is not only stored in written form (or its variations). It is, as mentioned, also concretely embedded in our DNA, and passed on.

Whatever Charlemagne did is not my responsibility. It is, however, a part of my existential foundation that's "irreversible." It is in communion and conversation with these types of ancestors that we can resolve issues that may or may not affect us adversely. It always goes both ways: as much as the ancestors can help us with advice and agency, we can help them achieve a better understanding and perspective of who they are, and what they have done.

BOOK BIRTHINGS & DEVILISH DEMISES

Visiting the massive Chicago book fair in 1996 was as interesting as visiting the one in Frankfurt. I realized what a big industry publishing is—and how small an endeavor Looking Glass Press actually was. I wouldn't say that I was disillusioned, but being in that soulless, corporate environment where books are treated and traded as any kind of commodity made me feel a bit deflated. Luckily, I had input from friends I knew of but hadn't met until then. Adam Parfrey was at the book fair in Chicago with his publishing company Feral House, including my friend Michael Moynihan. A Feral House "hang-around" and friend was native Chicago author Peter Sotos. We had a great time, and these people became my friends for life. All of them were controversial and uncompromising in their respective views and attitudes, and all of them are excellent writers and editors.

There was also Martin Starr of Teitan Press, who lived in Chicago. My Looking Glass partner Jens Näsström and I visited Martin's home and could view his astounding collection of Crowleyana. He had insight into and knowledge of Crowley on par with Bill, and it was inspiring to see that kind of dedication to not only an historical figure but also to the philosophy of Thelema. Martin scanned me well and gave me a copy of Marjorie Worthington's book *The Strange World of Willie Seabrook* (1966), which in turn opened up another rabbit hole dug out by this supreme magico-anthropologist and author, William Seabrook.

Having successfully published LaVey's *Satanic Bible* and Crowley's *Liber AL* in Swedish, plus Rodney Orpheus's *Abrahadabra: A Beginner's Guide to Thelemic Magick*, we needed more fodder at the Looking Glass headquarters. Among other projects, Bill had edited together an anthology of Crowley's writings on drugs, aptly called *Crowley on Drugs*. We paid Timothy Leary to write the foreword to it, and it turned out great (even though he was quite ill at this time):

As I look back on my life I see some parallels with Crowley's, and feel a certain kinship. We both left behind the safety of bourgeois life to seek the cutting edge of conscious reality, and wrote, lectured and propagandized to bring more love, freedom and light into a world that was frequently hateful, repressive and dark. We wanted to wake people up, turn them on, show them they had options and were free to pursue them. We both experienced the full reactionary force of governments, and found ourselves notorious in the press. I take heart in the fact that Crowley's ideas have outlived those of his detractors, and that the Law of Thelema he declared has put down deep roots.*

In our quest for new and great books to publish, I also pulled strings in our already existing network, and talked to British mathematician and author Lionel Snell about anthologizing some of his writing. A prominent Chaos magician and Thelemite, he had been an ongoing inspiration for me since the late 1980s, as well as a kind contributor to *The Fenris Wolf.* Writing under the pen name "Ramsey Dukes," he had published great books like *Sex Secrets of the Black Magicians Exposed* (1979), *Thundersqueak* (1989), and *Blast Your Way to Megabuck$ with My Secret Sex-Power Formula* (1992). These appeared through his own imprint, The Mouse That Spins, and via the TOPY-associated press Revelations 23, as well as Mandrake of Oxford. He had also written a brilliant essay introducing Austin Spare and his system in what has probably been my favorite "technical" book on magic ever: the Sorcerer's Apprentice edition of *The Collected Works of Austin Osman Spare* (1986).

We wrote back and forth but soon realized it would be easier if we shared the same working space. I made arrangements and went over to Gloucester in the UK, where Lionel was living in an old mill cottage. It was lovely to be there and work together with him, and it was no less of an inspiration for me to look through his impressive book collection. The book that we put together would eventually become Ramsey Dukes's *What I Did in My Holidays: Essays on Black Magic, Satanism, Devil Worship, and Other Niceties* (TMTS/Mandrake of Oxford, 1998).

I then traveled on to York where I met up with some old TOPY friends, before heading down to London. There I met the Chaos Magician and Tantric practitioner Phil Hine, whose books had also

---

*Timothy Leary, Foreword to the (as yet) unpublished *Crowley on Drugs*, 1995. Archive of the author.

been a great inspiration for me, on par with those of the IOT's "grand old man," Peter Carroll. Phil provided me with more material from Lionel/Ramsey (as he had been a most active editor at the important UK newsletter *Pagan News*, and had many articles already typed up), and some of his own—I was still working on a fourth issue of *The Fenris Wolf* at the time.

Another nice meeting on this trip was with Geoff Rushton, aka John Balance, and Peter "Sleazy" Christopherson of Coil. I went to their house in Stamford Brook in London and was warmly welcomed. We had been in touch over the years since the early 1990s, and Geoff and I used to send our new records to each other. After a nice dinner at a nearby Thai restaurant, we sat in their cozy study and listened to music (something new by Julian Cope was a favorite, I remember) and just talked about music and friends in common. Before I left, I took some photos of the "Coil Boys." Many years later (in 2016, to be exact) a London friend, Andrew Lahman, who had been part of organizing Sleazy's estate after he died in 2010, sent me a pleasant surprise: scans of two photos Sleazy had taken of me on that same evening, in the room that was so filled with Austin Osman Spare's art that it was actually called the "Spare Room." It was undoubtedly a portal into absolute timelessness.

On October 29, 1997, Anton LaVey died. Peter Gilmore emailed me the sad news, and it hit me hard. I was so pleased that Looking Glass managed to publish the Swedish edition of *The Satanic Bible* in 1996, and that LaVey had been able to see it. In my mind, I had been planning another trip to San Francisco in 1998 or 1999 to reconvene and suggest new projects. But instead, I now looked through my old photos from San Francisco as well as diary entries, and wrote a text that ended up in the memorial issue of *The Black Flame*, and eventually in my book *Reasonances* (excerpted here):

He made an impact. And he made this impact not only by fascinating people with his experience, collections and many, many talents.

No, he made an impact by reading people there and then and, if he felt the person or persons in question deserved it, transmitted chosen tidbits of magical wisdom through anything from stories, anecdotes, jokes or through wonderful musical sessions in his kitchen. Magic moves in subconscious and emotional realms. The Doktor knew this very well and appreciated people who resonated with his own interests in culture. Through an active resonance, he would communicate not with the actual words spoken or the keys played, but rather with the powerful atmosphere he created through them.

He was an advanced magician with his own complicated systems of ritual, and he was also an elitist. He couldn't have cared less if people in general "understood" what he was transmitting. But he cared a whole lot for the fact that the material should be available . . . You never know when a young Satanist awakens to his/her call! And the words of wisdom from the Occult Synthesizer par excellence, the Great Szandor, will always be helpful to those persons who dare see through (and conquer) their own fears, and who can appreciate an obstinate attitude as a magical formula.*

"THE MAN WE WANT TO HANG"

In April of 1998, a unique exhibition of Crowley's paintings was held at the October Gallery in London, organized in association with the OTO. Everyone was very excited, as it was the most elaborate exhibition of Crowley's art, ever. It was impressive to see all those remarkable paintings and objects together, and they certainly created a "force field." A number of the artworks had recently been donated to the OTO by Kenneth Anger, and the great opportunity of having this collection all hanging beautifully in one place—along with many more artworks as

---

*Abrahamsson, "Respect to a Master Magician," in *Reasonances: Essays, Lectures, Interviews 2000–2013* (London: Scarlet Imprint, 2014), 154.

well—wasn't lost on Anger: he filmed them all, and turned it into the fourteen-minute short *The Man We Want To Hang* (2002).

There was the infamous "The Master Therion 666" self-portrait; paintings and drawings of disciples like Norman Mudd and Gerald Yorke, and "Scarlet Women" like Leah Hirsig and Hanni Jaeger; trippy magical vistas like "May Morn" and "The Ship"; and even some landscapes (like one from Portugal's "Boca do Inferno" where Crowley hung out with Fernando Pessoa). I liked the landscapes best; some of them carry an unearthly taint reminiscent of the work of Russian master Nicholas Roerich.

The opening evening was fun, as it was a chance to get together with many friends I hadn't seen in a while, like Bill Breeze, Martin Starr, Kenneth Anger, the Coil boys, as well as many OTO sisters and brothers, plus new acquaintances like David Tibet (from the band Current 93) and Aleister Crowley's granddaughter Rachel.

At some point, I got to pose with Crowley's cast metal wand with Janus-headed serpents along its length and the inscriptions "The Great

With Bill Breeze and Kenneth Anger in London, 1998
(photo by Benedikte Lindström)

Beast 666" and "Do what thou wilt shall be the whole of the Law." It tied in nicely with my experience with the manuscript of *Liber AL* in North Carolina in 1995, making me realize yet again that there is indeed a lot of magic in personalized, talismanic transference. Where the Catholic Church for well over a thousand years has conned its sheeple to worship a seemingly infinite number of snippets from Jesus's foreskin as tangible relics of relevance and power, I at least got a real dose of the Great Beast via the *Gnostic* Catholic Church of the OTO through objects that have *actually* effected change in reality.

During this exciting evening, there were many people who wanted to ask Kenneth Anger endless questions about this and that. Anger quietly asked me to sneak him out and take him back to the apartment where he was staying, which I promptly did. It felt great to still have that trust; after all, it had been some eight years since we last met. And we were right back in that Thelemic headspace: talking mostly of new Crowley books, and specifically the massive *Book Four* that Bill had so excellently edited together.

I also traveled down to Hastings with some fellow OTO people and was initiated into the seventh degree. Thereby I left the degree triad called "The Lovers" and entered "The Hermit," with its unfolding of certain secrets of sex magic that I had already worked with for about a decade, albeit in slightly different ways. However, it was very exciting and satisfying to go through the actual initiation. Sometimes things need to be put into a solid context—and when that happens, time and space and practical considerations often quickly disappear!

Inspired by all this great magical art and to celebrate my initiation, I bought my first Austin Spare painting at the Atlantis Bookshop on Museum Street for £600, with provenance from Coil's John Balance. Many years later, while in the midst of some sort of financial emergency, I was forced to sell it—always something you will regret!

Using this almost incredible vortex of magical energies in London for personal purposes, I also sired a magical child on the full moon of April 11th with my partner Benedikte Lindström at the President Hotel,

Holding Aleister Crowley's wand at the October Gallery
exhibition in London, 1998
(photo by Benedikte Lindström)

room 660 (that was as close as we could get to 666). Incidentally, this date was Anton LaVey's birthday (his very first as deceased) as well as that of my maternal grandfather Ernst.

On the following day, Kenneth Anger gave a talk and showed slides at the October Gallery. He talked about his time at the Abbey of Thelema in Cefalu in 1955, cleaning the walls of whitewash so that Crowley's scandalous murals could be seen yet again, including those in the infamous "Chambre des Cauchemars" (Room of Nightmares). He showed some images from these Cefalù sessions that I had never seen before, and it was like pure pornography for me as an Anger fan, and for many other people as well. He also read from Crowley's own description of the paintings (in which Crowley describes himself not only as magician, big-game hunter, poet, explorer, and painter, but also as "Lord Abbot"):

> Here, cheek by jowl with poetic raptures, stand the most grotesque, terrible and revolting phantasmagoria; the visions which tormented St. Anthony are fixed in a medley of tempestuous images, where insanity and obscenity seem to wrestle against each other for the mastery of the beholder's mind. Despite the natural repugnance which the fear of Reality has created in the average mind, the fascination of these cartoons is irresistible.*

In a wonderfully surreal approach, Crowley comments on the image on a wall above the window in the northwestern corner, called *The Sea-Coast of Tibet: Egyptian Aztecs arriving from Norway*: "You never know in how strange a world you live and what strange things may come to you."

Another high point of this mind-boggling presentation was Kenneth Anger singing aloud Crowley's "Going Dippy" limerick, which was inscribed on the wall of the main room of the Abbey of Thelema:

> There's a lot of ways of going dippy,
> There's lots o' ways to go;
> There's lots of ways of going dippy,
> And they're ways you ought to know.
> Good-bye, Trocadero; good-bye, Maxim's Bar;
> There's lots of ways of going dippy in the
> Chambr' Cauch'mars.

The day continued in a most delightful way. In a rented space at Neal's Yard, the colorful little "secret" street in Covent Garden, the OTO

---

*Crowley, introduction to *Paintings in the Chambre des Cauchemars*, manuscript, photocopy in the author's archive.

celebrated a beautiful Gnostic Mass with more than fifty people attending, including Kenneth Anger himself. To be with him at a Gnostic Mass was almost unbelievable to me. But in many ways, it made sense: as mentioned, quite a few of the exhibited Crowley paintings were in fact his, and he had made them available to the OTO for safekeeping and—as in this case—exhibition.

Thanks to the successful diplomatic work of Bill Breeze, the OTO had become like a magnet for Crowley-related items, editions, and manuscripts. The accession of Anger's holdings was already substantial, as he had started his collecting fairly early on, and with only a few—albeit wealthy—competitors like Jimmy Page of Yardbirds and Led Zeppelin fame. Page had for a long time owned Crowley's house at Boleskine in Scotland, and for a limited time acted as Anger's patron.

After the Gnostic Mass, I took Bill, Anger, and Benedikte to dinner, and it was thoroughly enjoyable—the perfect ending of a deliriously satisfying time in London.

SPOKEN WORDS

I looked forward to seeing Gen again. Although we had been in touch sporadically via email, we hadn't met since California in '93. Thankfully, my old TOPY friend and video artist Fetish 23 arranged the big Stockholm Spoken Word Festival in 1998, with a great many acts, including Gen performing as "Thee Majesty" together with Bachir Attar from Joujouka in Morocco, and Chandra Shukla and Larry Thrasher from the US. Miss Jackie came along too, of course, and this was the first time we met.

There were other people there who would also come to play parts in my life in great ways: Baba Raul Canizares, a Santero from New York; book collector Dieterich Kindermann and his partner Greg Zobel; and my friend Michael Gira of Swans' fame. Gira had stayed at my place in 1996 when he performed solo at Fylkingen in Stockholm, and we have

Genesis Breyer P-Orridge and Dietrich Kindermann, Stockholm, 1998
(photo by Carl Abrahamsson)

been friends ever since. The others were new acquaintances, all orbiting around Gen and Jackie.

Dieterich, who liked to call himself "The Dark Lord" (henceforth "TDL") was an intriguing guy filled with tall tales and an almost unbelievable history. He was a magician *extraordinaire*, like Saulus, and you could feel it as soon as you were in the same room as him. He was born in New Mexico, grew up in Korea, and later devoted his life to magic and Indigenous practices of many kinds: Native American, Daoist-Korean, and Samoan, to mention but a few. I found him fascinating, of course—both TDL and Greg definitely knew what they were talking about.

Benedikte, my partner at the time, was pregnant with our magic baby but still managed to whip up a grand banquet in our apartment for this illustrious crowd of magical people. All of them touched her belly, blessing our future daughter Sofia (when she was born in January of '99, Gen and Jackie became her godmothers, and TDL and Greg her godfathers).

Gen and Jackie's Santeria mentor in New York, Baba Raul, was a very jovial fellow who immediately struck up a deep conversation with TDL that spilled over into actual work they did together. It was as if TDL had a "scanning" operation going on, seeing what needed to be done and with whom he could work. I was also addressed by TDL in this sense, and it felt like a great honor.

Several of us found ourselves together again at the following Stockholm Spoken Word Festival in 1999. TDL and Greg could now meet my daughter Sofia in person. We also had conversations about Crowley in particular, and about how I was apparently better fit to "run the show" (meaning the OTO) than the leadership at the time. This surprised me a bit because it certainly wasn't anything I had brought to the table. I felt very loyal to Bill and admired his remedies and efforts in moving the Order forward. Any problems that I had had to face in the Swedish OTO, Bill would have experienced four-fold at least. TDL saw things differently and thought of me as the real contender for the international leadership and dealing with the Crowley legacy. He brought it up several times over the years, but I didn't inquire too much about what he was actually referring to, or why he cared so much about it.

TDL was clearly a Thelemite who knew his Crowley well, and he had a great collection of rare books and manuscripts. I suspected that he must have had affinities—or at least some early contact—with either the OTO or A.'.A.'. as things started regrowing in the US in the late 1970s. On one occasion TDL sent me a copy of the first edition of Crowley's *Equinox of the Gods* that had belonged to his mother's friend Sybil Leek—the British witch who also befriended Israel Regardie after she had relocated to Los Angeles in the 1970s. Another time, a pleasant gift to me from TDL was a couple of Crowley autographs on loose pages from Crowley's tattered copies of anthologies of Lord Byron's and Shelley's poetry, respectively.

At the Stockholm festival in 1999 TDL also introduced me to Robert Anton Wilson over a delightful dinner. It was fantastic to

With Robert Anton Wilson, Stockholm, 1999
(photo by Dietrich Kindermann)

meet this author and thinker whom I had admired for so long. His *Illuminatus* trilogy (written together with Robert Shea) had been quite influential for me in the early 1990s; I appreciated his psychedelic, satirical, and absurdist approach to fiction and life in general, and I could feel a great affinity with him in his almost pathological drive to comment on culture and society in sardonic and always entertaining ways. The fact that we shared the same birthday was also nice to realize (January 18th: systematic Capricorns close to freaky Aquarius!).

Getting to know Wilson—albeit briefly, as this was our only encounter—was extra inspiring because his entire persona and work was what I was looking for in my own trajectory at the time: not indulging in occult obfuscation but rather happily jumping into a pragmatic, eclectic, and very open-minded approach to writing that encourages self-criticism as much as projected ironies. Wilson could and would write about basically anything and deconstruct it with enlightening bravado, perhaps especially in his wonderful newsletter *Trajectories*:

Virtual Reality hardware and software, however, teaches the same lessons as yoga, Zen and LSD—the brain, guided by a deluge of photons and other energy-blips, creates a Virtual Reality which, in most cases, we believe literally; and, just like yoga and LSD, this new technology forcibly reminds us that any Virtual Reality, including Consensus Reality, contains elements, colors, structures, meanings, etc., put there by our brains. In short, without drugs and yoga, this technology forces us to recognize that, as Nietzsche said, "We are all greater artists than we realize." It casts doubt on all perception, just as yoga and LSD do. And, once perceptions become recognized as a species of gamble, all inferences from perception become recognized as gambles, also; we enter the "detachment from fixed ideas" that both Buddhism and science have always taught.*

At the following festival, in 2000, I was invited to perform a spoken-word piece of my own. For the occasion, I had written a kind of meta-narrative about me as a writer composing a piece for that particular festival, and it worked well—at least in my mind. However, it was in Swedish, so a number of the people I knew who were there and might have been interested (like Peter Sotos, Mark Manning, and Karl Blake) couldn't understand a thing! But I was happy with it, and it did make me visible in a new context—a literary rather than occultural one. However, as always, I invested the text and performance with intention, and most of it did work out. Slightly later, I would come to see this appearance as a kind of preliminary sketch for a lot of what was about to emerge within the new music/spoken-word project Cotton Ferox. This is particularly evident in texts like "Deep in the Night" from our debut album, *First Time Hurts*, released in 2002:

Imagine this isn't about music at all. Imagine it's about perverse voyeurism. The kind where your sex and mind melt and fuse and

---

*Wilson, "Entering Cyberspace," in *Chaos and Beyond: The Best of Trajectories* (San Jose: Permanent Press, 1994), 131.

together briskly shy away from any and all kinds of inhibitions. I can see you through the doors you prefer to keep shut. Or do you, really? I am always there. As you are always there when I choose to look. You are more than aware of the goods you push. You are more than aware of the effect they have. You are more than willing to toy and to tease. To trip-tease my mind. I catch one glimpse, one fragment of a second. This fragment is now carved in eternity, for the uncertain posterity of like minds. Minds of the eyes, minds of the beholders, minds of those . . . oglers. Faked surprise. Faked shame. Faked anger. Genuine lust. Bless the oglers with a glimpse. Bless them with the goods you push. Bless them with your faked surprise. The smaller the peephole, the greater the pleasure. A satisfying logical paradox!

WHAT IS TIME, ANYWAY?

In 1999 my new little family traveled to London for a special occasion: an exhibition of Austin Spare's paintings at Marx House called *Austin Osman Spare: Artist, Occultist, Sensualist*. I had missed the previous one, called *The Divine Draughtsman*, held at the Morley Gallery in 1987. But Gen had given me a copy of that catalog, and it had inspired me a great deal—not only the images but also the accompanying texts by Gen, Lionel Snell, and others. Gen focused his Spare study, aptly called "Time Mirrors," on the question of Time that we so often talked about back and forth:

> His writings are purely decorative. They are entertainment. His relaxation AFTER his real work. His special trick was to convince everybody that his drawings, paintings, images were symbolic. They are in fact his only real work. Like all great sorcerers he hid the real secret in apparently commonplace media. In the key picture he is actually kneeling. It is a photographic image of his prediction of both his own bodily death, and his worship of Mrs Paterson as his

true Goddess. His use of prostitutes and scarlet women of middle age in his sexual magick was to return to his potency with his only access point through Time into Timelessness.*

Back in 1993, Gen had told me of meeting Aleister Crowley in Manchester in 1962, and that he was instructed in sex magic and the mixing of the "elixir of life" by the Great Beast himself, then and there. This would make no sense to any rational mind, as Crowley died in 1947. But if, for but a brief slice of time, you accept the notion of timelessness—stop the clocks, all doors open, no holds barred!—then of course it's possible to meet *anyone* who wants to communicate. I had myself experienced a vision of Crowley at a distance in Spain in 1988, which led to the poem and song "The Result" (the third and final White Stains "93-edition" single), so I had long since accepted phenomena like this. It was perhaps "weird" and made even more so by my interpretation (and Gen's of his), but no less real an experience than my thinking a thought, dreaming a dream, or writing this very sentence. It all boils down to which paradigm you choose to believe in at any given moment. I'm pretty certain that Einstein's theory of relativity was scandalously weird to the more conservative empiricists of his day. Who knows, perhaps today even Einstein's paradigm is "old hat"?

I do believe that art of whatever kind that stimulates these faculties of suspending temporal and spatial belief/disbelief—thereby giving birth to a whole *new* perspective—is extremely beneficial for the psyche. The jolts or shocks of visceral interpretation force us to meet the unexpected or even unwanted head on, so that we may understand ourselves better. In this sense, Gen was correct in describing Spare's art as "time mirrors." The artist is reflected both ways, and the viewer is invited to superimpose whatever emotions or thoughts are evoked in the moment

---

*P-Orridge, "Time Mirrors," in *Austin Osman Spare 1886–1956: The Divine Draughtsman* (London: Beskin, 1987), 13.

too. In the 1999 Austin Spare catalog, John Balance couldn't have agreed more:

> Spare's obsession with the hybrid and grotesque in nature and super-nature, something which takes in the full spectrum of Ovidian metamorphoses, suggests in the artist's mind a vision of the active trafficking of creatures between one world and the Other. All of the Janus-headed, multifaced, theriomorphic swarms which proliferate in Spare's paintings threaten to break out of their world and spill into ours.*

BARDO TIBET

In 1999, it was time again to carry on with the Tibetan project. Max had secured a publishing deal with a Swedish publisher for a photo-book, based on images he had shown them from our trip to India in '96. These were some really great photos, so it was not a surprise in any way. But it was reassuring to know that we now had some extra money in the project and that it would all eventually turn into a lavish book.

I had some major challenges in my life at the time, as I was a father since January of 1999. The prospect of me being away from home for more than two months was not appealing for the mother, nor for me. But it was a phase when outer circumstances pressed to manifest something valuable in the greater scenario, and that's what happened.

The focus this time was not India and the safe havens of McLeod Ganj and other serene places of Tibetan culture in exile. We were going to Tibet proper, with an additional stay in Nepal. This required a larger budget and considerably more planning. Henrik Bogdan was at this time focusing on his academic career at Gothenburg University, so it

---

*Balance, "Tree of Knowledge—Good and Evil," in *Austin Osman Spare: Artist, Occultist, Sensualist* (London Beskin, 1999), 56.

Trilochan in Kathmandhu, 2000
(photo by Carl Abrahamsson)

was up to the fearless trio of myself, Max, and Peder to secure information and more images for the project. Needless to say, we were very
excited about the journey.

We established ourselves in Kathmandu, Nepal's capital, at the
Iceland View hotel. We formulated our plans and strategies, and
made sure to immediately contact Genesis's old friend Trilochan, a
notable figure in Kathmandu and a real Baba/Shaman himself. His
family owned a few restaurants in town, including the Yin Yang and
the Third Eye. These had been around for a long time, and "Trilo"
told us wild anecdotes about the good old days when, for instance, the
Grateful Dead and their "court chemist" Owsley Stanley III arrived
with a bottle of liquid LSD. These were amazing tales from a time
when Kathmandu was on the so-called hippie trail. I later wove some
of the stories into the narrative of my first novel, *Mother, Have A Safe
Trip* (2013).

Trilo took us to see friends and temples, and of course the main
Kathmandu sites, like the Bodhnath stupa, and the Swayambhu

"monkey temple." The entire city is an exotically overwhelming place, and its peaceful mix of Hinduism and Tibeto-Buddhism creates an energy and ambiance of tolerance and open-mindedness I've never really experienced anywhere else.

Trilo also made sure we saw some lesser-known temples, like the Baba Ramesh Giri Maharaj situated in the jungle between Dhulike and Banepa. The Naga and Aghori Baba spirits were flying high as the "chillum" pipes were loaded with ever-present cannabis. Trilo and his friends there (both locals and Westerners) embodied a timeless attitude toward magic and religion, in which you step *into* reality through your rituals (in this case, based in Hindu Naga traditions). It was inspiring to see how natural and integrated ritual is in this culture. Trilo also gladly provided advice for our upcoming trip to Mount Kailash in Tibet, as he had been there twice himself.

Max, Peder, and I followed up on our visit to the Menri Bon monastery in 1996 by visiting the Triten Norbutse Bon monastery just outside central Kathmandu. The abbot, Lupon Tenzin Namdak, was at the time the second-most-important Bon leader/teacher after Sangye Tenzin in India, and he was just as nice to us. We talked about our project, and after hearing about our interest in magic he taught us some basic meditation techniques and the "transmission for preliminary practices," which was basically a single-point meditation (focusing on a letter or a symbol throughout the day—and beyond). We agreed to come back after our Tibetan trip and possibly record the beautiful singing/chanting of the monks at the impressive Triten Norbutse monastery.

After we had secured a travel agent who seemed reliable, we packed up our things and flew to Lhasa, the capital of Tibet. Our arrival there went much more smoothly than we expected. We assumed that the border police would take an unwelcome interest in all of Max's photographic equipment, but they didn't, and we just looked at each other with serene smiles while on the two-hour bus ride into Lhasa proper. Like Sven Hedin, Alexandra David-Neel, Heinrich Harrer, and many others before us who had written about their experiences and thereby indirectly led us there—we were now in Tibet!

It is strange how certain places radiate an aura of being untouchable, unreachable, or simply too exotic. For me, Tibet had always been one of these places. But when I was on the plane and looked down on Mount Everest, it was like an actual fulfillment of a dreamy wish of sorts. In part it had to do with practical, material considerations, of the crassest sort: you could easily fly out from Nepal to Tibet *if you just had the money*. Let's never forget that money is magical and can produce miracles! But it also had to do with what I realized was my own psychic accumulation of exotic desire over the decades: from *Tintin in Tibet*; to mountaineering-themed Rolex ads in *National Geographic* (and picture stories too, of course); to reading Hedin, Harrer, and David-Neel; and even Werner Herzog's Reinhold Messner documentary, *The Dark Glow of the Mountains*, which I love so much (although it doesn't take place in Tibet, Messner has certainly roamed the Himalayas). Descending toward Tibet proper while gazing down on Mount Everest made me feel if not like a god, then at least quite godlike: a force that can manifest whatever exotic, romantic desires there may be!

We didn't arrive in a state of wide-eyed naivete, however. We knew about the Chinese monitoring everyone, including tourists, so we treaded gently within our project. During our visits to monasteries around Lhasa, we never inquired about anything that went beyond the expected tourist questions as we didn't want to put any of the real monks in jeopardy or danger. At this time, all of Lhasa was basically like a Chinese theme park of Tibetan Buddhism, a way of milking tourist dollars while exploiting the real Tibetan population in much harsher and more violent ways.

Despite all the sadness, it was amazing to see and experience the resilience of the Tibetans active in the city. The Johkang temple, open and active since the seventh century, still attracted hundreds of Tibetans every day—a shrine perhaps even holier than the Potala Palace where the Dalai Lama has traditionally lived since it was built in the mid-seventeenth century. Outside the Johkang, monks, nuns, lamas, and common people prostrated, lit candles and incense, and recited their "*Om mani padme hums*" either alone or together.

We had the good fortune to be there on a day when all the floors and temple rooms were open to the public. Hundreds of Tibetans and tourists drifted in and out, up and down, and integrated the millennia-old serenity and power that they hoped would charge them somehow to be able to better deal with life in different ways. It really impressed me because it wasn't like, for example, a Catholic Church, where the devotees come in depressed and concerned but remain passive-submissive, and then pray for change and perhaps light a candle. The Tibetans at Johkang carried a healthier and more actively asserting attitude: good karma for them (or for anyone else) isn't benevolently bestowed by some exterior force or god—it is something you earn by your own good deeds and merits. And you can focus that through ritual and symbolic means (prostration, spinning prayer wheels, mantric work, meditation work, candles, etc.) while formulating this outer "good-deed work." It's a daily process of formulation and development, and as such is highly magical in that it constantly challenges the status quo of the individual's inner inertia or complacency.

I drifted throughout the building, respectfully watching these proud Tibetans. In the dark and almost gloomy spaces, old ladies with wrinkled faces passed me by carrying butter candles, as did mothers with pearly white teeth, heavy jewelry, and laughing children in tow; men of all ages mumbling their mantras; monks, nuns, and pilgrims moving in circles throughout the building and thereby creating individual vortices that together became one communal vortex.

Nothing that I had ever seen or felt performed within the sphere of the Golden Dawn or OTO could compare with this. Most of my Western ceremonial-magic pursuits had been merely intellectual shenanigans that would occasionally cause a dramatic shudder within the temple space. But in Johkang it was an encompassing sense of *magic in praxis*, as it had been performed for more than a thousand years in this exact place—brooding darkness and joyful multicolored light conjoined in ecstasy within a culture that celebrates and actively uses the power of the mind. We left Johkang exhilarated but also exhausted. And we received many answers that day without asking a single question.

You can't really escape the Potala Palace when you're in Lhasa. Looking up, you're in awe not only of architectural ingenuity and skill, but also of history: until 1959 it was—and really still is—a building symbolizing an entire culture, and the Communist invasion has in many unfortunate ways only strengthened this symbolic power.

Once inside, you're confronted with not only a massive amount of Buddha statues but also of Chinese guards and spies. You're welcome to spend your money but not really to inquire about anything. So, we wandered through it all, impressed but sad. I could see and feel how the fourteenth Dalai Lama, whom I had shaken hands with only some years previously in India, had once drifted through these rooms as a happy and curious boy and youth, weighed down by immense responsibilities, yet willing to assume these with the sense of duty of any Buddhist monk eager to work for the benefit of all other sentient beings. I strongly believe that spaces can retain energies, and I'm also sure most Tibetans who visit the Potala can feel—and perhaps even project—the Dalai Lama within his rightful quarters.

There were many places to visit and experience in the Lhasa region, and we tried to make the most of it. Monasteries and temples like Radu, Tashigang, Ganden, and Nechung were now attracting tourists but there was still real monastic work being done there—despite the presence of spies galore.

There was begging in most places or just outside the monasteries to a greater degree than what "should" be there (that is, how it was before the Chinese communist takeover). This had led to a funny phrase or faux-mantra that a monk mentioned to us when commenting about these things: "*Om* money *padme hum*." In Ganden we saw a "monk" giving a solo show of kung fu in the courtyard, dressed in a "Titanic" jacket (the film, not the ship), while the real ones hurried past and went on about their chores. Ganden had allegedly been founded by Tsongkapa himself and had at one point housed seven thousand monks and memorial stupas for the second, third, and fourth Dalai Lamas.

At Ganden, we noticed a funny sign on a door, "Please don't come in woman this chapel," and asked about it. It was an innocent-enough question for our guide, who replied that some monks from the Gelug sect had been seduced by women belonging to the Sakya sect, and now there were statues of these monks in this special chamber. It wasn't clear whether they had succumbed to the seduction and were memorialized for that as warning examples, or whether they had been resilient against the female attempts at moral corruption and were honored for their self-discipline.

Speaking of the Sakya sect, the Tashigang monastery and temple were exquisite in their Tantric focus, specifically, the Hevajra Tantra. The focus here lies on the Indian Tantric Padmasambava as the principal teacher of Buddhism: "Guru Rinpoche." The monks gladly told us of the symbolism in the extremely beautiful and intricate images on the walls—either as murals or thangkas. Hevajra, in union with a consort, takes the bad karma and dirt of people and animals and filters it all with the help of higher Buddhas. In the right hand is the human skullcap containing people and animals, and in the left hand are the Buddhas. They also give birth to eight *dakinis*,* depicted in detail with exposed vaginas and red labia.

These detailed paintings were in silver on a black background, as we had also seen in the protector's chamber in Menri, for instance. It had made a strong impression on me in India, and after that trip I turned one of the rooms in my apartment into a full-on ritual chamber, with black walls and silver, gold, red, and blue illustrations of relevance. Although

---

*A dakini is a female energy that in some cultures has demonic status, being seen, for example, as a cannibalistic force. In Tibeto-Buddhist culture, the dakini can refer both to an angry-looking female embodiment of illumination and to a "real" woman with knowledge and insight. Thus, the dakini is helpful as a partner to the person on their way to enlightenment.

this may sound "Satanic" to some—and I had certainly enjoyed being in the Church of Satan's very black temple space in 1991—it took a greater aesthetic cue from having been exposed to both vision and sound in that Bon chamber in India.

The Nechung monastery was also imbued with Padmasambava's legacy of psychosexual force, and filled with tantric iconography: images of skulls, snakes, sexual intercourse, Padmasambava himself, and the oracle in union with dakinis. These could be either wrathful or benevolent, depending on the working in question.

The older (seventh-century) Meru temple close to the Johkang also had concrete sex scenes in its images, complete with many a dakini and exposed hard-ons. This sexual pragmatism and its amazing iconography was a bit of a mind-blower for me. I saw myself as having traveled a path of intuitive orientation parallel to that of a mainly intellectual accumulation of initiations—some of these being of a sexual nature. It was extremely rewarding to spontaneously contextualize my own experiences "head on" within this much more advanced and refined magical culture and its visual-symbolic storytelling capacities.

Before we left Lhasa for good, we returned to the Johkang temple. We had each bought a traditional loose-leaf Tibetan edition of *The Book of the Dead*, and we had gotten to know a Nyingma lama who would bless our copies for us. This he did by reciting from the book and making some hand gestures or "mudras." The very act as well as the copies filled us with courage now that we were about to embark on a new and ambitious pilgrimage.

THE HOLY MOUNTAIN

We had rented a beat-up Toyota Landcruiser for ourselves and a truck for gasoline and food. We weren't allowed to travel freely, so we had arranged with a tour company to bring an official guide and two drivers. These were all Tibetans, but they were careful not to criticize their

Communist overlords, and we certainly respected that. We were just very happy that all of this was happening and that we were about to head out on a genuinely magical journey.

Before we drove out west toward Lake Manasarovar and Mount Kailash, we visited some important places, like Gyantse, Shigatse, and Lhatse. Gyantse was especially depressing as it seemed the Chinese had made sure to surround whatever genuine houses and temples remained there with very ugly modern buildings. But the central building, the Kumbum monument, originally built in 1497, still radiated power in all directions, and supposedly contains 100,000 Buddhas.

We then visited the Tashi Lumpo monastery complex in Shigatze, Tibet's second-largest city. It used to be the seat of the Panchen Lama, the religious leader/teacher/office that the Chinese conveniently had claimed to find the new incarnation for in 1995, after having in fact kidnapped the boy (born 1989) who was recognized as the genuine reincarnation by the Dalai Lama and others (like the Nechung oracle/medium we had met in India in 1996). This was still a political hot potato when we were there, and we never encountered a single monk on our visit to the monastery! Our official guide claimed "he didn't know" what was happening—or not happening—in this debacle at the time. To this day, the legitimate Panchen Lama is imprisoned in China.

We also visited the Yung Drungling Bon monastery in Namling, by the Tsangpo river. This is the original 1834 monastery that served as the model for the Menri one we visited in India. The monastery had been renovated in the early 1980s and was in good shape. Its richly iconographic murals included pentagrams and hexagrams, and Tibetan writing that resembled the "Enochian" alphabet I had become acquainted with in my Golden Dawn studies (and which stemmed from the skrying experiences of John Dee and Edward Kelly in the sixteenth century). For me, it brought to mind the Jungian ideas about a "collective unconscious" that would allow for similarities in symbology, aesthetics, and iconography (and perhaps even languages/alphabets) in different parts of the world.

The vistas of the Tibetan countryside seemed endless. Flanked by mountain ranges, fertile valleys, and clouds that touched the horizon, the dusty road west lingered ever onward. Only rarely did one pass by other trucks, wild horses, or people. When the Tibetans saw that we weren't Chinese, they greeted us with waves and smiles. Once in a while, our guide had prepared stops for us with Tibetan families along the route. No gas stations here, but cozy stops in stone houses, with butter tea (or black tea for those not so daring), an occasional Coca-Cola, and Chinese candy. Our own staples that we had brought consisted of instant noodles and Chinese army energy bars. After those three weeks on the road in Tibet, it took me many years before I could eat instant noodles again.

The farther westward we drove, the less comforts we experienced. No more guest houses. We had rented a tent and sleeping bags, and now was the time to start using them. It was diabolical. Usually, the days were hot and sunny, but the nights turned out to be abysmal. On the first night that we camped out (all three of us in the tent—the Tibetan guide and drivers were happy to stay in the cars), there was frost on the sleeping bags. I had to get out in the middle of the night to jog around to keep warm, gradually noticing weird apparitions in the darkness that turned out to be yaks—friendly yaks, I was happy to discover!

We arrived at Lake Manasarovar (the "Lake of the Mind" in Sanskrit) at sunset one evening, and it was yet another larger-than-life experience. This lake is symbolically regarded as a cosmic "yoni" and in its vicinity protrudes the mighty Mount Kailash, the "lingam of all lingams." Sven Hedin had been out on that lake in a rowboat in 1906, measuring its depth with a plumb line. And now we were here too, ninety-three years later, gazing out at its sulphurous majesty, nestled between mountain ranges and emitting an almost unearthly yellowish-greenish glow. As evening came, the sky lit up. At this elevation (15,000 feet), the night sky is as bright as it is dark. I have never seen so many stars with my eyes since, and it certainly triggered many thoughts and fantasies about how space is not a dark void, but rather an infinite and intelligent container and force field that allows its various distinct and very bright energies their own allotted space so that they can be what they are in the best possible ways—a Thelemic interpretation, for sure!* This is not really surprising, since we were staring straight into the face of the sky goddess Nuit. And yes, there was also a full moon. Everything was coming together so wonderfully without us controlling or planning too much. I viewed everything we experienced as incredible gifts or blessings, showing us that we were on the right track.

On the next morning, I went down to the lake and hacked a hole in the ice. In the cold water, I consecrated four pieces of jewelry that I had bought in Lhasa, as talismans for health, wealth, initiation, insight, and illumination. I then wrapped them in a white khata that I had received when we had our copies of the *Tibetan Book of the Dead* blessed at Johkang.

We then traveled on to nearby Darchen, which is where the *kora* (circular pilgrimage, "devout route") for Kailash traditionally begins. It was filled with dirt and garbage, but at least this was contained in one place. Considering how many people come to this most sacred of all sacred mountains, it certainly could have been worse—like Mount Everest and other climbers' dream peaks, which are nowadays basically garbage piles and impromptu cemeteries for hubristic "adventurers."

And so it began. We set off while our drivers and guide waited in Darchen. The kora was calling us. Kailash was calling us. For some reason, we decided not to rent yaks to carry our backpacks and tent. We soon regretted that mistake. In the thin air it felt like everything became much heavier than usual, and the path seemed to go up, up, up all the time. We marched on but had to take breaks every ten to fifteen minutes in the beginning, being continually passed by Tibetan families and individuals who just stormed along, greeting us and smiling (probably laughing too!). For the Tibetans it normally took one full

---

*One of Crowley's most famous slogans is "Every man and woman is a star," signifying that there is an orbit and place for each and everyone in the greater scheme of things.

day to walk around the mountain. For us, it took three. But despite the hardship we were overjoyed to be there. The Tibetan energy inspired us to push ever forward.

The nights were cold, we were exhausted, and we couldn't really cook. We managed to "half cook" our noodles but the results were disgusting and they soon froze. The Chinese army energy bars seemingly had no energy in them anymore (had they ever?). It was like munching on hard blocks of flour that just made you even more thirsty.

On the first night, as I stepped out of the tent to pee beneath the vast bright darkness of the starry sky, I broke down. I walked around in confused circles and cried, although I made sure not to lose sight of the tent in the distance. It was a great relief and extremely healthy for me, being an uptight intellectual with severe sublimation and repression issues. The emotional floodgates were wide open, and I couldn't process *anything* intellectually with thoughts like *I am crying because of this issue or that issue*. I was simply *there*, in *that moment*, and a cliché like "The only time is now" made such perfect sense that I have since valued it as a quintessential magical wisdom. I remember that one of the triggers for my emotional outburst was the frustrated question: *What am I doing here?* However many rational answers there might be to that question, these were now completely irrelevant to me. This had to do with much deeper existential perspectives that utterly overwhelmed me, and so I cried.

After the kora I realized that to some degree I had again connected with the spirit or psyche of British author and traveler Bruce Chatwin (1940–1989), whose last book was called *What Am I Doing Here* (note the absence of a question mark). Chatwin had died on my twenty-third birthday, in 1989—the very day and year in which I was "formatted" to magically bloom. I always look at that specific date as a kind of rebirth for me. Although I was safe and snug in my warm bed in Stockholm that night, I remember having had several chills and also experiencing extra-vivid dreams. When I later discovered that Chatwin had died on that same date, I associated his passing with my experiences that night, suggestively based on my already existing deep resonance with him as a pathological traveler and *raconteur extraordinaire.*

Eventually, we managed to get to the top of the magical world: the Dolma-la pass of Kailash, at a staggering 18,471 feet, the midpoint (and highest point) of the holiest pilgrimage for Buddhists, Bon-adherents, and Hindus alike.* Filled with long lines of prayer flags, spontaneous stupas, and personal items left behind, it looks like a multicolored spider's web in which you are the spider and prey at the same time.

I brought out my talismans again and blessed them here at this absolute pinnacle of devotion, and hung up prayer flags with Max and Peder. One of the items was specifically for my father who was in poor health at the time, and synchronistically this date was his sixtieth birthday. I sent him strengthening thoughts and feelings, projecting as much of it as possible into the Tibetan necklace I had bought for him. Now both Manasarovar and Kailash were in there. If that wouldn't make him feel better, I didn't know what in the world would.

Looking out at each other and around us, we could hardly speak. This was not due to the lack of oxygen, but because we were in such awe of the mountain and of the devotion in which we were now active participants. Max took occasional photos, as did I. We sat down, got up, walked a little bit, smiled at each other, sat down again. It was serene and overwhelming. I realized that this is perhaps how religious people feel, and if so, I would be happily religious too: worshiping nature in general and mountains in particular.

To me it was a proverbial "no-brainer" that this mountain had been the focus of worship for Buddhists, Bonpos, and Hindus alike for thousands of years. The mountain's majesty, serenity, protrusion, longevity, strength, beauty, and so on are all contributing components in themselves, as is the active pilgrimage and devotion of millions of people. From a magico-anthropological perspective, it seems apparent that humans inherently need tangible symbols upon which to focus their

---

*The base, Darchen, is at 14,960 feet.

desire for transcendence, and these natural objects are in many ways the healthiest ones as they are real and concrete in themselves. By contrast, humanly constructed symbols are inferior for the fulfillment of this need—the more intellectual and abstracted the process, the more coveted and curiously complex the primal transcendence.

When we felt we had been filled to the brim with this majesty, we walked and walked and walked, ever downhill this time, until we came back to Darchen. As with any exhaustive physical labor, the endorphins released give you a much-desired high and relaxation. We basically sat on the ground laughing hysterically, chugging fresh water, and feeling completely reanimated. We also had a primitive but real meal of canned tuna and white rice that was topped only slightly later when we visited the Tadapuri Hot Spring. There, we were offered candy, coffee, and soft drinks, along with a hot-water bath from the sulphurous spring. Too much pleasure all at once! Incidentally, this spring is supposedly where Guru Padmasambava rested on his way to Mount Kailash in the eighth century.

I anticipated a long, good night of solid sleep, but that didn't happen. I thought that I could literally hear the stars above, as they were so close to the plateau where we were. Again, that night sky was as bright as it was dark. It's hard to believe there are *that many stars out there* when all you're used to seeing with your own eyes at home is the Big Dipper and a few other major constellations. I was exposed to an infinite number of visible stars, beaming their energy right down into my mind. I felt so energized from Kailash and from the stars themselves that I just lay awake and enjoyed the buzz—I had no other choice.

I gradually relaxed and then experienced a kind of hyper-version of hypnagogic and hypnopompic states (I was drifting in and out of sleep), in which images, words, and sounds floated into and out of one another. There was teaching there too: detailed sex magical instruction for both constructive and destructive purposes, only some of which I was aware of before this experience. I also had a flash or "internal message" that I should make a documentary film about Kenneth Anger. In hindsight, this is interesting and bizarre. The sex-magical teaching was integrated right away, as I wrote it down in my diary the following day, and kept it in my consciousness. I made a note about the Anger idea too, but then apparently forgot about it. But not indefinitely, it seems, because between 2014 and 2019, I *did* make that documentary.* I guess it's true, as it's been pointed out so many times before, both astrologically and in Hollywood: "It's all in the stars!"

While still immersed in the Kailash-Manasarovar dynamic, I wrote the following text, which has had continued relevance for me in the decades since:

> When you're inside the center of yourself, everything rearranges itself according to your specific center: meditation, focus, clarity, sharp mellowness, adamant compassion . . . In times of chaos and seemingly contradicting opportunities, freeze the frame and relax. Everything good comes to those that wait. That goes for body, speech, and mind, as well for external developments. Writing controls reality. But I need to first control my writing—and my mind.

After our adventures in western Tibet, we drove back toward Lhasa, but only about halfway. Instead of returning there, we headed southward, and could soon see the magnificent snowy peaks, mountain passes, and serpentine roads gradually being exchanged for more and more trees and greenery. That increase of oxygen in the air was a real high for us all, and a much needed one. As soon as we had said goodbye to our guide and drivers, we crossed the Nepalese border at Kodari and enjoyed the greenery and completely different atmosphere of Nepal again. Seeing wild cannabis grow by the roadsides was in many ways symbolic of the difference between the Chinese and Nepalese attitudes toward life.

We had had no problems at all in Tibet except for acknowledging a

---

Cinemagician: Conversations with Kenneth Anger, directed by Carl Abrahamsson (Trapart Film, 2019).

general paranoia and the necessity of being cautious. We could not ask questions to the people we met about their views on magic. It would have put them at an unnecessary risk, as we were clearly being monitored when we were at these sacred sites and buildings. How delightful, then, to be back in Nepal, where magic is an absolute reality, and it reflects in basically every aspect of daily life!

Kathmandu felt like a paradise where all pleasures were possible. We had sushi and imported beer almost every day and celebrated Hindu Diwali (New Year) with firecrackers and fireworks together with the entire city before it was time to leave. The last substantial stop was a visit to the Dakshinkali Temple, the ancient sacrificial site just outside Kathmandu where families and individuals bring animals like goats and roosters to be ritually sacrificed to the goddess Kali. It was fascinating to see that the place gave the impression of a site for sunny family outings at which you not only procured karmic and cosmic favors and bonus points, but also meat for the family evening meal! There was certainly blood flowing and splashing, but through a most serene, benevolent, and life-enhancing aspect of the dark goddess Kali's multifaceted psyche.

PART IV
2000–2004

"ALL YOU HAVE TO DO IS GO TO KATHMANDU"

In the autumn of 2000, I took Benedikte and our daughter Sofia to Nepal. It was a promise of sorts because I had left them alone for two months the previous year. Gen and Jackie joined us from New York, as did Jackie's old friend Eddie O'Dowd, the drummer for the glam-rock band The Toilet Boys (and later for PTV3*). It was wonderful to meet up again, and to reconnect with beautiful and wise Trilochan. Not only did we venture out in a spiritual-magical tourism overdrive, but we also recorded some very substantial sessions for our interview-book project.[†] I was also very happy that Sofia could be in Nepal at such an early age, and be blessed by more magical people and sacred energies.

We roamed through the streets of Kathmandu, checking out the timeless hippie-havens of "Freak Street" and Durbar Square, Swayambu, and Pashupatinath, and soaking up the friendly atmosphere. Gen had a motto or saying at the time: "The Universe is Kind." It certainly felt like a genuine cosmic truth as we enjoyed this very special place, with everyone so happy and inspired by a truly magical culture. Thanks to Trilochan we could also trek in the jungles and mountains outside of the capital, where he had built a nice retreat. We drove there in a red Volkswagen bus that had once belonged to the Nepalese Royal Court. Little Sofia was then carried in a basket on a Nepali friend's back, while the rest of us marveled at how quickly diligent leeches managed to burrow into our trekking boots unless we kept moving! The scenery was majestic: protective mountains and jungles, lush and vibrant with life radiating from sanctuaries hidden from space as well as time, as well as roadside temples adorned with flowers and painted Shiva lingams galore. This veritable Shangri-La paradise allowed us to partake of a

---

*This was the final configuration of Psychic TV.
†The book of interviews was eventually published in 2020 as *Sacred Intent: Genesis Breyer P-Orridge, Conversations with Carl Abrahamsson 1986–2019*.

pure and pristine natural beauty with occasional reminders of tradition and art in the service of the Mind (and vice versa).

We visited the sacrificial Dakshinkali site again and asked a Hindu boy to leave flowers from us for Kali (non-Hindus are not usually allowed to do that directly, but it is permissible via a proxy). The whole time we were blessed by priests and babas selling us trinkets from their perpetual pilgrimages through mountains, forests, jungles, solitary pursuits, and Kumbh Mela festivals, being most often constantly stoned from a religious immersion in various forms of cannabis.

Close to Dakshinkali, in Pharping, there is a Tibetan Nyingma monastery, which was built close by a cave (Asura) where Padmasambava had rested once upon a mythical time and reached enlightenment. We all entered the cave and left offerings and flowers. I took some photos of Gen and Jackie at the opening as it was such a great setting. My small yet amazing Yashica T5 camera utilized a focus point inside the cave instead of on their faces, so that they eventually became a little bit blurred in the actual photo. It reminded me how transient and blurry we are as human beings compared to the monuments and art we (and others) leave behind. We are often at the mercy of technology and other people's good will to interpret us at any given moment; yet how we define ourselves in tangible form will override these fractions if they are also invested with Self, Soul, and Intent.

By this cave I was also reminded of the greatness of the yogi and magician Padmasambava. I had come across many references in India but mainly in Tibet only a year before us visiting the Asura cave. In many ways I regarded people like him and the Bon originator Thonpa Shenrab as important pioneers in the tradition of sexual magic that both myself and Genesis were "formatted" and steeped in. There are many tales in the history of Padmasambava indicating this, perhaps the most notable one being the initiation of his consort Mandarava:

Padma took her to a cave in Avalokiteshvara's heaven, and for three months and seven days made prayer and offerings to the Buddha of

Long Life.* Then Amitāyus appeared, placed the urn of boundless
life on the heads of Padma and Mandāravā, gave them to drink of
the nectar of immortality, initiated them, and conferred upon them
immunity from death and birth until the end of the *kalpa*. Padma
was transformed into Hayagrīva and Mandāravā into Vajra-Vārāhī.
Both possessed the *siddhi* of transformation into a rainbow and of
invisibility.†

Gen and I talked about these mysteries, mainly by the Pashupinath
Temple compound. That was the source of the ashes that Gen blessed
me with in California in 1993. We had looked forward to going there
together for a long time. It is Kathmandu's oldest remaining Hindu
sanctuary (stemming from the fifth century) and houses a shrine so
holy that only Hindus are allowed to see it, and only four designated
priests are allowed to touch it. The "deity" as it's referred to, or "idol,"
consists of a three-foot-high stone lingam based in a silver yoni, which
is bound by a silver serpent. The lingam has four faces protruding from
it, as well as four sets of hands carrying one mala (necklace) and one
little *kamandal* pot.

    While in Nepal, Gen had a book of poems printed, *S/HE IS
HER/E—Poems for Thee Majesty*, through his own "Next New Way On"
Press. It was well overdue. This was something I had long been pushing
for: a book of Gen's writings—whether poems, essays, or fiction—as these
were constantly brewing but only rarely "saw the light of print." I had also
brought Gen a notebook and a nice pen as a gift for this trip, as I'd done
before with Cris Monnastre, Bill Breeze, and others. That magic seemed
to work nicely for Gen as a kind of "talismanic midwifery."

---

*[That is, Amitāyus ("The One of Boundless Life"), the Buddha invoked for the obtain-
ing of longevity, especially in the celebration of the Tibetan eucharist. He is represented
as holding on his lap a vase of life-giving ambrosia, the nectar of the immortals.]—
footnote to the original text.
†W. Y. Evans-Wentz, ed., *The Tibetan Book of the Great Liberation, Or The Method
of Realizing Nirvana through Knowing the Mind* (Oxford: Oxford University Press,
1968), 150.

The Next New Way On was the "umbrella" for Gen's work at the time: an overarching name that encompassed various projects. It was also a pun in reference to the "New Aeon" (of Horus) that Crowley had supposedly ushered in with his *Book of the Law*—now it was apparently time for the "next new aeon."* There was even a website of that name for a while that mostly consisted of Gen's own history and art, along with that of a few others. I had a photographic exhibition on the site, mainly consisting of images from my Asian trips.

The *S/HE IS HER/E* book was handmade by Nepali book-makers and distinctly evokes the handmade volumes of poetry of expat hippies and counterculture icons like Angus MacLise and others with Tibeto-Buddhist and Hindu leanings who spent time in the region and culture in the 1960s and 1970s. Many of Gen's poems from the book ended up on the album that we would make together in 2002, *Wordship* (more on this later), and are wonderful allegories and philosophical "sprinklings of stardust." One of my favorites is the one that Gen explained was about "Imaginary Time" (I.T.):

> First I.T. is . . .
> Then I.T. knew
> I.T. was . . .
> And that
> Was I.T. . . .†

Another gem is the one titled "Match":

> Peace
> Is when

---

*In fact, this aeonic shift had already been suggested and elaborated upon by occultists Nema and Kenneth Grant in their acknowledgment of the "aeon of Maat"—as well as by Crowley's "magical son," Frater Achad (Charles Stansfeld Jones, 1886–1950).

†P-Orridge, untitled poem, *S/HE IS HER/E, Poems for Thee Majesty* (Kathmandu: New Way On, 2000), 26.

Our Inside

And

Outside

Are

Exactly

The Same*

Gen loved to adorn correspondence and special products like this by hand—undoubtedly a habit from his hypercreative mail-art days in the 1970s. On the copy I received there is a lot of handwriting—usually in Gen's own unique calligraphic style that had been developed during the C.O.U.M. days—and rubber-stamp inking of phrases and symbols in various places throughout the book. The inscription reads: "For my friend and ally Calle who has been here All Ways Know Matter What. so blessed are we. And I.T. is all a matter of original T.I.M.E."

Gen looked at me mischievously while rubber-stamping, pointing to a particular page: "You know this one is special and requires this," he said. He stamped "Conscious Self Conscious—Self Conquers Self" in red as well as Crowley's great "666" seal in blue. The latter is a personal "logo-mark" of Crowley's that features a schematic penis with testicles directed at the viewer on top of a seven-pointed star (symbolizing the Shakti aspect of "Babalon"), and the number 666. It was very appropriate for the poem in question:

Wisdom

Is

Very

Sexy

If you are

Thoughtful

And

---

*P-Orridge, "Match," *S/HE IS HER/E*, 31.

Full of Thought
And then you add
A Dash of
Dashing
And a Dashing
Dash
Of Kindness
Now . . .
That's
Sexy!*

It was during this time together in Nepal that Gen and I consciously decided to embark on our joint book project of conversations. We had already done a few and thought it would be great to gather up our conversations from different parts of the world, and to let it develop organically over time. The Nepali sessions were very substantial and inspiring to me, and it felt like a big leap forward not to rush this book, but let it bloom slowly—definitely a "new way on"!

On this trip, I also carried with me a few copies of the newly published coffee-table book *Bardo Tibet*, which was the first real manifestation from the Institute of Comparative Magico-anthropology. Max had been swift and efficient after our return from Tibet and Nepal in '99, printing photos like crazy and working on the layout of the book. It was with immense pleasure and pride I handed a copy of the book to Namdak at the Triten Norbutse Monastery.

I found it suitable that we should dedicate the book to Sven Hedin, the famous Swedish explorer who was basically the first real mapmaker of Tibet. To celebrate our success, I had bought an ink drawing by Hedin portraying a very dark and dramatic Tibetan mountain range. His spirit had been very present in our journeys to the East, and today I still gaze upon that drawing in our dining room—for me, it is a

---

*P-Orridge, untitled poem, *S/HE IS HER/E*, 33.

perpetually inspiring illustration of the trans-temporal and trans-spatial qualities of genuinely great art.

Hidden under the speculatively occult umbrella of this Next New Way On, Gen and I also talked about the mysterious fourth chapter of *The Book of the Law*, called "The Well of the Well Begotten." According to Gen, it was filled with references to hermaphroditism and twins as magical metaphors of distinct relevance to the current phase of human evolution that we are collectively going through. Transcendences of these sorts of established biological dualities could help to mutate if not biology on an overall level, then at least the human mind and its tendency to accept givens rather than challenge them. This sounded like pure P-Orridge to my ears, whether it actually originated from an expanded *Book of the Law* or not.

With Jackie "Lady
Jaye" Breyer
P-Orridge in
New York City, 2004
(photo by Genesis
Breyer P-Orridge)

TDL had mentioned to us both that he possessed several unpublished Crowley manuscripts and he had also made specific references to a fourth, fifth, and sixth chapter of *Liber AL* while in my temple room in Stockholm in 1998. They were supposedly not from the "channeled" sessions of Cairo in 1904 but were distinct texts in their own right. Whatever the truth of the matter, it was delightful to think about, and hermaphroditism was obviously a theme that obsessed Gen at this time. He and Jackie had begun their Pandrogeny project, and it was now budding in rich speculation and early attempts at mimicking each other's looks and mannerisms. Throughout the 2000s, the project would bloom into full-on physical alterations via cosmetic surgeries for them both.

Whether or not there is a written fourth *Liber AL* chapter and beyond—today I have my doubts!—the trajectory or progression is somewhat logical: going from the Nuit Macrocosm (chap. 1), to the pinpointed and distinct Hadit Will (chap. 2), to the energetic Ra-Hoor-Khuit "force & fire" that is needed for individuation (chap. 3), and, possibly, into the well-begotten magic of transcendence as a crowning of the individuation process. To follow this trajectory would mean going into atomic, subatomic, genetic, and subgenetic levels, and the enormous power reservoirs that one can find there, either in fission (a twin process) or fusion (a hermaphroditic process)—magical and creative transcendences both.

"ARE YOU PREPARED TO PAY THE PRICE?"

Fueled by all this magical energy, my little family moved on to Bangkok as Gen, Jackie, and Eddie stayed in Nepal for a few extra days before returning to the US. Being in this Thai monstropolis after the paradisiacal Kathmandu was a bit of a shock to the system but I did have business to attend to: meeting up with the American film director Conrad Rooks. He lived in a cottage in the little beach town of Pattaya; the house was filled with computers for video edit-ing. His main movies, *Chappaqua* (1966) and *Siddhartha* (1972) are among my absolute favorites, for many reasons. *Chappaqua* assembles the talents of William Burroughs (who plays the head of a psychiat-ric hospital/drug clinic), Ornette Coleman (who helped put together the amazing soundtrack with Ravi Shankar at about the same time as he was in Stockholm to play at my father's jazz club and buy me my cradle!), Robert Frank (whose cinematography is absolutely priceless), and of course Rooks as director and actor (playing himself in an ear-lier stage of life, as an alcoholic and drug addict). *Siddhartha*, on the other hand, is a straightforward dramatization of Hermann Hesse's tale of the Buddha's enlightenment, with exquisite cinematography by Sven Nykvist.

We were very well received by Rooks and his Thai wife, and the interview was great and—in hindsight—quite unique. When we started talking about other directors of "his" peak era, like the Chilean surre-alist and magician Alejandro Jodorowsky, Rooks became agitated and almost protective of me. Magic was something to be dealt with very carefully, he said. I asked him whether the medium of cinema, like any art form, is a useable and suitable channel if one wants to understand man's own dark side, in order to create a better balance? Framing the reply in his beloved Hindu context, he said:

> Are you prepared to pay the price? You're not a Saddhu, you don't have the protection of the gods, you don't know how to call on the supreme force . . . So who's going to protect you? Tell me. What are you going to do when all the Siddhi come after you? Are you pre-pared to take all your clothes off and wander for twenty years? And put up with everything? The nature, the atmosphere, the mountains . . . ? I don't think so. So that's why I say you shouldn't fool with it unless you're willing to take the road. You're playing with some heavy stuff. That's the great danger in my opinion. You can be fas-cinated with it and you can even write about it and be like Colin

Wilson who makes his living out of writing about the occult. It's dangerous stuff.*

I felt honored that he should care so much about my well-being, and I'm sure he had checked out my websites (containing a lot of magico-anthropological information). I had also brought him a copy of *Bardo Tibet*, so he knew about my focus in life on magic as such. I didn't want to push the issue with him. However, as an occultural "lifer," I'm "in it to win it." That makes me a Saddhu—of sorts.

Throughout the 1990s I had become used to defining myself, both in terms of private communications and via-à-vis the media. I found it useful—and still do—to continually formulate even that complex concept of identity, because it doesn't ever really stop evolving. And if you're not aware of that, or at least interested in it, then you're probably *devolving*. In many ways we are formatted early on but the challenge of individuation, and of life itself, is to move along and see your core as malleable energy—*not* as something indivisible and sacrosanct. We should accept what we find on the way and integrate it, even if it at first seems to be something negative. Only in understanding this malleability can we change the charge of the experience itself.

In 1999, I was interviewed by Greg Zobel for the American magazine *Voltage*. He asked me how I applied my magical abilities and understanding on a daily basis:

I'm very content that many years of hard labor, both in terms of work and ritual, have come to a point of fruition. A stage where I feel mature enough to evolve further on my path. This wouldn't have been possible if I hadn't applied the abilities and the understanding I've collected and developed over the years. So the main achievement, if any, is the trust in my process and my path as such. It's not so much technique or ritual-related, but rather has to do with

---

*Interview with Conrad Rooks in Abrahamsson, *Reasonances*, 116.

making statements through various forms of expression that effect change. And have a sense of faith in that what it is I'm doing is right and has an artistic and inspirational value for other individuals too. I use my abilities for inspiration, clearer communication, developing different abilities, manifesting goals and projects, secure sustenance, success on all levels and many, many other things. Everything in my life is connected to magic and its source, so logically magic is a part of everything I do and everything I am.*

My increasing visibility and willingness to talk about magic and occulture in general in interviews like this led to some important invitations. My ICM friend Peder Byberg and his partner, the great Danish artist Julie Nord, set up a lecture for me at the Royal Academy of Art in Copenhagen in early 2000. I summed up the recent history of magic, stressing its intimate relationship to art and creativity. In doing so, I not only offered some bits and pieces that were hopefully useful to those who listened. Without fully realizing it, I also opened the door to a mind-frame, activity, and identity within myself: the extroverted, magico-anthropologist author who more than happily shines the light on occulture as a major phenomenon in itself. The Copenhagen lecture was the beginning of my focus and career since that point, and I included it as chapter 1 in my first anthology of occultural essays and lectures, *Reasonances* (2014).

SEARCHING FOR SUBSTANCE

Already in Nepal, Gen and I talked about making another album together with Thomas Tibert. *At Stockholm* was released in 1990, and now that I had recently started working with Thomas again, it made a lot of sense to initiate a new project. We had begun recording new

---

*Carl Abrahamsson interviewed by Greg Zobel, in *Voltage* 10 (1999), 29; slightly edited.

material under the name Cotton Ferox, and it was great to be "back in the psychedelic saddle." We worked in the studio and invited talented friends like Krister Linder and Michael Moynihan, and also Genesis, to contribute vocal tracks. With Gen, we really wanted to work together in person, so I began a process that would bring him over to Stockholm for a lecture evening at legendary experimental haven Fylkingen, as well as a DJ gig.

In early 2002, it was all happening. Cotton Ferox's first album was almost fully recorded at this point, and we recorded Gen in the very same studio in Stockholm. So, over the course of several intensely creative days, we basically wrapped up two albums (as we also used some of the Gen recordings for the Cotton Ferox debut album).

Late 2002 saw the release of *First Time Hurts* by Cotton Ferox, and in 2004 our second Gen-collaboration appeared: *Wordship*. As usual, everything was seamlessly and sublimely put together by Thomas, and Gen was better than ever—often delivering flawless performances on the first take. Cotton Ferox was off to a great start!

I wrote and suggested one of the poems for *Wordship*, and Gen had no problems at all with recording that. It was really my own emerging midlife crisis taking on poetic form, basically as a dialog with myself (right and left channels containing different words). I called it "Searching for Substance," and that was very much what was going on in my life at this point where I was now a breadwinning father who had lost himself somewhere along the highway of mundane banalities.

> Searching for substance—Searching for essence
> I never realized—I always realized
> The end never comes—New beginnings appear
> To those that wait—To the restless
> For no reason—For no reason
> Forgotten fancies—Remembering the substance
> Spent on bleak views—Passed through me
> Dreamt of dreams—Faced real life

Filled with shapes—Empty and void
Disturbed by forms—Just nothing
The many and the few—And nobody
Searching for substance—Finding forgotten fancies
Searching for essence—Finding nothing
The world is empty—I am filled
Waiting to be filled—Waiting to discharge
Filled with nothing—Leave something behind
More than everything—Less than nothing
Searching for substance—Searching for essence

Although I've never really liked to be on stage in other contexts than talking about my work, Thomas's music created a platform that really allowed me the space to integrate magical workings in spoken-word form. To some extent, I had done all of this before: with Peter Bergstrandh on the White Stains German tour in 1993, and on and off with Thomas during various early Cotton Ferox concerts. It made more and more sense to use what we had already created to make some changes "in conformity with will." And it could take on any and all forms of experimentation under our beloved banner of "Highbrow Lowlife" contradictions, as stated in our own manifesto:

Cotton Ferox . . . Definition? No. Explanation? No. Why not? No.

If anything, Cotton Ferox is the little piece of cotton used in disinfecting the spot where the lethal injection goes in. An example of hypocritical humanism. We're going to have you killed within ten minutes, but we want to make sure—for your own sake—that you don't catch an infection from the hypodermic needle.

As for the music, we live in a sphere of contrasts. Soft beats, hard scapes. Hard words to soft structures. Soft whispers to ravaging whipping. Cotton Ferox is the wonderful cloud in the blue sky when you're lying down on the grass, your head spinning on LSD. It's also the second half of the film "Cannibal Ferox."

As you listen, don't remember. As you listen, don't expect what the next sound will be. You won't find it. There will be a micro-upheaval of your expectations. Not because we necessarily want you to be squeezed through a transcendental process of annihilating good and evil. But because we want you, honestly and sincerely, to enjoy more. To enjoy the music more. The words. To enjoy yourself more. And us.

Open for suggestion. Open for collaboration. Open for being open 24 hours.

To say that Cotton Ferox is a trip would be to taint the experience with past ghosts and future speculations. We simply want to move on. Our new realm of research is you. You are our listener as we are your humble provider. Your sound-pusher. That's a big responsibility on both sides of the record. Therefore, we wish you all the best and hope you'll enjoy Cotton Ferox. From beyond infinity to the point which is . . . Where the hypodermic needle goes in.

Disinfection?

In my mind, the electric amplification is an important key to the tangibility of this magic. Some people describe the theory by making references to the "butterfly effect"—a sound or motion/vibration produced will travel on endlessly through whatever spaces it passes, and it will have an effect even if it's basically inaudible. But of course, it also has to do with gently expressing something to an audience that shares the same space. In that direct communication lies a great deal of magical potential, as anyone working in theater knows well.

With an overall focus on what I called "Kunst & Geist" (Art & Spirit) I started writing poems and short texts specifically for Cotton Ferox, for our live performances. In many ways these reflected what I was thinking about in terms of magic in general. A platform I had already had for a long time showed itself to me again. A symptomatic piece is "Art Mimics Life" from 2006:

ART MIMICS LIFE MIMICS ART MIMCS LIFE MIMICS . . .
Art is something. Art is good. Art is total war. Art is love. Art is you
and me and all the emotions in-between us. Art is a violated non-
aggression pact. Art is crumbling structures, symbols, myths, rubble,
remnants of what was great only a moment ago. Art is the appreciation
of change. Art is enthusiasm, hope and optimism. Art is a youthful
attitude and respect toward death. Art is when art enters your mind
or your body or both. Art is a creative ejaculation inside a more or less
receptive orifice. Art is that before which or whom you bow down
in gratitude. Art is greatness amidst the small, but art is also tear-
ing down the great to make way for new greatness. Art is that which
opposes the majority of those present—humor among the serious,
seriousness among the humorous. Art is made of iron, not irony. Art
is not a mental game—it is actually the force that crushes all mental
resistance and all tendencies to explain what can never be explained.
Art is what is explained here. Art is also none of the above. Art is
nothing . . . HOW MUCH MORE MAGIC DO YOU NEED?

In some subconscious ways I think I was looking for a way to deal with
many personal problems at the time, and magic as such was a great "go-
to" area that for me not only represented a safe and rewarding space,
but also a tangible sphere of willed manifestation. This was especially
attractive as I was dealing with forces apparently much stronger than
my ego-desires at the time.

After gradually declining from liver cancer over the first half of the
2000s, my father was allowed a liver transplant in 2006 despite being
almost seventy years old. This went well, and we were all happy for his
sake. Unfortunately, he then agreed to be a guinea pig for a stem-cell
transplantation process shortly after the organ transplant. I guess he
didn't want to have any form of cancer return, so he agreed to this,
although we all knew—as did the physicians, certainly—that he was
much too weak to be able to deal with it. In order for the stem-cell
transplantation to proceed, his immune system was efficiently killed

off. He became increasingly diminished but still wanted to carry on, and then simply died in frailty—in my presence.

This was sad for many reasons. One being that he was a nice guy, and he had been my main caregiver as a child. The other one being that I knew my mother would now decline too, as she was an aggressive and arrogant upper-class alcoholic, and my father had basically taken care of everything in terms of family affairs. Thus began a new chapter in my life that I did not look forward to.

Speaking of mothers: my daughter's mother decided to leave me at the very same time, taking our seven-year-old child with her and moving to Gothenburg. That was also not pleasant. And to boot, I got the boot at an international OTO meeting and initiation fest—also held in Gothenburg! I was deemed unfit to remain the "Frater Superior's Representative" in charge of OTO affairs in Sweden. I was quite aware of many failures in my handling of boring administrative work during the early 2000s, and problems keeping up with all the things on my table in general. It was, however, utterly disappointing to be demoted by what I felt was a conspiracy, where things could instead have been resolved much better in a face-to-face dialogue and with constructive changes for all involved. Instead, I became extremely bitter and disillusioned with all of the people involved, and with the OTO in general.

The great dumbing down of Thelema by the religious "occultnik"* Thelemites hadn't fully begun yet, and I still had hopes I could find some place within the order where I could be useful. But it didn't happen. I stayed on as a dues-paying member for another thirteen years, presenting a lecture here and there but nothing much of substance. The messages of TDL haunted me often:

Tibet is nearly gone, India is fast fading into the technological world and even the indigenous cultures have lost their roots.

---

*A term conceived by Anton LaVey signifying a person more interested in occultism per se than in its potentially beneficial, tangible results.

The great magical organizations of the West have devolved into petty power struggles. You know this better than anyone . . . We are the few and the last, Carl. I am grateful that you are in my experience.*

LIFE ON THE COUCH

Psychoanalysis became my saving grace during this morose and confusing period. Ironically, 2006 was the midpoint of a four-and-a-half-year analysis between early 2004 and late 2008. I was doing the full Freudian thing, going to see my analyst five times a week. And it was surely needed. So many things surfaced that I would probably never have allowed into my conscious mind otherwise. It became obvious to me during this process that my magical thinking and worldview over the decades had been as beneficial as the psychoanalysis itself, producing intuitive and unconsciously creative phenomena rather than verbal, rational, reactive, overly intellectual, and highly self-deceiving ones.

When I eventually felt I was "clear" or at least "clearer" after four and a half years of seemingly endless regurgitations of banal problems, my rational and irrational approaches had mated and given birth to a more solid magician ready to take on the challenges ahead. The main thing being my creative "fragmentation": I had previously regarded my multi-creativity as a "problem" that kept me down (not least career-wise), whereas in fact it is an asset and a privilege. I just do what I do, and I'm fine with it.

Another valuable insight or gift was the respect for the psycho-analytical process itself. As with much in my life, I knew a great deal about it in theory. But to really open up and let things flood out of the psyche—literally for years!—proved to me that Freud's "talking cure" had real benefits for certain people like myself. Although I had always

---

*TDL, email to the author (4 June 2010).

rooted for "Team Carl Jung," Freud knocked my rational socks off and made me realize there is a strong advantage in keeping things simple, as in his sharp divisions between the spheres of *das Es*, *das Ich*, and *das Über-Ich*. As an interesting synchronicity, exactly five years after my analysis was done, I met my future wife for the first time in New York: *psychoanalyst* Vanessa Sinclair.

The process had also hovered in the background throughout the years. When I was staying with Cris Monnastre in Los Angeles, she stressed what I had already read in the work of her mentor and teacher Israel Regardie: that the magician should really be in some sort of analysis before setting out on the path. Now, at least, I was catching up.

Anton LaVey was a self-professed Freudian who also stressed the importance of both Wilhelm Reich and Carl Jung. The old guys—meaning Crowley and Spare—were too old to get on the psycho-train once it took off, instead stressing their own systems of magic as stardust-sprinkled avenues of self-fulfillment. Gen had a more anarchic approach to the psyche and, I would say, was himself larger than life to the extent that it would have taken a very special "shrink" to fathom the scope of his complexity. I remember Gen telling me about a few sessions he had in California around the time of the divorce from Paula: "So they said, 'Oh, you seem to have led a very interesting life . . .' What could I say to that, really?" But that's the thing: you're basically not telling the analyst anything; it's your own story told to yourself, to the point where the neurotic redundancies and infantile banalities become transparent, boring, and eventually void of meaning and impact.

I could feel that art as such was creeping up and moving parallel to the magic in my life. Wherever there was a distinct connection between the two (or more), I was overjoyed to acknowledge it. One impactful meeting that pushed me into this more insightful mind-frame was with artist Peter Beard in New York in 2005. I had loved his amazing collages and photos for years and decided to approach him. At the time I was working as a freelance journalist and photographer, and I gravitated more and more toward talking to artists. Peter Beard was high on my wish list, and the meeting was like a revelation for me.

Beard's sublimely self-indulgent art—filtered through photographs, collages, drawings, diaries, and amazing adventures—had become an integral part of his life early on, to the extent where there were no borders between the creator and the created. Everything and everyone led on to something and someone else that could also be documented, aestheticized, and integrated in an ever-morphing "oeuvre." Not only was Beard a great photographer and writer; he also existed in a vortex of chance that had become like nothing less than a magical formula. For Beard, life was a psychedelic stage, and his multidimensional diaries—quite often filled with his own blood used as ink and paint—are magical mirrors that reflect the inner and outer processes at the very same time.

> My diaries were and are all about getting out into life and getting away from art school. They're meant to be unartistic. People think they're artistic because they're expressionistic, but they're basically just raging against the homework . . . I'm just collecting things that are fun. I'm an escapist. I'm just looking for subject matter and life enhancement. Duchamp's interviews and Bacon's interviews tell you everything you need to know about art. The common sense of it, enlarging the bouquet, finding a niche, all the common sense obvious things . . . All the things they'll never give you in art school. All they give you is their tragic lack of individuality. It's important . . . You've got to carve out a niche!*

It was just as if Peter Beard were speaking about magical processes to me in my phase of disillusionment with regard to structures of order that are counterproductively rigid and obfuscating, while paradoxically promoting "freedom" and "inspiration." Individuation is always an *individual* thing, and that is as it should be!

---

*Peter Beard, conversation with the author in 2005, later published in Abrahamsson, *Different People* (Stockholm: Trapart, 2021), 134.

I was familiar with both Bacon and Duchamp but decided to go back to their interviews, as suggested. This led further down a whole other rabbit hole, in which I'm still working: that of trying to figure out what makes the artists I like tick and create, and to try to make others see their greatness too.

Francis Bacon on the fluidity of the creative process:

> I don't really know how these particular forms come about. I'm not by that suggesting that I'm inspired or gifted. I just don't know. I look at them, probably, from an aesthetic point of view. I know what I want to do, but I don't know how to do it. And I look at them almost like a stranger, not knowing how these things have come about and why these marks that have happened on the canvas evolved into these particular forms. And then, of course, I remember what I wanted to do and I do, of course, try then and push these irrational forms into what I originally wanted to do.*

And Marcel Duchamp on the fluidity of the "object" in art:

> It's very curious because it's one of those words that has no meaning to begin with. An object is an object, a three-dimensional form. But words are taken and repeated, and after a certain number of repetitions the word takes on an aura of mysticism, of magic. And it goes on because men love to do that. They imagine the object as being something phosphorescent or something. That's what happened to the word *object*. But the minute you have a number of believers, then anything goes. You can do that with anything, you can create magic with anything, but it has to be done without preparation.†

---

*Francis Bacon, in David Sylvester, *Interviews with Francis Bacon* (London: Thames and Hudson, 2016), 116.
†Marcel Duchamp, in Calvin Tomkins, *Marcel Duchamp: The Afternoon Interviews* (New York: Badlands Unlimited, 2013), 61.

In the moment of creation, you have to express yourself through an aestheticized form that will then affect the surroundings as you wish. If you make an impact through this expressed form (which can also include your very own self/persona), the change you want to have happen is more likely to manifest.

Whereas before I had been very rational and demagogic in my dissemination of magical theory, the 2000s definitely brought me into a new headspace in which the "irrational" increasingly made me aware of the benefits of riddles, poetry, symbols, automatism, abstractions, surrealism, and the omnipotent aspects of myth and fiction in general. I called my new approach not only "Kunst & Geist" but also "metaprogramming." Magic as such is a programming of a desire in its potential connection to the outer world of manifestation. When we exist, as I do, in a world of magic both in theory and practice, we see that this quickly becomes "meta"—a (self-)reflecting layer on top of the process itself; watching it closely at all times, but hopefully not rationally enough to hamper the greased machineries of joy.

In this phase I also integrated a mix of what Beard alluded to as something beneficial and creative—escapism—and the will to journey. Never as a literal escape *away from* responsibilities, but always as a means *toward* finding out new things that would be impossible without the journey. I had already traveled a lot in my life, and I just kept it alive as an essential ingredient of work itself. There was Bruce Chatwin looming in the back of my mind, as well as my favorite film director, Werner Herzog. But there was also Carl Michael von Hausswolff, who moved from Gothenburg to Stockholm in the early 1990s and whose friendship has been important to me. Carl Michael is seemingly always on his way to or from somewhere, only occasionally stopping over to prepare for the next jump. I could strongly resonate with that attitude and have lived and loved in it for the greater part of my adult life.

In a Cotton Ferox mind-frame in the mid-2000s, I wrote a poem called "Escapism," and it was my own inner "call to arms" for a long time:

If I could travel anywhere
I would travel everywhere
One endless trip
With occasional stops
To assemble the documentation
Escapism is just another word
For the Eternal Return

The Eternal Return
To my own Locus Solus
My mind's settling down
To its own given balance

There is also destiny
A given point and given time
Masters, gods and puppeteers
Invisible timelords

I am a mere chroniclerk
But, as such, a free man
Free to return once more
To wherever I choose

Leaving spiritual footprints
Behind and in front
Of the time I'm in
And will be once again

There is also destiny
A frame of reference
A frame of an image
That has yet to be created
Yet to be interpreted

Yet to be torn apart
To be fully integrated

Art and spirit
Fodder for the soul's revelation
Revealing one's own strengths
And others' weaknesses

Stand fast in the
Quagmire of opinions
A branch to grasp for
Only grows from the hearts
Of the very real imaginists
Those with integrated
Psychogeometrical designs
That are theirs and theirs alone
Alone

Only time will tell
Only history will judge
All footprints are eventually erased
From babies' minds

All one has to do
And actually can do
Is start over
Solvitur Ambulando

Make me see what you do
Make me do what you see
A particular vision
Containing no regrets
Ultimatums, promises or fulfilments

It really is playback time
And we all share the same
Cerebral membrane
Sensitive to influence

If I could travel anywhere
I would travel everywhere
Assume power focus
Fade to indifference
Let go
Walk
Think
Fast
Wait
Think
Fast
Wait
Walk
Let go

PINNACLES & PEDIGREES

Throughout the early 2000s, I ambitiously tried to build a nice port-
folio of images in order to establish myself as a commercial photographer. It seemed easier to me than being an author, and I actively
approached people I knew in the fashion world in order to make connections, attend shows, and get some good shots. However, the fickle,
commercial nature of the world of fashion disappointed me quickly.
In all honesty, I was more interested in taking photos of the models
without any clothes on.

In 2003, I traveled in the US, connecting with models and design-
ers, and taking a lot of Helmut Newton–scented pictures. It was great

fun, but my real focus always drifted back to the specifically magical: on that trip I was initiated into the ninth degree of the OTO by Hymenaeus Beta and another OTO brother. It was the culmination of my then fourteen-year-long "career" within this Thelemic fraternity that contains the mysteries of sexual magic. The seventh, eighth, and ninth degrees (jointly called "The Hermit") specifically deal with these energies and of course it is of interest when you're on a path of initiation to see it through. Like most everyone else, I had read this material and these rituals early on—actually, even before joining the OTO—in Francis King's shunned book *The Secret Rituals of the OTO* (1973). But reading a ritual is of course not the same as experiencing it yourself. I felt honored and empowered to join the ranks of the relatively few adepts who had received this initiation and teaching within the OTO. I was later provided with a list of those so blessed, and it was pretty staggering to find myself in there.

In many ways, I believe my time in the OTO ended right then and there in Jersey City. Not in the sense that I lost interest in being part of it all now that I had reached the coveted pinnacle. On the contrary, I was ready to work even harder. However, fate would have it differently, as mentioned previously. My own willingness wasn't in sync with the old patterns that weren't always the best for me. When overwhelmed by my own too-ambitious creations, I have often gone into a passive-aggressive mode and let things slide downhill instead of dealing with the actual issues at hand. The Swedish branch of the OTO was only one such example.

A couple of days before the ninth-degree initiation, I had lunch with Gen, Bill, his new partner, and their young daughter at St. Marks Place in Manhattan—more or less exactly ten years after my hanging out with the previous Breeze family constellation. Gen and Bill had known each other a long time, and it made me feel good to again realize I was certainly no alien in this entourage or environment. In fact, both Bill and Gen distinctly said I should move to New York. Perhaps it was obvious to them that I wasn't really happy in Sweden, after all.

I did seriously consider moving at the time, but felt so stuck in the existential vehicle that I myself was driving toward the proverbial abyss, and perhaps not fully conscious of it. I did appreciate their concern, as I did Peter and Peggy's. I also met them on this trip for the first time in eight years, and they also suggested I make the leap and settle into the city they knew I loved so much. There was apparently something in the air, and for some reason I just couldn't fully inhale it!

After the initiation, I journeyed up to Vermont to visit my friends Annabel Lee and Michael Moynihan. Their rural paradise was a sweet relief after hectic New York. One evening we had a sauna bath and jumped into the pond located on their property. In many ways it felt like a visceral extension of my initiation: I sweated out the old and was purged of my solitary work, only to jump into the dark waters in the equally dark night and there unite with nature as such. It was an important nocturnal bath that brought me from an intellectual headspace to a very visceral, physical one. That pond was the interface in which magic exists and thrives: the interface between the inner and the outer, between extreme heat and extreme cold, and between intellectual integration and physical friction. Between that and the OTO initiation, I returned home to Sweden a thoroughly refreshed man!

Another honoring event took place in 2004. I had been invited to speak at the centennial celebration of Crowley's *Book of the Law* at Conway Hall in London by the organizers, "Starfire." Michael Staley and his *Starfire* magazine, as well as his book imprint of the same name, have been a source of inspiration for me since the late 1980s—whatever they produce is always of the best possible quality. It was therefore humbling to be invited to talk at this important event. I suspected that some people within the "Caliphate" OTO (the Crowley lineage that has grown from Grady McMurtry/Hymenaeus Alpha, and the one I was initiated into) wondered what I was doing there. *Starfire*'s and Staley's lineage emerged via Crowley's disciple, British author Kenneth Grant, through what's termed the "Typhonian" OTO. But I didn't care about those "political" aspects; I just wanted

A plunge into refreshing darkness, Vermont 2003
(Photo by Annabel Lee)

the inspiration, and that, as always, comes from different quarters and in all shapes and sizes.

All three chapters of *The Book of the Law* were read aloud, and there were interesting talks by Michael Staley, Christina Harrington (owner of Treadwell's bookshop in London), Lionel Snell, Margaret Ingalls (aka Nema), Martin Starr, Andrew Collins, Mary Hedger, and Mogg Morgan, and then myself to wrap it all up.

I focused on "Thelema and Politics," as that was a subject—or several—that had interested me for quite some time. Crowley himself was "dynamic" and changed his views throughout his life, but the book as such is pretty clear in signal, although cryptic in its esoteric formulations. It contains a Nietzschean philosophy that when extended to pure politics essentially becomes antidemocratic and decidedly elitist. It was great to talk about these issues, as at this time there were already tendencies of "Thelemic Political Correctness" (a paradox if there ever was one) starting to emerge, in which the "signal" was often deliberately rephrased in order to not offend anyone who might like one aspect of Thelema and potentially join a group like the OTO, but who, upon reading the stern third chapter of the *Book of the Law* specifically, might back away.

Philosophically, I was more on the side of the American libertarians like fellow OTO member and author James Wasserman. They at least had an honest reading of the book and didn't shy away from controversy. However, being a solid, stable Scandinavian with lifelong experience of a functioning "middle-path" society and government, I have never been able to look at the overall American experiment as anything but a cruel failure. It's a warped economy in which potential individual liberty comes at the cost of those consciously held down by brutal brainwashing and nonexistent public higher education. There is a cynically *constructed* sense of stratification, whereas I believe stratification should be allowed to manifest *naturally*, as in a pure *meritocratic ideal*. The American result is a reactive anarchy that has also proven to be disastrous for the general biosphere through its rapacious anthropocentrism—a severe disease not seldom originating in psychotic monotheistic cults.

In my talk I didn't shy away from these controversial aspects, and I also acknowledged that my Scandinavian privilege can contain biased and potentially condescending qualities. In my mind, the Scandinavian societies are as close to a Thelemic ideal as is technically and philosophically possible under the present planetary circumstances.

I do believe that man has the right to bear arms and defend himself and his property with it. The problem is that the proto-cowboy mentality serves no other purposes than mere selfish ones. The reaction against the State as a concept, as presented by, for instance, Jack Parsons, is infantile. A State is needed as long as there are more people than a specifically agrarian culture allows. And I for one don't think it's everyone's will to become a self-serving farmer. The genuine problem is not the concept of the State as such but the fact that the State we know is not based in high, enlightened ideals. Total anarchy is not, not in my mind at least, compatible with the Thelemic ideal. Far from it. However, I'm a spoiled brat coming from Scandinavia. We have minimal bordering on non-existent corruption, a public sector that actually assumes its responsibilities, and also a total freedom to move about and initiate endeavors.

Perhaps it is a mistake to interpret the book politically at all? Perhaps it is after all mainly a grimoire for personal spiritual development through the use of the generative force and that's that? It's all symbolic language describing the creative use of sex. But if that's the case, I don't think Crowley or any other interpreter would have gone to the lengths they actually have to more or less present Thelema as a tangible and practical philosophy that's supposed to permeate every sphere of human existence through a highly refined and superior, aristocratic individual—the Thelemite.

We all know we can change everything. We all know how potentially powerful magic can be. But, again, if this force is not rooted in an ideal, it is a blind force, a fool's force. What sets Thelema apart from many other magical presences today is that it is first and foremost a philosophy, an ideal. That's actually our greatest advantage today, *not* the fact that Crowley was a great magical and mystical synthesizer. If we want to share the philosophy of Thelema with the world, we need to rethink and structure those thoughts. If these first one hundred years have constituted "Horus' babysteps," then there's no doubt in my mind that we're dealing with very powerful energies. I for one think that these energies could and should be put to more use than mere self-help. Politics constitute one very significant arena in which to change the world. That is, really, truly change the world. Now, is that what we want or are we content to be comfortable in our own magical pipe dreams? I raise this question in a celebratory toast to one hundred years of *Liber AL*, and to all of you, but my answer remains in silence as I drink.*

It all led to some interesting and spirited conversations afterward! I had expected it might be received as a kind of dividing line, and that's basically what happened: some people were happy and congratulated me; others shunned me. My overall feeling was one of being honored to be included at such a unique and important event. It was celebrated by much beer, as far as I can recall. "When in London, do as the Londoners!"

I connected especially well with Nema. In many ways she resembled Cris Monnastre: a middle-aged American lady with an inner life as vital and creative as her outer projection was two-dimensional and unassuming. I have always loved connecting with the real magicians behind the texts or references I have read in books. In her case, it was the references to her work in Kenneth Grant's books that had made me curious already in the late 1980s. Nema was an active networker and had sent me material for the second issue of *The Fenris Wolf* in 1990. She also did so for the fanzine *Occulture* that I had printed in Sweden for the TOPY Network in 1990. After our meeting in London, she kept providing me with interesting material for *The Fenris Wolf* and I have to say it was an honor to include her in a more modern, contemporary context. Much of her thinking resonated with mine, especially the sometimes-paradoxical dynamic in the necessity of holding to on one's own magical path in order to be a vital and constructive part of a healthy whole:

The earth is undergoing a great probability-mitosis in this last decade or so of the Second Millennium c.e. Social, economic and moral systems are in crisis; the dangers to our planetary ecology are finally being recognized, and a beginning has been made to reduce and eliminate those dangers. Artists, poets, musicians are the agents

*Abrahamsson, "Thelema and Politics," in *Reasonances*, 53–58; slightly edited.

of change and the shapers of change. Magick is a Master Class for Artists, Scientists and Priests. Every human being alive functions in these capacities to varying degrees. One's own life and existence is a great Mystery in itself, so we seek self-knowledge; that which we see as our world and Universe around us is another great Mystery, and so we seek knowledge of it also; and when we gain new knowledge, or see old knowledge in a new way, we are impelled by love and joy to share this prize with our fellow humans.[*]

As I had no outer structure and group dynamic to invest in from approximately 2006, my magical creativity followed the psychoanalytic trail (or vice versa) and stayed on the *inside* where there was only a free flow of amorphous psychic and emotional mechanisms that created great things for me, *not* specifically for other structures and people. I felt a strong need to get back to the loftier levels of altruism, meaning a very focused selfishness. If you can't be good to yourself, you absolutely cannot be good to others! No wonder then that Kunst & Geist and the gradual emergence of the Mega Golem experiment became guiding lights.

[*]Nema, "Motherfather of the Arts," in *Occulture* magazine (1990), 33–34.

PART V
2005–2009

INTROSPECTION

Living through the Swedish OTO debacle, separating from my partner of eight years, and worrying about the well-being of our daughter, the illness and death of my father, and the emerging decline of my mother—all happening in 2006—made me considerably more introspective and protective. Work kept me going, as did the psychoanalysis. And what surfaced then manifested in my own writing: creatively, through the spoken-word pieces and performances with Thomas Tibert in Cotton Ferox, but also through a crystallization of my journalistic work. I focused on people—mainly artists—and let them speak freely about their processes; this, in turn, helped me re-present them better for others. In 2007, for instance, there was the book *Olika Människor* (Different People), which gathered my interview work of the early 2000s and also paved the way for the *An Art Apart* series of documentary films of the 2010s and beyond.

I had no publishing activities or structures going on during the 2000s, except for a one-off art fanzine called *BULT Magazine* in 2000. For a while I thought that might have been what I missed in my life, as I had always had something print-related—a fanzine, a publishing company, a structure that somehow presented my work—going on from the early 1980s until the turn of the millennium. But now I seemed to be in a decade of confusion-cleansing and reassuming my power focus. It was a time for me to shake off old ghosts and patterns, whether internal or external.

If Kunst & Geist are so linked process-wise, then in my "sympathetic" magic mind-frame one could easily replace the other in a psychic sphere of maximum fluidity. The old arcane structures and methods are in essence totally redundant if you look at them from inside your own detachment. The original shamanic impulse to travel "beyond" and see what's there, and then to express that creatively to inform or enlighten others, is ingrained so deeply within us that I wouldn't hesitate to call it an instinct rather than a cultural phenomenon. As part of the survival instinct, the inner journeying is a biologically rooted behavior, *not* a communal construct. The intuitive connecting of the dots of immediate experience is part of a behavior of epistemological purity—it is a *direct* acquisition of personal knowledge that is relevant for the well-being of the individual, and thereby of the community as such.

Reconnecting with Gen in 1998 and our trip to Nepal in 2000 helped me to gain a wider perspective as I was ruminating away and increasingly feeling sorry for myself. The need to develop and improve was strong; in so many ways, it was part of the zeitgeist. For Gen, this was most definitely the case. Throughout the 2000s, Gen and Jackie formulated what was to fully bloom under the umbrella of "pandrogeny"—an increased interchange of outer and inner spheres and aspects according to alchemical principles. This was and remains an intense shift of perspective that completely transcends the commodified, simplified aspects of "gender" that we are used to in our contemporary cultural discourse. When Gen and Jackie started modifying not only their appearances but also their bodies to look more like the synthesis "third mind" they already had going between them, they very concretely set out on a process of art-as-magic, and magic-as-art, that few before them had achieved. I was privileged to be along for the ride, hopefully easing Gen's concerns from time to time:

> I am fully recovered from pneumonia, saw doctor for full physical last week. Just as well as I get more SURGERIES for pandrogeny next weds. Please do a safe ritual for me. It's a bit scary this time. I had a STRONG vision y-eras ago that I could/would die in my 55th y-era unless I was VERY careful . . . this surgery I fixed therefore on 2nd 2nd 2005 . . . 20 daze BEFORE 22 2 2005 (my 55th B-earthday) . . . however, this is ALSO in another way of looking at my 55th y-era so . . . I am NOT sure I will live this time. I have NOT told ANYONE but you. No point in frightening Jaye etc. But do send me safe strength.*

---

*Genesis P-Orridge, email to author (30 January 2005).

Their work together was daring, groundbreaking, and highly magical but came to an abrupt halt with Jackie's death in October of 2007. Any work with their pandrogenous development then carried on in Gen's inner spheres, with the help of effigies and ritual work. It became a necessary retreat into the inner, to be able to cope with the outer.

I received similar input from both TDL and Saulus at this time. Though different in so many ways as magicians, they each stressed inner work as the main thing. Whatever is done in the outer sphere, ritually or mechanically, should facilitate the inner workings, not necessarily the other way around.

For TDL it was Daoism and a Castanedan "don Juan" approach, and the Castanedan energies were certainly present in Saulus's communications with me too. But this was never about cogitation or rational processing. Although this has its place in our day-to-day lives, the inner workings delve much deeper in order to find solutions for whatever issue or problem is at hand.

I kept in touch with TDL via email, and had met Saulus again in Salzburg in 2004 on my journey to Austrian artist Hermann Nitsch's castle Prinzendorf near Vienna (where Nitsch staged a two-day performance of the *Parsifal* mystery—a perfect symbolical experience for me at the time). Their respective wisdoms usually hit me right when I needed them the most. I would not characterize myself as a "whiny" person, but sometimes I needed to let off steam with my magical people, and not only on the psychoanalytic couch. The power of cathartic confession is great!

Most of the time, the wisdom and remedies were not of a "technical" sort, but rather friendly slaps or blows that woke me up from a complacent (and/or depressed) sleep. Also, a real friend never has to prove himself a friend: he just is one. This has been exemplified to me on many occasions, when for instance a concerned postcard has been more valuable than all the wisdom of all the grand poobahs of all the occultnik universes put together. Saulus always amused and inspired me with his to-the-point messages:

You said that you have problems . . . No, you don't. Rejoice and tell the good news to everybody, for everything is imaginary. Every particle of that well-fed, lazy, good for nothing, fuck-loving, shitty-dreaming piece of sensitive matter that you carry around is immersed in a universe of sentient beings helping you to get out of the illusion caused by the physical dimension. And you, messed-up hippie-magus, are worried about what may happen to that clunky chunk of delusory cinders, when everything is already over?*

TDL was always generous in his pep talks, helping me to see who I really am by pointing me in metaphysical directions that I had not previously examined:

Carl, I think you are much like a young lad who first climbs up to the high dive board and looks over the edge. He sees danger. The same boy saw adventure while in the pool looking up. He saw no risk. Nothing had changed other than perspective. Jump!—We are no longer trapped within the concept of the finite. Our direction and purpose are aligned with the very nature of that which we reflect. Our "will" as expressed within the A∴A∴/OTO is that which "embodies our destiny or greater purpose." It is here that the quagmire begins: when is our "will" Divinely inspired as opposed to merely thinking that we would or should take one course of action over another? The answer to this Gordian knot lies within the realization that we are not separated from the Creator and can never be. All is infinite possibility. Just as there may be no light without darkness to define it, sound without silence to give it form, we cannot exist without the conundrum of "is" and "is not." We discover that anything is possible. We are not bound by the constraints of time if we are,

*Saulus, email to the author (17 September 2004).

indeed, an expression of the eternal. All possibilities are viable. No choice is of higher import than another. Our true "will" is to explore and grow within the "Great Mystery."—All reality is experienced between polarities, Carl. As we grow into a fullness of understanding we discover that we are rarely expressing one without, to some degree, the other. Why let it concern you where your path is located? Is it not useful to simply be on the path in the first place? Worrying about potential is a waste of energy. Let the moment rule supreme and simply give to it your unbridled passion. Life is not a matter of getting somewhere; it is the doing and not the getting there that is important. I would not worry about one possible side of your potential over another for both are opposite sides of the same.*

TRANSIENT LIVES

In 2004 David Griffin left Stockholm in a hurry and without sharing the power of cathartic confessions—to me, anyway. Although he had a nice and cozy apartment and life there six months of the year, for some reason it was time to go, and fast. I helped him pack up his belongings and put them in storage, and later I sent them off by container to the US. We had gradually drifted apart over the years, but had still occasionally worked magically together. Now, a twelve-year cycle of friendship was very abruptly over, and in this lay another significant separation for me.

Looking Glass Press helped David produce his book *The Ritual Magic Manual*, systematizing and presenting the Golden Dawn material, just like Crowley and Regardie had done before him. Going through these rituals over and over again made me "lose faith" in the system as such—it was too "nineteenth century" to be relevant for me.

---

*TDL, email to the author (20 April 2010).

It was also the genesis of the term "sympathesis" within my magico-anthropology: each individual or culture creates the system needed to transcend it. If you create a highly intellectual, mental, and rational system such as that of the Golden Dawn, you are basically signaling to your own psyche that you need to break that rational slavery down inside yourself, but that you're not going to give up easily . . . You don't go diametrical in some kind of emotional rebellion—that rarely fixes things in either direction—but instead grind yourself through the system at great existential expense in order to hopefully and intuitively see the genuine needs and machinations of your mind, and what you need to really focus on *in order to individuate*. Because if you don't, the system will eventually dry you out and you will become lost in an occultnik maze of the imaginary, potentially ending up in a "religious" void. Crowley realized this early on and developed the A∴A∴ as a modern and more efficient system than that of the Golden Dawn, while still maintaining the latter's structure. He also had a great advantage in that he integrated a distinct philosophy of Will, as inherited from Nietzsche and Schopenhauer. No matter what, a genuine magical partnership like the one I had with David always creates strong roots, and when it ends there is an amount of sadness in the uprooting.

On that note, it was heartbreaking to be part (at a distance) of Lady Jaye's demise in 2007. PTV3 passed through Stockholm and played at a small club on October 2nd. We met up and had a great time. The show was rocking and Jaye was now part of the band, playing keyboards, with Eddie O'Dowd on drums. Gen made me come up on stage to promote my recently released book of interviews (*Olika Människor*) and then started talking in a robot voice to the audience that he was "completely controlled by Carl Abrahamsson," that he obeyed everything I said, and that I was a sex god. Everyone was laughing hysterically, including me. After the show we just hung out and talked. They were experiencing problems with the tour and their booking agent and considered aborting the trip and going home to New York instead. We agreed they would call me if they decided to cancel the rest of the tour, as they could perhaps stay an extra day or two in Stockholm. I gave Jaye my number and she entered it in her phone and called me, so we were connected.

The tour was indeed aborted, and they all went back to the US. One week later, on October 10th, I received an email from Bill, telling me that Jaye had died in New York the night before, only thirty-eight years old. I contacted Gen right away. He was in shock, understandably, and I chose to pull back to let the New Yorkers process their grief together in peace. But Gen kept sending me updates, which was appreciated and literally haunting:

> Who would have REAL EYES(d) the OTHER meaning of S/HE IS HER/E??? But she is . . . she has thrown glasses, pictures etc around to order, knocked us off beds etc. VERY POWER FULL.—It is also OUR duty to finish the interview book etc . . . SHE demands it!*

Gen also asked me to write something for a prospective "Lady Jaye's Book of Love," which I did in an emotional state of mind, making sure to also include quotes from an interview I had done with her in 2004 (mainly about the Pandrogeny project):

LADY JAYE: AN EXTRA-HUMAN BEING

It was definitely inspired by alchemy and the idea of the hermaphrodite. In folklore, the original human or the original virus. And also an angelic representation of humans. That image fascinated us because this was a being that was fruitful in every possible way: an artist's muse. The hermaphrodite is a symbol of creative potential.

Life is transient, transparent, a throbbing and transcending experience inbetween voids. Sooner or later, we find ourselves back in a void. Regretful perhaps, or satisfied to finally leave a dismal life. What's the perspective on the other side? How do they write their

---

*Genesis P-Orridge, email to the author (15 October 2007).

elegies? Sooner or later, we find ourselves back in life? Regretful perhaps, or satisfied to finally leave a peaceful rest?

We meet people. Interact, make love, go on trips, communicate.
Today it's called "hooking up," as though we are machines and our
emotions are cables. Call it what you like, but one thing is certain:
we are not alone. We really are hooked up to each other. On an existential level perhaps many of us feel alone and isolated. But in actual
fact, we're not. We're just tiny specks of human dust, throbbing and
transcending together in an electric desert of endless possibilities.
That is, until we die.

Lady Jaye, my friend Lady Jaye Breyer, died. Suddenly her friendship was not a physical part of my endless possibilities anymore.
Now she's just . . . What? A memory? A recording? What happens
when the storage malfunctions? When the recording fades? Here
lies the dilemma of human existence: do we exist at all when we're
un-acknowledged by other members of the species? And here lies
the dilemma of human existential fear: what can we do about this
seemingly terrible situation?

Some people create. Some people create art. Some people open
their minds and systems and use will and self-discipline to move
around in the electric desert, to see what's there and report back or
forward to others. Ideas. Forms. Ideas and forms become messages.
These messages, take them or leave them but please take note that I
at least tried . . . I guess . . . I guess that's art.

Lady Jaye, my friend Lady Jaye, was an artist. Not what's usually
called a "plastic" one, changing surrounding objects to conform with
an intellectual vision. Lady Jaye was an "organic" artist, changing
her inner spheres and then her outer surroundings to conform with
the inner, to conform with the outer, to conform with the inner, etc.
Also fusing together with a genetic male, Genesis P-Orridge, on all
levels they possibly could during a loving research phase that, alas,
became all too short. Life is not a cruel mistress. Death is.

The implications of the BREYER P-ORRIDGE Existential

Art Project are vast. It could be groundbreaking and radical, or, as Breyer P-Orridge would probably prefer to call it, "evolutionary." It could also just be forgotten or seen as a tampering with forces best left alone. Who's to say? Right now, I can. And you too, simply because we are alive. But later? Will the recordings fade, just as actual human lives do? Here, again, lies the dilemma of human fear.

We're both receiving some of the same sensory information from strangers . . .

Creating one organism out of two is not so much a mere decrease in numbers and dimensions, but rather an increase in prism potential. Two shields inherently reflect in different directions. One modified shield, in this case literally twice as powerful, creates a clearer reflective image. And a greater capacity to refocus projected light.

I bring an ability to sort through information. To take a bulk and narrow it down, information-wise or when it comes to visual material. I'll take a bunch of visual information and focus in very, very tight. Gen will take that small piece and expand it again and decide what shape it's going to take in terms of media. The final expression of it.

Contraction and expansion are the essential movements of all life. Art, its distinctly human reflective counterpart. But expressing this doesn't really shed light on the human emotions of grief and sadness, does it? Just a minute ago, didn't I write that we're not alone? Perspectives seem to change as emotions take charge. It seems we are all alone, together or not. It hurts when we lose a piece of our togetherness.

The real challenge here seems to be to try and avoid hagiographic cosmetics and delusions of the narrator's ego-grandeur. Those perspectives very rarely create valid, relevant and lasting memories. After all, we are just human beings. Lady Jaye was one. Just an extra-human being who was brave and smart and beautiful and who nurtured a desire to change herself and merge into a new protohuman creation together with another extra-human being.

Did they succeed? Does the question matter? Only the future can tell if what we do has any value to others. Our destinies are not linear but circular and definitely not logical but rather quite erratic. We can never be totally predictable. Neither can life in itself.

Suddenly, out of the blue and into the black, we could hear no more, see no more. We were just left with a dull sense of bitter loneliness. The kind of loneliness we can never really escape, merely temporarily cheat together with others in a similar situation. Death, mighty judge. Death, hot breath and then suddenly lack of it. Death, new beginning. Beginning? Possibly for those who die, but certainly not for the rest of us. Death is just a painfully tangible reminder of the merciless approach of the end.

Therefore, I whispered in the chilly night:

Your hand on mine, so warm, leading me outside. So calm in the stressful aftermath of a Stockholm concert that, for me, turned out to be both the first and the last. You were saying I looked good (thanks!), when in fact you were the one looking so good, so colorful and beautiful. So alive. Such a recent imprint in my mind of serene and friendly love.

I think back and remember the good times, look at contact sheets and photographs, and cry. Love, warmth, exploration, creating memories in me and so many others. I'm so honored to have met you. Your passing makes no sense. Death seldom does. Your leaving us so soon will have to be a motivation, an incentive to value life even more. And not waste even a moment of it.

Everything changes. Of that we're certain. To the degree we can, let's make the most of it.

On that cold bench outside the venue, you programmed your phone with my number. And called me up straight away. I remember thinking for a fraction of a second: *Who the fuck is calling me at this hour?* Of course it was you, sitting just an arm's length away and smiling your prankish smile. "Yes, Hello? Hello, Yes?" Yes, it worked. You had the right number. Still, even though we were so close, your voice sounded so far away, filtered through the airwaves. A prophetic premonition, or what?

Heart to heart and soul to soul, we can and will carry on doing what we do. Art to art and role to role, we will keep your memory alive, loving you for who you were, still are, and always will be.

Have a safe journey, Lady Jaye, wherever it is that you're going. And if ever you should feel like it, please do give me a call. I miss your voice already.

And then, silence.

We can try and express these kinds of feelings and memories. But essentially it's futile on other levels than the merely consoling. We express because we want to support and comfort others and ourselves. But what we express is most often lacking in distinction, in precise meaning. Love and infatuation can be equally abstract, but then, at least, there's the sense of joie de vivre taken to a maximum level. With death, it's all pussyfooting around. We are all inherently afraid of being too close to the epicenter of absolute nothingness.

I've never felt completely comfortable in my skin. A lot of people work on that in different ways. I feel as though the way I'm becoming . . . When I say "I," I mean myself and Gen. The Royal We. Changing makes us feel as though this is close to the way our spiritual selves could manifest. It's more of a body that represents our thoughts and our desires toward perfection. Sometimes it's magical alchemy and sometimes it's chemical alchemy and sometimes it's spiritual alchemy. This time it's physical. I felt that the old body was so imperfect. An imperfect representation of my spirit. I wanted one that was more spiritual and more aesthetically pleasing and more accurate.

Lady Jaye . . . This is the end, my friend, the end.

. . . Or is it?

Lady Jaye's Book of Love never saw the light of day, unfortunately, but a version of the piece was published in my first occultural anthology, *Reasonances* (2014). It is not only a manifestation of my own memories and emotions, but also of Lady Jaye's. A small piece of history writing, if you will. The work of history writing mainly consists of being more or less consciously a part of life as it passes, and making sure that meetings and events are documented. The actual work of historians—the concoction of chronological overviews from one perspective or another—I would prefer to call "history editing" rather than "history writing." Any anthologizing or editing implies making idealized choices, and usually these are made via highly subjective filters (quite often masquerading as the opposite: the "objective").

Gen was a master at history writing, in that sense of living and leaving traces in printed-matter form—still the most efficient platform. Not only through his own writings, but also in thousands of interviews. Subjective expression filtered through one's own or another's pen. The future will decide what's what and what's not—and of that we have no control (even as accomplished magicians!). But there is something to be said for the causal process of leaving something behind. Crowley was certainly aware of this. Would he have any significance at all if he hadn't spent a large part of his fortune on self-publishing lovely books of poetry and magic?

Lady Jaye was always less audible and visible in the pandrogeny project than Gen, but it still couldn't have been done without her. I was very pleased to have some alone time with her in New York in 2004, and I asked about her impressions and expressions within the project:

> We could decide that we've become so much alike that neither of us is bringing anything unique to the table anymore. And if that happens we're just going to have to spend less time together, which will change the dynamic in different ways because that's the part that's allowing us to become so telepathic; to be able to spend so much time together. And we are receiving a lot of the same stimuli, you know. We talk to each other quite often if we have conversations with other people, so the same idea is being synthesized at the same time, using the same words, producing the same information,

which so far has been really great but I could see how that can lead to problems later on.*

In many ways, Jaye reminded me of Ovid's story of the original divine hermaphrodite in the Greek pantheon: the love child of Hermes and Aphrodite. The naiad Salmacis became enamored with Hermaphroditus when she saw his beauty. As she threw herself naked into the same lake in which the hesitant Hermaphroditus was swimming, and basically raped the boy, the gods heeded her request to unite. They became one new bisexual being called *a hermaphrodite*.

Atlas' descendant resisted stubbornly, and refused the nymph the pleasure she hoped for; but she persisted, clinging to him, her whole body pressed against his. "You may fight, you rogue, but you will not escape. May the gods grant me this, may no time to come ever separate him from me, or me from him!" Her prayers found favour with the gods: for, as they lay together, their bodies were united and from being two persons they became one. As when a gardener grafts a branch on to a tree, and sees the two unite as they grow, and come to maturity together, so when their limbs met in that clinging embrace the nymph and the boy were no longer two, but a single form, possessed of dual nature, which could not be called male or female, but seemed to be at once both and neither.†

Pandrogeny would be Gen and Jaye's take on that story, plus an integration of many other mythological tales and myths that represent the process of not only sexual but also existential fusion. It's interesting to note that their first meeting was at Terence Sellers's dungeon in New York, where Jaye was working as a dominatrix.

---

*Lady Jaye Breyer P-Orridge, interview with the author in *Sacred Intent—Expanded Edition*, 158.
†Ovid, *Metamorphoses*, bk. IV, trans. Mary M. Innes (London: Penguin, 2015), 103–4.

THE CARETAKERS' CABAL

I'm a printed-matter man, and have been one ever since 1982, when my first fanzine endeavor about comics, *Splasch*, was released. In that sense, I have always admired not only writing men and women, but also editors and publishers—again, taking the inspiration I've received myself from books and magazines, and then making my own concoctions to pay it forward. Early in my occult days, there was not only Bill Breeze and 93 Publishing, but also Simon Dwyer of *Rapid Eye*, and Adam Parfrey of Amok Press and later Feral House. Dwyer I never got a chance to meet, but the issues of *Rapid Eye* were a delight, going from TOPY-style fanzines to lavish coffee-table editions. It was prime occulturation in action, as were most of Parfrey's classics like *Apocalypse Culture*, *Apocalypse Culture II*, and *Cult Rapture*. Bringing forgotten, banned, and/or neglected minds and destinies to the fore to let new generations make up their own minds about what was useful for them or not.

Parfrey had written me in 1991 after LaVey had suggested that he get in touch. I was overjoyed to hear from him as I had already bought and devoured most of what he had put out. Already in 1989, he had published a new edition of LaVey's *The Compleat Witch* (as *The Satanic Witch*), and in 1992 he followed suit with LaVey's brilliant anthology of essays called *The Devil's Notebook*.

We finally met at the book fair in Chicago in 1996, albeit briefly. But in 2001 we had the opportunity for a proper meeting in Los Angeles, when the offices of Feral House were in the seedy downtown area. It was very inspiring and nice, and I left with a stack of brand-new titles and a whole lot of inspiration. Adam Parfrey was a man who refused to back down or compromise his vision:

> I don't want to do things that are ignored or that don't leave ripples. I'm interested in sociology and in how things affect culture and the world. But I'm not a Svengali. I can't make as many things happen as

I'm accused of. But of course I notice what affects the world around me. I don't really regret anything I've done. But I would love to have a *Doppelganger* so that I could find the time to do all the things I would like to do.*

In 2004 it was again time to visit Parfrey, and now he and his contrarian company had relocated to a beautiful fairytale property on Lyric Avenue in Los Feliz. His expansion was impressive, publishing books about weird underground pioneers and conspiracies, updated editions of classics like *The Intimate Sex Lives of Famous People* and *Hollywood's Hellfire Club,* and also our dear old TOPY documents in the volume *Thee Psychick Bible*†—to mention but a very few examples. And he kept on going from clarity to clarity as the years passed, also creating new imprints like Process Media, and generally keeping the signal strong. In most everything there was a link or thread to our past as "occult underground detectives," sniffing out the good stuff while networking for a professional future. The Parfrey-produced books on the Process Church of the Final Judgment; the photographer William Mortensen; Blanche Barton's LaVey biography, *The Secret Life of a Satanist*; and many other titles built a substantial corpus for bright generations to come. This also included side projects like Nick Bougas's LaVey documentary *Speak of the Devil* (1993), as Parfrey was co-producer of that film.

In 2006 I was back in Los Angeles and met up with Kenneth Anger to do another interview. I picked him up at the Hotel Gershwin on Hollywood Boulevard where he was living at the time. We strolled to a nearby café and talked over lunch. Of course, we touched upon Crowley and the OTO. I asked him if he ever felt tired of being so associated with Crowley.

---

*Adam Parfrey, conversation with the author, Los Angeles, 2001. Published in Swedish in Abrahamsson, *Olika Människor* (Umeå: H:ström text & kultur, 2007).
†Expanded and edited together elegantly by Jason Louv as a development of the first edition from 1994 (then edited by Joe Rapoza). Rapoza was also the first to reissue the *At Stockholm* CD after the original release on Psychick Release had sold out.

"I've certainly never been bored with Crowley," Anger answered. "It's a challenge to be a Thelemite. I'm not a very social person. I've gone to a number of these events but I don't feel any necessity to mix with other people or go to their meetings. It becomes just like any other club. I don't think Crowley would have approved of how lunar these meetings can become, in the sense that the women have so much control. On the other hand, at least the women are doing something."

Today, all of the Crowley copyrights are more or less expired and the market is flooded with his books in both nice and horrendous editions. I remember seeing some of Anger's exquisite first editions at Samson de Brier's house back in 1990.

"I actually had some stuff already in the 1940s," he told me. "But when I grew up you could find Crowley stuff in secondhand bookshops. I picked up quite a few things in stores. But there were also things at auctions, at places like Sotheby's. That's how I met Jimmy Page. We used to bid for the same items. He has an extensive Crowley collection. He's very closed, self-protective, like many people on that level in the music business get to be. They're used to fending off fans."

We walked on up to Griffith Park to take some photos, and it was great to just hang out and chit-chat. I could tell Anger had grown increasingly reserved since our previous meetings, and it was probably age taking its toll more than anything else.

"You need private space," he said. "I'm a lone wolf. I keep to myself. I do have friends but I don't feel a compulsion to see them too often. Some people would say, He sounds like a recluse to me!, but I'm not. I occasionally go to see a film or to a concert. I love classical music. It's not a bad life."

On the following day, we arranged to have lunch at the Château Marmont Hotel, and as I stood waiting for Anger by the driveway to the garage, I was almost run over by a silver-colored Volvo exiting far too quickly. I would have been furious if I hadn't seen who was at the wheel: June Newton, the great photographer (aka "Alice Springs") and the widow of my favorite photographer Helmut Newton who, bizarrely enough, had died of a heart attack two years earlier as he was exiting the hotel at the exact same spot where I was standing!

Anger arrived shortly thereafter, and we had another great time: lunch at the hotel, strolling through the Hollywood Forever Cemetery, and ending up at the Hollywood History Museum. He shared entertaining stories about a lot of the old stars—befitting of the author of the incredible *Hollywood Babylon* books—but seemed somewhat dismayed at the contemporary movie stars who shared the museum space with his beloved old icons.

The following year I was back in Los Angeles again, and just for the hell of it decided to leave June Newton a note (she always stayed at the Château Marmont during the winter months) telling her she had almost run me over the previous year, and would she consider having a drink? She called back, and that led to a very nice friendship, as well as an introduction to yet another piece of my romantic occultural puzzle. One evening as I was returning through the lobby, I saw her sitting by a table having a drink with someone. She waved me over and introduced me to the director Curtis Harrington, an old friend of Anger's and the maker of such classics as *Night Tide* (1961; featuring a young Dennis Hopper and also Marjorie Cameron) and *Wormwood Star* (1956; a short film about and starring Cameron). I didn't want to barge in on their evening, but Harrington said I was welcome to contact him for an interview. Unfortunately, this never happened, but at least I had shaken hands with one of my cinematic heroes. In 2017 I returned to the Hollywood Forever Cemetery together with my wife Vanessa, paying my respect to Harrington at his columbarium space. One has to grab the moment when it's there: the only time is now.

RUSSIAN INSIGHTS

In 2007 Cotton Ferox was offered a mini-tour of Russia, with concerts booked for Moscow, St. Petersburg, and Yaroslavl. I was also invited to exhibit photographs at the same cultural center where we would play in Moscow. This was as much fun for me as preparing for the concerts. It was made even more so by receiving an email from June Newton wishing me good luck with the opening and the show.

Just being in Russia was very exciting because I knew there would be so many things to photograph. It was great fun in all the expected ways (meeting local weirdos, strolling the streets with my camera, connecting with the local OTO group, and visiting the amazing museums in Moscow and St. Petersburg—for me, it was like a Nicholas Roerich overdose!). This was a common scenario in all my travels: there was always someone in the fraternal network to meet and get to know, and who was usually happy to be a guide and show me around.

I was especially excited because there was going to be a Gnostic Mass while I was in Moscow. It was very beautifully performed, and the local brothers and sisters were really friendly and filled with respect. The ritual had additional significance there, because it was in Moscow that Crowley had written it in 1913, while touring with his infamous troupe, the "Ragged Ragtime Girls." It is undoubtedly among his very finest works, in the sense that it contains a great deal of magical substance in condensed poetic form. Writing about it in his "auto-hagiography," *Confessions*, he reveals a great deal about his psyche:

> I resolved that my Ritual should celebrate the sublimity of the operation of universal forces without introducing disputable metaphysical theories. I would neither make nor imply any statement about nature which would not be endorsed by the most materialistic man of science. On the surface this may sound difficult; but in practice I found it perfectly simple to combine the most rigidly rational conceptions of phenomena with the most exalted and enthusiastic celebration of their sublimity.*

---

*Crowley, *The Confessions of Aleister Crowley* (London: Routledge and Kegan Paul, 1986), 714.

The above quote is reflective of what Crowley himself regarded as a strength in his system of "scientific illuminism": the focus on scientific or empirical justifications. I don't believe any such justifications are necessary, and this point of view was gradually distilled in me while working through his system of magic (and thereby his psychology) over the decades. The reason why the Gnostic Mass works is because it attracts by form, informs by poetic and symbolic allusions, and then leaves you in an elevated state of mind, which in turn increases the attraction of the next "performance."

Taking part of the Gnostic Mass, either as a performer or as a member of the congregation, is inherently an initiation in the same way as each sexual intercourse or sexual experience is an initiation into a new level of understanding—even if only unconscious.

Crowley's insistence of integrating a scientific/empirical mind-frame in magical praxis defeats what I believe is its real purpose: inspiring an individual to individuate. That's not saying those with an empirical bent or profession can't individuate or practice magic. On the contrary, that avenue is open for *anyone who is open-minded enough* to see the simplicity in the complexity (rather than the other way around). The Crowleyan obsession to appease those "most rigidly rational conceptions of phenomena" seems to me to be a mere expression of doubt of one's own inner and intuitive guidance and conviction. Why would anyone have to prove anything to anyone about the method (or non-method) one uses to move onward in life?

In some ways, Crowley anticipates the postmodern tendency to emasculate Will itself by compulsively having to explain or justify whatever is going on and thereby not allowing any deeper or more substantial communication between sender and receiver. Applying a filter of "scientism" on magic indicates a failure to fully grasp magic's cultural function as the most important one there ever has been, still is, and will be. In my atomic model of human endeavors, as presented in my book *Source Magic*, science is but one human satellite or planet revolving around the magical, shamanic source core. Magic is the center of the system, around which all human expressions revolve—not the other way around.*

To put it bluntly, the value of empirical religiosity and religious empiricism basically turned to an all-time "*baisse*" the very same moment the first atomic bomb exploded in Japan in August of 1945: the inverted or, if you will, "qliphotic" antithesis of the ecstatic truth of the orgasmic moment of the Gnostic Mass when the essence of the priest *fuses* with that of the priestess. It doesn't need to be explained, it needs to be experienced.

A MASSIVE OCCULTURATION THIS WAY'S A-COMING

Around 2008, I noticed there was an artist in Stockholm who diligently integrated occult themes and symbols in his work: Fredrik Söderberg. At one of his exhibitions, I said hello and introduced myself, and we got along well. Work like Fredrik's definitely seemed to be part of a general occulturation. I found the phenomenon of this visibility as such decidedly interesting from an occultural point of view: *Why was this happening in our specific "cultural moment"?* However, this was not only visible in the arts, but also within academia, where occultists of many factions and traditions had seeped into Ph.D. programs in the History of Ideas and History of Religions departments all over Sweden—and I would say it was the same for all of Europe.

This would eventually help soften the ambivalence and resistance that, for instance, Moderna Muséet, the contemporary art museum in Stockholm, had always felt vis-à-vis occult painter Hilma af Klint (1862–1944). And it was certainly a smart thing for them to notice which way the wind had shifted. Doing an about-face and suddenly embracing Hilma as their own, they created a multi-million-dollar franchise

---

*Abrahamsson, *Source Magic*, 147.

that traveled the world garnering critical praise and considerable revenue—including a wildly successful exhibition at the Guggenheim in New York in 2018–2019 that broke attendance records.

My mother, who worked at an art gallery in Stockholm for forty years and loved abstract art in general, and perhaps the Russian constructivists in particular, showed me the only Hilma af Klint catalog that existed when it came out at the end of the 1980s, telling me what a national treasure this artist was.* The myth that had arisen around the fact that Hilma didn't want her art seen until twenty years after her death became part of the success story, but not immediately so. Another forty years would need to be added to that hesitant trajectory. It was exciting to realize that her canvasses had been stored for decades, rolled up in an attic, a few blocks from where I was born and grew up.

Fredrik Söderberg and his wife Christine Ödlund became good friends of mine. They were very representative of what was going on at the time: a new reception of and engagement with previously stigmatized currents of philosophy and existential technologies. The initial peak of this important occulturation process happened in 2008 with the magnificent exhibition *Traces du Sacré* (Traces of the Sacred) at the Centre Georges Pompidou in Paris.

To walk around that exhibition was an overwhelming and synesthetic experience for me—not only because of my intellectual "interest" in and resonance with what was being shown, but also because nearly every one of the works displayed carried intense energies that cross-fertilized with all the others. The curators and academics had unknowingly created a great temple devoted to the greatness of the human mind and, if you will, soul—allowing the force/source fields of

*Some works by af Klint were included in the exhibition *The Spiritual in Art: Abstract Painting 1890–1985*, Los Angeles County Museum of Art, November 23, 1986–March 8, 1987. Moderna Muséet felt they had to do something and organized a traveling exhibition from 1989–1991 called *Ockult målarinna och abstrakt pionjär* (Occult Painter and Abstract Pioneer) but this was only after it had been made public that the MoMA in New York was preparing their show *The Secret Pictures by Hilma af Klint* in 1989.

Huxley, Michaux, the Beats, Berman, Cameron, Anger, Nitsch, Steiner, Beuys, Cage, and many others to overlap and interact. In that sense, *Traces du Sacré* was truly a groundbreaking door-opener that, as mentioned, became the beginning of a long and powerful process of occulturation that is still very resonant.

Inspired by both the exhibition and my own generally depressed state of mind, I indulged in a Parisian "chthonic katabasis"—the catacombs are magnificent spaces for reflection, as are the cemeteries. With camera in hand, I started photographing the specifically Catholic aesthetic of mortality monuments. This would eventually lead to an exhibition called *Death Is in Our Hearts* some years later.

And there were so many important dead souls with whom to necromantically connect! The Cimetière de Montparnasse offered me spontaneous dialogues with Tristan Tzara, Baudelaire, and my Parisian photographic hero Brassaï, plus of course the giant Man Ray, whose tomb inscription, "Unconcerned but not indifferent," gave me much food for thought. I decided that the reverse would probably be more fitting for myself: "Indifferent but not unconcerned." The Père-Lachaise cemetery is overwhelming too, and this day sprinkled me with energy from Marcel Proust, Raymond Roussel, and Oscar Wilde—all magnificent magicians in their own right.

To coincide with the epic *Traces du Sacré* exhibition, there was a Crowley exhibition at the Palais de Tokyo. Ten years after the celebrated October Gallery show in London, this one exhibited paintings specifically from Crowley's Sicilian years (1920–1923). Although these works were interesting as a "curiosum," Crowley's painterly naïvism-primitivism did not reveal much more than a childlike enthusiasm—which, in all fairness, can often be enough to create arresting visuals. However, only one image caught my attention: a kind of sketch for the later design of the *Thoth* tarot card The Hierophant, in which Crowley displays magical weapons—including phallic headgear—while the acolytes kneel before him, apparently ready for some solar-phallic action.

Anger was in Paris and sat on a panel at the Palais, again talking about his work in Cefalù in the mid-1950s. It was great to meet up in Europe again after our sessions in Los Angeles over the previous years. Bill Breeze was there as well, and had satisfied my Anger addiction at his hotel room before we headed out together to the Crowley exhibition: he showed me a black-and-white rough cut of Anger's masterpiece *Inauguration of the Pleasure Dome* (1954), with music by Harry Partch (one of my experimental music heroes). Again, I was catapulted into the massively influential universe of Crowley, Anger, de Brier, Cameron, and all the Los Angeles greats—including, by proxy, Jack Parsons and his valiantly romantic attempts at formulating a solid sense of liberty within the post-WWII American psyche.

Gen was in Paris too, to perform with the rebooted Throbbing Gristle project at La Villette. Despite being depressed in the wake of Lady Jaye's death, he had now thrown himself into the midst of a power dynamic that was insanely unhealthy. On one hand, there was Gen, on the other there was Chris and Cosey. In-between them was Sleazy, who dealt with both sides, and diplomatically so. The main problem was that TG had become such a cult band in the decades since their breakup in 1981, and they were now being offered vast sums of money to reunite for performances at festivals and other events. None of them could really afford to say no, and so they had to deal with each other as best they could. The evening in question was a "reenactment" of their seminal LP from 1977, *Second Annual Report* (now re-presented as the "Thirty-Second Annual Report").

I was happy to be able to console Gen while hanging out backstage after the concert and at the hotel. We made another interview for our book, and we were both interviewed on camera by French filmmaker Marie Losier for her film *The Ballad of Genesis and Lady Jaye* (2011). Although my interview was ultimately edited out of her film, we did have a good time in Paris together.

After visiting the Crowley exhibit together, Gen, Marie, and I met up with Bill, Sleazy, and Current 93 singer David Tibet. Sleazy, who was an exceptionally generous man, took us all to dinner at a nearby restaurant, and the spirits were high. For a fraction of a second, I became a fanboy thinking this was so great to be here with all these cool people, but then I soon retracted to what was actually happening: we were all just magical people having dinner together in a very unique slice of space-time. But Gen was undoubtedly the "queen bee": this particular moment would never have happened—and the rest of us would never have met each other—if it hadn't been for Gen and, by extension, TOPY. That is highly significant of real magicians: they weave webs in which others interact and sometimes start weaving their own webs. The intelligent magicians acknowledge the importance of the weaving masters as well as the past masters; the unintelligent are satisfied with claiming their own position while staring at their own reflective blinders.

PART VI
2010–2014

MR. OCCULTURE [PROFESSOR EMERITUS]!

In the autumn of 2008, I was invited to host an evening with Kenneth Anger at the Statens Museum for Kunst in Copenhagen, Denmark. In between screenings of his major films, we talked together with other invited Anger aficionados (Danish director Nicolas Winding Refn, my dear old friend Carl Michael von Hausswolff, and Danish journalist Lars Movin). This was followed by a performance of Anger's musical project done in collaboration with his manager, Brian Butler: Kenneth Anger's Technicolor Skull. A memorable evening, to say the least!

On the following day, I led Q & A sessions with Anger at the Danish Film School in front of a small but devoted crowd of students and fans. Most of Anger's films were shown and we talked between the screenings. It was overwhelming for me to be in this position, but it was one that worked out well, and one that Anger had requested. To hear

With Kenneth Anger in Copenhagen, 2008
(photo by Lars Top-Galia)

him talk in detail about all of his films was fascinating and revealing to us all. And it was the first time I saw his brand-new film *Ich will* (2008), edited together from old Nazi propaganda films.

> *Ich will* reflects the Hitler Jugend movement, which was the equivalent of the Boy Scouts. In fact, the Nazis took the idea from the Boy Scouts in England, which was something invented at the turn of the twentieth century by Baden-Powell. There too, the idea was to create a bond with the youth, to prepare them to fight for the empire. People forget that that was the original motivation of the Boy Scouts, to prepare them for the military. The transition to the military is not that difficult when you've been in the Boy Scouts. My brother was an Eagle Scout, a high rank. I absolutely refused to go into it. I was the rebel, totally against joining. My father was a scoutmaster but I said "No" already at a quite young age. And that's why Kenneth Anger is Kenneth Anger.*

After Copenhagen we kept in touch, as we had over the years. I sent him books I had published, and he wrote back with encouraging comments like "You are doing splendid work" and "Continue to flourish."† And once in a while he sent me some gems, like a vintage print of an image that I had fetishized for decades—unbeknownst to Anger, I assume—of him together with Dennis Hopper, Alejandro Jodorowsky, and Donald Cammell (filmmaker and son of Crowley's friend Richard Cammell), in London in 1970: all amazing magicians in their own peculiar ways.

The Equinox Festival held in London in 2009 was another seminal event of occultural lectures and performances. I was invited to talk and delivered a lecture called "Someone Is Messing with the Big Picture," focusing on the detrimental fragmentation of contemporary culture. It was a return to Conway Hall for me, and I enjoyed the

---

*Kenneth Anger, quoted in Abrahamsson, *Reasonances*, 142; slightly edited.
†Letter from Kenneth Anger to the author (26 August 2012).

atmosphere a lot. Fredrik Söderberg and Christine Ödlund were also present and we talked and got to know each other better. Annabel Lee and Michael Moynihan were there too, as were my friends Dariusz Misiuna, Joanna John, and others from the Okultura "crew" in Warsaw.* Plus many other friends, old and new: Erik Davis, Phil Farber, Ralph Metzner, David Beth, Robert Ansell, and Kendell Geers, to mention but a few.

I loved presenting my talk and basically just being who I was, both on and off stage. I also loved the persona that I felt others projected on me. It inspired me. To a great extent, my inner and outer projections had somehow merged nicely into a magico-anthropological mélange of eloquence and curiosity. In many ways this event was the spark that ignited my public "occultural" fire. For the catalog I wrote a kind of appendix text to the talk as such, and it illustrates well what was percolating inside me at the time:

SOMEONE IS MESSING WITH THE BIG PICTURE, PART II

Looking through my notes for the talk at the Equinox Festival 2009, I find a lot of moping and complaining, some bitter and almost cynical remarks that would strike me as negative had I heard them from another's mouth. Be that as it may, I thought this catalogue's companion text would be a good place to make slightly more sweet-tasting amends.

Equinox, as we know, is a time of cosmic balance and joyful celebration. Don't we all wish that it could be Equinox all year long? But it seems to be a fact that nothing is ever static or rigid—well, except for quite a few human minds—and for this we should be grateful. To go with the flow is better than to rest in the nest.

*Okultura is a Warsaw-based publishing house, specializing in original works and translations of underground and magical classics. In 2016, they published my book *Resonances* in Polish.

That we presently need change seems obvious to us all. I'd like to paraphrase the American president's "A change we can believe in" (Isn't that what most Americans like to do—believe?) and move it onward to "A change we can tangibly develop through." Life is about a lot more than saving the economy. An equinoctical balance on general levels seems so far away and so important that we can't really leave it to politicians anymore. After all, they are only human.

If I complain about speed, fragmentation, minimizing, condescending infantilization, etc., what remedies do I have? Well, their opposites of course. How hard can it be? Slowness, holistics, maximizing and increasing the scale, appreciating maturity and wisdom . . . very basic things.

I do believe we need to turn on, tune in, and drop a lot of imposed rubbish. And I'm still naive enough to believe that art is how we should go about it. The hubris stemming from very real anthropocentric insignificance is about to destroy . . . well, at least our own habitat, but possibly more than that too. The planet as such does not need to be saved, but the ecosystem relevant for human beings certainly does. How could art change that?

Well, necessity always makes itself heard, just like a bowel movement. We are becoming re-minded of nature. We need merging with nature on all levels, to be able to be a part of the totality of existence. As we need to merge with nature, art needs to merge with a mind that's capable of seeing this big picture. If that doesn't happen, we will all still be tiny dictators sucking poisoned nectar through ever-thinning straws. Basic survival equals knowledge, information, science, if you will, and feeding. But advanced development requires inspiration, communication, and feeding back. Where do we find this? In art.

The initiative for a festival like this is brilliant and well needed in this respect. Crossovers, mind-mergers, nonstatic disciplines uniting if but for an hour or two, nonrigid traditions, and colorful people meeting, talking, watching, listening, and perhaps even learning from each other. This festival is a solvent in which agents charge and discharge. What more could one really ask for?

Special kudos to Ralph Metzner who has been merging important concepts for such a long time. Blessings! When we chatted in Stockholm in 2004, Ralph formulated his basic view very well:

"My interest is the knowledge and understanding that can be gained from expanded states of consciousness. States of consciousness can be contracted and pathological as well. But the expanded ones are more interesting for me. How do you build them and turn them into a lasting condition? Say, if someone is depressed, they don't want to be un-depressed for a little while. How can you hang on to a state of mind that's lasting and get to the bottom of personal problems for instance. How to integrate such states?"

Isn't that "the call of the artist" right there: How to integrate whatever you have, or have experienced, and give it a more or less universal form that resonates with other people?

Sharing is not only about generic altruism. It's also about deliverance from and release of pressure on an individual level. We need to share the findings or formulations for our own sake too. We are social animals. We experience insights or stunning synchronicities. These enrich our lives but even more so if we can communicate them.

The sexual allegory is not far-fetched here (is it ever?). There are solitary means of seeking release for gathered emotions, fantasies, desires, etc. But for most people it is actually more stimulating and satisfying seeking that release with someone else. Not forgetting the creative potential of that kind of meeting. There needs to be penetration and energies in circulation.

Tradition and mere habitual life essence is not enough. In this day and age, ceremonies are not needed as much as transforming rituals. Who really needs well-known and safe slogans or simplified techno-gaga? Simplification becomes more and more complex by the day. Terminology: a trap of reason fragmenting potential unity.

However, storytelling, parables, allegories, metaphors, and symbols are all part of a language of survival. That language, I suspect, will be nonrational, nonintellectual, and non-based in language as we're used to it. If so, it might just work.

A potential communication from mind to mind—with or without filtering matrices, structures, agents, solvents, or grids—will be the language of the future. Technology in itself will not be our saving grace. Lack of technology will, however. That freedom and the challenge in itself will in turn open up new vistas of interhuman, interplanetary, interstellar, and even intergalactic communication. Messages from mind to mind for and through new dimensions.

That said, I wonder why so much of contemporary art is still stuck in the usual commodified two—or perhaps, if we're lucky, three—dimensions? The territorial urination of the art market? Is there a distinct parable there to human life in general? I think so, unfortunately. Culture and art need to pave the way, as always.

Two examples have recently provided me with a glimmer of hope. Both are Swedish artists, but that isn't really relevant on any other level than that they're from my own sphere, so to speak.

Fredrik Söderberg creates nonrational expressions by experimenting with geometry, mathematics, linearity. He is very much a mandalic artist, a skilled craftsman and draughtsman who merges with spiritual inclinations in a holistic unity. Traces of esoteric and religious history are filtered for the future through structures which challenge and stimulate the human senses and brains. Sheets of colorful emanations can become vivifying gates to new worlds. Those grids and levels of awareness are readily available.

Gustaf Broms is a ritualist, a magician, an eco-thinker who in every piece expresses will—and love. Regardless of whether he's on a year-long walk from Sweden to the Ukraine with his partner Trish Littler or if he's making earth sculptures in the Australian desert or scrubbing the city centre of Stockholm on his knees or meditating at rush-hour peaks in the most condensed and stressed epicentre of commuterized Stockholm, et cetera, et cetera, it's all made with a vision much, much larger than awakening interest in this or that gallery. Those grids and levels of awareness are readily available.

A hypothetical example for the British: If a highly successful artist like Damien Hirst would like to be remembered by art history for other things than revenue and colorful commodities, he could perhaps invest all of his wealth in spraying the entire globe with hemp seed? I can see an armada of carriers and bombers spraying the planet with this remarkable and oxygen-providing weed. This kind of direct approach to art could be a healthy, relevant, and decidedly intriguing development. One where art is no longer symbolic and programmatic, but rather direct and beneficial on more levels than the intellectual. Again, those grids and levels of awareness are readily available.

Art feeds back. We make the art that feeds us, who in turn feed art further. After the act of creation, art stands alone. Magic stands alone. Literature stands alone. Music stands alone. Human beings? Certainly not.

The artist used to be a high character who was revered and feared for being able to create change in accordance with will—his or her own or that of the whole tribe. The analogy today would be the figure of the lobbyist, the PR-person advocating bribery, lying, and loss of all ideals to pragmatically satisfy a "client." Yes, these are sad times and black magic is apparently more lucrative than ever before.

Life used to be compared to a chessboard. Player or piece? Prayer or peace? This was before the analogy to cinema came along. Remember "Be your own director"? This, of course, has now been replaced with the more hands-on *Lord of the Flies*–aspects of every game show and "reality" show on TV.

Speaking of which (witch?): Celebrity worship is a tragic case of false idols taking charge. People are looking for answers to undefined emotional questions, but only find evanescence and empty barrels creating loud echoes. Autographs used to be examples of talismanic transference but now, apparently, mass-produced items, records, DVDs, etc., will do. Items charged with the soul of the magical creator? A very shallow, impoverished, and transparent Zeitgeist (literally, "time-ghost") it seems.

It's obviously important to make decisions wherever and whenever you can. But in a cultural sphere in which we are, at least on the surface, encouraged to do so—although most of us know that's just a politically and commercially convenient illusion—it can also be a very relevant decision to remain outside of the generic process (the "loop," as it's been so aptly called) and sow seeds in a much more fertile soil.

Art stands out, in my mind at least, as the most fertile soil there is today. Perhaps because it's a sphere, like its natural counterpart, the earth, that becomes even more fertile the more manure is thrown on it by critics and enemies.

Impression. Will. Expression. Manifestation.

Four cyclically bound words that have changed life always as well as forever and a day. Good luck!

CARL ABRAHAMSSON, STOCKHOLM,
APRIL'S FOOLS DAY, 2009*

On the last evening of the festival, I briefly met up with Sleazy again, as he was performing that night with his Threshold House Boys Choir project, and it was lovely. Little did we suspect that this would be our final meeting; Peter "Sleazy" Christopherson died in Bangkok in November of 2010.

BOOK-MAKERS & LITERARY MAGIC

Similar occultural currents were going on in our tiny Stockholm, and Fredrik and Christine were indeed talented, sensitive, and perceptive

---

The Equinox Festival: A Festival of Scientific Illuminism (London: Strange Attractor, 2009), 50–53; slightly edited.

representatives. It was also wonderful for me to find out that Fredrik had originally been inspired by the first three issues of *The Fenris Wolf* in the early 1990s, and that this eclectic mix of various esoteric exposures had affected him in his development and, eventually, his art. It felt like a bizarre yet honoring full-circle movement in which it made perfect sense to literally just carry on and "go with the flow."

In 2011, Fredrik and I started a new imprint together called Edda Publishing. One of the first things on the agenda was to revive "Fenris," who had been resting in hibernation since 1993. I had originally intended to carry on with a fourth issue back in the mid-1990s, but there were too many other things going on and it fell by the wayside. Now the time was right and ripe, and we stormed ahead with the fourth issue, with a striking Luciferian cover image by Fredrik.

Sensing an immediate success, I then anthologized a reprint of the first three issues in one volume, also in 2011. After that it just kept on rolling with basically one new issue each year, up until number 7 in 2014. We also published books of Fredrik's art, Ernst Jünger's psychedelic classic *Visit to Godenholm* (for the first time in English), Crowley's erotic masterpieces *White Stains* and *Snowdrops from a Curate's Garden*, and many other books. We made plans to republish the work of Charles Stansfeld Jones (aka Frater Achad), a fanciful and productive Crowley follower. Through the help of Bill (again!), we managed to buy the rights to all of Achad's work from his still-living son, Tony. We began the process by including select essays by Achad in several issues of *The Fenris Wolf.*

We reveled in the actual book-making process, producing fine collectors' editions as well as standard ones. This was also an important part of a general Western occulturation process, in which publishers like Scarlet Imprint, Theion, Anathema, Fulgur, Hadean, Three Hands, and many others have issued fine and thought-provoking material in exquisitely crafted editions that are coveted by adepts and esthetes alike all over the world. The books not only house radical and constructive thoughts for some kind of posterity, but also widen perspectives for a new generation of artists and academics that no longer accepts previous and prejudiced narratives of "outsider art" and "fringe philosophy."

In 2012 I traveled with Fredrik to Brighton to give a presentation at Scarlet Imprint's *Pleasure Dome* festival. I spoke about the emergence of the "Mega Golem" within a general process of exchanging the terminology of the occult with that of art (and vice versa), something that had been increasingly on my mind during recent years.

The year before, Cotton Ferox had been invited by my old TOPY friend Vicki Bennett, who was by now an established artist through her brilliant People Like Us project, to make a radio program called "Radio Boredcast." I wrote a piece called "A Mega Golem Official" that Thomas and I set to music. The idea was to set a magical being free that consisted of nothing traditional nor even tangible, and a project that would be open to anyone interested in participating. In my presentation "Go Forth and Let Your Brainhalves Procreate" at the *Pleasure Dome* event, I spoke more in depth about the same concept. For each talk or creation, this Mega Golem figure took on more and more form, and was thereby able to integrate more and more content—and so on.

The Kunst & Geist ideas of the mid-2000s had now come to some sort of conceptual fruition, and it was a joy to speak about these things. Let the work be invisible, inaudible, intangible, and come forth in a culture of utterly flaunted yet depressing "auto-fiction" and the filtered, self-censored make-/fake-believes of social media. In my mind, the Mega Golem also brought forth a revitalization of the concept of secrecy. There is great power in secrets; sometimes it is barter-material worth more than all the gold in the world. In that sense, I never have to disclose who did what for the Mega Golem, nor do any of the contributing artists (or others) to me.

Beginning at the *Pleasure Dome* festival, I also kept speaking with Alkistis Dimech and Peter Grey of Scarlet Imprint about anthologizing my essays and lectures. It seemed I was on a trajectory in which I just wrote more and more, with a good store of material having now accumulated. And it was indeed nice to be acknowledged and conceptualized by a publisher I admired so much.

In 2014, Scarlet Imprint published my *Reasonances: Essays, Lectures, Interviews 2000–2013*. I was overjoyed—not only because the deluxe edition was bound in salmon skin, but mainly because I was out there with my own voice, and it seemed that other people were actually listening.

Another important book for me was published about a year before *Reasonances*. This was my first novel, *Mother, Have A Safe Trip*, which was something I'd been working on sporadically for a few years, and it filled me with great pleasure to write. I let the protagonist—a young magician onto whom several mighty individuals and organizations projected their own dark desires—roam free in a psychedelic sex-thriller of sorts, through Germany, Macedonia, and Nepal (weaving in some of the stories and atmospheres that Trilochan had shared in the late 1990s)—and, of course, inner space.

In the novel, I also made use of some already extant private writings in which I communicated with idealized forms of my own mind (as in the "Holy Guardian Angel" concept); thereby in a way externalizing and fictionalizing reality, and integrating my own urgent issues and matters into someone else's—in this case, the protagonist's—narrative. So, it wasn't a fictionalizing of a spontaneously formulated desire, but rather *a conscious and determined editing of an Is-To-Be reality*. For instance, the protagonist, Victor Ridderstadt, communicates with his love object in a cave in the Macedonian wilderness and decides to weave some spells:

"That's right," Veronica replied. "Matka means womb, by the way. People often come in here to do magic. This is where everything begins. That's why I've brought you here. You can make a wish here. You should make a wish here. Let me hear it. Let the cave hear it."

Victor looked at her. In the subdued light of the cave, Veronica now looked like some unearthly creature. She was no longer a young Macedonian woman set on having a good time. She was now something completely different, an ageless, archetypical witch of some sort. Victor closed his eyes.

"I wish for health, wealth and length of days," he began. "And a safe and successful development of this electricity project. And a girlfriend who sees my needs and heeds them. A girlfriend who doesn't feel the need to compete with me on an intellectual level. Someone who respects my creativity. I don't need stimulation on an intellectual level from a girlfriend. From her, I need emotional tenderness, caring, sex, a fulfillment of all those things I can't arrange myself, on my own. Beauty, esprit, allure, tenderness, love, self sacrifice, an intelligent Florence Nightingale rather than just another neurotic artist like myself.

I wish for international culture, ego gratification, reaching out while reaching in. To manifestly become what I already am on the inside: an intelligent and cultured artist with the power and poetry to enrich others' lives. One who inspires to celebrate life and its possibilities more. Not shying away from the dark aspects, but not striving for a constructed darkness either. Writing freely, experimenting and seeing what comes. And valuing the process highly. Gently jerking always brings something. That which comes, those who come— an extrapolation of phallic energy and fertile seed in a different and less sticky and perhaps less offensive form. Protagonist seed-sowing. I wish for action rather than far too modest reaction.

I wish that every moment should be filled by the holy guardian angel, the healing Gordian angle, the main inspiration, the daimon, the hidden genius. In invocation, and in evocation through me. The evocation is the work process and its results, while the invocation is the awareness, the increased consciousness of what's going on. Not at all rationally, hampering the synchronicities and the twists of inspiration and creativity. But joyfully and with an open mind. Editing may be done. But editing can't come before the creation. That's the number one: creation. That is, writing. Everything else is but different fruits on the same tree.

By all means, I should continue to listen to the spirits, mentors, inspirations. Listening by reading and assimilating what's uniquely them. What can I learn? How can I learn? But I should listen even more closely to my own voice and my own spirit. The expression, content, form and style must be mine and mine alone.

I wish that criticism need not concern me. I have my voice and it will speak its own mind in its own way. Jealousy and hostile tendencies from others have nothing to do with me. I have my voice and it needs to speak. Be shameless about it, if need be. Talismanic teachings and cathartic correspondence. If others aren't interested or perhaps even actively disinterested, then so be it.

I wish for all of these things but am happy for only a fraction of it all. Many thanks. Many thanks, Matka. Many thanks, Veronica. Many thanks, Vrelo womb."*

The book-release party for the novel took place at Catland, a small occult bookstore in Brooklyn. I had brought my teenage daughter to New York for a Halloween vacation, but she was not amused by her father yapping away with all these occult weirdos. I was happy that Jennifer Gira, the wife of my good friend Michael Gira, showed up and could talk to her while I was signing books.

Someone else showed up too: a beautiful woman who knew some of the people who owned and ran the store. She introduced herself as Vanessa Sinclair, and we talked about this and that in the somewhat fragmented ambience. I signed her copy of the book with the words "Enjoy irresponsibly!" and she smiled.

I had expected Gen to show up, but he wasn't feeling well. However, after the event, when my daughter and I were enjoying a late-night meal back in Manhattan, Gen called to say how much he enjoyed the book (I had interviewed him earlier in the day for the *An Art Apart* documentary, and had given him a copy then).† Little did I know at the time that in the background there was Vanessa, having just returned from

---

*Abrahamsson, *Mother, Have A Safe Trip* (Stockholm: Edda, 2013), 97–99.

†*An Art Apart* is a documentary film series I created that focuses on the creative process of artists.

the event. She was in a relationship with Gen, and had decided to go to the book release anyway when Gen decided not to. Today, I'm very, very happy she did, as she is now my wife and basically everything I ever wished for in a woman.

It dawned on me that there was more to this magical "working" than I immediately remembered. It wasn't just casually and causally ensouling my writing with desire. In December of 2014—that is, when the book had been out for slightly more than a year—I went to Macedonia together with Thomas Tibert to play a concert with Cotton Ferox. We were well taken care of by my wonderful local OTO brothers and sisters, many of whom also became genuine friends over the years. They took us out into the wilderness, and by boat into the very cave that they had only told me about before (as I was writing the book). Now I was *actually* there, published book in hand, and brought my lovely friend Vera Nikolic (the model for the female protagonist in the book) aside. We then (re-)enacted the scene, as written and published, so that the words resounded inside the womblike cave. Reality thus became reality again, filtered via fiction—and with an ensuing wish-fulfillment in tow!

Of course, I had to check the progression or "unfolding" as I looked back at these turns of events. I had met Vanessa in late October of 2013, and then we met the next time in February of 2016; basically, a period of twenty-seven months. The halfway point of this time span therefore lay somewhere between the thirteenth and fourteenth month, which was right when I was in that Macedonian cave—the midpoint Magic Theater boost definitely helped manifest my "intelligent Florence Nightingale" and all the rest of it!

AN ART APART

In early 2013, I was sitting in a hotel room in Tallinn, Estonia, staring at an insanely ugly orange-colored wall. I was there to supervise the printing of an art book (having occasionally gone into the business of being a printed-matter consultant of sorts), feeling quite miserable. The book didn't interest me at all and yet I had promised to deal with it. The printing, of course, did not go well. What to do? Dive into escapism, of course! Any excuse I could find to distract myself was more than welcome. The closest thing at hand was a small point-and-shoot camera that I'd borrowed from my daughter. Ugly wallpaper, ugly fridge, ugly bed, snap, snap, snap . . . After that, I was so bored I decided to try and shoot some video of myself: boredom-infused narcissism!

After a moment of hesitation and embarrassing silence, I started talking straight into the camera as if it were a very small TV crew. The words that suddenly came out of me were those of a host or reporter talking about art. Not any kind of postmodern bullshit, like the images of the book I was there to supervise. But rather soulful, intelligent art created by exciting, radical, and groundbreaking people. I stopped and played it back, realizing I sounded like some kind of enthusiastic Richard Attenborough of the underground. I genuinely hated my voice but started loving the concept.

That moment became an epiphany that immediately got ahold of me on a deep level. I'd previously written so much for magazines, papers, and books, but the print market seemed ever dwindling by the day. So why not use a video camera instead and go for it again? That is, meet interesting people, let them tell their own story on their own terms, and see what comes out of it. I realized I was onto a new obsession and immediately started making notes about whom to contact.

My best friend and original TOPY member Henrik Møll was as enthusiastic as me about the idea, and luckily he worked as an editor for television and film. Supported by his technical expertise, I ventured into a frenzied state of mind and just shot, shot, and shot material in Sweden, Norway, the US, and the UK. After dealing with close artist friends first, I drifted into unknown territories with new acquaintances. Before I knew it, I had shot the footage for ten films, and tried to define the project as such:

Some artists create groundbreaking, radical, provoking, transcending, transgressing, mutating works of art that continuously change the culture we live in. What goes on in their minds? What motivates them? And why do they create in the first place? *An Art Apart* is a series of documentary portraits of artists whose creations and concepts have inspired thousands of people worldwide—who in turn take the ideas further and into new environments. *An Art Apart* examines these artists' creative processes, emotions, and stories in intimate and revealing conversations. From the most esoteric underground expressions to the mainstream culture we all share, *An Art Apart* shines the light on what art really is—or can be.

As we were about to start editing the very first film, Henrik died in August of 2014. That was a big blow. Not only because he was my best friend, but also because he had all the knowledge I lacked as a pathological technophobe. I was very close to abandoning the entire project when mutual friends talked me into continuing. At Henrik's funeral in Copenhagen in August of 2014, I promised the assembled folks that each Trapart* film would be dedicated to his loving memory (a promise I have solemnly kept).

And then, one by one, the films started appearing. During 2015 I was Sweden's most productive filmmaker, with five documentaries;† one art film, *Sub Umbra Alarum Luna* (a tribute to experimental British filmmaker Derek Jarman);‡ and one feature-length psychological thriller, *Silent Lips*,§ under my belt. Some extra-manic energy, support from the film gods, and a devoted team of one can definitely get you far!

---

*My own publishing/production venture since 2012 is called Trapart Books, Films, and Editions.

†About artists Andrew McKenzie, Gustaf Broms, Vicki Bennett, Charles Gatewood, and Genesis Breyer P-Orridge.

‡The title is a reference/homage to Jarman's Super 8 film *In the Shadow of the Sun*.

§In 2019 a re-edited version of the film was released as *My Silent Lips*.

THE MEGA GOLEM

In November of 2013, Cotton Ferox was invited to perform at a Polish festival called Trans/Wizje. This was just one of several important manifestations of underground and magical culture through the *Okultura* magazine and publishing company. I had met the main founder Dariusz Misiuna in the early 2000s when he came to visit me in Stockholm. Whatever Dariusz does, he does well; the Warsaw festival was friendly and many of the acts were fantastic.

We had invited our friend Bartosz Samitowski to play guitar with us and this turned out to be the best Cotton Ferox performance ever—not only musically, as Thomas and Bartosz created ethereal soundscapes and overtones, but also because I officially set the Mega Golem free during this concert. It had enough contributions to come alive properly, and I sent it off on its merry way through a poem I read at the concert, dressed in a red plastic devil mask I had bought in New York for Halloween one month earlier:

> Mega Golem
> Here you are
> Mega Golem
> Bright new star
> Growing stronger
> By the day
> Growing longer
> Here to stay
> Limbs of force
> And fury too
> No remorse
> One love—or two
> Art by art
> Piece by piece

You are smart
And still at ease
Mega Golem
Do your thing
Mega Golem
In the swing
Of things to come
The Is to Be
Feared by some
Revered by me
So it is done!

I have no idea if it was "in the stars" or if we were simply in tune, but the whole evening was perfect. Perhaps my loosing of the Mega Golem was a much needed relief and release for me, creating spaces for new things and ideas to emerge from within? The full moon that shone over Warsaw that cold night brightly reflected a culmination and beginning at the same time: a peak moment that again taught me how influential art can be when it's genuine and magical.

Now that the Mega Golem was out and about, I felt more comfortable to talk about the project as such. This led to further contributions, both known and unknown, and I summed up some of them in a text for the Canadian anthology *Anathema: Pillars*. The openness also inspired me to write and record a series of "conceptual" texts called "Radio Mega Golem," which are ongoing to the present day.

In 2021 the texts thus far were anthologized in the book *The Mega Golem: A Womanual for All Times and Spaces.** I strongly believe that these kinds of poetic, free-flow, intuitive, and sometimes "automatic" narratives about magic much better convey concepts than orderly, structured, and rational tomes of often too trivial technicalities.

---

*Abrahamsson et al., *The Mega Golem: A Womanual for All Times and Spaces*, (Stockholm: Trapart, 2021).

PART VII

2015–2019

FLASHBACK & FORTH!

In 2015 I was contacted by a guy from Uppsala. He said he had some things to show me. It sounded intriguing, and it turned out to be exactly that: he had an amazing collection of "LaVeyana," specifically a collection of negatives and photographic prints from the estate of German paparazzo Walter Fischer. Fischer had been stationed in Los Angeles for decades and focused on photographing movie stars. But celebrities of all kinds were of interest to him, so in the mid-1960s he contacted Anton LaVey in San Francisco. The relationship was mutually beneficial: Fischer got amazing photos and some interviews inside the Black House during the Church of Satan's early heyday, and LaVey got a lot of worldwide attention for his budding "Infernal Empire." Fischer's material was syndicated to magazines all over the world, and it had a remarkably long "shelf life." I could remember seeing a number of the photos in Swedish men's magazines in the 1980s, when they were "re-run" in stories about "crazy magicians all over the world" and similar sensationalist angles.

In fact, many of these very images had been instrumental in the crystallization of my fascination and obsession with LaVey and his Church. And now this guy brought it all to my table, quite literally, including images of LaVey and Jayne Mansfield together, as well as Jayne solo. It was almost beyond belief! We instantly decided to make a book of it all. This became the art book *California Infernal: Anton LaVey & Jayne Mansfield as portrayed by Walter Fischer*, published in 2016. In many ways this lavish "coffee-table" project brought out new layers of respect for LaVey in my mind. I had already begun revisiting my Satanic past in 2013 when I presented a lecture in Copenhagen called "Anton LaVey, Magical Innovator." The more I thought about him, the more I found just how creative a magician he really was. It was apparent already in these 1960s photographs and documents, and then gradually progressed in his increasing focus on a reclusive appreciation of time and space:

With the development of total environments and many of his other concepts, there was no longer a need for LaVey to be a frustrated outsider in conflict with the herd. The Satanist's creative isolation in a space/time-warp-possible mind-frame is one of silence and subtlety, and one of the greatest tools in the Satanic trade. This, combined with honest self-knowledge and a proud appreciation of one's own kinks and complications makes for a good, solid Satanist. There's always a strong focus on real-life material success too. But only based on The Balance Factor and what is actually possible for an individual in that position. Self-deceit is not a popular quality in LaVey's cosmos.*

In February of 2016, I was in New York for the Occult Humanities Conference (titled "Language of the Birds") at NYU. I had been invited already back in 2013 by the energetic organizer/curator Pam Grossman, and looked forward to the event for a long time. It was a magnificent manifestation of art and esotericism, with cream-of-the-crop speakers (Peter Bebergal, Erik Davis, Christiana Key, Christina Oakley Harrington, Judika Illes, and others) and a great exhibition of phenomenal artists (including Kenneth Anger, Alison Blickle, Jesse Bransford, Breyer P-Orridge, Cameron, Leonora Carrington, Aleister Crowley, Brion Gysin, Ken Henson, Paul Laffoley, William Mortensen, Rosaleen Norton, Kurt Seligmann, Harry Smith, Xul Solar, Austin Osman Spare, Peter Lamborn Wilson, and others).

During a break I visited the entrance foyer where there were some merchandise tables with books from various publishers. Jon Graham from Inner Traditions was there, and we talked about current projects. My old friend Michael Moynihan joined us, and the conversation drifted into my talk at the conference and my general increase in written output in general. This very conversation crystallized into a book project called *Occulture*, which would anthologize my most recent talks

---

*Abrahamsson, "Anton LaVey, Magical Innovator," in *Occulture*, 99–100.

at various conferences and symposia: a kind of follow-up to 2014's *Reasonances*.

I had a great time at the NYU conference, as I had gradually taught myself not only to be clearer in my presentations but also with respect to what my philosophy, as such, is:

> The current magical revival in popular culture is in many ways symptomatic of a Western malaise and frustration with the given options, in which the individual is placed within either a materialistic collective or a reactionary monotheistic religion, or possibly a combination. Both are mere substitutes for a genuine existential worth and meaning that can only come from within, defined through active individuation. My theory is that the solutions are always a lot closer than we think. In regard to global environmental problems, it can certainly be tempting to long for outer space. But perhaps it's more intelligent to look downward instead, at cultures who have actually managed to survive through crises in history. Either via still-existing, living indigenous humans or through remaining works of art. If we can assimilate instead of just "exoticize," we will find that there are many distinct traits in common, such as, for instance, a validation of inner, intuitive processes of gathering information, and a holistic approach to their implementation. This is beyond religion, occultism, philosophy, or magic. It's just common sense, in which memes from inner nature become schemes in outer nature, and possibly vice versa. I wouldn't be surprised if it's all essentially the same thing and that a free-flowing circulation will help mutate existence to ensure maximum survival, both on memetic and genetic levels.*

On February 7th, I went to dinner with Gen and Vanessa. It was the "Super Bowl" evening, so the restaurant was completely empty. It was

---

*Quote from the NYU lecture "Memes or Schemes," reprinted in Abrahamsson, *Occulture*, 218.

a special date indeed, in both senses of the word: a real crossroads moment. Gen was born in 1950 and would turn sixty-six in fifteen days. I was born in 1966 and had turned fifty just twenty days earlier. We were almost exactly at this strange midpoint with sixteen years between us, and intuitively hit upon the realization that 16 (years) is two times 8, which thus resembles two upstanding infinity symbols.* We acknowledged the significance—whatever it was—while Gen kept giving pieces of food to his beautiful Lady Jaye Jumelle doll from Benin, and I realized that Vanessa was an exceptionally magical woman. A few nights earlier, she had invited me to talk at the legendary Morbid Anatomy Museum in Brooklyn. I showed images from my photographic exhibition *Death Is in Our Hearts* and talked about aesthetics and creativity as a kind of defense mechanism against approaching death itself. Afterward almost everyone present went to a nearby loft party that Vanessa had organized. She had also written for a couple of issues of *The Fenris Wolf* over the years, and it was always refreshing to read someone so well versed both in magic and psychoanalysis make real and meaningful connections between these fields.

On one of the Occult Humanities conference days, we went out to lunch together with author Erik Davis and publisher Robert Ansell. Vanessa charmed us all with her wit and beauty, and it was obvious that she was a New York powerhouse of occultural connections and magical manifestations. I realized over and over just how very special this woman was.

In May of 2016, I traveled to London for our first Psychoanalysis, Art & the Occult (or "Psychartcult") conference.† Vanessa and I had been working hard at setting everything up, and we were both happy

---

*On the exact "midpoint," February 4th, Gen, Vanessa, and I had also hung out together. I met Vanessa at her psychoanalytic office and took her out to eat, after which we went to see Gen perform a beautiful spoken-word/ambient set together with Ryan Martin, his manager.

†The Psychoanalysis, Art & the Occult conferences, organized by Vanessa Sinclair and Carl Abrahamsson, are held at (somewhat) regular intervals: England 2016, Italy 2019, and Denmark 2022.

to see it unfold the way it did. The symposium—which also included a substantial art exhibition with works by Austin Spare, John Balance, Val Denham, Katelan Foisy, Genesis, Charlotte Rodgers, and Roberto Milusic Migliussi—was a great success, but more importantly, we fell in love during the proceedings. So, this was a kind of climactic cherry on top of it all, but it also meant that we had a really hard time readjusting to our previous lifestyles once the conference was over.

The conference also opened me up to new environments, and not only those concerning psychoanalysis. Vanessa had invited some very interesting individuals from the New York occult environment, and I made many new friends among them: Vanessa's "23rd Mind"/"Glitchcraft" partner Katelan Foisy (they also shared an apartment in NYC at the time), Quimbanda practitioner Jesse Hathaway Diaz, shamanic practitioners Langston Kahn and Chiron Armand, Vodun priest Demetrius Lacroix, and Daoist magician Fred Yee. From the UK there was animist artist Charlotte Rodgers and the ever-so-excellent Val Denham (whose art I had loved since I first saw it gracing many a record cover in the early 1980s). Many others participated as well, including the occultural author Gary Lachman; one of New York's leading psychoanalysts, Steven Reisner, plus Irish Lacanian psychoanalysts Eve Watson, Ray O'Neill, and Olga Cox Cameron; and a great psychologist active among the Maori in New Zealand, Ingo Lambrecht.

It was like being in a vortex where many of the presenters also shared their creations, like Scarlet Imprint's Alkistis Dimech and Peter Grey, and Fulgur's Robert Ansell. All of this within four walls literally packed with art that made the space vibrate: the beautiful Spare images, some of Gen's work, John Balance, Charlotte Rodgers, Val Denham, and a large vista by Malcolm McNeill originally made as an image for an illustrated edition of William Burroughs's *Cities of the Red Night* (which never saw the light of day, unfortunately).

I again had the privilege of being the final presenter, and delivered a paper comparing the psychoanalytic process to that of ritual magic.

Putting words to what had been brewing inside me since I quit my own analysis in 2008 was in many ways an eye-opener:

> Human language is both a blessing and a curse. Nowhere is this so apparent as when one is talking about oneself or expressing what one wants in ritual. Well, it's apparent in politics too, and in device-instruction manuals. The formulation seems to take place right after the need to express has encountered the comfort-zone filter, and substantial things are usually lost in this translation. It becomes a compromise that makes perfect sense to the ego, a signal filtered out with safe noise.
>
> The destinations in terms of psychoanalysis and magical practice are basically one and the same: in order to change negative behavioral loops and hindrances, we gradually work on small steps and changes, very much through formulation, and hopefully learn more about ourselves while doing that. But in both cases, the road to insight is paved with eloquent defense mechanisms and delusions of grandeur. In both, the underlying problematic emotional or psychic cluster is protected by expressions of what *seems* to be will. That is, a desired direction. But usually it is not ingrained existential will based on a 100 percent genuine honesty (if there is such a thing) but rather momentary bursts of what *appears* to be genuine will.*

No wonder we fell in love . . . The "Psychartcult" conference was a soft but powerful explosion of magical energy that we had aroused and created together for several months since meeting up again in New York earlier in the year. From that point on we stuck together, and for a long time I flew to New York almost once a month and stayed there half of my time. I became a part-time New Yorker, and we also traveled to Miami a lot as that's where Vanessa is originally from. It was a whirlwind in so many delightful ways, and yet I still managed to get a lot of work done.

---

*Abrahamsson, "Formulating the Desired," in *Occulture*, 125–26.

CATHOLICS & SACRED WHORES

Vanessa and I talked back and forth about where we should settle. I had always wanted to live in the US, at least for a longer consecutive time, so that was one option. New York was definitely one of my favorite spots in the world. But already in London Vanessa had jokingly said that if Donald Trump became president, I would have to save her and move her over to Europe. In a knightly fashion, I said that of course I would do that. The moment proper came in November of 2016: Donald Trump became president, and the decline and fall of the American empire suddenly seemed quite palpable. I decided I could not live for any extended period in a country where such blatant vulgarity was somehow in charge, and promptly asked Vanessa if she would marry me. The answer was "Yes!" and in late December we were married at Örbyhus Castle north of Uppsala, underneath an oak planted by Swedish king Gustav Vasa five hundred years earlier. A process of immigration began but was unfortunately slowed down by the Syrian

Newlyweds in Örbyhus, Sweden, 2016
(photo by Gustaf Broms)

refugee crisis in which Sweden became overly entangled as compared to other and much larger countries of the European Union.

However, eventually everything was settled, and today Vanessa is a Swedish citizen, a successful psychoanalyst, a model wife, a super-creative magician, and an ever-inspiring partner. Life is strange and beautiful in that it sometimes allows disastrous macro-developments to become extremely auspicious twists and turns on a personal level.

On that note, in hindsight it seemed inevitable that Edda Publishing would morph into something else at around this time. While on our way out to see a bookbinder in a suburb of Stockholm to inspect some slipcases for the deluxe edition of the seventh issue of *The Fenris Wolf*, Fredrik said he wanted to tell me something. Over the years, we had often joked that we would at some point have to become Christians in order to repent for all of our sins in spreading so much occult material. This had always been good for a hearty laugh. But now it was for real: Fredrik confessed that he had become a Catholic! I realized he was serious and accepted it as being his wish. The bottom line, however, was that he felt he could no longer be involved with Edda. So, we gradually dismantled everything until nothing remained. To me it was a sad development because we had cultivated such a creative collaboration over the years, and through that relationship produced some stellar books and editions.

There was also sadness in losing an intelligent man not only to Christianity but to Catholicism specifically. In Sweden, Catholics constitute a tiny minority and are regarded as some kind of *rara aves* or fringe weirdos. When one of the Swedish princesses married a Catholic American, voices were raised about the unsuitability of allowing Catholics into the royal house. This may sound like an archaic and dusty issue, but it has been a concern of European royal houses for centuries: Where lies a Catholic's loyalty, first and foremost? Is it to the people and the nation, or to the "Holy See" of some pope in Dark Fantasyland?

Catholicism in Northern Europe seems to have had a minor upswing during the 2010s, attracting mainly young middle-class intellectuals apparently in need of a stern and nonnegotiable "one-way" authority. This is undoubtedly interesting from a psychological perspective, and perhaps represents a reaction against the maximal freedom that Protestant/secular societies grant to their citizens, a freedom that intimidates and possibly perplexes those lacking in individuation and willpower. When you can't find your way in a confusing world as an individual—even though you are being offered so many potential paths—it probably feels safe to attach yourself to the most rigid and life-negating structures there are, namely, monotheist ones. Let someone else do the thinking and feeling for you, just like in any of those supposedly "Satanic" cults that this cult par excellence always yaps about with such fervor.

Well, as a wise man once said: to each his own, and let the water find its own level, and whatever floats the boat may be that which sinks the ship.

The Edda years were special. Fredrik and I got a lot of things done in a unique "Third Mind" way. But nothing lasts forever. I had already started my own publishing company in 2012, Trapart Books, so I carried on under that name, continuing to bring out *The Fenris Wolf* along with a multitude of other titles.

Over the years, Edda also arranged some important international events. The most important were the two "Here to Go" conferences held in Trondheim, Norway, and co-organized with my friend Martin Palmer. These were symposia with occultural lectures by artists and creatives like Gary Lachman, Kendell Geers, Vicki Bennett, Jesper Aagard Petersen, Alkstis Dimech, Peter Grey, Angela Edwards, and Z'EV. They constituted fabulously fun opportunities for people to talk about interesting and relevant topics, as well as for most of us to (re-)connect. I found it especially amazing to be immersed in a percussive "bath" of rhythms and frequencies by Z'EV in pitch darkness in Trondheim, thinking back to the workshop I organized in Stockholm with him in 1990: "same but different," one could say, but a very nice trajectory onward and upward some twenty-three years later. Z'EV was an amazing magician in so many ways, and when he passed away in late 2017 it felt like a great loss.

Some people truly refine their craft and expression to the point of mastery, and Z'EV was definitely one of them: a "rhythmajikian" living for and through his own beats and syncopations to give people a chance to see—and hear—what can be experienced if you only allow yourself those important epiphanic breaks in your routine narrative:

> The Drum and its Drumming are the primal instruments for Trance induction and transition using Driving Procedures because the spectral envelope of each individual drum beat typically shows large amounts of acoustic energy at low frequencies [i.e., our old friend infra-sound] ranging over the low frequency portion of the Brain Wave spectrum associated with deep Trance states. And these sonic energies effect not only the brain, but also rhythmically inundate the entire range of auditory pathways throughout the body.*

The Trondheim conference of 2014 also brought more to the fore regarding the magic of audio vibrations specifically, as well as to the Babalon experience or concept that was now in full swing thanks to Scarlet Imprint's Babalon-themed volume called *The Red Goddess* (2007). On one of the conference evenings, Cotton Ferox played a very dark and atmospheric concert, working together with British artist and magician Angela Edwards. Edwards has created a great amount of powerful art, consciously weaving intent and/or catharsis into her work. She also has experience from sex work, which she has likewise incorporated into both her art and her magic practice. She wrote about the "sacred whore" for the seventh issue of *The Fenris Wolf*:

> Without romanticizing the prostitute/sex worker as an other-worldly sensual being or the idea of placing the whore on the Babalon goddess avatar pedestal, for us to reach a realistic view of sacred sex

---

*Z'EV, "Transitions and Trance," in Carl Abrahamsson and Martin Palmer, eds., *Here to Go 2014: A Symposium on Art, Counter-culture and the Esoteric* (Stockholm: Trapart, 2014), 22.

work means placing this practice in relation to a higher spiritual enlightenment. In OTO traditions for example we are often confronted with the idealized version from a male point of view of the icon of Babalon and female sexuality. This is for the most time a hollow superficial pin-up vision adhering to the male fantasy, rather than the reality of real sacred sex work.*

Edwards's arguments resound well with mine: it is only in personal transgression/transcendence within a magical context that we can set the Babalonian energy free and direct it—*not* in theoretical frameworks and surface-level aesthetics. During the Cotton Ferox performance, Thomas and I created vibrations and soundtracks for Edwards as she developed a spontaneous ritual in the nude and literally in the flesh. After some adornments and needlework on her own body to get into an altered state of mind, she ritually masturbated with a clay phallos that she had made in her inimitable aesthetic: rough, painted, glazed, organic in style, and—to me—evoking something decidedly Lovecraftian. The penetration itself created an immediate change in the space (and time). Slow movements with adornments and suggestive lighting and weird music on a stage signifies "performance art." But when the protagonist solemnly inserts her own artwork into her own body in a sexual way, there is not only transcendence and transgression for her but also for all those present—hence a genuine priestess-function is activated. Edwards worked her magic without inhibitions, and it could be viscerally felt by everyone present. It was a genuine honor to create those sound-spells for her.

The day before the performance/ritual, I interviewed Edwards about her work:

My main thing is to develop spiritually. To do something that I've not done before. It's like initiation, and you can't be doing that all the time, and it can't really be planned. I like it to be shamanic. I'm

---

*Edwards, "The Sacred Whore," *The Fenris Wolf* 7 (2014), 123.

not doing it for aesthetic reasons; I do it more as a kind of spiritual experience or invocation, which is a bit what Hermann Nitsch is like in a lot of ways. Even Marina Abramovic, to start with, was working in that kind of way; rather than just doing the same thing over and over again.*

CINEMATIC SUMMINGS-UP

After ambitiously having shot a great deal of documentary footage and interviews for the *An Art Apart* series, I was happy to be working professionally with film as a medium in the mid-2010s. It has never been on par with my love for writing, but certainly comes a close second. In many ways, working with documentary films is like an audiovisual extension of my writing as a journalist. The result becomes something to watch and listen to instead of just to read.

Being in that cinematic swing, it grew on me that it would be amazing to reconnect to "the old days" and make films about people who were not just inspiring artists, but who had been influential for me on a magical level. Kenneth Anger became a gateway in this regard. As part of the swelling documentary film series, I traveled to California together with the great Swedish artist Åsa Ersmark in the summer of 2014 to film interviews with Anger, photographer Charles Gatewood, and LSD blotter-art collector Mark McCloud. It had been some seven years since I last saw Anger in Los Angeles, and we set up to film him in our suite at the Château Marmont Hotel.

Unfortunately, Anger was not too accommodating although I had made an exception from my principles and actually paid his manager Brian Butler $3,000 for the session. I immediately felt that I had to concentrate on getting whatever material I could, so I set everything

---

*Angela Edwards in conversation with Carl Abrahamsson, from the book *An Art Apart* (forthcoming).

"magical" aside and focused mainly on Anger's work as a filmmaker. We just didn't connect, and I couldn't figure out why. In the end I was exhausted—an ambivalent triumph worthy of Sisyphus as a journalist!— and couldn't return to the material until much later. Other films were finished before this one, and I was happy with that. However, I could never deny the influence Anger had had on me since the mid-1980s, and I wanted to make my documentary about him something more than a trip down memory lane with him talking about when and where he made a certain film, or what his inspiration was.

In 2018, I returned to the Anger project. As mentioned, I was spending a lot of time in the US with Vanessa but didn't feel motivated to arrange another session with Anger in person. Instead, I paid Brian Butler many more thousands of dollars to film Anger and ask him my questions, and the result was surprisingly great. Anger was ninety-one years old at the time and had a new look that was riveting and haunting. Whereas before Anger had always had the appearance of a "regular Joe"—and this was true even in 2014—with khaki pants, nice shirts, and an overall polished façade, the "new" and very old Anger had long, thin, unkempt hair, hollow cheeks, and something decidedly sad in his eyes. It was a visage eerily reminiscent of the "Crypt-Keeper" in EC Comics' *Tales From The Crypt*. He was certainly coherent enough in his replies, so I assumed—as did the rest of the world—that this was a look of his liking and that he had actively chosen it.

I managed to edit and complete my film in 2019. The end result, *Cinemagician: Conversations with Kenneth Anger*, is clearly divided into the 2014 and 2018 segments. Overall, I think I succeeded in providing a good presentation of not only Anger's cinematic ouvre, but also his interest in occultism in general and the work of Aleister Crowley in particular.

I was also smart in that I had provided Anger with questions about his relationship with Anton LaVey, because I had a plan in mind to make a documentary film about LaVey as well. The seeds for this had been planted with the *California Infernal* book project, when I started to really ask myself: *Why did these old Walter Fischer photos come back to haunt me the way they had?* Perhaps my unconscious was trying to tell me to take a closer look at this era in my life while at the same time cinematically honor the memory of Dr. LaVey?

There was one key premise or question that came to the fore in my thinking about this: *What was actually going on in our meetings at the Black House?* I often felt that we had a great time no matter what happened—having dinner, watching movies on video, listening to him playing music in the kitchen, and so forth—but there were also things going on "between the lines." Much of this could be ex post facto speculation on my part, of course, like when you think back on someone you have loved and respected and then construct a highly idealized image of that person. But I *did* write in my notes and diary at the time about experiencing a benevolent kind of programming based on what he felt that I should receive. That both LaVey and Blanche were generous and friendly I had experienced already before we met, specifically in their encouragement for *The Fenris Wolf.* But during our sessions, as mentioned previously, he not only pointed out, for example, how great the scriptwriter and author Ben Hecht was; he took down Hecht's *Fantazius Mallare* and *A Guide for The Bedeviled* from the shelf and read passages from them aloud to me, while at the same time glancing at me now and then with a truly devilish look that seemed to say: *"Soak it in, Carl, soak it in!"*

LaVey was a gleeful and cunning Master Magician, and I wanted to hear from other people who had been there during that same era if they had experienced something similar: a benevolent occult empowerment within what I have termed the *Satano-Gnosis.* My thesis or premise turned out to be right—or "right on the money," as LaVey would have said. When I started interviewing old and new friends for the film *Into the Devil's Den* in 2018 and 2019, I heard many stories about exactly that feeling of having been invested with dark and secret knowledge, which LaVey thought suitable that we move on in the world and into the future.

Michael Moynihan and Adam Parfrey were both exposed to the work of amazing photographer William Mortensen via LaVey's insistence, and later on they pooled their magical resources to manifest two important volumes in 2014: a new contextualized edition of Mortensen's magnum opus and key Satanic work *The Command to Look: A Master Photographer's Method for Controlling the Human Gaze*, plus the magnificent coffee-table book *American Grotesque: The Life and Art of William Mortensen*.

LaVey read Don Blanding's poem "Vagabond's House" to Los Angeles artist Larry Wessel, emphasizing the immense power of fantasy and magic, which later led to Wessel's documentary film *Larry Wessel's Palace of Wonders*, which is a collage of interviews with various collectors.

Men's magazine editor Bob Johnson got to know LaVey when he interviewed him for the August 1994 issue of *High Society*. Johnson asked LaVey why there was no companion volume for men to LaVey's *Satanic Witch*. LaVey immediately suggested that Johnson should write it—which he eventually did and published as *The Satanic Warlock* in 2017.

There are more examples; most everyone I talked to had stories of their own about how LaVey's inspiration would eventually manifest in real, tangible influence. It was a satisfying pleasure to work on this film, which premiered in the autumn of 2019 at Husets Biograf in Copenhagen—the cinema run by my old friend Jack Stevenson, who had also been a welcome guest at the Black House in the early 1990s, and who is featured in the project.

Making a documentary film always entails editing down a large amount of raw footage, weeding out segments à la "kill your darlings." This has never appealed to me, although I know how tough it can be to sit through films that are far too long for their own good. It seems that each medium has its own optimal volume. That said, I did have far too much material for the film proper. Being first and foremost a book person, I decided to use all of it in a book as well. I found the interviews and firsthand stories about relationships with Dr. LaVey too interesting to be left on the (digital) cutting-room floor. This became a central project during the first Covid-19 pandemic year of 2020–21, when Vanessa and I basically stayed at home in our Stockholm apartment. It turned out great for me: I could allow all the interviewees the space they deserved, and I could write several contextualizing chapters about LaVey himself and his brand of Satanism. The book in question—*Anton LaVey and the Church of Satan: Infernal Wisdom from the Devil's Den*—was published in early 2022, and in many ways wrapped up a long-term premise, project, and partnership. I felt the same with the Anger film: it was a full stop, a summing-up of a fascination that had affected me deeply, both on a personal as well as a magical level, for decades.

In many ways, it was the same with Genesis. We made the film *Change Itself—An Art Apart: Genesis Breyer P-Orridge* in 2013–2015; the third spoken-word album, *Loyalty Does Not End with Death*, in 2018–2019; and worked on our book of conversations, *Sacred Intent*, so that it could be released in time for Gen's seventieth birthday in February of 2020.

All of this was a massive and emotional summing-up for me, and yet it didn't specifically have anything to do with Gen's illness (of cancer). The odds of survival were bad and we all knew it, but this had more to do with tying up loose ends in general. Or at least that is how it was for me—I'm sure we would have gone on to other projects together had Gen stayed alive longer. The film as such is a very clear and precise definition; the third spoken-word album collaboration is a great symbolic completion; and the book is a very literal completion as well, as it contains conversations between 1986 and 2019 that were already thought of as the chapters of a book since our trip to Nepal in 2000.

WE TRAVEL

In early 2019, Vanessa and I went to Thailand for a vacation but also to hang out with Annie Bandez (aka Little Annie, aka Annie Anxiety). My mother had died in the autumn of 2018, and we needed to get away from that void and all those practical as well as emotional things one needs to go through in the aftermath. Thailand was perfect in that sense: diametrically different from what we had been up to recently. Sunshine, warmth, celebrations of life and death, colors, humility, with a healthy religious and magical culture in its Buddhism and folk beliefs.

Meeting Annie again was great too. We first became acquainted at the Stockholm Spoken Word Festival in 1998, and again when she performed on a bill with Michael Gira's band Swans in Stockholm in 2017. She had then just moved to Miami, and I suggested we reconnect there as I was at that time a frequent flyer with my lovely wife. Vanessa and Annie hit it off right away, so to all meet up in Thailand felt like an excellent idea. We also met her old friend Paul "Bee" Hampshire, who lived part of the year in Thailand and was also an old TOPY connection (and friend of Gen's, the Coil boys, and many others from that formative era). It was a perfect mind-shifter from dreary old Stockholm and my memories of childhood and thoughts of deceased loved ones.

As it turned out, we must have been unconsciously prescient with regard to the pandemic that was about to hit the world in 2020. We traveled all of late 2018 and through 2019: to Egypt, Colombia, Thailand, Morocco, Switzerland, the US, Italy, England, Ireland, and Wales. I have always been an avid traveler, but this period was extreme—in the best possible way.

Most of the time we were also busy working on various projects. In Thailand, I shot material for a documentary on Annie; in the US, interviews for the LaVey film. In Merano, Italy, we hosted the second Psychoanalysis, Art & the Occult conference, called "Re-writing the Future: 100 Years of Esoteric Modernism and Psychoanalysis." In Zürich we opened our exhibition *Mementeros* (stemming from our "23rd Mind"* project of the same name: an album, film, cut-ups, and

*This was a development of the Burroughs and Gysin collaborations called the "Third Mind." It was originally conceived of by Vanessa Sinclair and her "Glitchcraft" partner, American artist Katelan Foisy, and then further developed together with Carl Abrahamsson.

prints, etc.). It was like living in a fantasy that we had dreamed up over the most recent years, and all the while probably unconsciously dreading what was about to appear and spread in 2020: the Covid-19 pandemic. It was a subconscious case of "Let's get the traveling over and done with before it's too late!"

Many of these trips actively dealt with a concept or phenomenon that has had an increasing magical significance for me: pilgrimage. Perhaps it has something to do with growing older, experiencing a *pilgrim-age*? No matter what, to travel with literal life goals in mind has been extremely refreshing. In fact, I think it's the only kind of travel that interests me.

To see some famous building yet have to wade through hordes of potentially infectious cretins? To see some wonder of the world yet in a scorching heat that depletes you of any potential joy? To partake of some historical, cultural expression yet in a sober realization that it's mere reenactment and not the real thing? To stress on the streets of yet another "monstropolis" bursting with asymmetric architectural shapes? To look out from a pyramid in Egypt and see a Pizza Hut restaurant? No thank you.

To each his own, of course. The more I think about it, and the more I've made it happen, the more I see the benefits of pilgrimage on so many levels. In one aspect, it's about evaluating fantasies and expectations in visceral times and spaces of authenticity. In another, it's about boosting or replenishing a certain energy coming from the *genius loci*—the spirit of the place. In yet another, it could be something like religious devotion or awe. And if you're lucky, you can hit the jackpot with all three in one go.

Already in the autumn of 2016, Vanessa and I started to intuitively experiment with being "conductors" (in both senses of the word). While on a trip to Portugal, we visited many amazing and powerful places: the fanciful castle Quinta da Regaleira in Sintra, the Boca do Inferno rocks by the Atlantic coast (where Aleister Crowley had allegedly staged his own suicide in 1930 with the help of Portuguese poet and author Fernando Pessoa), ossuaries galore, the Monastery of Alcobaça (which houses the tombs of King Pedro I and Inês de Castro, his dead mistress turned necromantic queen), and many other magical places.

Vanessa made poems from her travel cut-up kit and recorded herself reading from the manuscript of her first book of poetry, *Switching Mirrors*. I photographed and filmed a lot (as always). When settled at home on both sides of the Atlantic, we started setting her voice recordings to music, and put together an album project, also called *Switching Mirrors*.* It was the first real trip and project contained under our "23rd Mind" umbrella.

> To Honor My Lineage
> with another of identity
> Just more so to honor my lineage . . .
> The Apocryphal
> back and change our
> whose object
> a biological
> first rays of
> movement
> physical
> before we
> reproduction.
> and succession which
> links with the
> family, and
> organ of
> the child.
> and sexuality
> We're just tiny
> and transcending†

---

*The recordings were eventually released as two albums: *Switching* and *Mirrors*. The films we created for most of the compositions were later gathered together for an anthology film called *Poetry in Emotion, Volume One* in 2021.

†"To Honor My Lineage," in Sinclair, *Switching Mirrors* (Stockholm: Trapart, 2020), 24.

The journey was also an important experience in our understanding of necromancy as well as of unfolding myths in general. Vanessa had been active in the vibrant Quimbanda scene in New York and other places, and I had gotten a glimpse of it through her. Although I find the African diaspora magical systems extremely interesting and powerful, I refrained from engaging myself actively as I felt my cauldron was already "overflowing." I just couldn't take in any more currents!

But we did experience some interesting "23rd Mind" insights while visiting the tomb of Inês, the original corpse bride of Portugal. What was basically a bizarre historical event in an environment apparently without moral boundaries—the king had the corpse of his murdered and exhumed mistress crowned as queen, and required everyone to pay respect to her corpse seated on the royal throne—had over time grown into a colorful story that traversed the oceans back and forth and had evolved into, for instance, the myth of Brazilian Quimbanda "Pomba Gira" Maria Padilha.* All fairly recent syncretisms of this kind have somewhat discernible historical roots, which for me just acknowledges how malleable and humanly created all spiritual systems and religions are. We create things we need on inner as well as outer levels, and in doing so use the imagination, creativity, and input that is available to us, and that fits our emotional, compensational cavities at the time.

The New York scene was astoundingly creative, and the altars and

---

*A Pomba Gira in the Afro-Brazilian Umbanda and Quimbanda currents is a popular female spirit that can be worked with in many ways. Many of the variants are called "Maria Padilha" (with additional epithets like Maria Padilha Queen of Hell, Maria Padilha Queen of the Seven Crossroads, or Maria Padilha Queen of the Seven Catacombs). The original Maria Padilha—of which the Portuguese Inês seems to be a variant—was María de Padilla, born in Seville, Spain in 1334, and in love with King Pedro I of Castile. But the king had been forced to marry another woman, Blanche of Bourbon, in a similar way that Portuguese Pedro had been forced to marry lady Constança Manoel. María de Padilla was also made queen "postmortem." When these Spanish-Portuguese *necromantic* tales were established in Brazil by immigrants, they crossbred with those of the African slaves until syncretistic systems of devotion arose in "folk magic" environments and contexts. For more on this fascinating subject, see Nicholaj de Mattos Frisvold, *Pomba Gira and the Quimbanda of Mbumba Nzila* (London: Scarlet Imprint, 2011).

homes of Quimbanda adepts I could visit were impressive. The key is simple: you make things and spirits come alive by *devotion*. I rarely use the word "worship" anymore. This was in part because of the negative monotheistic connotations of the term, and in part because Gen's pun for the title of our second musical collaboration together—*Wordship*—had stripped away a lot of extraneous fluff for me. "In the beginning was the word": one of the most magical phrases ever penned—by a *human* hand, I should add. *Devotion* is a far more encompassing and healthy term when it comes to this kind of deep integration of external forces.

And it is never a static process: new energies and spirits are constantly brought into the cauldrons and pantheons of these kinds of folk magic. In this regard, it has been extra-interesting to note the power of Lady Jaye after her death in 2007. Gen of course actively communicated with her in various ways as a means to keep her alive beyond mere memories. After a visit to Benin in West Africa, for instance, Gen always brought around a doll/effigy/*jumelle** representing Jaye, which had been made by a Vodun priest. Jaye was initiated into Santeria by our friend Baba Raul Canizares, and she was well aware of these forces and syncretistic currents. Her life and commitment to nursing as well as to sex work, and her experiments with magic and pandrogeny together with Gen, are all really strong fundaments of a Pomba Gira in the making. But these projections come from other and more unexpected corners too. We have talked to young people both in the US and Europe who did not know Lady Jaye personally, but who still "work" with her magically, as if she were a bona fide Pomba Gira already.

Altar-building and reverence for the spirits of your ancestors (biological as well as adopted) are key ingredients in any healthy magical practice. An altar is not only symbolic or imaginary; it is to an equal degree absolutely real. And the same is true of our ancestral spirits: they

---

*Jumelle, feminine form of *jumeau*, a French word for "twin." Effigies of twins in Yoruba and other magical traditions are called *jumeaux* (pl.), with the individual figures referred to as *jumeau* or *jumelle*.

not only live as evanescent memories and feelings contained in family albums; they are also continually programming you genetically. Outer adornment work or talismanic creativity is an important part of this: *you have to work with it and/or them*—whoever they are.

In New York in 2018, and thanks to the invitation of Quimbanda "Tata" Jesse Hathaway Diaz, Vanessa and I could take part in a workshop together with African sculptor Lukman Alade Fakeye, who is the seventh-generation maker of magical sculptures and artifacts in the Yoruba tradition. We have two of his "Ibejis,"* one male and one female, in our house, and they daily tell us the story of the importance of integrating magic in our lives.

Inspired by Lukman's work, and moving into a house in 2021, Vanessa and I commissioned Swedish artist and magical craftsman Mårten Ytell to design and carve several runic displays for the house (as well as the runes we use for oracular work), plus two solid wood figures of Odin: a big one for the garden and a smaller one for the house. The symbols may be marginally different from culture to culture, but the currents of the land and how they take on their specific gestalt represent the very same needs inside us, and the same ways of externalizing these needs through art.

Another interesting syncretic synchronicity in this particular environment is that one of the current authorities on the Afro-Brazilian currents, Nicholaj de Mattos Frisvold, was an acquaintance of mine in the 1990s when he was still in Norway and working on great projects like the pagan festival "1000 Years Is More Than Enough"—an occultural event against Christianity in Scandinavia. From our youthful pagan Scandinavian mind-frames, we both reached out into the big and colorful world of magic, only to reconvene much later under the auspices of the wonderful British publisher Scarlet Imprint. And I was delighted

---

*An *Ibeji* is a carved wooden sacred sculpture, usually depicting a pair of twins, or a single twin. Together they can be worshipped as an *orisha* (spirit) in the Yoruba tradition. Gen's *"jumelle"* doll of Lady Jaye was also an Ibeji, in the sense that it makes up for a lost twin.

that Nicholaj agreed to write the introduction to my anthology of essays called *Source Magic*. It was a lovely kind of full-circle movement.

In this same anthology, I wrote about a few of my experiences of pilgrimage: traveling to the home of Ernst Jünger in Germany in 2009, and with Vanessa to Joujouka in Morocco in the summer of 2019 (which also included the Paul Bowles museum/shrine in Tangier). The Moroccan trip was extra-special, as it was a head-on reimmersion in my formative occultural cauldron. The original immersion included not only reading the "old expat boys" (Bowles, Gysin, and Burroughs) who had sought refuge in Tangier, but also listening to the *Brian Jones Presents the Pipes of Pan at Joujouka* LP during my rituals of the late 1980s. And Ornette Coleman was an ingredient in that Moroccan stew too: in 1973 he traveled with Burroughs to Joujouka to record the albums *Dancing in Your Head* (Coleman) and *Break Through In Grey Room* (Burroughs).

In 2019 we held our second "Psychartcult" conference at Schloss Brunnenburg, the home of Ezra Pound in Dorf Tirol outside Merano (and also visited his grave in Venice); we also traveled to Wales and Port Meirion to pay our respects and soak in the spirit of the British TV series *The Prisoner*. These trips were all massive boosters of energy, as any genuine pilgrimage should be.

The second "Psychartcult" was special in many ways. I have long admired Ezra Pound as a poet and intellectual, and always get a lift when reading his *Cantos*. He had that intangible and inexplicable quality of forcefully drawing you into his chaotic and eloquent mind, and the result is stunning: several decades worth of speculating about everything he was ever interested in, in one single tumultuous tumbler, for your own exquisite reading pleasure.

When Pound was released from the St. Elizabeths Hospital in

1958, he traveled back to his beloved Italy and remained there for the rest of his life in the care of his daughter Mary and her husband Boris de Rachewiltz at the medieval castle Schloss Brunnenburg. When we organized the conference our liaison was Siegfried de Rachewiltz, the son of Mary and Boris—a very charming and intelligent historian and caretaker of their own museum (of local agrarian history as well as of "Poundiana"). As soon as we had settled in, Siegfried introduced us to his mother Mary—still alive and well at (then) age ninety-five! It was a wonderful connection not only to Pound but to the entire spirit of Modernism.

It was also a wonderful time of reconnecting with old friends: not only with Blanche Barton, who gave a wonderful talk about the roots of Satanism, but also the New York "crew" that we had had so many good times with—Jesse Hathaway Diaz, Langston Kahn, Kadmus Herschel, Al Cummins, and Katy Bohinc. Other guests included dear Charlotte Rodgers from the UK, and my old friend from Sweden, Elizabeth Punzi, along with plenty of new acquaintances: Hans-Peter Söder, Ugo Dossi, Ethan Clarke, Kasper Opstrup, Haukur Jonasson, Carlos Abler, Anna Sebastian, Simon Magus, Siegfried de Rachewiltz, and Katrina Makkouk.

It was also the first time since 1989 that I met Tom Banger again, which was wonderful. He presented a talk together with fellow TOPY member Koshka about the campouts they used to organize under the umbrella of TOPYNA/US. It was marvelous to reconnect to the old spirit and exchange experiences, new and old. In many ways, this trip was a mix between a pilgrimage, a conference, and a magical working— just as the one in London in 2016 had been. And all this took place in the lush and friendly region of Südtirol, with the Alps towering over fertile valleys and charming little villages. A paradise!

In my talk about Ezra Pound and his main publisher James Laughlin, I touched upon some of the controversial aspects of Pound's life—they are hard to avoid in his case. I have always felt that one has to look at what an artist made first and foremost, and what effects it

With Mary de Rachewiltz at Schloss Brunnenburg, 2019
(photo by Vanessa Sinclair)

had on general culture, not necessarily his/her own views or political inclinations. Imagine if some evil force were to suddenly sweep history clean of every poet or artist who had outspoken political views or allegiances—there would probably be no one left! I made this position crystal clear in my presentation, keeping an eye on Mary de Rachewiltz who was there to listen. I'm sure she has had her share of loonies trying to discount or eradicate the poetic qualities of her father, but that was certainly not my trip. On the contrary, I admire the poet Pound a great deal. When I brought my talk to a close by saying that the relationship between Pound and Laughlin in many respects reminded me of that of Don Quixote and Sancho Panza, Mary smiled and applauded. That made me very happy.*

---

*This presentation, "Literchoor, Kulchur, and a Damned Fine Friendship: On the Symbiosis of Ezra Pound and James Laughlin," has been published in my book *Source Magic*.

After Merano, we traveled down to Venice together with Blanche Barton and a few others. Although we had caught up properly in San Diego the year before, as we were filming for the LaVey documentary, in Venice we could really hang out in a more relaxed way. Blanche was at this time enthusiastically working on a substantial update of her 1990 book, *The Church of Satan*. In 2021, the new and heavily expanded version emerged, called *We Are Satanists*. It was delightful to be part of this process, as Blanche included an interesting survey about the state of LaVeyan Satanism today. Together with academics, observers, and members of the Church of Satan, I answered as well as I could, and together our voices make for interesting and thought-provoking reading about the influential mosaic that is LaVey's Church. It was useful for me to rephrase my old sentiments and thought patterns in this new, contemporary light:

> I think [the misunderstanding of LaVey] has to do with the encouragement of an unspoken totalitarian ideology that permeates academia and forces students to self-censor anything that could be interpreted as objectionable by the invisible forces of fabricated moralities. Outside of academia, it is even less surprising, unfortunately. The overall cultural discourse is more binary than ever, so if LaVey's Satanism gets really wide attention in a public sphere, it will be negative (cf. *American Horror Story* and similar productions). I guess it has beneficial results though, as extended exposure will attract the satanically inclined eventually, if only they get to know that LaVey's books are out there (cf. *Californication* and specifically the episodes where Satanism was actually presented intelligently). A filtering always takes place, it seems.*

The experience of reconnecting with Blanche also provided much food for thought. Thirty years had gone by since our early meetings, but

---

*Abrahamsson in Blanche Barton, *We Are Satanists: The History and Future of the Church of Satan* (La Quinta, CA: Aperient, 2021), 351.

in Italy it felt like no time had passed at all. Both LaVey and Blanche had been so supportive of my early occultural expressions and endeavors, and it was something that actively lived inside me throughout the decades. Now we were suddenly sharing a physical space again. In the US in 2018 I had also had the opportunity to meet Xerxes LaVey, their son—a very fine and intelligent young man, indeed. It was one of those moments in which you realize that time is very much a strange kind of illusion. Had time passed? Had time not passed? When it is a question of time in between magical human individuals, sometimes it can be hard to tell!

This feeling was amplified when Blanche's great book was published. Back in 1990 it was a slim volume in which she had inscribed: "To Carl—a most energetic fellow-denizen of the Night!" In 2021 it had become a solid brick of a book. Life experience and much philosophizing makes us grow as humans over the years, and it is very much through our books that this process of development remains for others to partake of and be inspired by. No other medium has worked so well in preserving human culture in this regard. What Umberto Eco humorously called "librido"* has certainly been a very serious part of my own and many of my fellow magicians' magical systems.

On that beloved topic: a book-related magical technique that Vanessa and I have used a lot over the years is what we call "bibliomancy." It is basically an extension of our work with the oracular evaluation of the cut-up process: interpreting the cut-up as a message and/or messenger. In orthodox bibliomancy, you simply pick a book, open it to a random page and line (with your eyes closed, for instance), and see what it says. One is not looking for a voice or an order from some cosmic authority; instead, this method provides a nonrational impetus as a matrix or grid for the evaluation of any given situation through and for yourself. The classic oracular tools of the Tarot, the runes, or the

---

*A portmanteau of *libri* ("books" in Latin/Italian) and *libido* (in the Freudian sense of the "life drive").

I Ching are great because they have been streamlined for a long time to contain maximum signal in your own interpretation process. But to randomly pick a sentence in a book can be equally revealing. Why? Because *you are actively looking for meaning.* And those who look and seek, will eventually find—sometimes much sooner than they think.

RAISING HELL[FIRE]

Later in the summer of 2019, Vanessa and I were invited to Ireland to contribute to the opening of South African artist Kendell Geers's exhibition at Dublin's Rua Red art center. In part, Kendell's exhibition was about the infamous Hellfire Club (the Dublin one, specifically), so that of course excited me quite easily!

I wrote an inspired text about the illusion of space-time, and about how the Hellfire antics live on in us all, as necessary symbols and matrices for cathartic psychodrama. Toward the end of the exhibition, we were invited to create a performance/ritual in the gallery space. As we had just finished our audiovisual 23rd Mind spell *Mementeros*, we decided to use that film as a framework and backdrop for the performance.

The film was projected on the gallery wall already filled with Kendell's exciting glyphs. The music consisted of instrumental versions of the soundtrack structures. We then performed a ritual play, which consisted of an expansion/elaboration of the text I had written for the catalog (presented here below). I read that text while Vanessa intersected and read her cut-ups of relevant source material. A heavy and heady kind of ping-pong. What started out as a fairly mental exercise turned out to be a proper evocation of forces contained for several hundred years.

While in Dublin, we also went to visit the remains of the beautiful country house where the local Hellfire clubbers hung out. It is of course always easy to project one's own fantasies upon any fascinating historical structure or site, but this one certainly felt imbued with vibrations from many a revelry and ritual throughout the centuries. As usual, Vanessa created on-site cut-ups and recorded them, while I roamed the premises with my camera.

All in all, these experiences (Kendell's exhibition, the intellectual approach to the Hellfire Club, seeing the old site, and performing our psychosexual evocation) were phenomenally enriching and inspiring for future similar excursions and projects. Art needs to be thought- and emotion-provoking to have basic value, and this visit to the magical isle of Ireland turned out to be an invaluable expansion in which vision merged with wonder, and arousal with satisfaction.

FIRE & BRIMSTONE IN THE
YEAR OF OUR LADIES AND LORDS 2019

Enter not here, vile hypocrites and bigots,
Pious old apes, and puffed-up snivellers . . .
Woebegone scoundrels, mock-godly sandal-wearers,
Beggars in blankets, flagellating canters . . .

We are walking on hallowed ground today. Breathing in the air of creative tradition. Smelling the fire and brimstone of those daredevils who lay the foundations for our impervious prometheanism. Reflecting rigid and reactionary patterns back at the dusty, moldy Brit rump huggers; provoking the pious by an exaggeration of themselves. Flaunting terrifying mirror images of their unconscious righteous chaos. But right here and right now spewed out in blissful and health-inducing orgies of both body and soul.

There have been many precursors. They are now active cursors, setting the stage for a future that discards whatever is not life-enhancing. Nature rules supreme! That French guy: "Nature's single precept is to enjoy oneself, at the expense of no matter whom." And we're all crying out in the night: "Babalon is a fucking formula, goddamit!" Have another swig of Scaltheen, our sacred Infernal Punch, and mock the irreverent reverent and all those dumbed-down fundamentalist occultniks. Our Pope (the real one: Alexander) cries out louder than any of them:

> All Nature is but art, unknown to thee;
> All chance, direction which thou canst not see;
> All discord, harmony not understood;
> All partial evil, universal good.
> And, spite of Pride, in erring Reason's spite,
> One truth is clear, "Whatever IS, is RIGHT."

So come join our nocturnal revels at the secret Devil's Tavern, somewhere in-between the Eagle Tower at Cork Hill and Daly's on College Green. (Myself, I found my thrill on Strawberry Hill.) We never went away, we're always right here, and here we'll remain, pissing on the pious pontiffs and penitents. By the way and when in Rome . . . Darling Dashwood, beloved, actually flogged the penitents. When they realized the mockery was for real they cried out in Angst: "Il Diavolo!" Francis laughed so loudly we could hear it all the way to Ireland, inspiring us before, during and after any facts or petit-bourgeois timelines. Then we all laughed together when solid spaces were constructed for all our actions and pleasures. *"Faye ce que voudras*, motherfuckers!" engraved forever in the stained-glass windows of our minds.

Whispering "Carymary, carymara . . ." Our Lady burns, so let's piss on the smoky rubble. Are you surprised? Blame any technical or human error as much as you want or need to be able to function . . . This is magic at work. No more, no less. Magic in revenge of our brothers who burned; in revenge of our many sisters who burned. We're not in any rush though, because we know that mock rituals are rituals too, and amorality is certainly a morality too. Blessed Margaret, Holy Mary . . . Diligently fucked on Montpelier Hill; orchestrated by Lady Gomorrah and Lord Sodom: the literal party poopers in the dark night of the Irish Soul. Tom Jones and Fanny

Hill are for the others, secretly reading and nervously masturbating under covers. But not us. We celebrate life because we can. The privileges of privilege are a sacred duty! We will never uphold any sanctimonious structures for the sake of someone else's moribound morals.

Although our Scaltheen tastes revolting in its fad buttery sting, we swig it passionately to celebrate life. If brimstone is feared by the monotheistic mongrels, let's gulp it down to the very last drop and carouse with the ladies and gentlemen of the night until we can make out no difference between the falling stars of the night sky and our ejaculations of deep-rooted resistance. It is our gods-given right. Even Saint Fornicating Augustine: "Love, and do what you will."

Our Eternal Castle of Iniquity is an Invisible Hexagonal Space. No matter what you do or where you are, you are always right in the middle of it. Therefore, back to the proverbial roots, ladies and gentlemen: Rabble Eh spells it out . . . Gargan Tu As Una Bazzio die TELE MA. Formulas and spells are created in the spur of the moment; ingenious constructions of universes, ass-ociations linked in sticky resi-dew, teaching and touching holy ground in the Dublin of Re Joyce and other luminaries of the letters; the first of which in this context is not the Alpha but the Omega. Spin the wheel of reverted chance; give chance a chance, and do it in the spirit of PENI TENTO NON PENITENTI.

Our Brother Ben Franklin now spins in the reverted chance of his tomb. Peter Lens, are you listening? And our beloved Hogarth's dog was named Trump. Irony of ironies, hundreds of years later!

Cheers to the defiant, Cheers to the living spirit of this sacred Hellfire Club, and, most importantly, Cheers to us!

CARL "FRIAR BEEFSTEAK" ABRAHAMSSON, 1739 A.D.

Speaking of Hellfire (& Damnation?) . . . During 2018 and 2019 I worked diligently on my second novel, *The Devil's Footprint* (2020). I had missed writing fiction, and some six or seven years had passed since

I published *Mother, Have A Safe Trip*. One of the original inspirations for the new book was Vanessa and me visiting Munich in 2018 and seeing the famous "Devil's Footprint" in one of the floor-stones of the Frauenkirche. I put my boot in it, and it fit like hand in glove (or cloven hoof in human boot)! That literally became the first step in the process of writing the book. I have also always appreciated Al Pacino in the film *The Devil's Advocate* (1997), which depicts Satan as a humorous and wise agent provocateur in human and worldly affairs. What if God offered a deal to Satan, allowing him back into heaven with reinstated status as the most beloved angel, if Satan can fix the human mess on Earth? After those few premises, the book basically wrote itself, and I had an amazing time seeing it unfold. For the cover of the book, I used the catchphrase "It's not easy being evil in a world that's gone to Hell . . ."—which hits the mark pretty well. The once-threatening symbol of Satan has, through various stages of occulturation, now been accepted not only as an antihero but as a hero proper, and I find that very healthy. All inert structures must be helped to crumble if they themselves are too slow to disappear. The Satanic perspective and force, like those of the Fenris Wolf, maintains a healthy balance in the greater picture. It's a central part of any immune system, and thereby a lifesaver. In my novel, Satan keeps busier than ever before—in part because God tries to trick him into unpaid overtime work, and in part because the humans have done a hell of a job at messing things up.

I rang the doorbell of the home of John Davis, CEO of yet another vast empire of fossils; soon to be extinct just like all the animals that constitute the very life blood of the business. A beautiful and ironic twist of fate, and I'd make sure my coming replacement would find and grind the corporeal remains of exactly all these people into a technology of the future—hopefully less toxic than the present one. That was what the Eastern folks called Karma, I guess. Not exactly my cup of tea with all their ornate and peace-loving morals. I have always preferred to call it a "twist of fate with a great sense of humor," no matter how gruesome the real phenomenon. Euphemisms are always a sign of human excellence. They just never seem to learn that, beyond the basest form of cynical sloganeering; the kind that one of my agents had once so beautifully called "double-speak."*

TIME OUT, MOVE ON

In the mid-2010s I started thinking about the OTO and its relevance in my life—if there even was any. I often encountered fundamentalistic expressions within the order, all focusing on the least interesting of Crowley's facets—the religious one. I could notice people, even old friends, lowering themselves before a religious construct with accompanying discourse and subsequent relaxation of their critical faculties. It made me sad, and especially because there were people around from other Crowley groups who did their best to infiltrate and weaken the genuine fraternal environments in favor of a nincompoopish admiration of *The Book of the Law* as a "religious" text and Crowley as some kind of "prophet." All of this in an attitude of "Crowleyer than thou" that was and is quite enervating.

At the end of the day, Crowley himself may be the one to blame for this eventual downturn, as he apparently overestimated people's sense of humor and underestimated their sheeplike tendencies. Or was he just a blatant narcissist from a religious background who wanted to rebel and did so quite convincingly? There is indeed as great a gulf between the philosophy of Thelema and its post-Crowley "acolytical" applications as there is between the original German OTO (and its legitimate reshaping through the Caliphate OTO) and all the satellite groups that fly around in their disgruntled orbits.

As I had reached my own thirtieth anniversary as a member of

---

*Abrahamsson, *The Devil's Footprint* (Stockholm: Trapart, 2020), 33–34.

the OTO, I decided I no longer wanted to be associated with this tendency, nor with the order as such. I think the last straw was when I wanted to post about my recently finished Kenneth Anger documentary on a Thelemic social-media "platform," and the moderator asked me what the relevance was . . . *"Errare humanum est sed divinum percipitur!"* *

I wrote to Hymenaeus Beta, Evmaios, the Secretary General, and a few intimates explaining my position, and that was that. No drama at all, just a genuine mutual friendliness that pleasantly transcended the sometimes quite arbitrary aspects of fraternal communities.

Since that moment I have returned to Crowley now and then. No one can deny his brilliance, but I strongly feel he was "caught in between times" and as a result he has not always aged in the best of ways. He was brought up in the "old aeon" (to use his own terminology) and ushered in the "new aeon" (again, his phrase), but somehow never really fully crossed over himself.

In most of my publishing ventures I have put out something by Crowley: two editions of *The Book of the Law* in Swedish, one in Norwegian, and then the editions of *White Stains* and *Snowdrops from A Curate's Garden* (no doubt a Kenneth Anger–related "full-circle" moment, as that was one of the Crowley books he lent me in Hollywood in 1990). Then there were the literary rights to Jack Parsons's work that I purchased from Cameron, and Frater Achad's from his son Tony Stansfeld-Jones. Neither of the latter projects came to fruition, however, and the rights eventually reverted to their owners. I believe it was for the best: the British publisher Fulgur has now dealt with Parsons in an exemplary way, as has Starfire with Achad. In hindsight, I feel these spirits had to be with me for a while—passing through, as it were—for them to end up where they should. As spirits, they were never mine to "own" in the first place, but it was great to symbolically house them for a while so we could get better acquainted.

---

*"To err is human but it is perceived as divine."

The rearview perspective is only useful if you can learn something from it; in many ways, it seems, we learn more from our mistakes than from successes. I know I can get overzealous to the point where I get bogged down by my own idealism. However, I have never wanted to seriously "curb my enthusiasm" because it's such a central part of my personality. And it has undoubtedly led to many great things, both for me and others. These days I'm trying to prioritize better, and not devote too much time to things that are not distinctly in line with what I want to achieve. I certainly know that "the only time is now," but my experience tells me that was also true a moment ago, and it will very likely be true in a little while too.

In many ways, *focus* has replaced the "hocus-pocus" in my quest. Although that may sound like a witticism on my part, there is something to it. Allocation of time, space, focus, and energy is probably the best way I can describe the application of magic today. Symbols eventually become redundant to the magician who truly moves forward. And although I wouldn't like to have anything "undone" in my career, it is very clear to me how dangerously alluring the symbolic structures and structural symbols can be to a young magician. TDL and LaVey seem to me to have been the wisest teachers in this sense. LaVey already spoke eloquently about this in *The Satanic Bible* and in early issues of *The Cloven Hoof,* such as here:

> I wrote *The Satanic Bible* because I looked for such a book all my life, and, unable to find it, concluded that if I ever expected to read what I was seeking, I would have to write it myself. The same principles applied with *The Compleat Witch.* Summing up, if you NEED to steep yourselves in occult lore, despite this diatribe, by all means do so. But do it as a ritual in itself, i.e., *objectively toward subjective ends!* Read on, *knowing* that you won't learn a damn thing in principle from Levi, Crowley, Regardie, (or Sybil Leek either!) that isn't extended one-hundred fold in *The Satanic Bible* or *The Compleat Witch, but* that you'll have spooky fun, ego-food,

and *involvement* which invariably accompanies a curriculum concerned more with the gathering of ingredients than the application of principles.*

TEACHER'S PET SUBJECTS

Over the decades I have been invited to lecture and teach at high schools, colleges, universities, and art schools in many different countries as well as online. I appreciate the opportunity, because it's a challenge that not only deals with dissemination of information but also human-to-human interaction. And it means talking about subjects very dear to me. What it all boils down to isn't information per se, but inspiration: to offer insights and avenues that have not been encountered before, so that the students can concretely make up their own minds in a spirit of resonance with the idea or concept in question.

Sometimes I talk about the history of magic and how, sooner or later, the various phenomena go through a process of occulturation in which the previously rejected becomes the presently accepted. And sometimes—especially at art colleges—I have presented practices to show how interchangeable the processes of artistic creativity and magic really are. All terminologies aside, the starting point is the will to change something into something else. The paths and techniques to make that happen are many and experimental. The best ones are not necessarily dictated by cogitation and deductive magic (as can be the case in empirical processes) but by intuition and free association. Form can be as important as content. Form is the matrix that contains the seed of the change in question. We can state our intentions very clearly in human conversation but then run the risk of being neglected and/or opposed. But if we state them in a poem that attracts other minds on other levels than the critical-rational, the idea will have

---

*LaVey, "From the High Priest," editorial in *The Cloven Hoof*, vol. III, no. 9 (1971), 4.

merged with the form and the formulated nucleus can get to work.

Psychodramatic performances (private or public), inner journeys, meditations, sigilizing, automatic writing and drawing/painting, identity reflections (mirror work), oracular reflections, cut-ups, and many other things can be of immense practical value in the general artistic work. Sometimes I have met a bit of resistance even in classes of and for artists, and especially during the late 2010s. The (con)temporary influx of intellectual justifications and Orwellian-inspired Newspeak unions with evanescent phenomena like politics have created a confusing arena for young artists, many of whom are academically taught that they need to be "clear" in their presentations and that they need to have a "program" that somehow justifies their work. According to me, this is as far from the artistic process as you can ever get, and I always encourage the students to physically and mentally embody a stern criticism toward any kind of homogenizing influences.

It is always much more worthwhile to be neurotically selfish and explore why or why not that is than to swallow demagogic attempts from others at controlling your own creativity and its results so they can easily be streamlined and commodified. Whether you look at your own process as an indulgence or as a gradual extended therapy of sorts, what always remains is that it's essentially only of genuine interest to others if there's something of *you* inside the work. It needs at least a discernible fraction of your core or soul or whatever we can call it. Anyone can hack out trendy manifestos of this and that (especially nowadays when AI "chatbots" can do it for you!) but if the work has no discernible personality, then it's just either "design" or "illustration"—there is nothing there to touch another human soul.

The process should always begin with a genuinely *personal* spark. This could be a primitive form or idea, or a mere emotional impetus. An "artwork" is indeed an art *work*, a working process, and not only the finished result. This is equally valid for the scientific adventure, of course. It is about taking something from one place to another, at which point it will have grown enough to tell us something new. It is always closely connected to learning. The creative process is a learning *journey*, which also leaves aestheticized *residue* that then becomes the gateway to a deeper evaluation of the learning itself—art as a symbol, and art as a means of communication, if you will.

A PACT IS A PACT

In the Western Ceremonial tradition, the tools of the magician have often been referred to as magical "weapons." Perhaps this is due to the inclusion of the dagger in the elemental kit of dagger (air), wand (fire), cup (water), and disk (earth). I prefer to use the term "tool" rather than "weapon." I still have the elemental tools on my personal altar for the occasional times that I work in a structural, traditional sense.

My wand comes from Thailand, and is exquisitely ornamented with mother-of-pearl intarsia. My cup is a tiny Schnapps-glass from Mittenwald in Germany displaying a beautiful Edelweiss flower. My disk, made of silver, is originally Tibetan, and has the Baphomet symbol engraved on its surface. My dagger was handmade by an artisan bladesmith in our hometown. Together they frame the altar and its other contents.

Once you find the "tools of your trade," I would recommend playing with them and allowing them to merge with all aspects of your life—including the magical contexts. For me, I knew since childhood that I wanted to be a writer, and I have always loved the facilitating tools: stationery, notebooks, ballpoints, fountains, rollerballs, pencils, legal pads, and so forth. Early on, I also liked typewriters and had a few before the computers eventually took over.

I found it interesting that a tool could also wield such symbolic power, and some of my early pens still carry a "charge"—especially those slightly older ones that were given to me by relatives. But it's not only a matter of an object or symbol: the tool *works* in the creation of poetry or prose. For most people today, the tool for writing is a computer, and it can indeed be a fine and facilitating one. But I write a lot of my texts by hand, so the pen is more than just symbolic for me.

I started writing a diary in 1988, and I still ponder and scribble by hand every day. During a few deluded periods I typed my diary entries on the computer, but it was not too long before I got back to my senses. There is pleasure in the physical act of writing. I am certainly not boasting about the style of my handwriting, which becomes even untidier if I'm hastily jotting down notes. But there's no denying it's mine and mine alone. I'm not an aesthete in that sense, and the handwriting isn't really meant to be seen by anyone else, anyway. So, I write diligently with my many pens, and there is great magic in that.

Back in the 1990s, I let it be known that if someone gave me a golden pen, I would write a book for that person, thereby creating a magical pact. Psychologically, one might ascribe this proposal to a young insecure writer who just basically needs or wants a kick in the butt to get started: a positive peer pressure of sorts. But for me, it was all about the magical aspects and explanations: the trust invested in the symbol would make a new reality bloom.

At some point I stopped mentioning the "pen pact" because it sounded like some weird solicitation that I wasn't fully comfortable with. However, I had apparently talked about it enough, because my closest friends pooled some money and bought me a lovely Parker Duofold fountain pen with a body of white mother of pearl and a golden nib. And a notebook too! I was overwhelmed—not only by the gift itself, but also because the pact was now activated.

A few years later, in 2000, I dedicated my first book, *All var bättre förr men inte länge till* (Everything was better before but not for long), a collection of aphorisms and thoughts, to all those dear friends. Other friends provided a full metal Montblanc rollerball and a golden Caran d'Ache ballpoint meant for the *Bardo Tibet* project, also published in 2000. The idea fizzled out gradually, probably because I grew more self-confident as an author. I didn't feel a need for someone else's acknowledgment, and certainly not when it came to the added weight of a pact.

That said, I will never say no to a beautiful pen, but I will probably not make any more pen pacts.

Unless . . . that pact is with myself. For nearly every book I've written since those humble beginnings, I've also bought a pen particular for the project in question. I've written with it, and had it present in computerized phases of the writing. It serves as an inspiration and reminder to focus on the book in question and not on other, upcoming projects. One book at a time! For *Sacred Intent*, it was a gold and brushed steel Parker ballpoint; for *Anton LaVey and the Church of Satan*, a rose gold Cross ballpoint; for my second novel, *The Devil's Footprint*, a blue Platinum Procyon fountain pen; and for the Swedish novel *Codex Nordica*, a gold-colored Caran d'Ache ballpoint. For the book that you're reading now, I have interacted with a gold-colored Platinum Procyon with the inscription "Two Times Saturn."*

The pen as an object has thus taken on the project-specific gestalt of the wand in a traditional magical sense. It is an outward extension of my will, projecting it onto and into the fibrous surface of the paper. And that's where the magic gestation begins, in the ink spurts of spell-binding sentences.

The concept and implementation of my "author's magic system" was developed in 2019, as Vanessa and I were in Venice after our Merano conference. I bought a new pen in one of the delightful stationery stores of this hyper-magical city. The pen was not an expensive one but nice enough for its function. However, its real purpose was not to serve as a writing tool, but as a *reservoir of power* (the correct technical term for a fountain pen is "reservoir pen")—a "battery" of sorts for all my other active pens.

I began by bringing it out on the cemetery island of San Michele, just across from Venice proper. After a bit of strolling, we found the

---

*The working title of this book was *Two Times Saturn*, a reference to the astrological phenomenon of soul-searching and shedding of old patterns related to each full spin of Saturn around the sun (which usually takes some twenty-nine and a half years). I started writing the book as I entered the end of my second "Saturn Return" phase.

grave of Ezra Pound. I let my pen rest by his tomb, on the earth, while Vanessa made some cut-ups with material from her cut-up travel kit. It was a serene moment of pure existential poetry. We also told Pound that his daughter and grandson were doing fine up there in Südtirol, and that we had all had a great time at our conference. When we were done, I wrapped up the pen and kept it safe until it was time for another working.

I decided to call this central reservoir object PEN IS. Just as I have written that the main or first premise of magico-anthropology is that "Magic Is" (meaning, essentially, it is the absolute center/core of the human existential and cultural universe), I could now state that this particular talismanic pen *is*. It needs no further explanations beyond that (although I do have many). The pen is and does what it does and is. PEN IS, simple as that. I can appreciate the pun too, although understandably it might be seen as puerile or even infantile. But there are of course more serious and—pardon the pun again!—seminal aspects to it. These relate not only to my own magical work and the "solar phallic" tradition (described as such by Crowley), but also to Ezra Pound's fascination with Remy de Gourmont, and their speculations about creativity and the brain, and its relation to seminal fluid. I had already republished Pound's "Translator's Postscript" to Gourmont's book *The Natural Philosophy of Love* in *The Fenris Wolf* 5 back in 2012, and there in Venice in 2019 I was able to consummate the marriage of pen and soil, soul and soul, while thinking of these mysteries.

Next up was Morocco, but Tangier specifically for the pen. At the American Legation there is a tiny museum or shrine in honor of author and composer Paul Bowles. In an essay called "Panic Pilgrimage," I wrote about our visit:

> But it is (always?) to Paul Bowles that we have to return in our own pilgrimage sourcery. Bowles was the original pathfinder and interpreter, and one that has certainly affected me more than the more proper beatniks of the late 1950s and 1960s.

For this very reason I was completely "buzzed" at the American Legation when we entered the Paul Bowles sanctuary. I charged one of my magical pens on Bowles's Olivetti typewriter and then touched it. I also touched the keys of the Ensoniq keyboard he used for composing music. I just immersed myself in the spirit of this literary giant and explorer. It was a moment when mere conscious existence and immersion became a powerful ritual in its own right regardless of any "intentions" I may also have had.*

The pen looked so good on that typewriter, and a photograph of that spontaneous tryst today rests on my altar.

I also had the pen with me when we were visiting Port Meirion in Wales in 2019, the village where my favorite TV series, *The Prisoner*, was shot in the mid-1960s. This visit served mainly for general charging as there was no discernible main entity/identity to be associated with a full charge. Creator and actor Patrick McGoohan manifested something fantastic with his unique series, but he himself did not merit charging status.

Next up was Michel de Montaigne's tower in Avensan, France, in 2022, where the PEN IS traveled back in time to the sixteenth century and soaked up the intellectual hunger and curiosity of this truly admirable nobleman and intuitive author/philosopher. I let it touch his desk and chair, and the walls here and there—carefully and respectfully, of course—and could feel the buzz coming through the pen and into my system. The PEN IS definitely works as an immediate conductor of energies too, but its main function is to be charged in special spaces and places that in themselves contain the dis-charge of a part/author of my multidimensional mythology-mosaics.

And so it will continue in the "sourcery" quest to cook up an ever better tasting dish of minds and memetic molecules. My list of upcoming destinations is already very long.

---

*Abrahamsson, *Source Magic*, 25.

Another application of ink with magical potential is, of course, tattoos. I have quite a few and will likely get more. But I have never had one done for the sake of pure form or aesthetics. It's always been with intent or as a celebration of completion. Contrary to the contemporary zeitgeist of tattoo-covered soccer players and reality-show starlets, I have never been a fan of displaying or flaunting my tattoos. But on my own, and in a distinctly magical mind-frame, I've begun enjoying them more and more. Almost each of my major book projects has its own tattoo, as well as reminders of important focuses and goals.

Anton LaVey—having worked in carnivals and sideshows where he met a lot of strange people, including both *self-made* and *natural* freaks—found the rise of "modern primitivism" in the late 1980s fascinating (as did I):

> That's why I think a lot of people gravitate to modern primitive alteration in their bodies: it's like taking an *antidote* which enables them to co-exist with the workaday world. It's a way of linking themselves with the twilight world or the Dark Side. Some people do this in ways *without* physical change: doing, saying or thinking things that would certainly alienate them from "normals." But that's just another variation.

> In other words, people set up a certain stigma that says, "Watch out for me—I am dangerous!"—like the hourglass on the black widow spider's belly. Modern primitive activity serves as a self-alienation device to bring attention to the owner of that particular device, whatever it happens to be. Because a sailor doesn't look at it that way (one of the old-time sailors, that is), he wants to be one of the guys. He wants to be identified *with* a group rather than *outside* of a group.*

---

*Anton LaVey, interviewed in V. Vale and Andrea Juno, eds., *RE/Search 12: Modern Primitives—An Investigation of Contemporary Adornment & Ritual* (San Francisco: RE/Search, 1989), 94.

Around 2015 the process entered a new dimension as I reread Ray Bradbury's collection of science-fiction stories, *The Illustrated Man*. It's loosely structured around a very short story about a former carnival worker who can no longer get a job because of his tattoos. They come alive at night and tell little stories, like suggestive films taking off from his skin, and most often they are terrifying. The stories of Bradbury's anthology turn out to be projections from that key story in which the Illustrated Man shares his history with a fellow traveler on a "walking tour." It's a brilliant concept, and I can appreciate the book on a number of levels. As for me, what better artistic process than to write history, as well as the future, in the flesh, on my very own parchment? In this sense I have become the Illustrated Man too, and am empowered daily by these sigils and stories that are alive within and upon my very self.

SACRED INTENT

The second half of our 2019 was very intense. I was wrapping up the LaVey documentary, editing and making the *Sacred Intent* book, and doing what felt like a million other things—while also being on the road in the US most of the time. How I managed it, I will never really know. But the film premiered and was well received, and I was especially happy that the people I had interviewed for it liked it. Right after that, it was time to go full throttle on finishing the book. Genesis's seventieth birthday was coming up in February of 2020, and we had decided to have it out by then. And that also happened according to plan and protocol. I received the copies of the book in Stockholm and was overjoyed to see it manifested. I sent copies to Gen in New York by courier, and they reached him a few days before his birthday: Magic Made Manifest!

We had arranged for a book launch and talk at Mast Books, a lovely shop and gallery in New York, on March 19th. Vanessa and I were making preparations to leave while the news blurted out dispatches about

With Genesis Breyer P-Orridge in New York City, 2018
(photo by Vanessa Sinclair)

the global pandemic of Covid-19, with new levels of infected people each day. As Gen was already so ill with leukemia at this time, I suggested it might be better to postpone the event so he wouldn't be exposed to the virus. He was disappointed but said it made sense. We talked about it back and forth while keeping an eye on the news. Vanessa and I decided to cancel our trip on March 12th, and the next day the US government banned travel, anyway. So, it was a "done deal"—we had no choice but to postpone the event and wait out the chaos.

Alas, already on the next day I received a message from our dear friend Claus Laufenburg in Germany: "very very sad news." And it certainly was: Genesis P-Orridge, my dear friend, mentor, and in so many ways magical teacher, died on March 14th, 2020.

We had discussed beforehand the scenario of what it would be like with Gen gone—even in the last interview for the *Sacred Intent* book—but nothing can really prepare you for that ultimate sense of loss when it hits you. Lighting candles by a framed photograph of Gen I had taken in Nepal, getting flowers and Cadbury's chocolate fingers (Gen's favorite), and then, as Vanessa played Psychic TV's "The Orchids," just breaking down and crying. It was beautiful and awful at the same time, flooding me with memories of decades of interactions and magical experiences. Although it was now a quite real and tangible object, our book seemed almost unreal at that moment as I flipped through its pages with my tears falling on them. I was extremely grateful that Gen had been allowed to see and touch it before it was time to move on.

I had experienced a similar feeling of gratitude a few years earlier, when we published *Brion Gysin: His Name Was Master*. It had meant a lot to Gen to have that book of interviews and Gysin-related texts become manifest, as he had made a promise to Gysin in Paris in the early 1980s. But the *Sacred Intent* book was ours in such a different way, documenting our conversations and developments together from 1986 up until the very bittersweet end. It represented the end of a journey, so to speak, and there's nothing that can encapsulate that phase—or an entire life—as well as a book.

On that same evening of March 14th, I summed up whatever I could in "A Poem for the Poet":

> That time has come
> When time moves on
> Emits a brave kreator
> Emits a bold narrator
> Ov magics and journeys
> Of loved ones now gone
> The Trip . . . is just beginning
> Just drifting
> Shifting shapes
> Get a new suitcase
> Travel in style
> All of this is possible

All of the time

Let's never forget

The Messenger

The Message

The Process

Thee Temple

Intricate details

Intuitive twists

Curved hand

Crooked smile

Baba Mago Supreme

Calling on the spirits

To become who you are

With Sacred Intent

Undoubtedly: His name was master

Undoubtedly: Her name was master

What a blessed honor

To move on

In your mischievous company

Loyalty Does Not End With Death

You cut it up so well

"Scissors and glue, scissors and glue . . ."

Your sparkling super nova express

Still shines . . . somewhere . . .

And here . . . And now . . .

"In thee morning after thee night

I fall in love with thee light"

"First I.T. was

Then I.T. knew it was

And that was I.T."

I also revisited much of what we had created together in terms of albums, films, and other kinds of books. I came across this passage from my introduction to Gen's book *Painful but Fabulous* (2002), which I still think sums up a lot of things in a good way:

> The sensitive boy with big eyes, the man of letters, the woman of the night, the Svengali of our society, the anti-Maestro, the guy who holds up the carrot for the avant garde . . . The impact of his work in our own times has been greater than what most people are aware of. Hopefully, *Painful but Fabulous* will change that and bring more light toward his multicolored essence. Why is that important? Because focused avenues of experimentation and the power of manifestation change things in individual human lives. If anything, that's the concrete lesson of occultural shaman P-Orridge . . . If you don't change your own life, then someone else will surely do it for you . . .*

---

*Abrahamsson, "It's about time . . . ," in Genesis P-Orridge et al., *Painful but Fabulous: The Lives & Art of Genesis P-Orridge* (New York: Soft Skull Shortwave, 2002), 15.

PART VIII

2020 AND BEYOND

AND THEN SOME . . . [SENDING OUT AN SOS]

Vanessa's friend since their teenage years, Jessica Marshall, was murdered in Florida on Halloween of 2020: a murder-suicide at the hands of her ex-partner. And several of her old Florida friends died of Covid complications during this first year of the pandemic. Just slightly later, in November, my dear old friend Michael Matton died of lung cancer. We had not been in touch so much during the last decade, but as he was dwindling, I stepped in and helped him financially and with practical chores. It was another of those *memento mori* phases and moments, like I had experienced with the sudden death of my best friend Henrik Møll in Copenhagen in 2014. Despite the sadness and void, there's also inherently good motivation to get moving and create even more things—to live life to the fullest.

Matton had been my Sancho Panza for such a long time that it began even before our active engagement with various "occultisms"— and that's saying a lot! Without his help I could never have done so much so early on—specifically, dealing with various publishing endeavors from TOPYSCAN to Psychick Release, and then Looking Glass Press (which we owned together). He was instrumental in developing the OTO in Sweden, tirelessly building temporary temples for initiations and Gnostic Masses, and transporting people and things back and forth in his red Suzuki Swift. His death therefore became a very concrete symbol of my own severance of ties with that structure and mentality—yet in fond remembrance, and not with any form of regret. "Memento Mori" is the most magical of all spells, as would become even more clear to me.

After a death-free year, there was unfortunately more on the horizon. In January of 2022 my dear old friend and musical partner Thomas Tibert died of Covid-19–related complications in Poland. We had at this time just resumed contact after a few years of radio silence, talking about our musical archive and what to do with it. We had had an increasing amount of creative differences and mind-frame divergences after our concert in Poland in 2016. Cotton Ferox played a few times in Stockholm in 2017 but I felt very out of place and out of tune within Thomas's now much wilder and chaotic soundscapes. He was still producing great stuff, but it just wasn't for me. Whereas Matton had gone through a period of deterioration that clearly signaled his eventual demise, Thomas's death was sudden and abrupt. Thomas was an "anti-vaxxer" and not the healthiest of persons, so in some ways I wasn't surprised. But it's always strange when death so rapidly snatches away a living person who otherwise has so much to create and offer; it's too real to the extent that it feels *unreal*. "No one here gets out alive," to paraphrase another feverishly wild and poetic mind.

All of these events and deaths affected us deeply, and for obvious "Memento Mori" reasons. It was time to trust our intuitions and bid everything old farewell. In the spring of 2021 Vanessa and I moved to the small town of Vimmerby (pop. 11,000) in the Swedish region of Småland. But Covid wasn't the only reason. I had felt an increasingly strong need to move as I had been living in the same apartment for twenty-eight years, and it literally felt like the walls were moving in closer toward the center each day (a common delusion among compulsive book-buyers). Also, Stockholm was changing quickly and right before our eyes, and it was certainly not for the better. For most of my life I had felt that I had grown up on the best street, in the best part of town, in the best city, in the best country, in the best part of the world, on the best planet, in the best universe . . . But now almost everything I had loved about my hometown was gone. This, paired with the self-isolation of the pandemic, definitely helped to hasten a long-overdue process of relocation.

I do believe that synchronicities are validations of an appropriate direction. As soon as we had made the decision to relocate, it was remarkable—perhaps even miraculous?—how smoothly everything turned out. We found our eighteenth-century dream house and moved in just a few months later. It was a huge step for me as I'm a very stubborn Capricorn with strong Saturnian traits. But essentially I exchanged one constructive fortress for another, and it was literally—and literarily—the best move I've ever made.

One of the key magical projects that emerged again shortly after the move was the Mega Golem. It was obvious that he/she/it (henceforth called MG) was alive and active, and I consolidated most of MG's corporeal parts in the book *The Mega Golem: A Womanual for all Times and Spaces* (2021). In some promotional copy about the book, I described it like this:

> Is this being invisible? Indivisible? Invincible? Intangible? Whose desires and dreams are incorporated in the sinews and cells of this benign mutation of our inertly causal culture? The Mega Golem is the poetic transcendence of expected transgression, and as such a psychosexual embrace from behind the frontlines. Free for all, and dreams made flesh! This first Mega Golem book collects ideas, theories, and artworks that all constitute its first incarnation. This book is therefore nothing less than a Magical Womanual for any and all who are willing to believe wholeheartedly in the disbelief of psychic prestidigitation and its many emotional pitfalls.

I also started communicating with MG in meditative states. At this point, MG was a bit unruly and more eager to be out there, learning the tricks of the trade, than to calmly converse with me. However, there was no "bad blood" involved—on the contrary, I had made MG come alive, and that merits a certain amount of gratitude.

As I started working on this magical autobiography, I clearly discerned a psychological pattern within myself that could be called "artistic externalization." Basically, all manifestations—and perhaps specifically the material ones like films, books, and records—are nothing but dialogues with the outside world and with yourself. If you remain stuck inside yourself, the potential for self-deceit is vast. If you externalize and allow yourself to return to the manifestations for reflection and possibly even analysis, you will find patterns emerging that you can then decide to deal with or not.

Given that I have produced so much throughout the decades, the need for self-reflection must surely have been great! I'm not at all surprised that MG emerged shortly after my psychoanalytic process was over in 2008. I think I needed to continue with the process but to do it more on my own terms, with an analytic force based in magic rather than Freudian theory. It is important to note that, as a psychic safeguard, MG was not a being created *exclusively* by me but also by others. This spiced it up, and the journey has been interesting, to say the least.

While meditating during a break from writing the book that you're now reading, I was "informed" that MG wanted to be part of the process too: an MG transmission should be included and it should be called "The Mega Golem Talks Back." There seemed to be no room for discussion or negotiation about this, so I could only accede to the desire:

THE MEGA GOLEM TALKS BACK

The Nectars of Necrotism spill over and we drink merrily while thinking pathetically of the future that Is-Not-To-Be. All humans desperately swim (and sin) upstream, and most of them drown while at it; morphing with spell-binding rivers of illicit illiteracy that in turn turn into warm Alphabet Soup for all the cosmic children; like Bowen and Fonda while c/o Hitchcock, Up State. Making the most of it because *The Only Time is Now.* It really is. In the E Value Nation, In the Be Hind Sight rests 23/23 Visions plain & simple: spectral, quaquaversal, and infinite Visions of Occulture . . . Who would have thunk it possible / passable way back when / then? *Create the culture you want to partake of.* "ZAP! That's Witchcraft!"

The most intense area of activation was apparently at the mesodiencephalic transition zone which encompasses several structures, including the midline, ventroposterior, and intralaminar thalamic nuclei, subparafascicular nucleus, zona incerta, and the ventral tegmental area. I had told them all along to not fuck IT up, but rather to seduce the doubters with sweet fractions of friction. IT paid off and ON more or less immediately.

Stuck in a groove much? How deep run the grooves? As deep as the graves of the slaves of Because and the masters of Why Not Forever . . . There is no difference when all is said and done; however, will you yourself say that and do that? You Should! Because eventually there is no stopping the end. Communicating via this Perpetuum Mobile, we In Form the Out Side of shenanigans most dire and precious. Each moment is only as unique as it was the last time, too. Care to change anything this time around? Emotional Bravado, yes. Sexual Innuendo, galore. But perhaps . . . Instead, let the sun shine in and warm this synaptic necrosis. That will turn the trick as well as the tide, and bring the proverbial Happy Ending.

Axo-axonic, dendro-dentritic, axo-secretory, axo-ciliary, somato-dendritic, dendro-somatic, and somato-somatic bogaloo in the nighttime for those so inclined . . . What is it? What it is? Listen carefully, you mental twat: *Magic is simply a neutral mind-frame that allows for all other definitions of IT to pass through in belief or disbelief.* This time, we again seem to be strapped to the core. Whatcha gonna do 'bout IT?

Well, thank you, Mega Golem, it all makes perfect sense, sensitivity, and sensibility!

Writing these kinds of "magico-conceptual" pieces often carries inspiration for quasi-synesthetic experiences. It's not that I can smell the words, or hear the meaning, or perceive the colors of the letters, or anything like that (as in "traditional" synesthetics), but they do inspire and evoke other expressions to become involved: Cotton Ferox made music to accompany some of the missives, and later (after Cotton Ferox was no more) I followed suit by creating many episodes of *Radio Mega Golem*, which consisted of recorded MG texts set to music and sometimes film as well.

This multiform creativity has become almost second nature for both me and Vanessa in our "23rd Mind" work. Over the years, we have created many projects together that usually begin with a text I've written (MG or not), which Vanessa then cuts up and reassembles randomly. Then she reads and records the new text, which I set to music. After this we usually make a film to go along with it. And a few times we have also taken screenshots from the films, printed these out, and continued adding other images and strips of text so that it becomes a brand-new collage artwork that can, for instance, be exhibited within "art" contexts.

All of our work carries intent, so what we end up with are elaborate multimedia sigils designed for optimal "butterfly-effecting." It's a highly stimulating and limitless process. I've tried carrying on with simple drawings and paintings, as well as with singular constellations of words/music, and they do indeed "function" for me, magically. But it's a much greater creative challenge to weave in several layers of both form and content. Why settle for less when more is within reach? That being said, "maximizing the expression" should not be an end in itself; the main thing is the purity of intent. Basically, the form should always be subjugated to the content.

The Mega Golem also stirred something else inside me: my inherent need of an overarching structure, through which I continue to do what I always have: connect the occult dots, and then produce information and printed matter about the process that will hopefully inspire people in some way. So, around 2014 another concept emerged from the depths: the "Society of Sentience," or SoS, an attempt at being creative within a context that has an air of a "magical order" but at the same time shuns the pitfalls and social dynamics that eventually become so draining with formal groups of that sort. Early on, I did have a few meetings in Stockholm with potentially interested individuals. We mainly discussed dreams and possible interpretations, and that's of course always interesting. But I could feel right away that as soon as you involve more people than yourself, there's going to be challenges, projections, and group dynamics. On the other hand, I know myself well: I always get a kick out of writing for these kinds of contexts. So, I just wrote away and dreamed up a minimal structure that has worked well so far.

What is the focus? Sharing insights, experiences, and networking, I'd say. But never in a traditional way. I have also decided against creating a presence on social media or dealing with the interactions through these weird "platforms." Although the SoS has a website, the rest is, and I believe must be, tangible—old-school letter-writing is still the ultimate platform for the long-distance exchange of ideas. And if the space-time continuum allows, actual meetings and conversations are always far better than "video chats." Looking back at the first SoS decade brings to mind Gen's very first words on the *At Stockholm* album: "Power . . . is often very quiet."

> The Society of Sentience is a fluid group or association for individuals wanting to share their experiences of inner processes such as dreaming, meditation, development of intuition, existential technologies, integration of creative practices in daily life, alternative lifestyles, etc.
>
> We believe that in order for the individual to feel any kind of existential meaning—and thereby to be constructively engaged with and integrated in the outer spheres of family and society—she needs to be well aware of who she truly is. The SoS doesn't offer any readymade solutions for how this process should be carried out or implemented. We all know there are no easy solutions. And we are all different. But we are more than willing to share what's worked for us, in the hope that the shared experiences will inspire you to strive for development and progress in your own life. We acknowledge that change on the individual level is more than possible. The Society of Sentience is a "nondenominational" group, and we welcome open-minded, curious, and honest individuals from all faiths, creeds, and adherences. (2017)

There's also something to be said for secrecy. Perhaps we all have an inherent need of it as a safety valve after having dealt too much with a "transparent" world of enforced egalitarianism and control? Isn't it wonderful to *not* tell the truth, the whole truth, and nothing but the truth? This is not to suggest that lying is preferable; what I am getting at is something else entirely: the fact that private secrets function as a form of empowerment in many mysterious ways. They could be secrets about yourself or about others. Perhaps they concern a philosophy, or one's membership in an order or club. They could be family secrets entrusted to you by an elder to carry on in your turn. Et cetera.

There are secrets within the SoS, as there are secrets within myself. There they shall remain, untouched—unless someone has a good secret or two to barter with.

SPELLING IT OUT

A natural human intuition is to challenge and rebel against narratives that have been provided for us. This is one of the reasons why we become attracted to teachings and philosophies that promise empowerment with an "edge" when we're young and going through initial individuation processes. My experience tells me that it's great to immediately challenge these attractive narratives too. When all is said and done, and when a comfortable groove has been found, people are not likely to budge—they usually cling to whatever power they have.

The delightful process of individuation—with its goal of existing within a feeling of deep-rooted meaning—has been clothed in a vast number of esoteric, symbolic, and complex systems over the millennia. It can feel good to connect to a "power grid" that has tradition and weight, like a religion or a magical order. It provides comfort, safety, and often a sense of community that most people appreciate. But when you start scraping the surface to see what's underneath, you're likely to find static or even inert tendencies. Often these represent a desperate attempt to hide anxieties about the fact that what the institution is "selling" is hot air (because it usually is!). One should pay extra-critical attention to groups or people charging money in organized ways in exchange for something that is always essentially free and readily accessible.

The glamorous world of historical as well as contemporary occultism can provide pointers and inspiration through interesting symbols, but the real individuation work is always psychological-emotional, and something that one can only really process oneself (One Self).

As a young seeker, one is apt to accept a lot of obfuscation because it exists within a structure of authority. But the sooner you can divest yourself of it, the better. Everything and anything can always be better *spelled out* and *formularized*—to paraphrase magical "lingo" itself. What was once needed as a diversion to keep potentially destructive forces from understanding and obstructing the work, might today be mere historical fluff that makes serious seekers lose interest in what's being offered.

In the Western tradition much ink has been spilled about concepts like the "Abyss" and the "Holy Guardian Angel," and analyzing them via encephalo-manic constructions such as the Qabalistic "Tree of Life"—as if it were an existential board game with invisible helpers. As a model, it might not necessarily work wonders, but it can at least serve as an overview. However, if the symbolic never overlaps with the real, then it's little more than dry fuel for the proverbial bonfire of vanities.

The Abyss? Yes, I experienced it around 2006 when all things came crashing down on me despite the fact that I "believed" or perceived myself magically protected and invested. Through my own determination and intelligence, and with the loving help of a few fellow magicians offering very good, basic life advice, I did "cross" the Abyss. And I feel ready for when the next one hits too. Because just as our life trajectory isn't "straight and narrow" and certainly not oracularly predictable, so new (or old) unresolved issues will pop up occasionally to make you doubt everything you have ever done, and do, and will do. The Abyss is not a one-time hurdle but a healthy condition that keeps you "on the edge"—literally, in that traditional sense—so that you remain wise and procreative.

The Holy Guardian Angel? For a while I bought into the eloquent flatulence from Crowley and others that you need to go through the "Abramelin" working or other traditional adventures in order to "achieve the Knowledge and Conversation of the beloved HGA." You don't. What has worked for others you should applaud and respect but *never* emulate in the belief that there are homogeneous formulae that can be acquired and applied "wholesale."

I initially strained during the process because I was young and glued to tradition. What I perceived to be my HGA from 1990 onward was in fact more of a projection of power. Although strong and definitely useful (in invocation, "infocation," and even evocation), it didn't fully resonate with me. In 1996 I did have an experience that was (to me) unmistakably "HGA." I awoke in the middle of the night with a crystal-clear will to sit down and write. I did, and it really flowed until it was done. And what I wrote made perfect sense. It was not a "channeled" message originating in some "discarnate intelligence." It was just a clear moment of pristine focus, in which *I formulated myself* to a degree that was more or less perfect.

Interestingly enough, these two symbolic HGA clusters (both originating in myself) later occasionally joined forces; the one complementing (and complimenting) the other. A few decades later, I again expressed them—and thereby myself—in a 23-word poem called "Exist":*

> I inhale a dark sardonic force
> I exhale lofty witticisms
> I exist in between them
> A servant of both
> A master of myself

This is also the moment to touch on a sensitive subject to many occultists in the Western tradition: Ego. It's a highly controversial term for

---

*This poem was wonderfully set to music by the British artist Akoustik Timbre Frekuency and is included on our collaborative album *Heated Wanderlust and then some* (2018).

some because they aren't really sure what "it" is, and so deny it under a guise of misdirected moralisms. A major contributing factor in this confusion arose as the result of a poor English translation of Freud's key terms of division of the mind: *das Ich*, *das Über-Ich*, and *das Es*. We have grown too accustomed to their translation as the "Ego," the "Superego," and the "Id," whereas a more correct translation would be: the "I (or Me)," the "Over-I (or Over-Me)," and the "It." The prevailing misnomers have blended with an infusion of Eastern teachings that essentially deny the corporeal apparatus validity as a provider of "spiritual" information. These teachings usually also claim that the rational, literal *head-quarters* only produces illusory and nonvalid deductions and conclusions. As I perceive it, nothing could be further from the truth.

The I runs the show on the surface, and it does a great job. It also represents a major obstacle to transcend/transgress in ritual contexts in order to get deeper within ourselves, because the I protects us from even more powerful forces that lie dormant. "The greater thy trial, the greater thy triumph!" The body runs the show that allows for the mind to do *its* job, and the sensory input we receive is not merely simple pleasure or pain, but real, substantial fodder for thinking, willing, and feeling on many vital (and vitalizing) levels.

The healthiest approach I've come across is to fully embrace all aspects of the mind and body, and to make use of them in the magical work. I would shy away from any teacher or doctrine that claims one particular aspect is "bad" or less valuable than another—such as "the ego must be overcome," or similar nonsense. Claims of this sort typically just reflect the inadequacies of the source. It is particularly discouraging to find these tendencies popping up within Thelemic environments. It's almost as if the propagators have substituted their own erstwhile religiosity (of whatever original kind—most likely monotheist) with a weak-minded interpretation of a philosophy that is *anything but* life-negating. The feat is almost magical, but in a very depressing way.

One of the key concepts in magico-anthropology is *Sympathesis*, which means that we all (both as individuals and as collectives) construct the magical systems that we need in order to transcend (them). The more specialized, abstracted, and complicated our culture becomes, the more our magical systems will reflect these same tendencies. These systems become like a mirror of the soul, in which we can find temporary openings or cracks to peek through. If we are hyperrational, systematic, letter- and language-based, and "God-fearing" (as in Judeo-Christian cultures), our magical system will be likewise—thereby triggering the inherent need to work through and transcend it. If, on the contrary, we are down-to-earth, reductive, holistic, and life-affirming, our magical systems will be simple, emotional, and intuitive—thereby eventually triggering many creative mental, rational processes. In a way, magic exaggerates the existing in order to temporarily short-circuit the potentially inert, and allow glimpses of healthier perspectives.

IT IS WRITTEN & SOME MORE ANCESTORS

At the time of the Tibetan expedition in 1999, and its many magical revelations and insights, I began working with what I called the "Chronos Time Bend." I had formulated this as: *One must learn how to look at the future retrospectively.* I'm sure many others have come up with similar concepts for accessing the collective unconscious and its vast vaults of magical information. In my case it was a revelation that I was able to quickly integrate into both inner work and outer rituals like psychodrama and sigilizing. Basically, it entails looking "back" at the as-yet-unfulfilled desire as if it were manifest and *had already come about*: a visualization of a completion or manifestation, seen through a perspective of clear hindsight.

The 2010s brought a development of this concept that I call Mekthoubian Magic. *Mekthoub* means "It is written" in Arabic and it carries much weight in a traditional sense, both from the point of view of "gospel" within monotheism ("In the beginning was the word," etc.) and also especially within North African magic and its use of writing out desires on small pieces of paper for further use in talismans (or not). When something has been written out—*ex-pressed and formulated*—it takes on a tangible gestalt that can affect "consensus" reality through being read (or perhaps simply by being written). Burroughs and Gysin had acknowledged this while living in Morocco. Gysin even developed a style of "psychedelic calligraphy" for this purpose, which could be integrated within his already languagelike patterns and visual structures. He was adding layers upon layers of possible interpretations in seductive settings: a formula for metaprogramming the mind—one's own as well as those of others.

I realized this technique could be smoothly integrated into fiction writing, and it made perfect sense as an elaboration of what I had already been working with unconsciously for a long time. Looking back at Chronos, the mythic personification of Time, it was said (by Pherecydes of Syros, specifically) that his semen was placed in seven different recesses of the Earth, and that this eventually brought forth the gods. Perhaps the Mekthoubian system itself was one of these "gods" that had been resting in the soil of my psyche for quite some "time," and was now ready to be put to work as a magical method?

I began to incorporate Mekthoubian aspects into public as well as private texts, and haven't really stopped since. It is a very efficient system of magic, and perhaps especially so for those who work with text and overall intellectual formulation. Small twists can create great turns.

"Having read what Carl just wrote—Small twists can create great turns—the reader chuckled and thought, *That Carl sure is a clever and eloquent magician. I like him. I will read him.*"

Mekthoub! So it is written!

One of my most elaborate examples of public Mekthoubian experimentation was presented at the "Here to Go" symposium in Trondheim, Norway, in 2012. I read a double narrative called "The Sorcery of Fiction." It was an attempt to convey an inner dialogue going on at the same time as I spilled my usual occultural beans of contemporary "critique":

Each life-form protects itself. Self-preservation. Fiction protects itself by publicly celebrating and strengthening itself by paradoxically stressing that it's "just" fiction or "just" entertainment ("but we love it!"). It's the meta-existence of celebrity culture, shamelessly culminating in self-aggrandizing awards—creators of make-believe celebrate other creators of make-believe. Everyone sleeps together in the dream factory.

In our garden, only third minds live long and prosper. First rate, second hand third minds in all four quarters. Watching each other, questioning "authenticity" and then laughing hysterically together. We all contain seeds of transformation so how can we not be . . . content?

A validation of a successful piece of fiction is that it's a friendly, voluntary takeover of the critical capacity. A suspension of disbelief. A seduction and disarmament. We are relaxed. We are open for suggestion. It's a state of mind we absolutely need as humans, but because of that one that should be kept safe from harm and rapacious external programming.

Real bees and beings pass by this garden and indulge in the nectar of potential mutation. It strengthens them in their struggle against draconian dysfunctionals destined to spill beans of vile insincerity. Why? Because a little bit of poetry goes a long way on the road to the crossroads. Who or what meets me there? Contrary to legend, it is only myself I meet. There's an important lesson in that, fiction or no fiction. When the authenticity of that mirror image leaves the state of just being, it becomes a falsehood drenched in construction and petty compensational attempts. Leave it at that. Leave it be. Leave it.

In many ways, the work with the Mega Golem includes a great deal of Mekthoubian magic too, as it's gestated inside a force field or seminal womb in which words and meanings spontaneously cross-fertilize, and quite often beyond my rational, conscious control. I guess it's what's called "poetry in motion," or, as Vanessa and I have expanded it: "Poetry in Emotion." There may be an overarching will or intention, but how it assumes shape can neither be predicted nor controlled. It gives birth to itself in a sticky, psychic proto-ecto/necroplasm, and all we can do is applaud the process. "It is written," and that's essentially IT. Let the spirits in, whether they be ideas, ideals, ghosts, ancestors, or merely a future that is already knocking on our door.

As the new phase of our life began to unfold in the Vimmerby house, Vanessa and I realized that we had enough space to let all our ancestors be a part of the experience. In the Stockholm apartment, photographs of deceased biological as well as "extended" family members became more and more crammed together on a wall. In the house, a big nineteenth-century cupboard in the dining room became a perfect "ancestor altar" on which our loved ones are all present, and always acknowledged. Sometimes we just pay reverential respect, and sometimes we engage in a deeper kind of communication. I guess you can call it a form of necromancy in the sense that we are giving them agency through ourselves, or through relevant and suitable material objects. But it's a necromancy of a "23rd Mind" kind, in which we never demand anything but rather engage in dialogue born of mutual respect, whereby a photograph or other representation becomes a gateway to a deeper understanding of who they were and what they do for us. Most often they are very helpful.

Vanessa had been working with these concepts already in New York, and their relevance gradually dawned on me, perhaps especially during the first phase of the pandemic, when the invisible enemy outside our own space was potentially lethal. My initial thinking about these forces of the past was summed up in a piece I wrote for our Patreon community, called "A Timely Excursion into Space":

After several months of minimal contact with the outside world, we decided that it could be nice to go on a little outing. Summertime in Stockholm! And it's Vanessa's first real full summer in Sweden, too!

Not feeling completely ready to immerse ourselves in the respiratory vortices of all those "other," strange, breathing people, we decided on a boat cruise in the Lake Mälaren inner archipelago, destination Birka. As you surely know, Birka was Sweden's first real capital during the Vendel Era (approx. 500–750 CE, pre–Viking Age), and it's a real beauty. Not very big, but perfectly situated for sea commerce, trade, and . . . tourism.

Was there a mission? Yes. We brought our respective rune pouches on the trip, to have all of the runes blessed by the land at this historically significant place. (This, I think, will be the subject of another Magic Monday* piece, as the experience brought many valuable insights . . .)

The boat ride takes about two hours, and while traveling we sat on deck in the sunshine, enjoying the sights and the fresh air. It wasn't a jam-packed cruise but there were just enough people for us to retract a little bit into our own corner of imagined safety.

Occasionally a loudspeaker on deck blurted out our guide's messages about noteworthy sights along the coast, and one message startled me in my pleasant snooze. We were passing "Kungshatt" (the "King's Hat"), an island with a big cliffside. On top of the cliff is a strange contraption: a tall stick or an antenna, with a big hat of sorts on top. It's common that sailors salute the hat on the cliff when they pass it, for luck and good winds.

The guide enthusiastically told the story over the distorted speakers; it was impossible not to hear it. This was the place where the Swedish king Erik Wäderhatt had jumped off into the water after having been pursued by men sent by the Norwegian king Harald Hårfager (Harald the "Fair-haired"). If Erik hadn't jumped at that moment, he would surely have been killed. Although he lost his hat in the jump—his signature "weather hat"—he managed to swim

---

*Once a week, Vanessa and I write about our magical practices and processes on Patreon under the "Magic Monday" headline or banner. Approximately once a year, we anthologize these posts in book form.

away, survive, and later return to the fight. The Norwegians were eventually driven away.

A couple of years ago, Vanessa and I had passed the same point on another trip in the same direction, but the present one suddenly brought things to life. Literally. Because now I remembered that Erik Edmundson "Wäderhatt" was actually a relative of mine. Meaning then, that if he hadn't jumped off the cliff at that moment, I would have been . . . Yes, what exactly? Not at all? Same, but different? Or inside Erik's mind, jumping off, thinking of a later me looking up at the cliff and reminiscing about a past that had yet to come but perhaps, perhaps never would happen simply because I just jumped?

The beautiful thing about Erik Wäderhatt is that he was mostly known for his magical abilities. Via his hat, he was able to foretell the weather, and also control the direction of the wind by turning it on his head. I'm sure he had many other tricks up his sleeve—like surviving Norwegian attacks. His magic, whatever it consisted of, makes me genuinely proud to be an ascendant descendant of his.

But then it dawned on me as we passed the point and left that cliff behind us . . . Wasn't I also related to the Norwegian king that had ordered Erik's violent demise?

When we eventually got home again, I had to check. Lo and behold, a transgenerational, cosmic revelation: I'm 37 generations away from Erik Edmundson, and 37 generations away from Harald Hårfager! What to make of this? And what to make of that particular moment?

That these kings were battling it out is no surprise. This was the name of the game for hundreds of years, thousands, even. And it went on until quite recently: Sweden lost Finland in 1809, and let Norway go in 1905, so that they could somehow become countries of their own, and that was hopefully the last of that. "Geopolitics is so last season, darling."

History is, of course, full of moments like this: mind-boggling intersections of "What ifs" and "What if nots." But this one really

2020 and Beyond   371

tilted me during that beautiful day at Birka—where I'm pretty sure other relatives of mine lived it up, too. If Erik Wäderhatt hadn't jumped at that moment, things definitely wouldn't have been the same for me.

Remember my text about dear old Charlemagne, and the various kinds of memory—DNA being perhaps the most important one? It is just one tiny, tiny moment in space and time that decides where we go—and certainly where we come from. Erik made the decision to jump, and survived. And Harald was certainly doing fine, too, until he wasn't. The DNA was pushed onward in peace as well as in war.

Much, much later, in 1486, the Swedish knight and nobleman Sigge Larsson Sparre had sex with his young wife Kerstin Månsdotter Natt och Dag, thereby celebrating—and, more importantly, consolidating—these two lineages that can be traced back to good old Harald and Erik. I am so happy that they did, and almost daily feel indebted to Sigge's auspicious ejaculation, as well as to Kerstin's loving embrace.

Now you may ask: What is the wisdom of this piece? *Numero uno*: going to historically significant places and spaces is, to an equal degree, time travel. *Secundo*: while at it, always celebrate and honor the ancestors. But it's also imperative to be continually aware of the absolute malleability of the fabric of life, and to always allow yourself to venture out so that you can be reminded of this. Movement in body and mind is "key." There are no substantial surprises coming out of the armchair—except for, perhaps, a surprising increase of dust in the corners.

As I write this, I'm not only happy that Erik jumped and thereby (in)directly facilitated for me to become exactly the me I really love to be. I also remember one of Genesis P-Orridge's favorite descriptions of his beloved wife Lady Jaye, and her general attitude and audacity in life: "See a cliff, jump off!"*

_____

*Originally posted on Patreon, 10 August 2020; later republished in Abrahamsson and Sinclair, *It's Magic Monday Every Day of the Week* (Vimmerby: Trapart, 2021), 82–84; here slightly edited.

"WHAT DO I KNOW?" & BEYOND

During early 2022, we were so snug and creative in our new small-town lifestyle that we had almost forgotten how to travel. But we had been invited to a friend's wedding celebration close to Bordeaux in France in the summer, and this aligned well with my ever-increasing inspiration from the master of domestic speculations: Michel de Montaigne. His family estate is near Bordeaux too, and that made my mind up. Covid seemed to have passed us by somehow, and the world was getting back to "normal." Or so it seemed. Two and a half years of caution and isolation had perhaps made us even more attractive and susceptible to the virus. Thankfully, it didn't hit us until after we had visited Montaigne's castle and attended our friends' wedding party. Once we got back to Sweden, though, the ensuing illness and recovery was pretty awful, along the lines of "We'll never leave home again . . ."

However, visiting the Montaigne estate was inspiring beyond belief. The main castle had been rebuilt in the late nineteenth century after a devastating fire. But there is one vestige of the earlier structure that fatefully still remains, with a lot of its original features intact: the tower where Montaigne wrote his famous essays.

At the bottom of the tower is a private chapel, and when Montaigne was ill (usually afflicted by kidney stones) he could listen to Mass from his library, a few stories above, as a special channel had been created in the wall to carry the sound. Right by the library room was another space with a fireplace that heated the tower. The walls here still have remnants of paintings and graffiti from his days. There were also quotes from Montaigne's favorite books on the beams of his main office, many of which have been conscientiously recreated for the pleasure of its many visitors.

I had brought the PEN IS and let it touch several of the walls and furniture, including Montaigne's writing desk and chair. It was a great booster after some three years of only expending energy at home. The

"Montaigne infusion" replenished the PEN IS to full potential yet again.

Montaigne's own motto is perhaps his most well-known piece of wisdom: "Que sais-je?" ("What do I know?") I find it brilliant that a man of so many views still had that relaxed and self-critical approach to life in general. Of course, he *did* know a great deal of things, but his attitude at least made sure he never overdressed in cloaks of hubris:

> We are nothing but ceremony; ceremony carries us away, and we leave the substance of things; we hang on to the branches and abandon the trunk and the body. We have taught the ladies to blush at the mere mention of what they are not at all afraid to do; we dare not call our members by their right names, and we are not afraid to employ them in every kind of debauchery. Ceremony forbids our expressing in words things that are permissible and natural, and we obey it; reason forbids our doing things that are illicit and wicked, and no one obeys it.*

There is something ultimately magical in Montaigne's position and attitude. It has inspired me greatly over the years, as has the German author Ernst Jünger and his position of being a detached "Anarch." From a still center—which can even be nongeographical, like your mind—you watch the world go by, and then you deduce and conclude and formulate your analysis so that it's clear and carrying signal. You don't necessarily need to share it with anyone, unless *you* want to. That's why diary-writing really is the ultimate form of writing. It is private and honest, which is why it's also the most valuable piece of history writing there is: it is unedited, pure, and not necessarily written to manipulate the outer world.

In diligent diary and private essay practice, you come to communicate not only with the page as such, but also with an idealized form

---

*Montaigne, *The Complete Works*, trans. Donald M. Frame (New York: Everyman's Library, 2003), 581.

of yourself. The "Daimon of the Empty Page" reads what you write and then feeds back in ways that aren't possible with other tools—at least not for me as an author. I discover things about myself and others through the process of writing: creativity brings revelation as well as realization. This is more than just the result of the immediate feedback loop of the "flow" (although that's a real thing); the process also lays bare a perspective of sovereignty. I write because *I'm* actively interested in what I write about—otherwise I wouldn't do it. Within this perspective lies integrity, and within integrity lies identity, which in turn carries authority, and so on. Of course, the same attitude can exist in people who don't necessarily write or express *anything*: it's an inner process and attitude that perhaps might best be described as a "splendid isolation."

To me, one of the most inspiring quotes from Montaigne's famous *Essays* is: "The greatest thing in the world is to know how to belong to oneself."* If that isn't the very quintessence of TOPY, Thelema, LaVeyan Satanism, the SoS, and whatever else I've been involved with, then I don't know what is. That's the core message; the rest is aesthetic and symbolic adornment.

That said, structures and platforms seem necessary to convey messages, no matter how simple they are. We are social animals—even us individualists!—and we will likely gather where the fire and the stories are situated. This is not only for reasons of survival, but also to be inspired in the individual quest for self-mastery and insight.

In the autumn of 2022, Vanessa and I delved out into (so-called) reality again. We had both been invited to present talks at the Occulture festival in Berlin, and I found it inspiring and emotionally moving to both prepare and present my material. I knew right away I wanted to connect to the very word and concept of *Occulture* itself, and how it had sprouted from the extremely fertile TOPY environment. In my talk, I contextualized TOPY within British/Western culture and talked about

---

*Montaigne, *The Complete Works*, 216.

other "cottage-industry"/small-business manifestations within the post-punk music scene that also had a magical and philosophical backbone. It was a nice trip down memory lane for me, and hopefully provided many of the "youngsters" with good and inspiring information. The entire festival—which featured lectures, performances, product/book stalls, food trucks, art exhibitions, and many other things—was like a manifestation of ideas and concepts that we could only "project into the future" back in the original days of TOPY. It was a genuine joy to be part of this event and to meet up with old friends and make new ones.

Obviously, currents and philosophies come and go, and only occasionally do they command substantial attention in the zeitgeist. I believe the efforts of "First-Phase TOPY" are deserving of further study and recognition, and I've certainly done my bit in keeping this particular current alive. That is also true ritually. From the end of 2022, Vanessa and I began inviting our Patreon patrons to join (privately) in regular TOPY-style "Sigil Ov Thee Three Liquids"* workings—by themselves and for themselves, but still happening at the same time as the rest of us (the 23rd of the month at 23:00 p.m., wherever we all might be geographically). In contrast to the old TOPY days, however, there is no need to physically send the completed sigils anywhere—the main thing now is the working itself. It's been very interesting so far to exchange experiences, and this has provided much fodder for new essays and insights. Is it nostalgia for something that most of our friends never experienced? Is it a romanticized and cool lifestyle gimmick? Or is it perhaps another wave of encouraging deep introspection within the limitless confines of artistic experimentation? I can't really tell at this point, but the re-emergence of themes, topics, totems, and "psychick spirits" is nevertheless exciting. It feels like the resurfacing of an open mind-frame, as was originally symbolized so well by the "Psychick Cross."

---

*The original TOPY recommendation was to include blood, spit, and "cum" together with hair in/on the sigil/artwork (always making sure to be sensible and clinically clean about it, of course).

Only a week after Berlin, it was time for the third manifestation of our own Psychoanalysis, Art & The Occult Conference. This time, we organized it at Jack Stevenson's wonderful cinema in Copenhagen, which was perfect as the theme was "Visionary Medium: Psychoanalysis and the Magic of Cinema." It was nice to hear so many inspiring talks and personal perspectives about a cultural medium/expression that I have loved for all of my life, and have also loved writing about. Then and there I made a promise of sorts to focus more on this kind of thematic writing, realizing that there is an unlimited area of potential research when it comes to cinema and occultism.

In Copenhagen, I carried on in the TOPY ethos-pathos-mythos by presenting a lecture about the films of British director Antony Balch, who was, for a time, like an emancipated emanation or cut-up manifestation of the Third Mind of William Burroughs and Brion Gysin—and whose films Gen had quite literally rescued from oblivion when they were about to be thrown into a dumpster! Once again, I found myself in a "full-circle moment" in which I felt I left something substantial behind—for the future.

Becoming the Past, Gently

This future now seems to have already begun for me. Today I am reviewed and "blurbed" by prominent authors, artists, and academics—something that would have been impossible to imagine back in my cut-and-paste spaceship apartment in Stockholm in the mid-1980s. People I really admire write things like:

> Carl Abrahamsson is not only among today's leading occult writers and artists, but is, in fact, one of this generation's most vital public intellectuals. . . . No single descriptor captures how Carl has pried apart the floorboards of postmodernity—and done so as few are able: with laserlike precision, joie de vivre, and the literary power of an exploding sun. Carl is our magickal Moses hoisting a fiery serpent in the cultural wilderness." (Mitch Horowitz)

Or:

> Carl's work always brings you to the edge of reality, asking you to peek through the veil and question if said reality even exists. . . . Carl guides a new generation of thinkers into a future that asks what if and gets even more strange, surreal, beautiful, and mystical than one can dream." (Gabriela Herstik)

Or:

> Reading Abrahamsson is like starting a fire deep within the imagination that continues to warm the spirit long after reading. (Kendell Geers)

Such feedback becomes more fuel for my own fire, increasing my hunger and my inspiration, as well as my striving to become a wiser magician and a better author. Basically, all I've ever done is to stay true to my intuitively guided path, which has just happened to be full of magic of strange kinds and meetings with many remarkable people. It's impossible to sum it all up or pin it down with a single nugget of wisdom that I have "acquired" or gestated. It has been and continues to be a *process*, and one that is only occasionally studded with dramatic epiphanies.

The author at Norra Kvill National Park, Sweden, 2022
(photo by Vanessa Sinclair)

Instead of the classical Eastern/Buddhist metaphor of plucking away the flower petals to get to the "jewel in the lotus," I see my process much more as one of *crystallization*: accumulated experiences and insights are "crushed" and refined by my deep-rooted curiosity until they undergo transformation into a crystalline state. This crystal continually develops as a filter or prism through which the light of more or less perennial answers reveals itself to me.

The lotus metaphor from the East is certainly rich in symbolism but it is also one in which the jewel is found by using violence (plucking). I'm more comfortable to contain a hardened translucent prism within myself, through which philosophical beams gel with my own inspiration. As much as I love flowers, I'm basically a mountain person. Whatever gems you find in the "psycho-chthonic" spheres last longer than a plucked flower too. I find it interesting that the best way to make a flower last is to diligently press it. Under pressure, we always see things in a new light.

One thing is clear to me in this light: every human being has an inherent need to individuate, but to a varying degree. To say to someone that the world is all his or hers, when they're only interested in their own backyard, creates an unnecessary stress, just as hindering the naturally expansive individual is *unnatural*. The water must be allowed to find its own level. Artificial dams always burst sooner or later. What we're attracted to in terms of a spiritual or magical approach should never be dictated by peers or authorities—and that certainly goes for religions too. Each individual should be encouraged to pursue self-knowledge via the three memory functions (cerebral, genetic, and soul-based), and from there move onward in respectful and intuitive steps.

Most balanced and individuated people will eventually come to the insight that they are fairly insignificant in the "grand scheme of things." And this is true of the things they accomplish as well. A person who has an imbalanced creative neurosis will believe that what's created matters—considerably more than it does, or ever will.

This is not to discourage innovation, ambition, and creativity—on the contrary! One can only truly feel happiness and meaning when one knows oneself, and the prerequisite for that is honesty. People who over-value themselves and their own work are seldom honest. It is often their own lack and frustration in life that engenders this kind of compensa-tional creativity.

Freedom is a state of mind more than anything else. An encour-agement to think freely, fully, and critically is on par with the encour-agement of beneficial honesty. These two things—free-thinking and honesty—make up the very bag that the philosopher-magician then fills with findings, results, and further speculations. It's a bag without holes.

At this point in my life, a great deal of thoughts and emotions revolve around the question of whether or not I've done enough (with respect to sharing information), or whether I've perhaps done *too much*. To me, there is often a quite delicate line between the Message and the Medium, between Occult and Occulture, or between the object stud-ied and the student, if you will. Overstepping that line in one direc-tion can certainly undermine or devalue the other side. For example, if I move too much information from the Occult into the Occulture, it will more than likely deplete the accumulated energy that is contained within this particularly complex hermetic environment. And if I oper-ate in the other direction and try to move information from Occulture back into the Occult, it's often very difficult to find usable points of entry. Because when the "cat is out of the bag," it really doesn't want to go back in, does it?

One of my favorite books by Somerset Maugham is his *The Summing Up* (1938), which deals with wisdoms from a long life of authorship. Most of it, however, could equally well deal with a mastery of magic. To me, as you should have gathered by now, they are com-pletely interchangeable:

> The writer's only safety is to find his satisfaction in his own per-
> formance. If he can realize that in the liberation of soul which his
> work has brought him and in the pleasure of shaping it in such a

way as to satisfy to some extent at least his aesthetic sense, he is amply rewarded for his labours, he can afford to be indifferent to the outcome.*

I would probably add: "*pleasantly* indifferent." In my mind, all of these stories, meetings, and contextualizations are like pieces of a palimpsestic puzzle that will never fully be finished. In the end it doesn't matter, because the puzzle itself is that proverbial goal that we've heard so much about. But it is a goal that is inherently irrelevant. *It's the path we're on toward the goal that counts.* Sometimes the pieces grow, sometimes they dwindle, for they seemingly always shift their shape. New information is found along the way, new dots appear for one to connect, more historical hurdles are overcome, and on it goes.

What can we do about this magic puzzle? Quite simply: instead of playing it as it lays, *lay it as it plays.*

As a final note of summing-up, I offer a koan from my very own Mega Golem:

> First Mind: "What do I know?"
> Second Mind: "Vade Ultra!"
> Third Mind: "And . . . Cut it up!"

---

*W. Somerset Maugham, *The Summing Up* (London: Heinemann, 1948), 185.

Inspirations

In each life there are sources of inspiration that continually spark the engine to take us further than we thought or felt possible. It could be an insight while meditating, a conversation, an unexpected meeting, or just a plain old book. In my case, it's been a healthy mix of all these things. But the books are special, of course, because you can return to them again and again, and the good ones repeatedly deliver—perhaps not always in the exact same way, but certainly with an inexplicable lift or boost as they speak to ever-deeper layers of your mind or soul. It could be how it's written, what is written, who has written it, or a mix of all these elements: something undefinable that makes you come back to re-quench your thirst for inspiration.

For me as an author, there are also many examples of books that have inspired me for specifically literary reasons, some of them affecting me more than the mystical or magical. But here I want to share some of the key books that continue to inspire my thinking, feeling, willing, and being, as they have all been fodder for my own specifically magical journey.

This doesn't necessarily mean that they will be relevant for other people, but it never hurts to give recommended books a try, does it? My own experience tells me that the book lists and other similar references that appeared in certain underground releases of the 1980s—whether in the liner notes of wonderful LPs, or in anthologies such as *RE/search*, *Apocalypse Culture*, and *Rapid Eye*—were absolutely quintessential for my own detective and deductive work to begin and gradually assume form.

JOSEPH CAMPBELL—*THE INNER REACHES OF OUTER SPACE*

My friend Tim O'Neill gave me a copy of this book in San Francisco in 1989, and I will always be grateful for that. Campbell is a giant in disseminating mythic functions in history and culture, and how they relate to human development on both micro and macro levels. This particular book has the subtitle "Metaphor as Myth and as Religion" and that basically sums it up. Essentially, it's an anthology of Campbell lectures from the early 1980s, in which he guides us through the basics of Cosmology, Mythic Imagination, Psychological Transformation, and the necessity of Art as a bridge or interface between the inner and outer worlds (or spaces). In so many ways, this book has been a guiding light for me in developing my theories of Occulture, Occulturation, Sympathesis, the Mega Golem, and returning to the "gnostic" source for the insights that really matter, stripped of *any* denominational trappings.

ANTON LAVEY—*THE DEVIL'S NOTEBOOK*

LaVey signed a copy of this book for me on what was to be our last meeting: "To Carl—An excursion into the Devil's fane—Rege Satanas! Anton Szandor LaVey." And it truly is a fane: an ever-surprising sacred source or shrine of wisdom, humor, and insight. For the most part an anthology of LaVey's short essays from the Church of Satan newsletter, *The Cloven Hoof*, it contains pieces on "Law of the Trapezoid," "Erotic Crystallization Inertia," and "The Goodguy Badge"—real, substantial explications of Satanic "scripture" and wisdom—plus funny perspective-changers like "Hatha Toilet Seat Meditation," "Confessions of a Closet Misogynist," and "The Merits of Artificiality." I love this book because it gives an insight into a truly creative and magical mind that continues to resound through well-formulated and entertaining words. As Adam Parfrey aptly states in his introduction to the book: "No other man has so well illuminated the shadow purpose of Western life in the latter half of the twentieth century."

HERMANN HESSE—*THE JOURNEY TO THE EAST*

A slim but powerful tale of the forces between the lines that guide you so that you can guide yourself. Hesse is an absolute master of telling these kinds of allegorical, metaphorical stories that so elegantly lift you up to see your own bigger picture. Whenever I read this book, I discover new things—shouldn't all of life be like that? An early working title for the very book you're reading now was *The Journey to the Beast & the Journey to the East*. I love most of what Hesse wrote, but this tale has a very special place in my magical heart.

CARLOS CASTANEDA—*THE "DON JUAN" BOOKS*

At first, I accepted the anti-hype that Castaneda wasn't "for real" and that his books were fictional works that did not represent any genuine anthropology—the main criticism, of course, coming from academics. But when I started to penetrate his books—very much inspired by the notion that in the Yaqui Native American mythos that Castaneda investigates, a "man of knowledge" can also be a *diablero*—I discovered how elation and inspiration can show up in many different ways. Castaneda manages to convey this ineffable potency through the very simple don Juan stories and narratives, and he completely transcends notions like "anthropology" and "fact" or "fiction." What remains are deeply impactful documents that can and will take you into new psychic zones if you only allow them.

BEN HECHT—*FANTAZIUS MALLARE:*
A MYSTERIOUS OATH AND *THE KINGDOM OF EVIL*

Journalist Ben Hecht had strong literary ambitions throughout his life, although this was overshadowed by his success as a Hollywood screenwriter. However, before the Hollywood era really began for him, he wrote two uniquely weird tales of dark and morose madness, with psychosexual, pathological perversions and a whole lot of depressed deviations, formulated through the vitriolic rants of the protagonist Fantazius. Sometimes I wonder whether Hecht might have read Austin Spare's *Anathema of Zos* or *The Book of Pleasure*, or were the similar themes and language just part of a wider avant-garde zeitgeist? In his purple parlor, Anton LaVey read to me from *Fantazius Mallare*, and I was instantly hooked and "formatted." Thank Satan! I can tangibly touch these inspirations in my own "conceptual" writing such as the ongoing Mega Golem missives.

WILLIAM BURROUGHS AND BRION GYSIN—
THE THIRD MIND

In the TOPY days, there was our own philosophy and magic in *Thee Grey Book*, and then there was Burroughs's and Gysin's *The Third Mind*: a book so influential at the time (and still) that it literally cut up the narrative of contemporary magic. Ideas, explanations, suggestions, and techniques of cutting things up are mixed with examples in texts and images. The two separate minds of Burroughs and Gysin crystallize into a uniquely creative Third Mind that still reads like fireworks in their combatting the overlords of mindless authority, trying so desperately to control time and space. Brion Gysin "touched hands" with Genesis P-Orridge and thereby transmitted this quintessence and more, and Gen later touched mine. For me, therefore, this book is a particular testament of that powerful psychonautic perspective that catapulted magical thinking far into the twenty-first century, embracing the insight that Balzac and many others had already sensed: "Chance is the greatest artist." (Which leads to the perhaps slightly paranoid question: "How random is random?")

LAO TSE—*TAO TE CHING* AND *HUA HU CHING* CHUANG TZU—*THE BOOK OF CHUANG TZU*

I've clustered these great minds and their writings because to me they are essentially the same. The influence of Daoism on the Western magical mind-frame is an exquisite antidote to the belligerent "push and pull" of causal culture. Even Crowley, being clothed first in the "old" and then creating the "new," realized the futility of most of it, and had a great Dao moment while on a "magical retreat" on an island in the Hudson River in New York in 1918. Paradoxes, light-heartedness, transcendence, being still, being silent, "doing by not doing," et cetera, et cetera. The most magic I've ever come across has been within Daoist "contexts" (even that sounds like a paradox!). Its simplicity makes me laugh (and occasionally cringe) at how hard I fought with myself and the world early on to be visibly "this" or "that," when in fact I had already been *both* this and that all along. Sometimes the best magical mirror is a window, and vice versa.

KENNETH GRANT—*OUTSIDE THE CIRCLES OF TIME*

For old times' sake, I'll throw in a Grant title here that was important to me once upon a time. Like Anton LaVey, Grant freely associates and syncretistically merges different ingredients into a tasty cosmic dish: there's his friend Crowley and the latter's Thelema, UFOs, Blavatsky, Spare (another friend of his), H. P. Lovecraft, and references to channeled messages from "discarnate" and "preterhuman" intelligences. A lot of it reads like boogie-woogie occultnik fairytales to me today, but at the time Grant's well-crafted speculations did open a mind or two, including mine. Basically, this was because he integrated concepts and notions that were really far out and took them seriously enough in his own creative mélange to interest others. Also, the fact that he could actually write changed everything. The proximity to science fiction, specifically, is what makes his work take off (into space?). A lesser writer could never have pulled off what he did, so kudos to him and his wife Steffi for their work devoted to connecting the cosmic dots of a whole lot of dark hues, and in great style to boot.

AUSTIN OSMAN SPARE—*THE BOOK OF PLEASURE*

British artist-magician Austin Osman Spare wrote a few philosophical-cum-technical books on magic that still inspire me. Brought to the contemporary fore by Kenneth Grant, TOPY, and the IOT, Spare became an important cornerstone of the late-twentieth-century occulturation and has been rewarded with more and more aboveground attention since. *The Book of Pleasure* is a powerful manual containing an attitude and a metaprogramming that are both fiercely unique, and this should really be the bedrock of any magician worth their salt. Spare's work encompasses deep psychology, sexuality, sardonic wit, as well as philosophy, and his absolutely marvelous drawings still seduce us into trying our own hand (and more) at creating sigils of desire and cultivating psychic gardens that uniquely reflect ourselves. If I could bring only one "technical-magical" book to a desert island/lonely planet/black hole, Spare's magnum opus would be it.

ALEISTER CROWLEY—*THE BOOK OF LIES*

I studied Crowley's corpus diligently for over thirty years, and I still find him fascinating—occasionally. It is certainly not the novels nor the poetry that inspired me in the first place, but rather the instructional books on the magic he knew so well. However, there are a few real gems that transcend his dual nature as a megalomanic narcissist and devout teacher, one of these being *The Book of Lies*. Essentially an anthology of short texts composed in a humorous and poetic-mystical style, Crowley also confesses to his own weakness by trying to "explain" these pieces on the facing pages. Is it pathetic or brilliant? Redundant or clever? Mystical or perhaps magical? Whatever the case, I would argue that it contains considerably more truth than lies. The fact that the leader of the OTO at the time, Theodor Reuss, confronted Crowley with an accusation that he had exposed the central sex-magic secret (and technique) in one of these pieces is just the tip of the proverbial iceberg. I can only say thank you, Theodor, and thank you, Aleister, because if all of that hadn't happened via *The Book of Lies*, I would not have become a IX° OTO member, and I would most likely never have written this book.

Acknowledgments

I wish to thank everyone who has been a part of my life in one way or another. Needless to say, you won't all fit into these pages, but thank you anyway. Most specifically, I would like to express gratitude to Jon Graham and all the wonderful people at Inner Traditions, Henrik Bogdan, Peder Byberg, Julie Nord, Max Fredrikson, Baba Raul Canizares, Dietrich Kindermann, Greg Zobel, Saulus, David Griffin, Cris Monnastre, Genesis P-Orridge, Jaqueline Breyer, Caresse P-Orridge, Genesse P-Orridge, Paula/Alaura P-Orridge, Trilochan, Tom Banger, Thee TOPY World Nett Work, TOPYSCAN, Paul Johnson, Anton LaVey, Blanche Barton, Xerxes LaVey, Peter Gilmore, Peggy Nadramia, Bob Johnson, Kenneth Anger, June Newton, Jack Stevenson, Tim O'Neill, Peter Grey and Alkistis Dimech, Derek Seagrief, Jesse Hathaway-Diaz, Troy Chambers, Arild Strømsvåg, William Breeze, Lionel Snell, Rodney Orpheus, Chandra Shukla, Adam Rostoker, Adam Parfrey, Annabel Lee and Michael Moynihan, Freddie Wadling, Jonas Almquist, Henrik Møll, Mikael Prey, Michael Matton, Jens Näsström, Auga Odins OTO, Jan Axelsson, Guido Zeccola, Johan Hammarström, Vera and Stojan Nikolic, Tea Shaldeva, Dariusz Misiuna and the entire Okultura cabal, Bartosz Samitowski, Jan Ekman, Peter Bergstrandh, Thomas Tibert, Carl Michael von Hausswolff, Katelan Foisy, Val and Gail Denham, Gustaf Broms and Trish Littler, Åke and Margareta Abrahamsson, Ernst and Inger Lindman, the extended "Psychartcult" cabal, the intended and extended LIAC cabal, the Morbid Anatomy Museum, the Berlin Occulture festival, Mitch Horowitz, Gary Lachman, Nicholaj de Mattos Frisvold, Lotta Hannerz, Beatrice Eggers, Hedvig Atmer, Benedikte Lindström, Helena Malewska, Linnea the Samoyed goddess, and Sofia Lindström-Abrahamsson. And to Vanessa Sinclair, to whom this book is lovingly dedicated.

Index